Dictionary of World Place Names

Derived from British Names

Dictionary of World Place Names Derived from British Names

Adrian Room

ROUTLEDGE
London and New York

First published in 1989 by
Routledge
11 New Fetter Lane, London EC4P 4EE
29 West 35th Street, New York NY 10001

Typeset in 9/10pt Baskerville Linotron 202 by Input Typesetting Ltd, London
Printed in Great Britain by T. J. Press (Padstow) Ltd, Cornwall

British Library Cataloguing in Publication Data

Room, Adrian
Dictionary of world place-names derived from British names.
1. British place names. Etymology
I. Title
910'.01'4

Library of Congress Cataloging in Publication Data

Room, Adrian
Dictionary of world place-names derived from British names.

Bibliography: p.
1. Gazetteers. 2. English language—Etymology—Names—Dictionaries. 3. Great Britain—Gazetteers. 4. English language—Influence on foreign languages—Dictionaries. 5. Civilization Modern—20th century—English influences—Dictionaries. I. Title.
G103.5.R65 1989 910'.01'4 88–18492

ISBN 0–415–02811–6

Contents

Sed nunc terminus Britanniae patet ('But now the bounds of Britain open wide'), Tacitus, *Agricola*

Introduction

One has merely to glance at a map of the world to see that, especially in English-speaking countries, there is a liberal distribution of place-names of British origin. That is, not merely names such as Cape Town and Northwest Territories that are composed of English words, but names that are based on, and sometimes exactly the same as, British names. Moreover, it is not simply British place-names that have been 'exported' to other countries in this way, but personal names, too.

Let us take a brief survey of this world map. Across the Atlantic, we can see that many place-names in the United States and Canada are derived from British names in this manner. The names of states are conspicuous here, such as New York (from York), New Hampshire (Hampshire), Pennsylvania (Penn), West Virginia (Virginia, or 'Virgin'), Carolina (Charles), Georgia (George), and so on, while north of the border, we find the Canadian provinces of New Brunswick (Brunswick, the royal house), Nova Scotia ('New Scotland'), Alberta (Albert), British Columbia (Britain) and, in major natural features, Hudson Bay, Mackenzie River, Baffin Island, Foxe Basin, Beaufort Sea, M'Clintock Channel, and many more. And this is to say nothing of the names of major cities in North America, such as Boston, Baltimore, Pittsburgh, Birmingham, Halifax, Regina ('Queen'), Edmonton, Vancouver, Victoria, and many others.

This pattern is repeated in the newer 'New World'. In Australia, for instance, we instantly notice New South Wales, Queensland, Victoria, Adelaide, Sydney, Perth, Darwin and Melbourne, while New Zealand easily reveals such names as Wellington, Christchurch, Dunedin ('Edinburgh'), Auckland, Nelson and Napier, with Stewart Island to the south. Then there is South Africa, or indeed Southern Africa, with Durban, East London, Port Elizabeth, Kimberley, Livingstone, and, further north, Lake Victoria, Lake Albert and Lake Edward. Nor was it all that long ago, historically speaking, that names such as Rhodesia, Salisbury, and Fort Victoria were familiar and in the news as much as Zimbabwe, Harare and Gwelo are today.

Elsewhere in the world, there are still many island territories with British names, such as the Falkland Islands, Gambier Islands, South Georgia, South Sandwich Islands, Pitcairn Island, New Caledonia, New Britain, New Ireland, Cook Islands, Society Islands and Prince Edward Islands.

Down in Antarctica, that unique and complex continent, names of British origin are almost embarrassingly prolific. We note Graham Land, Coats Land, Enderby Land, Princess Elizabeth Land, Queen Mary Land, George V Land, Victoria Land, Ross Sea, Prince Albert Mountains, Scott Coast, Beardmore Glacier, Cape Crozier, and many, many more. At the other end of the world, similarly, British names can be found without much difficulty inside the Arctic Circle, such as Scoresby Sound (in Greenland), George Land (Franz Josef Land), Herald Island (eastern Siberia), and the many islands and other features with British names in northern Canada.

Nor should the rest of the world be overlooked, for there is Abbottabad in Pakistan, English Bazar in India, Wingate in Israel, Victoria in Hong Kong, Kingston in Jamaica, Londres in Argentina and, until recently, there was Port Arthur in China. (The Dictionary contains a few 'recent' names of this type.)

Thus despite the fact that the heady (and in many cases bloody) days of the British Empire are long past, there remain hundreds of place-names of British origin round the world to testify to the former influence of the English-speaking mother country and to the worldwide dissemination of the English language itself.

This new Dictionary thus aims to present a fairly wide selection of such names, and to give their origins, where they are known, as they mostly are, for Britain's colonial history is relatively recent and fairly well documented.

It should perhaps be stated here, at this point, that many names that *seem* to be of British origin are not in fact so. For this reason, many well-known names are absent from the pages that follow, and there will be no further mention, except incidentally, of Washington (the state), Lincoln (the mountain) or Nashville (the city), for example, all in the United States, for these names honour two American presidents and a Revolutionary officer, not Britons. Other apparent omissions, such as South Africa's Johannesburg, Australia's Tasmania, and Oceania's Caroline Islands will also not be represented, for they are the wrong nationalities (respectively Dutch for the first two, and Spanish for the third).

So it is on the British names pure and simple that we must concentrate and like all place-names, they will be found to be very much a creation of their time. That is, the sort of British names one finds will have been inspired by one (or more) of a number of motives, ranging from the patriotic to the political, and the religious to the military.

A very little history therefore cannot be avoided, for the earliest British place-names of a country will date from the time of its original colonisation and possibly even discovery.

Bearing in mind, therefore, that all countries with British names will have had indigenous names before the arrival of the British, and in many cases names given by other colonising peoples, such as the Dutch and the Spanish, we can present a simplified picture as follows for the six major lands involved: the United States, Canada, South Africa, Australia, New Zealand and Antarctica.

Seventeenth century
English settle in Virginia, USA (1607); Hudson Bay, Canada, entered by Hudson (1610); English settle in Massachusetts, USA (1620) and Virginia (1624); English settle in Maryland, USA (1634); Hudson's Bay Company formed (1670) to trade and find Northwest passage; English settle in Pennsylvania, USA (1681); West coast of Australia navigated by Dampier (1688)

Eighteenth century
Hudson Bay region and Newfoundland pass from French to English (1713); Cook visits New Zealand (1769), makes first landing in Australia (1770); American Revolution (1775–83), Declaration of Independence (1776); British occupy Cape, South Africa (from 1795)

Nineteenth century
Australia circumnavigated by Flinders (1801–3); Cape, South Africa, ceded to British by Dutch (1814); 5000 Britons emigrate to South Africa ('1820 Settlers');

Entire Australian continent claimed by British (1829); New Zealand colonised at Port Nicholson by New Zealand Company (1840); Expansion to American Midwest after gold discovered in California (1848); 2nd Maori War, New Zealand (1860); Dominion of Canada established (1867); British annexe South African republic (1877); 1st Boer War, South Africa (1880–1); 2nd Boer War, South Africa (1899–1902)

Twentieth century
Scott's 1st expedition to Antarctic (1902–4); Union of South Africa formed (1910); Mawson's land expeditions in Antarctica (1911–14, 1929–31); American Richard Byrd explores and maps Antarctic in 1930s and 1940s; by 1940 Britain, USA and Norway have own named territories in Antarctic; Commonwealth Transantarctic Expedition (1955–8); Zambia proclaimed a republic (1964), followed by Botswana (1966); Independence of Tuvalu (1978), Kiribati (1979), Vanuatu (1980); Zimbabwe proclaimed a republic (1980), Salisbury renamed (1982)

The above basic outline contains several 'firsts', but is obviously not comprehensive in this respect, and does not include, for example, James Ross's discoveries in the Antarctic of the early 1840s, nor the achievement of the South Pole by Scott (but after Amundsen) in 1912. Even so, it does give an overview of the period and place of the various discoveries, settlements, annexations, conflicts and reorganisations that occurred in the main countries of the English-speaking world, and will thus serve as a guide to the introduction of British place-names in those countries, and to the reversal or abolition of those names (e.g. in Southern Africa) in recent times.

The kind of names that were given at any period will have depended, as mentioned, on the aspirations and credos of the colonists and settlers. It was not enough to colonise a country; it had to be done in a cause. Often as not the motive was a religious one, and moreover a Protestant or at any rate non-Catholic one, for it was the French and the Spanish who were the great introducers of Catholic names. There are exceptions, of course, but broadly speaking the British naming pattern was Protestant, even Puritan, and the famous 'Pilgrim Fathers' who founded the first permanent European settlement in North America (at Plymouth, New England, in 1620) were careful not to give 'saintly' names. It has to be said, however, that they did not give noticeably religious names, either, and one might have expected biblical names to have been bestowed. The same applies to the many Quakers who settled later in Pennsylvania, and in that state, too, biblical names are not common.

But just as the 'Catholic' names are conspicuous by their absence, so in this part of America are the 'royal' names, for the Puritans were hardly royalists! Again, there are exceptions, but such royal names as there are will usually have been given at a later date, and one of the most famous of them all, New York, honouring the Duke of York, was not given until 1664, after it had been captured by the English from the Dutch (who had called it New Amsterdam, in a rather stolid way). By this date, the monarchy had been restored (in the person of the Catholic-sympathising Charles II), and royal names were the fashion of the day.

This latter fact explains the wealth of royal names in Canada, where colonisation by the English occurred rather later than it did in America. In Canada, too, all the 'saintly' names will have been given by the French Roman Catholics, and can still be found prominently in Quebec and Newfoundland.

If it was the Puritans and the Quakers who were predominant in colonial America, it was the Church of England that played a similar influential role, although much later, in New Zealand. Hence such well-known names there as Canterbury and Christchurch. In Australia there had been a Scottish Presbyterian influence, especially in Tasmania, while in South Africa the Presbyterians and Nonconformists generally were also strong. (In the latter country the Presbyterians had much in common with the Dutch Reformed Church, and many of the new settlements there were named after local ministers of either church.)

Royal names can be found in reasonable representation in Australia (for example in the names Victoria and Queensland, relating to one and the same monarch), but to rather a lesser extent in New Zealand and South Africa, although the latter does have its King William's Town, and Port Elizabeth there, although not itself of royal origin, was formerly known as Port Rex. (For the story of this name, which is not quite straightforward, see its entry in the Dictionary.)

After religion and royalty, there next comes politics and statesmanship, taking in military heroes on the way. All English-speaking countries thus without exception contain many names based on those of 'great Britons', from prime ministers to colonial governors, and from admirals and generals to local leaders and administrators of all kinds. New Zealand is heavy on the 'heroes', and has many names familiar from the history books, such as Wellington, Clive, Nelson, Palmerston and Napier. This particular country was colonised at a time of considerable patriotic fervour, when the Indian Mutiny had occurred and when, rather earlier, there had been the still fresh memories of the Napoleonic victories of Trafalgar and Waterloo. The battle names themselves were not so much transferred as the names of those who had been victorious. Hence such names as those just mentioned.

The considerable Scottish contribution to British naming cannot be overlooked. The Scots were great pioneers and missionaries, even if not always in a strictly religious sense, so that many transferred Scottish names will be found among the more conventionally English. This is particularly so in Tasmania, as mentioned, and in New Zealand's South Island, where the Scottish Presbyterian names match the Anglican ones further to the north. The southern half of South Island thus has names such as Dunedin, Balclutha, Invercargill, and (on Stewart Island) Oban.

Another important source of names can be found in those of the original discoverers and explorers, especially in the more 'adventurous' or hazardous parts of the world, such as the polar regions. The Antarctic is thus almost a fifty-fifty blend of the royal and the reconnaissant, that is, of the men who first came here and the monarchs and their families that they honoured.

Some of the greatest explorers and discoverers were also the greatest namers, and James Cook must have given hundreds of names to the new places that he sighted and surveyed. (Sometimes, he seems to have been in such a hurry to press on his pioneer way that he failed to identify some features correctly, or simply noted an inlet or a bay without entering it.)

Cook was thus the man ultimately responsible for the naming of many familiar places in Australia and New Zealand, including Hawke Bay, Port Jackson (otherwise Sydney Harbour), Botany Bay (which he initially noted as Stingray Bay) and, most significantly of all, New South Wales, as well as many island groups such as the Society Islands, New Hebrides, New Caledonia and Prince Edward Islands. One or two of his names have now been superseded by others, such as Davis Land, which is now known as Easter Island, and the Sandwich Islands, which are now better known as Hawaii. But many of his original names remain on the map, especially on the chart of the South Pacific, so that his epitaph there might be, like that of Christopher Wren before him, *Si monumentum requiris, circumspice*. His own name is preserved in that of New Zealand's highest mountain, Mount Cook, and also in the Cook Islands (South Pacific), the Cook Strait (between North and South Islands, New Zealand), Cooktown (Australia) and the Cook Inlet (Alaska), these representatively illustrating the worldwide range and scope of his travels.

The reader will encounter many other names in the Dictionary bestowed by Cook, as well as those given by other British explorers and namers, such as William Dampier, Francis Drake, Matthew Flinders, Arthur Phillip, John Smith and George Vancouver. (See their respective surnames in the main entries for examples of the creation, and for details about the less familiar among them.)

It will be noticed that for the larger landmasses, such as the continents of North America and Australia, and the southern portion of Africa, most of the British names are still to be found where they were originally planted on or near the coast. Many of these names are among the best known internationally, and include several cited at the beginning of this Introduction. The reason for this is obvious. Why go far inland when you lay out a new settlement? If conditions are favourable by the sea, preferably at the mouth of a river, then all-important communications will be favourable. Even in Europe this principle operates, so that unless a country is itself far inland and removed from the sea, its most important cities will be near the coast. This applies to a large number of capitals, and among those so situated are London, Amsterdam, Copenhagen, Oslo, Stockholm, Helsinki, Lisbon, Rome, Athens and Istanbul. The former capital of Russia, Leningrad (then St Petersburg) is a port, and even Paris and Brussels are not too far from the sea. (It is a geographical mystery why Spain's capital should be inland Madrid, instead of coastland Barcelona or Málaga.)

The converse to this principle is thus broadly true, so that most of an English-speaking country's indigenous names will be in the hinterland: North America's Indian names, Australia's Aboriginal names, New Zealand's Maori names, and Southern Africa's African names.

It is perhaps rather surprising, in view of the worldwide dissemination and establishment of British-based names, that there are no major countries with a British name. Of the four chief English-speaking countries, America has a name that is probably of Italian origin (although the claim of Amerigo Vespucci as the source for the name has been challenged in recent years), Canada has an Indian name, Australia has a Latin name ('southern land') and New Zealand has effectively a Dutch name ('new sea land'), while South Africa's name is simply geographical. Even 'United States' is purely a title, rather than a name. This situation is all the more unexpected when one finds that names given by colonising countries apart from Britain have persisted for the lands colonised. Thus the Philippines remain named for the Spanish king Philip II, and Mauritius still bears the name of the Dutch prince Maurice of Orange. (One can almost count Colombia here, named after Columbus, although he was Italian-born, if Spanish-serving.)

But the lack of any leading state with a British name is simply a matter of the breaking of colonial ties, and the achieving of independence, and until quite recently there was a country with a British name, Rhodesia (see the timechart above).

A word needs to be said about British place-names in Antarctica. The situation there is complex, because different countries have come to claim different sectors, and in the process of discovering and naming, by different countries, some features have come to be named (and even 'discovered') twice. This means that one country can carry out an Antarctic exploration of a region and duly chart it with its own names, while another country can subsequently chart more or less the same region and give it *its* names. In other cases, due to a genuine misunderstanding, one country can 'discover' and name a feature that had, unbeknown to it, already been discovered and named. There are other factors that complicate things, too, so that a misidentity may lead to a 'Land' actually being an 'Island', or a 'Coast' actually an 'Ice Shelf'. Although there have been strenuous efforts in recent years to sort out such difficulties, and to regularise and coordinate naming procedures in the Antarctic, discrepancies remain, inasmuch as there are still rival claims to different regions. Argentina, for example, has claimed the Antarctic Peninsula since 1942, and given her own names there, just as she still calls the Falkland Islands *Las Malvinas* (and in the 'Falklands War' of 1982 renamed Port Stanley, first as Puerto Argentino, then as Puerto Rivero). But the place-name commissions of the different claimant countries, especially Britain, Australia, New Zealand, France and Norway, have largely resolved their problems, and the British names in Antarctica, even if not always official, are sufficiently well established to feature in this Dictionary.

Purists or pedants – of which you, reader, are unlikely to be either – may object to one small category of names included in the Dictionary that are not, strictly speaking, British names at all. I refer to the so-called 'battle-names'. Of the six such names entered (see Appendix I, List 9, p. 203), four are of battles fought outside Britain. They are those of Aliwal (India), Blenheim (Germany), Camperdown (Holland) and Waterloo (Belgium). But although these are indeed not British names, they are of battles fought and won by the British (sometimes with the aid of allies), and as such have become 'adopted' British names, with the second and last now even found in Britain itself. (Blenheim Palace, Oxfordshire, is a familiar mansion and estate to tourists and visitors to Britain, and London's Waterloo Bridge and Waterloo Station are known to anyone who has been to the capital, and even to many who have not.)

It is thus almost as if, in winning the battle, the British 'won' the name. And it is certainly true that all six names have been transferred to places elsewhere in the world by British settlers and colonists. (For details, see the names in the Dictionary.) I therefore feel that the inclusion of such names is justified, for although they were *im*ported to Britain, they were also *ex*ported from Britain, so are in the right category as far as the Dictionary is concerned.

Readers who are interested in this particular phenomenon, that is, the import of names to Britain from elsewhere in the world, may like to know that the category is very small. There is the curiosity of Baldock, imported (in now almost unrecognisable form) from Baghdad, and there are a few American names such as California and New York, used mostly for isolated locations, and occurring as recent borrowings, but otherwise there are few such names to be found. (Battle names are perhaps the most familiar type, and for a rather fuller consideration of the process, readers may like to refer to an article of mine on the subject, published in the irregular 'Place Names' series in the *Geographical Magazine* for June 1987, p. 274.)

On the whole, however, it is the names of the battle-winners, not the battles themselves, that have been transferred to countries outside Britain, and as far as these particular four battles are concerned that will mean the names of Harry Smith (as in South Africa's Harrismith and Ladysmith), Marlborough (for the Battle of Blenheim), Duncan (for Camperdown) and the famous Wellington (for Waterloo).

Finally, something needs to be said about the actual form of the names that were transferred from Britain to other countries.

As mentioned, many of them were taken over 'neat', just as they were, whether place-name or family name (or even first name). At the same time, it must be remembered that the earliest such transferrals took place in Shakespearean times, when many of the names were spelt differently and when spelling itself was irregular, even capricious. This is not perhaps so evident in personal names, but in place-names it is frequent. One striking example is the name of Lexington, USA. This was transferred from the Nottinghamshire village now known as Laxton. But in the early seventeenth century it was known as Lexington (or some variant spelling of this), so that there is no actual corruption here, as might be supposed. This historical factor will account for many other differences between a New World version of a name and its original in the mother country. The same can also apply to pronunciations, so that the present American pronunciation of a name corresponds to the English one at the time of settlement. This often results in a difference between the present American pronunciation of a name and the English one. Compare the American way of saying 'Derby' with the English: the former rhymes with 'Kirby', the latter with 'Tarby'. (But in the case of Hartford, the American spelling has been altered to reflect the English pronunciation of 'Hertford'.) The mention of the name Hertford is a reminder that the place-names of the Midlands and East Anglia are particularly well represented in the United States (Birmingham, Warwick, Bedford, Cambridge, Boston, Stamford, to name just a few).

Where a name was not exported 'neat', it was frequently preceded by 'New' (as if 'reborn') or was given a suffix such as '-ton' or '-ville', the last mostly, but not exclusively, for transferred personal names (such as Canada's Drummondville). But 'Fort' and 'Port' were also popular prefix words, depending on the site and the purpose of the place, even though subsequently this first word was often dropped.

It goes without saying that the most popular names can be found in all kinds of varieties several times round the world, so that the basic 'George', for example, can turn up as Georgetown, Georgeton, St George, Georgia, and so on with further additions possible not only with 'New' and the other words mentioned but with 'North', 'South', and so on. *The Times Atlas of the World* (see Bibliography,

p. 217) lists ten *lakes* named George alone.

The Dictionary, it should be noted, enters 'one-off' names in full, such as 'Fury and Hecla Strait', but for the more frequently found names, such as 'George', only the basic form of the name is usually given where a geographical term such as 'Lake' or 'Cape' normally accompanies it, or an administrative term such as 'County'.

The reader who is specially interested in the different categories of British place-name is recommended to consult Appendix I, pp. 196–207, where seventeen such categories are presented, together with brief analytical comments.

'British' names, it should be pointed out, means not just English and Scottish names, but Welsh and Irish. The last nationality is included because when all these names were first given, Ireland was itself a British colony: it was subdued by Cromwell after the rebellion of 1642 and then united legislatively with Great Britain in 1801 (as the United Kingdom of Great Britain and Ireland), so that it was granted dominion status (as the Irish Free States) only in 1921. Northern Ireland is of course still part of the United Kingdom.

When deciding whether a 'nominee' (a person who gave his or her name to a place) is genuinely British or not, I have followed the principle that if his parentage was British, then he was, wherever he was born. On the whole, too, this means that a Briton is a Briton even if he emigrates as a child with his parents, and never returns to his native land. After all, his *name* is British, and that is what matters for our present purposes. Very occasionally, I have made a minor exception here, but always with a rider explaining why.

It will be seen from the entries that many names link up with many others, either for family reasons or simply because the name itself has been duplicated or multiplicated. In other instances, a name turns up in different countries simply because its bearer did, and it was not unusual for a colonial governor or administrator to be appointed first to one country, then to another, and then even to a third or fourth. All such correspondences and interconnections are indicated by a simple cross-reference system, so that a name appearing in **bold** print in an entry will have its own entry in its appropriate alphabetical place.

Where a name does derive from a 'worthy' of some kind, I have always tried to give his dates and to explain who he was or what he did. Where dates are missing, it means that they were not readily obtainable. Otherwise, in general, the information is given as succinctly as possible, for there are over 1000 entries, and there is simply not the space to go into much detail.

For similar reasons the Bibliography (pp. 216–21) is likewise selective, as the introductory note to it explains.

And although the selection of names for the entries has itself had to be restricted, the reader will find that all the best-known ones are there, and perhaps a few lesser-known ones besides. Every entry tells its own British-based story, and the reader will soon build up a picture of the naming process, as it has occurred round the world over the past four centuries.

ACKNOWLEDGMENTS

The few acknowledgments I have to make for help during the compilation of the Dictionary are none the less very real.

First, I would like to express my thanks to Dr G. Hattersley-Smith, Secretary of the Antarctic Place-Names Committee (Polar Regions Section, South American Department) at the Foreign and Commonwealth Office, London, who not only piloted me in the right direction for source books on Antarctic place-names but even kindly presented me with an original, unpublished document on the subject, which proved not only valuable but interesting in its own right. There cannot be many toponymists (place-name experts) employed by the Foreign Office for their speciality, but Dr Hattersley-Smith is one and I am pleased to have had the benefit of his professional advice.

Also in the world of place-names, I would like to thank Miss Anne Dunford, of the Permanent Committee on Geographical Names for British Official Use, who always efficiently and cheerfully (and promptly) answered the several queries I put to her over the months, and who enabled me to make the factual content of the Dictionary that much more accurate and reliable. Ever since I first took a close interest in place-names and their meanings, I have never ceased to thank my lucky stars that I came across the offices of the PCGN (as it is more conveniently known), whose members toil assiduously and devotedly for toponymical accuracy and consistency up in their fascinating premises over the august Royal Geographical Society's demesne in Kensington.

Third, I would like to give a special expression of thanks to Mrs Kate Musgrave, who kindly supplied me with much interesting private information about Midshipman Robert Pitcairn, who gave his name to Pitcairn Island. Robert Pitcairn's grandfather was a direct ancestor of Mrs Musgrave's husband, and the family tree supplied by Mrs Musgrave is conclusive in this respect, so that the reader can be assured that the entry for this particular place-name is as authentic and accurate as it could be!

Finally, I owe thanks to Mrs Elizabeth Murray, who is lucky enough to live on the doorstep of the British Library in London, and who kindly hunted down helpful titles there on my behalf, as well as pursuing other enquiries relating to 'colonial' names.

My acknowledgments are thus due to all four members of this quartet, who in their different ways have helped to make the present Dictionary a much better book than it would have been without them.

Adrian Room
Petersfield, Hampshire, England

Place-names exported from the British Isles

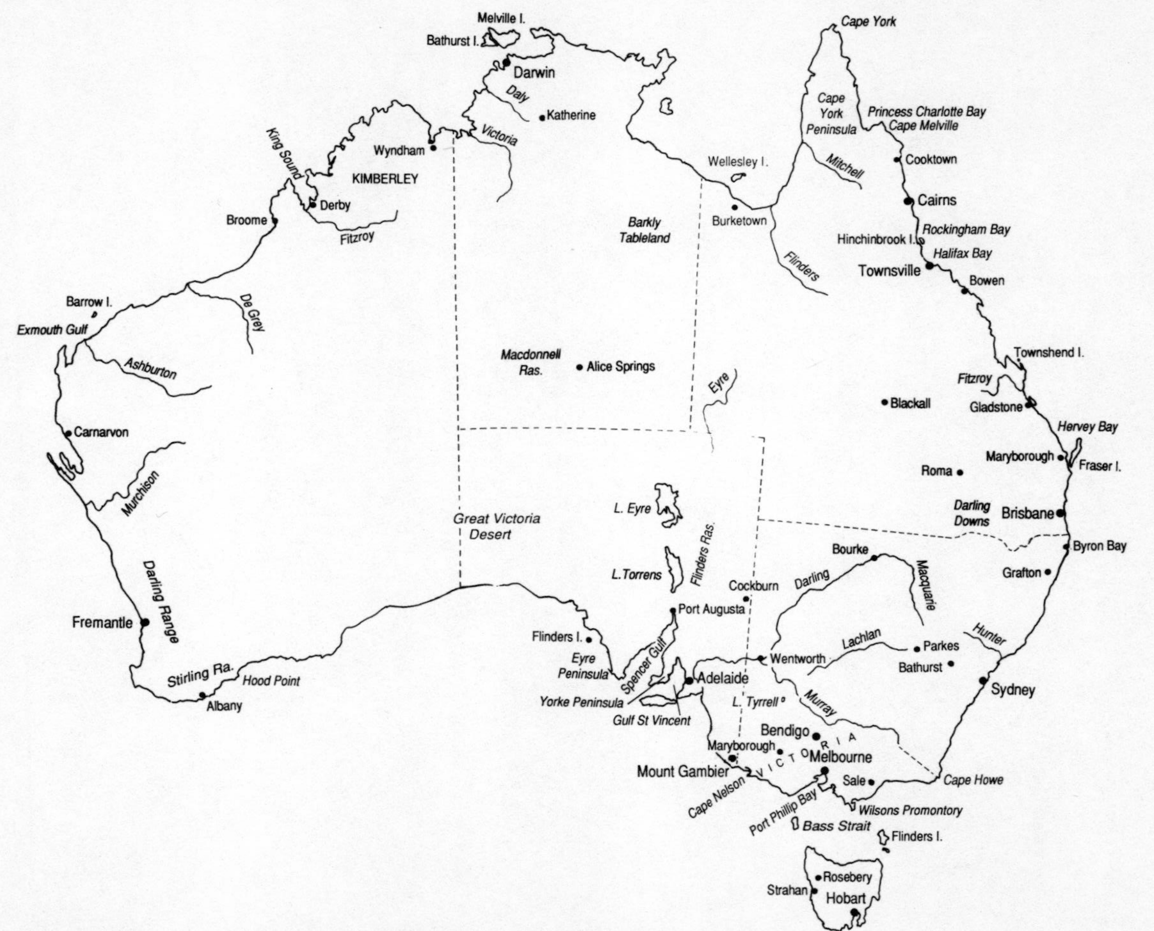

Australian place-names derived from British personal names and titles

Abbottabad (Pakistan)
The town, northeast of Rawalpindi, was founded in 1853 and named after General James Abbott (1807–1896), the first British deputy commissioner of the district of Hazara, annexed by the British in 1847. For his stand against the Sikhs and Afghans, Abbott received many awards and medals, culminating in a knighthood in 1894. In 1947, the town passed from India to Pakistan. '-abad' means 'town', as in the name Hyderabad. (Hyder is another name of Ali, son-in-law of the prophet Muhammad, or Mahomet.)

Abercorn (Swaziland)
The village, near Big Bend, was named after James Hamilton, 2nd Duke of Abercorn (1838–1913), who was a close associate of Cecil Rhodes, the founder of **Rhodesia**, and who became chairman of the British South Africa Company on its foundation in 1888. The Zambian town of Abercorn was also formerly named after him, until it was renamed (as Mbala) in 1968.

Aberdeen (USA, South Africa)
In **Maryland**, the town of Aberdeen was settled in about 1800 and was named after the Scottish city by settlers from there, while in South Dakota, the city of the same name was established in 1880 and was similarly named by Alexander Mitchell, the Scottish president of the Chicago, Milwaukee, and St Paul Railroad. Scottish emigrants also named Aberdeen, Missouri, and Aberdeen, Washington, after their native city (or possibly their native county, Aberdeenshire). In South Africa, the town of Aberdeen, Cape Province, was named after the birthplace of the Rev. Andrew Murray, Scottish minister of the Dutch Reformed Church at the nearby town of Graaff-Reinet.

Abingdon (USA)
The town of Abingdon in southwest **Virginia** was named after the English town in Berkshire (now Oxfordshire), which was the home town of Mary Ball Washington, mother of George Washington. Some sources claim, however, that Abingdon was named for an English Lord Abingdon (his family name would have been Bertie), or that the name was transferred to Virginia from Abingdon, **Pennsylvania**. The latter town was the home of the legendary frontiersman Daniel Boone, whose English Quaker parents had ties with the English town. Hence the name in that state. Compare the next entry below.

Abington (USA)
The Massachusetts town, settled in 1668, was probably named for one or other of the villages of Great or Little Abington, Cambridgeshire, from which the settlers had come, unless the name is actually a spelling variation of **Abingdon**.

Acton (Canada, USA)
In Canada, the Ontario town of Acton was originally know as Adamsville, after early settlers there named Adams. In 1844, however, the name was changed to Acton after the Middlesex borough near London (now in London), and it was this same Acton that gave the name of the United States town in Massachusetts, which is itself in **Middlesex** County. In England, Acton was a centre of Puritan activity in Cromwell's time, and this doubtless served

as the inspiration for the name among the early settlers. Compare the next entry below.

Acton Vale (Canada)
The town of Acton Vale, Quebec, was named after one of the many English Actons, and very probably after Acton, Middlesex, with the same Puritan motive as for the United States **Acton** in Massachusetts.

Addison (USA)
The names of Addison County, Vermont, and the village of Addison, Illinois, both come from that of the British essayist and statesman, Joseph Addison (1672–1719), who, although best remembered for his contributions to *The Tatler* and *The Spectator*, was also a commissioner for trade with the colonies and, near the end of his life, Secretary of State.

Adelaide (Australia, South Africa, Antarctica, Canada)
As the capital of the state of South Australia, the city of Adelaide was laid out on a site by the **Torrens** River in 1836 and the following year was named after Queen Adelaide, consort of William IV. The Adelaide River, in Northern Territory, Australia, was discovered in 1839, and was similarly named after the Queen. (The town of Adelaide River, south of **Darwin**, takes its name from the river.) Queen Adelaide also gave her name to the South African town of Adelaide in Cape Province, which was founded as a military post in 1834, while in the Antarctic Adelaide Island was likewise named in her honour, as was the Adelaide Peninsula in Northwest Territories, Canada. Adelaide Bay in **Prince Regent** Inlet, between **Somerset** Island and **Baffin** Island, off mainland Canada, was discovered by James Ross (see **Ross Sea**) on 13 August 1829, Princess Adelaide's 35th birthday. (She became Queen the following year.)

Admiralty Island (USA)
The island is in the Alexander Archipelago, Alaska, and was named by George Vancouver (see **Vancouver**) in 1794 in honour of the British Admiralty.

Ailsa Craig (Canada)
The Ontario community was named by Scottish residents after the small island south of Arran, Scotland. The town itself was founded as a result of development by the Grand Trunk Railway in 1858.

Ainslie, Lake (Canada)
The **Nova Scotia** lake was named in honour of George Robert Ainslie (1776–1839), the coin-collecting Scottish colonial governor who was Lieutenant-Governor of Cape Breton from 1816 to 1820.

Airdrie (Canada)
The town in **Alberta** was laid out in about 1893 and was named by its Scottish residents after the Lanarkshire burgh.

Ajax (Canada)
The Ontario town was established in 1941 as the site of a munitions factory, and its name was given in honour of the cruiser HMS *Ajax*, which engaged the German battleship *Graf Spee* off Montevideo in 1939. A military name for a military settlement in a military period historically, therefore.

Albany (USA, Canada, Australia, South Africa)
The capital of the state of **New York**, and one of the oldest permanent colonial settlements in the United States, was at first named Beverwyck when it developed from a Dutch trading post in the early seventeenth century. When it passed to the British in 1664, together with nearby Fort Orange, it was renamed Albany in honour of the then Duke of York and Albany, the future James II of England. Virtually all the other places of the name in the USA are taken from the New York city. In Canada, Albany River, Ontario, was named after Fort Albany, the trading post at its mouth established in 1684 by the Hudson's Bay Company. In Australia, the town of Albany in Western Australia was originally a penal settlement de-

veloped in 1826 as Frederickstown, after Frederick Augustus, Duke of York and Albany, the second son of George III. By 1832, however, the name had become Albany. It was this same duke who gave his name (or title) to the South African region of Albany, in Cape Province. It was established in 1814 by the former Governor of the Cape Colony, as it then was, Sir John Cradock (see **Cradock**), in an area previously known as the Suurveld (literally 'sour veld', referring to the type of grass there). Albany itself is an ancient name for the Scottish Highlands, but is no longer in use in Britain except as a later local name derived from one of the dukes.

Albemarle (USA, Galápagos Islands)
In the USA, Albemarle Sound is an coastal inlet in northeast North **Carolina**. Although first explored by the British in the late sixteenth century, it was not named until the seventeenth century, when it came to be called after George Monck, 1st Duke of Albemarle (1608–1670), who was one of the Lords Proprietors of the territory between **Virginia** and Florida (including present-day North and South Carolina) granted to him and seven others in 1663 by Charles II. The Galápagos Islands, in the Pacific, belong to Ecuador and officially have Spanish names. The islands have alternative English names, however, and Isabela Island, the largest of the group, is also known as Albemarle Island. It is almost certainly not named after the 1st Duke, however, but after his son, Christopher Monck, 2nd Duke of Albemarle (1653–1688), governor of Jamaica from 1687. The namer was the English buccaneer navigator William Cowley, who arrived in Galápagos in 1684.

Albert (Southern Africa, Canada)
One may be almost certain that any place named Albert will have been named after Prince Albert, consort of Queen Victoria. Lake Albert, on the border between Zaire and Uganda, indeed was. It was discovered in 1864 by the English explorer Samuel Baker, and he was the namer. However, the lake was renamed Lake Mobuto Sese Seko in 1973, after President Mobuto of Zaire (from 1965). But the old, more familiar name still appears on many maps and in many atlases, leaving the new name as purely an official one. In South Africa, Albert is the name of a region between the Stormberg and the Orange River, in Cape Province, and is also named after the prince, as probably are the Albert Falls on the Umgeni River in Natal. In Canada, Albert is the name of a county in **New Brunswick**, and it, too, was named after Victoria's consort when it was established in 1845. (The Albert Mines near the present village of Riverside-Albert in the county gave their name to the mineral albertite.) See also the next entry for the best-known 'Albert' name.

Alberta (Canada)
The Canadian district of Alberta was established in 1882, becoming a province, with an enlarged area, in 1905. But the name does not commemorate Queen Victoria's consort! It was proposed by the Governor-General of Canada from 1878 to 1883, the Marquess of Lorne, in honour of his wife. She was Princess Louise Caroline Alberta, and the daughter of Prince Albert (see previous entry) and Queen Victoria. Obviously, the princess's own name was based on that of her father. See also **Lorn**, **Lorneville**, **Louise**.

Alberton (Canada)
Alberton, together with Alberton South, is a settlement near the western tip of **Prince Edward Island**. It was named after Queen Victoria's eldest son, Prince Albert Edward, the future King Edward VII, who in 1860 paid a visit to the Island (itself named after his grandfather). The larger Alberton in the Transvaal, South Africa, however, was not named after the Prince but for the purchaser of the estate in 1904, General Hendrix Alberts.

Albion (USA)
Albion was originally an ancient name for England (or for southern England only, or perhaps even for the whole of the British Isles), and it is found as the name of several settlements in the United States.

The first American record that we have of the name is when Francis Drake claimed what is present-day California for the crown in 1579 and named it **New Albion** (which see separately). Some of the modern Albions were also given the historic name directly, although they were founded much later. But it is still disputed in a few instances, as often happens, one Albion took the name of another in the United States, so made a secondary acquisition. This happened with Albion, Michigan, which was named after Albion, Maine. Drake is said to have given the name specifically because he sailed close to some white cliffs, which reminded him of the 'white cliffs of Dover'. But it is still disputed whether the original name actually derives from Latin *albus*, 'white', and even whether it is basically the same name as Albany.

Albury (Australia)

Albury is a city in **New South Wales**, on the north bank of the **Murray River**. It was founded as a police post in 1838 and is said to be named after the village of Albury near Guildford, Surrey, from where possibly one of the early explorers of this region had come or had been born.

Alden (USA)

The village of Alden, in the state of **New York**, was named after John Alden (1599–1687) and his wife Prescilla. John Alden was one of the 'Pilgrim Fathers' who arrived on the *Mayflower*, and who subsequently became Deputy Governor of Massachusetts. The courtship of John Alden and Prescilla forms one of the central (but fictional) themes in Longfellow's poem *The Courtship of Miles Standish* (1858), where John is described as marrying Prescilla after first wooing her for his friend Miles Standish.

Aldershot (Canada)

Aldershot, **Nova Scotia**, is a military base, like its English counterpart, Aldershot, Hampshire, after which it was named.

Alert (Canada)

Both Alert Bay, on **Vancouver** Island, **British Columbia**, and the settlement of Alert at the northern end of **Ellesmere** Island, Northwest Territories, are named after HMS *Alert*, the flagship of a British survey expedition to the Arctic that called at both places in 1875 or 1876.

Alexander Bay (South Africa)

Alexander Bay is south of the mouth of the Orange River, Cape Province, and was named after the British officer and explorer, Sir James Edward Alexander (1803–1885), who served in the Kaffir War of 1835 and later explored the region here (now known as Namaqualand). His actual post in the War was that of aide-de-camp to Sir Benjamin D'Urban, who gave his name to **Durban**.

Alexandra (New Zealand, South Africa, USSR)

The New Zealand town of Alexandra, on South Island, was named in 1863 in honour of Princess Alexandra, who married the Prince of Wales (the future King Edward VII) that year. The South African township of Alexandra, near Johannesburg, was also presumably named after Queen Alexandra, while Alexandra Land (Zemlya Aleksandry) in Franz Josef Land, USSR, certainly was, the latter by the explorer Leigh Smith in his exploration of the Arctic islands in 1880–1.

Alexandria (South Africa)

The town, in Cape Province, was originally known as Olifantshoek ('elephants corner') when it was first established as a police post in the first half of the nineteenth century. In 1873, however, its name was changed to Alexandria, not in honour of Queen Alexandra (see previous entry), but after Alexander Smith, a Scottish minister of the Dutch Reformed Church at Uitenhage.

Alexandrina, Lake (Australia)

Lake Alexandrina, a lagoon in South Australia southeast of **Adelaide**, was discovered in 1830 by the English explorer Charles Sturt (see **Sturt Desert**), who named it after Princess Alexandrina, the future Queen Victoria (whose full names were Alexandrina Victoria).

Alfred (USA, Canada, South Africa)
Both towns of Alfred in Maine and New York were named in honour of King Alfred, king of the West Saxons, in the latter case possibly because the terrain suggested that near Winchester, Hampshire, where King Alfred had his capital. In Canada, Alfred, Ontario, was named after Prince Alfred, the infant son of George III. In South Africa, however, Alfred County, Natal, was named after another Prince Alfred, the second son of Queen Victoria. He visited Natal in 1860.

Alice (South Africa)
The town of Alice in Ciskei was named in 1847 after Princess Alice, the second daughter of Queen Victoria. The Princess was only four years old at the time.

Alice Springs (Australia)
The town of Alice Springs, Northern Territory, arose in 1889 on a site surveyed the previous year and originally named Stuart, after the Scottish explorer John McDouall Stuart. The present name was given in 1933, when 'Alice' was a tribute to the wife of Sir Charles Todd, then postmaster of South Australia, while 'Springs' referred to the permanent water holes there in the bed of the Todd River. The town features in Nevil Shute's novel *A Town Like Alice* (1949).

Aliwal North (South Africa)
The town is in Cape Province, on the Orange River, where it was founded in 1849 by the Governor of the Cape Colony, Sir Harry Smith (see **Harrismith**). He named it Aliwal to commemorate his victory over the Sikhs at Aliwal, India, in 1846. Aliwal was also formerly the name of Aliwal South, some distance away on the south coast, but this town's name was changed in about 1850 to Mossel Bay (after the bay here) to avoid confusion with Aliwal North. See also **Whittlesea**.

Allerton (USA)
The town of Allerton, Massachusetts, and also Point Allerton, **Boston** Bay, were named after an English place of the name from which English settlers probably came. This is likely to have been the present district of Allerton in Liverpool, as there are other Liverpool-based names in the USA (such as **East Liverpool** and **Liverpool** itself).

Alliston (Canada)
Alliston, Ontario, is said to have been named in 1848 by the first settler there, William Fletcher, after his native Yorkshire village, Alliston. But English gazetteers do not list such a name. Perhaps the original reference was to Allerston, a village near Pickering, Yorkshire.

Althorpe Islands (Australia)
The Althorpe Islands lie south of Cape **Spencer**, at the southern tip of **Yorke Peninsula**, South Australia. Both the Cape and the Islands were discovered in 1802 by the English explorer and hydrographer Matthew Flinders (see **Flinders)**, and he named them both for the noted statesman, George John Spencer, Viscount Althorp and 2nd Earl Spencer (1758–1834), who was First Lord of the Admiralty (to 1801) at the time when his ship was commissioned. (See **Spencer** for more details.) Viscount Althorp's title came from the village of Althorp near Northampton, where he had his family seat in the historic house of the same name. (This was also the family home of the present Princess of Wales, formerly Lady Diana Spencer.)

Alverstone, Mount (Canada)
The mountain, in the Yukon, as one of the St Elias Mountains, bears the name of Richard Everard Webster, Viscount Alverstone (1842–1915), who was not only the Lord Chief Justice of England but, more significantly for the mountains here, a member of the Alaska Boundary Commission of 1903. Further south, just over the border with **British Columbia**, the boundary peaks in this same mountain group bear the names of other men who served on the Commission at a later date,

although these were mainly Americans, not Britons.

Alvinston (Canada)
The community of Alvinston, Ontario, has a name that is a corruption of that of the village of Alverstone, near Sandown, Isle of Wight, with which one of the settlers must have had a link. But this was not the place's original name. It was first named Gardner's Mills (after the first settler, Archibald Gardner), then Brooke Mills, then Brannen, these last two also presumably after settlers.

Amelia (USA)
Amelia is the name of both a county of **Virginia** and of the county seat ('capital') of that county. Both names honour Amelia Sophia (1711–1786), second daughter of George II of England, who gave his own name to **Georgia**, among other places.

Amery Ice Shelf (Antarctica)
The name was given by members of the Australian National Antarctic Research Expeditions (ANARE), who conducted research in the Antarctic from the 1940s, in honour of L.S. Amery (1837–1955), the British politician who did much for colonial territories as Secretary of State for, successively, the Colonies, Dominion Affairs, and India. Australia claimed the Amery Ice Shelf in 1933.

Amesbury (USA)
The town in northeast Massachusetts is near **Salisbury**, and so is named after Amesbury, Wiltshire, which is also not far from the English city of Salisbury. However, although Massachusetts has county names identical with English counties (such as **Berkshire**, **Hampshire**, **Middlesex** and **Norfolk**), it has no Wiltshire, and Amesbury is actually in **Essex**.

Amherst (USA, Canada, Burma)
In the United States, Amherst is the name of a number of places, almost all of which derive ultimately from Jeffrey (later Baron) Amherst (1717–1797), the British army commander who captured Canada for Britain and who was promoted to chief commander in America in the French and Indian Wars, although he refused a North American command during the War of American Independence (American Revolution). The same is mostly true in Canada, although the town of Amherst, **Nova Scotia**, for example, was originally called La Planche by French settlers, and other places had similar French names to begin with. The Amherst in Burma was named for another Lord Amherst. This was William Pitt (later Earl) Amherst (1773–1857), the nephew of Baron Amherst, who was British Governor General of India and who played an important part in the gaining of Asian territories after the First Burmese War of 1824–6. The present district of Amherst, in Lower Burma, took its name directly from the seaport and resort of the name which is now, however, called Kyaikkami. See also **Cobourg** (Canada) and the next entry below.

Amherstburg (Canada)
Both Amherstburg and Amherstview, towns in Ontario, take their names from Baron Amherst (see entry above), as do many other places in Canada, including Amherst Island in Frontenac County. Amherstview is really a descriptive name, as the town overlooks Amherst Island in Lake Ontario.

Andover (USA, Canada)
The town of Andover in northeast Massachusetts originally had an Indian name when it was settled in 1642. This was Cochicewick ('great cascade'). However, the name became Andover four years later, as tribute to many of the settlers who had come from Andover, Hampshire. In Canada, the town of Andover, **New Brunswick**, had a name of similar origin. In 1972 it combined with **Perth** (also a British name) to form the new community of Perth-Andover.

Anerley (South Africa)
The holiday resort near **Port Shepstone**, Natal, is said to be named after the London district of Anerley, in the borough

of Bromley. Possibly one of the original founders or settlers came from there. Alternatively, the original farm on the site here could have been given the Scottish name Anerley for its isolation, as the name itself means 'lonely', 'on its own'.

Ann, Cape (USA, Antarctica)
In Massachusetts, Cape Ann is a peninsula north of Massachusetts Bay. The name was placed on the English colonist John Smith's map of New England by Prince Charles (the future Charles I) in 1614, probably as a compliment to his mother, Queen Anne of Denmark, consort of James I. In Antarctica, Cape Ann is on the coast of **Enderby** Land, which was itself discovered (more precisely, rediscovered) by the English explorer John Biscoe (see **Biscoe Islands**) in 1831. Biscoe named the cape after his wife. There is another Cape Ann in Antarctica, a small peninsula on the equally modest Coulman Island, off **Victoria** Land. This was named after the wife of the famous explorer James Ross (see **Ross Sea**).

Annandale (Canada)
Annandale, on **Prince Edward Island**, was named in 1868 by James Johnston, a settler who emigrated to Canada from Annandale, Scotland, in 1840. The name is that of his native district, the valley of the Annan River, in Dumfriesshire (now Dumfries and Galloway). See also **New Annan**.

Annapolis (USA, Canada)
Annapolis, the capital city of **Maryland**, was settled by Puritans from **Virginia** in 1649 and was at first called Providence. After three changes of name, including Anne Arundel Town (after the daughter of Thomas Arundell, 1st Baron Arundell of Wardour, later the wife of Lord Baltimore, whose family gave **Baltimore** its name), the town was renamed Annapolis in 1694, partly retaining the former name, but chiefly to honour Princess Anne (the future Queen Anne), with *polis* the Greek for 'town', 'city'. In Canada, Annapolis Royal (originally Port Royal when founded in 1605), is the seat of Annapolis County, **Nova Scotia**, and was so named in 1710, also to honour Queen Anne. Annapolis Royal is Canada's oldest settlement, and was the capital of Nova Scotia until 1749, when **Halifax** was founded. See also the next entry below.

Anne Arundel (USA)
Anne Arundel is the name of a county in **Maryland**, given for the same reason as the early name of **Annapolis** (see entry above).

Anson (USA)
Anson is the name of a county in North **Carolina**, and it bears tribute to George Anson, Baron Anson (1697–1762), the English admiral who was responsible for defending the Carolina coast.

Antrim (USA)
Any place named Antrim in the United States is likely to have been named, either specifically or generally, by Irish immigrants for the Irish county (or its town of Antrim). This certainly applies to the county in Michigan and the town in **New Hampshire** (the latter, moreover, in the county of **Hillsborough**), and for Antrim, **Pennsylvania**, it is known that that the original settler was the Irishman Duncan S. Magee, from Co. Antrim. Records tell how in 1686 a company of promoters gathered round the spring here, and 'Duncan S. Magee, dipping a glassful of water from its crystal depths, formally christened the place Antrim'.

Archbald (USA)
The borough of this name in Lackawanna County, **Pennsylvania**, was originally a village known as White Oak Run until about 1846, when it was renamed in honour of James Archbald, an influential engineer in the Delaware and Hudson Company, who was born on the island of Little Cumbrae, Scotland, in 1793.

Arlington (USA)
There are several places of the name in the United States, with perhaps the best known being Arlington, Massachusetts, Arlington, Texas, and, particularly, the

Arlington National Cemetery on the Potomac River, opposite Washington. The last named was built in 1864 on the estate of the playwright George Washington Parke Custis, adopted son of George Washington and the father-in-law of Robert E. Lee, and he had named his mansion after Henry Bennet, 1st Earl of Arlington (1618–1685), the English statesman who, with Lord Thomas Culpepper, shared Charles II's grant of the colony of **Virginia**. The name was then transferred to other places today named Arlington, although many of them will have had different names previously. Lord Arlington was one of the members of the famous Cabal (group of ministers) whose names fortuitously spell out this word: *C*lifford, *A*shley, *B*uckingham, *A*rlington, *L*auderdale.

Armagh (Canada)
In the same manner as places named **Antrim**, Armagh, Quebec, was named by Irish immigrants after their native county (or its chief town).

Armidale (Australia)
The town, in **New South Wales**, was founded in 1839 by G.J. Macdonald, commissioner for crown lands, and he named it after his father's Scottish baronial estate of Armadale (as it is now spelt) on the Isle of Skye.

Arniston (South Africa)
Arniston is the unofficial name of the seaside village in Cape Province usually known by its Afrikaans name of Waenhuiskrans ('coach-house cliff', referring to a local cave). The name Arniston, promoted by a local estate agency, refers to the British troopship *Arniston* that was wrecked in the bay off the coast here in 1815 with the loss of over 300 lives. Arniston itself is a Scottish village near Dalkeith.

Arnprior (Canada)
The town of Arnprior, in Ontario, arose in 1823 as a Scottish settlement pioneered by Archibald McNab, the last laird of the Clan McNab, and he named it after the ancestral home, Arnprior, near Stirling, of his associates, Andrew and George Buchanan.

Arrowsmith (New Zealand, Australia)
Mount Arrowsmith, in the Southern Alps range, South Island, New Zealand, Mount Arrowsmith, in **New South Wales**, Australia, and Point Arrowsmith, in Northern Territory, Australia, were all named after the English cartographer John Arrowsmith (1790–1873), who published large maps and charts of many countries, including especially fine ones of colonial Australia.

Arthurs Pass (New Zealand)
Arthurs Pass is a route through the Southern Alps (see previous entry), which became especially important when gold was discovered in 1864. Two years later, a road was built through the mountains here, and it was named after the explorer Sir Arthur Dudley Dobson (1841–1934).

Arundel (Canada)
The town in Quebec is named after its English namesake in West Sussex, with which early settlers doubtless had an association.

Ashburnham (USA)
The town in Massachusetts was named in 1765 after Ashburnham, East Sussex, rather than any members of the Ashburnham family, as is sometimes claimed. (The best known of these was the seventeenth-century Royalist John Ashburnham, who advised Charles I to take refuge from the Parliamentarians in the Isle of Wight.)

Ashburton River (Australia)
The river is in Western Australia, and was discovered in 1861 by the explorer (and politician) Francis Gregory, who named it after Lord Ashburton, the then President of the Royal Geographical Society.

Ashcroft (Canada)
The community of Ashcroft, in **British Columbia**, was so named in 1862 by the English-Canadian senator and governor

Clement Francis Cornwall. It was originally the name of his ranch here, which he called Ashcroft Manor after his family home in Gloucestershire.

Ashley River (New Zealand, USA)
In New Zealand, Ashley River, South Island, famous for its scenic Ashley Gorge, was named after the famous philanthropist, otherwise known as 'Lord Ashley', Anthony Ashley Cooper, 7th Earl of Shaftesbury (1801–1885). The river in South **Carolina**, however, was named after the 1st Earl of Shaftesbury (see **Cooper River**).

Athelstan (Canada)
Athelstan, Quebec, was settled by Scotsmen, and the name is a shortening of their native village of Athelstaneford, near Haddington, Lothian.

Athol (USA)
Athol is a town in Massachusetts, where it was originally settled in 1735 with the Indian name of Pequoiag. In 1762 it was incorporated and renamed for Blair Atholl, the Scottish home (Blair Castle) of the Dukes of Atholl. The particular tribute was to James Murray, 2nd Duke of Atholl (?1690–1764), who was Lord Privy Seal at the time. Compare the next entry below.

Atholville (Canada)
The name of the community in **New Brunswick** derives from the railway station here, which was originally called Athol House, and which was built as a home for Robert Ferguson (1768–1851), a settler who was a native of Blair Atholl, Scotland. Compare the previous entry above.

Attleboro (USA)
The Massachusetts city was named after the town of Attleborough, Norfolk, from which early settlers had come.

Auburn (USA)
The many towns, cities and other communities in the United States named Auburn have almost all directly or indirectly taken their name from Oliver Goldsmith's pastoral poem of 1770, *The Deserted Village*, where he describes a village named Auburn as the 'loveliest village of the plain'. Goldsmith's Auburn has been identified both with Lissoy, Westmeath, where the poet spent much of his childhood, and with a village near Bridlington, Yorkshire (now Humberside), that has been swept away over the years by the sea. But although the Irish village was actually known as Auburn for some time, and recorded as such in gazetteers, the Yorkshire village was never known by any other name (prosaically, rather than poetically, it means 'eel stream'), and it seems likely therefore that Goldsmith's 'Sweet Auburn' was a blend of the two, with the name of the latter chosen for the idyllic village of the poem, which contains descriptions of features recognisable in the former. The city of Auburn, Washington, was originally known as Slaughter, after an American army officer killed in the Indian wars. It was renamed in 1893.

Auckland (New Zealand)
The name is best known as that of the seaport city of Auckland, North Island, and that of the Auckland Islands, an uninhabited group to the south of New Zealand. The city was established as the capital of the colonial government in 1840, when it was named in honour of George Eden, Earl of Auckland (1784–1849), Governor General of India and (subsequently) First Lord of the Admiralty. The Auckland Islands were discovered rather earlier, in 1806, but were nevertheless named, some years later, after the same Earl of Auckland. Auckland was superseded as the New Zealand capital by **Wellington** in 1865. The Earl took his title from Auckland, Durham, near Bishop Auckland. The administrative district of Auckland, North Island, was named after the city. See also **Russell**.

Augusta (USA)
The city of Augusta, **Georgia**, was set up as a fur trading post in 1735, and the settlement that developed round it was named after Princess Augusta, mother of

George III. Augusta, the state capital of Maine, however, was probably not named for the Princess but for Pamela Augusta Dearborn, daughter of the American general Henry Dearborn, who was Secretary of War under Jefferson.

Avalon (USA, Canada)
Avalon, **Pennsylvania**, had three earlier names before it acquired its present one in 1893. The surrounding countryside had many fruit trees or orchards, so the residents chose a name that has been interpreted as meaning 'island of apples', 'orchard'. (In Celtic languages the word for 'apple' is similar, such as Irish *abhall* and Welsh *afal.*) In Canada, the Avalon Peninsula in Newfoundland is on record as having been named by the English proprietor Sir George Calvert (1580–1632) for its plantation, which was 'officially styled in imitation of old Avalon in Somersetshire' (*The Newfoundland Journal of Aaron Thomas*). Other American and Canadian places named Avalon may have been generally so designated as a kind of 'paradise', with reference to the Avalon of Arthurian legend.

Avoca (Australia)
The town of Avoca, in **Victoria**, was founded in a gold rush in 1852 and was named for the romantic village and vale of Avoca, in Co. Wicklow, Ireland. The reference may have been partly topographical as well as 'idealistic', and the direct source of the town's name is that of the Avoca River, on which it lies.

Avon (USA, Canada)
Most of the towns, cities or other settlements named Avon will have arisen on an Avon River, and the reference is almost always to the English river on which Stratford-on-Avon, Shakespeare's birthplace, stands. However, compare the next entry below, and see also **Stratford**.

Avondale (USA, Canada)
Although the city of Avondale, Arizona, is named after the English Avon River, as mentioned in the previous entry, the Canadian Avondale, in Newfoundland, was named after the Irish village of Avondale, Co. Wicklow. Its original name was Salmon Cove, but this was changed in 1906 by order of the Newfoundland Nomenclature Board, presumably to avoid confusion with another place of this name.

Aylesford (Canada)
Aylesford, **Nova Scotia**, was named in honour of the 4th Earl of Aylesford, who was Lord of the Bedchamber to George III. The township was established in 1786.

Ayr (Australia, Canada)
The town in **Queensland** was surveyed and gazetted in 1881 and the following year named after Ayr, Scotland, the birthplace of the then State Premier, Sir Thomas McIlwraith (1835–1900). The Canadian community of Ayr in Ontario was also named after this town by Scottish settlers, one of whom was James Jackson, who named the **Nith River** in this province.

B

Babbage River (Canada)
The river, in the Yukon, was named by the English Arctic explorer Sir John Franklin (see **Franklin**) for the mathematician Charles Babbage (1792–1871), who was one of the founders of the Royal Astronomical Society, as well as of other learned bodies.

Back River (Canada)
The river flows through the **Mackenzie** and Keewatin districts, Northwest Territories, and was originally known as the Great Fish River, this translating its Indian name Thlew-ee-coh-desseth. The Arctic navigator (later Admiral Sir) George Back (1796–1878), who was a member of Sir John Franklin's expedition (see **Franklin**) of 1819–20, considered the original name to be too long. The river was therefore renamed after him, as a tribute to his exploration of it in 1833–5.

Baffin (Canada/Greenland)
Baffin Bay is a large inlet lying between Baffin Island, Canada and Greenland. It was discovered by the English navigator William Baffin (1584–1622) in 1616 and named after him as was, that same year, Baffin Island itself. Baffin was the pilot on several expeditions in search of the Northwest Passage in the four years from 1612 to 1616, and he succeeded in sailing to a latitude of 77°45′, a record unsurpassed for 236 years.

Bagotville (Canada)
The town of Bagotville, Quebec, was first settled in 1839 and came to be named after the man who surveyed it three years later, Sir Charles Bagot (1781–1843), Governor General of Canada (or 'British North America', as it was then officially designated). Bagot County, Quebec, is also named after him.

Baillie-Hamilton Island (Canada)
The island is one of the **Parry** Islands, and lies between **Bathurst** Island and **Devon** Island, Northwest Territories. It was named in 1851 as a tribute to the successful career of Captain W.A. Baillie-Hamilton, who was Secretary of the Admiralty at the time.

Baillie Islands (Canada)
The Baillie Islands, near Cape **Bathurst**, Northwest Territories, were discovered by Sir John Franklin (see **Franklin**) in 1826, and named after George Baillie, the then Agent General for the Crown Colonies. Also named after him is the Baillie River, a tributary of the **Back River**, and the namer was Back himself, who discovered it in 1834.

Bairnsdale (Australia)
Bairnsdale is a town at the mouth of the **Mitchell River, Queensland**, and is said to be so named because an early Scottish settler commented that 'bairns were born with unfailing regularity' there. The actual development of the town proper dates from the end of the nineteenth century.

Baker Lake (Canada)
The Lake is in the Keewatin district, Northwest Territories, to the west of **Hudson** Bay. It is named after Sir William Baker of the Hudson's Bay Company, and the namers, who discovered the lake in 1762, were the two Captains Christopher and Norton, themselves members of the same Company.

Balclutha (New Zealand)
The town of Balclutha, in Otago, South Island, was originally known as Clutha Ferry and thus takes its name from the Clutha River on which it stands. The river name, in turn, was given by Scottish settlers from an early, Celtic name of the river Clyde in their native land. The 'Bal-' of the name is a common element in many Scottish place-names, such as Balmoral and Balfour, and means simply 'village', 'settlement', so is appropriate for the New Zealand town. Compare **Clyde**.

Balfour (South Africa)
There is more than one place of the name in South Africa. Balfour, Transvaal, a town southeast of Johannesburg, was originally known as McHattiesburg, after the owner of the farm where it was founded in 1897. In 1905 it was renamed Balfour after the British Prime Minister, Arthur James Balfour, who visited South Africa that year. However, the village of Balfour in Cape Province, north of **Fort Beaufort**, was established as a station of the Glasgow Missionary Society in 1828 and was named after the first Secretary of the Society, Robert Balfour.

Balleny Islands (Antarctica)
The islands, a volcanic group in the Ross Dependency (see **Ross Sea**), were named after the captain of an English whaler who discovered them in 1839. This was John Balleny.

Balmoral (Canada)
Balmoral, **New Brunswick**, was named by Scottish settlers after the famous royal residence in Scotland, Balmoral Castle, as both a native tribute and a royal one. The name is quite late, as Balmoral Castle did not become a royal holiday residence until 1852, when it was purchased by Prince Albert. Compare **Sandringham**.

Baltimore (USA)
The well-known city in **Maryland** was established in 1729 and was named for the Lords Baltimore, proprietors of the colony of Maryland. Baltimore was the hereditary title of the Calvert family (see **Calvert**), and derives from their baronial seat of Baltimore, Co. Cork, Ireland. Aptly enough, in a metaphorical sense, the actual name Baltimore in the original Irish means 'settlement of the great house'.

Banff (Canada)
The community of Banff, **Alberta**, with its well-known Banff National Park, is named after the Scottish resort of Banff. The name was suggested by John H. MacTavish, Land Commissioner of the Canadian Pacific Railway, as the Scottish town was not far from the birthplace of the Railway's President from 1881 to 1888, Sir George Stephen (Baron Mount Stephen).

Bangor (USA)
There are two Bangors of note in the USA – and two possible Bangors in the United Kingdom from which they may be named, either Bangor, Wales, or Bangor, Northern Ireland, both ancient religious settlements. The city of Bangor in Maine was at first known as Kenduskeag Plantation after its original settlement in 1769, then it was renamed Sunbury in 1787. It acquired the name Bangor in 1791. The story behind the name runs that a Reverend Seth Noble was one day whistling the rather mournful melody of the hymn-tune 'Bangor' when he was asked the name of the new town. Not understanding the question properly, he replied 'Bangor', and the name was accepted. Bangor in **Northampton** County, **Pennsylvania**, however, is named directly after Bangor, North Wales. The town was founded in 1866 by a Welshman, R.M. Jones, who wished to open a slate quarry. The site that he found resembled the area of slate quarries in Carmarthenshire (now Gwynedd) near the Welsh town, and the name thus relates to both his native Wales and the quarries of both regions.

Banks (Canada, New Zealand, Australia, New Hebrides)
All these places and regions, as well as many others, are named after Sir Joseph Banks (1743–1820), the English naturalist

who accompanied Cook around the world on board the *Endeavour* and who subsequently became President of the Royal Society. Most of the names were given by Cook himself, and among the best known are Banks Island, Northwest Territories, Canada, Banks Peninsula, South Island, New Zealand, Banks Strait, between the **Furneaux Islands** and Tasmania, Australia, and the group of islands, Banks Islands, in the **New Hebrides** (which are now known as Vanuatu, renamed in 1980).

Banzare Coast (Antarctic)
The Banzare Coast is a section of the coast of Wilkes Land, and took its name from BANZARE, otherwise the British, Australia, New Zealand Antarctic Research Expedition of 1929–31, led by Sir Douglas Mawson (see **Mawson**), which mainly concentrated on this eastern region of the Antarctic. At least the first letter of the seven-letter abbreviation justifies the inclusion of the name here, even if Mawson himself does not for this particular entry!

Barkerville (Canada)
The town of Barkerville, **British Columbia**, was named for William Barker (died 1894), a Cornish sailor who jumped his ship in 1858 to try his luck in the gold rush in the Cariboo Mountains. Barker made a strike in 1862 that was valued at $600,000, but he died in poverty.

Barkly Tableland (Australia)
The Tableland extends for several hundred miles parallel to the Gulf of Carpentaria in Northern Territory, with its eastern end in **Queensland**. It was named by William Landsborough, the explorer, after Sir Henry Barkly (1815–1898), Governor of **Victoria** from 1856 to 1863. Compare the next entry.

Barkly West (South Africa)
The town of Barkly West, on the Vaal River in Cape Province, was originally known as Klipdrift ('rocky ford') when it first arose in 1869. The following year it was renamed for Sir Henry Barkly, Governor of the Cape from 1870 to 1877. Also named after him are the town of Barkly East, established in 1874, and the mountain route of Barkly Pass near here over the Drakensberg Mountains. Compare the entry above.

Barnstaple (USA)
Barnstaple is a town and port in Massachusetts, founded in 1838 by farmers attracted to the salt hay in the marshes nearby, and the site was named after Barnstaple, Devon, also a seaport. Doubtless some of the original settlers had come from the English town, although the location of the place by the sea could have been an added reason for the name.

Barrhead (Canada)
The town, in **Alberta**, was named in 1913 by directors of a local cooperative after Barrhead, Scotland, a manufacturing town where there had been a similar collective force.

Barrington (USA)
The town of Barrington, Rhode Island, was originally incorporated by Massachusetts in 1717, becoming a new township distinct from **Swansea** in that state. In 1747 Barrington was transferred to Rhode Island Colony, where it became part of the town of **Warren**. The separation from Swansea was made because of religious differences, and the town's name reflects this, as it derives from that of John Shute, Viscount Barrington (1678–1734), the English theologian and lawyer who advocated religious freedom. (His brother, Samuel Shute, was governor of Massachusetts.) Compare the next entry.

Barrington Passage (Canada)
Barrington Passage, **Nova Scotia**, was settled by New England planters in the 1760s. In 1767 it was named after William Wildman Barrington (1717–1793), later Viscount Barrington, who was Chancellor of the Exchequer at this time.

Barrow (USA, Canada, Australia)
Point Barrow, in Alaska, was discovered in 1826 by the British admiral and Arctic

navigator Frederick William Beechey, and named for Sir John Barrow (1764–1848), the member of the naval administration who promoted Arctic exploration. The city of Barrow on the headland here is named after the Point. Barrow Strait, Canada, between **Bathurst** and **Cornwallis** Islands, Northwest Territories, was discovered by Parry in 1819 and also named after him, as is Barrow Island, off Western Australia. Several other capes, bays, rivers and other natural features in the above countries are also named after Barrow, but not Barrow County, Wisconsin, USA, which is named after a local jurist.

Bartle Frere, Mount (Australia)
The mountain is the highest in **Queensland**, and was named in 1873 by the Scottish explorer George Dalrymple in honour of the Welsh diplomat Sir Henry Bartle Edward Frere (1815–1884), formerly Governor of Bombay. See also Mount **Frere**; **Lady Frere**.

Bass Strait (Australia)
The well-known strait between Tasmania and mainland Australia was discovered in 1798 by the English navigator Matthew Flinders (see **Flinders**) and his surgeon colleague, George Bass (1771–1803), and was named after the latter.

Batemans Bay (Australia)
Batemans Bay is both a town and an inlet of the Tasman Sea in **New South Wales**. The inlet, which gave its name to the town, was discovered in 1770 by James Cook and was named by him after Captain Bateman, master of the ship *Northumberland* (see **Northumberland**).

Bath (USA)
Bath, the city and port in Maine, was settled in about 1670 and named after the city of Bath, Somerset (now Avon). The town of Bath in North **Carolina**, however, was named for the 1st Earl of Bath, William Pulteney (1684–1764), while Bath, the village in **New York**, was settled in 1793 and named after Sir William's daughter and heiress, Henrietta, who at one time owned more than a million acres of land in western New York.

Bathurst (Australia, Canada, Gambia, South Africa)
All these places were named after one and the same man, Henry Bathurst, 3rd Earl of Bathurst (1762–1834), Secretary of State for the Colonies from 1812 to 1827, a period of rapid and intensive colonial expansion. The more important places of the name are as follows: the city of Bathurst, **New South Wales**, Australia, founded in 1815; Bathurst Island in the Timor Sea, Northern Territory, Australia, explored by Philip Parker King (see **King**) in 1818; the city of Bathurst, **New Brunswick**, Canada, named in the 1820s but founded by the French some two hundred years earlier; Bathurst Island, one of the **Parry** Islands, Northwest Territories, Canada, discovered by Parry in 1819; Cape Bathurst, in **Mackenzie** District, Northwest Territories, Canada, discovered by Dr (later Sir) Richardson (see **Richardson**) in 1826; Bathurst, the capital of Gambia, founded in 1816 (but renamed Banjul in 1973); Bathurst, the town in Cape Province, South Africa, founded in 1820 and named after the Earl by Sir Rufane Donkin, Acting Governor of the Cape Colony. The Earl himself probably derived his name and title from Bathurst Wood, near Battle, Sussex.

Bayfield (USA)
Bayfield County, Wisconsin, was named after the British admiral Henry Wolsey Bayfield (1795–1885). Its original name was La Pointe, retained for the only settlement on the Apostle Islands, in Lake Superior, off the Wisconsin coast.

Bay Roberts (Canada)
The town of Bay Roberts, Newfoundland, was named by fishermen from the Channel Islands, who settled here in the sixteenth century, and who must have included a man named Roberts. Compare **Jerseyside**.

Beaconsfield (Canada, Australia, South Africa)
The city of Beaconsfield in Quebec,

Canada, where it is now a suburb of Montreal, was named after Benjamin Disraeli, 1st Earl of Beaconsfield (1804–1881) (see also **Disraeli**), as were both the town of Beaconsfield in Tasmania, Australia, and Beaconsfield in Cape Province, South Africa, originally a separate town but now a district of **Kimberley**. (It was originally called Dutoitspan after the local diamond mine proprietor.) Disraeli was twice the English Prime Minister: in 1868 and from 1874 to 1880. See also **Hughenden**.

Beagle Bay (Australia)
Beagle Bay, in Western Australia, was discovered by the British admiral and explorer John Lort Stokes in the late 1830s, while he was surveying the western Australian coast in the *Beagle*, and the bay, as well as other features here, were named after the ship. (This was the same *Beagle* on which Darwin had made his famous surveying expedition in the Pacific and elsewhere in 1831–6.) Compare the next entry below.

Beagle Channel (Chile/Argentina)
The Beagle Channel lies between Tierra del Fuego and a group of Chilean islands off the tip of South America. The channel was discovered by the British admiral Robert Fitzroy (see **Fitzroy**) when he was making a survey of Patagonia on board the *Beagle* in the period from 1828 to 1834, and it was given the name of his ship. This was the same vessel on which Darwin made his surveying expedition in the Pacific, and Fitzroy was a participant in this later historic voyage. Compare the previous entry above.

Beardmore Glacier (Antarctica)
The glacier, which is one of the largest in the world, was used by Sir Ernest Shackleton as part of his route to the South Pole in his expedition of 1907–9, and was named by him after the shipbuilder and patron of Antarctic exploration William Beardmore, Baron Invernairn (1856–1936). Beardmore had sponsored Shackleton's expedition and had given him a motor vehicle to be tested for the first time in Antarctic conditions.

Beaudesert (Australia)
The town is in **Queensland**, on the **Logan** River, and when a livestock station was established there in 1842 it was named after the small village of Beaudesert near Henley-in-Arden, Warwickshire. Presumably one of the original settlers must have come from there, although the name, meaning literally 'beautiful wilderness', must have seemed appropriate and propitious for a new settlement.

Beaufort (Canada, USA, South Africa)
Probably the best-known location of the name is the Beaufort Sea, in the Arctic Ocean northeast of Alaska. It owes its name to the British admiral and hydrographer, Sir Francis Beaufort (1774–1857), who also gave his name (because he devised it) to the Beaufort Scale of wind speeds. Beaufort, the city in South **Carolina**, USA, was the subject of many early attempts at settlement, but was eventually named, in about 1712, for Henry Somerset, 2nd Duke of Beaufort (1684–1714), a proprietor of the colony of South Carolina. His title was fitting for the fort that had been built here by the British the previous year. In South Africa, the settlement of Beaufort was established in what is now Cape Province in 1818, and was named by Lord Charles Somerset, Governor of the Cape, after his father, the 5th Duke of Beaufort. In order to avoid confusion with Fort Beaufort and Port Beaufort, however, the name of the town was subsequently changed to Beaufort West. See also **Port Beaufort**; **Somerset**.

Bedford (USA, South Africa)
Many of the United States Bedfords are named for the English town, either directly, because settlers had emigrated from there, or indirectly, as a transferral of an existing Bedford. Among these are the towns in Massachusetts and **New York**. However, several others are named after John Russell, 4th Duke of Bedford (1710–1771), who was responsible for

negotiating the peace treaty that ended the French and Indian Wars (1757–62). These include Bedford County (and the county seat) in both **Pennsylvania** and **Virginia**, and the town in **New Hampshire**. The latter was named by Governor Benning Wentworth, who was a personal friend of the Duke. (The Duke is said to have presented a 'beautiful silken English flag' to the commander of Fort Bedford, as the Pennsylvania Bedford was formerly known.) In South Africa, the town of Bedford in Cape Province was named by the owner of the farm where it arose in 1854, Sir Andries Stockenström, after another Duke of Bedford, a friend of his. This was Francis Russell, 9th Duke of Bedford (1819–1891).

Beechey Island See **M'Clintock Channel**

Belcher Islands (Canada)
The islands are in **Hudson** Bay, Northwest Territories. They were first sighted by Hudson himself in 1610, and he named them after Sir Edward Belcher (1799–1877), the naval officer who made many coastal surveys for the Admiralty and who led an expedition in search of the lost explorer Sir John Franklin (see **Franklin**).

Belfast (USA, South Africa)
The city of Belfast, Maine, was named by a settler who came from Belfast, Ireland, and who helped establish the community in 1770. Like its Irish namesake, the United States Belfast is a seaport and port of entry. In South Africa, Belfast in Transvaal is a town that was established in 1890 on a farm whose owner's father, John O'Neill, had been born in Belfast, Ireland.

Belinda, Mount (Antarctica)
The mountain, in the **South Sandwich Islands**, was named by members of the *Discovery II* expedition of the 1930s for the daughter of the British oceanographer and biologist Stanley Kemp, later Director of the Discovery Committee.

Bellingham (USA)
The Washington city was probably named after Sir William Bellingham, who supervised the voyage of George Vancouver (see **Vancouver**). The name was given by Joseph Whidbey, under Vancouver's command.

Bell Lakes (Canada)
The lakes, in **Nova Scotia**, were originally known as the Baddeck Lakes, a corruption of an Indian name. In 1974, however, they were renamed in honour of Alexander Graham Bell, inventor of the telephone.

Bendigo (Australia)
The city, in **Victoria**, was founded as a sheep run in 1840, and was known as Castleton, then as Sandhurst, before acquiring its present name in 1891. It was named as a tribute to the English champion boxer and (later) Methodist evangelist who went by the name of Bendigo (1811–1880). His name was probably a corruption of the Old Testament name Abednego, and his real name was William Thompson. No doubt the boxer had a 'fan' here among the early Australian settlers.

Ben Lomond (Australia)
The mountain mass in Tasmania was named in 1894 by the explorer and Lieutenant-Governor of **New South Wales**, William Paterson, after his native Scottish mountain Ben Lomond. Other places of the name also derive directly or indirectly from the same source.

Berkeley (USA)
The places with this name do not commemorate one single man but several. Berkeley, California, probably the best known, owes its name to the University of California that was established here (as the result of a merger of two colleges) in 1868. Its campus, opened in 1873, was named after the Irish philosopher Bishop George Berkeley (1685–1753), who went to America in 1728 in connection with a scheme for a missionary college in Bermuda. Before leaving, Berkeley composed a set of 'Verses on the prospect of planting arts and learning in America',

containing the famous line, 'Westward the course of empire takes its way'. However, Berkeley County, West **Virginia**, was named after Norborne Berkeley, Lord Botetourt (1718–1770), a colonial governor of Virginia, and Berkeley County, South **Carolina**, was apparently named for John Berkeley (1607–1678), proprietor of South Carolina in the reign of Charles II. Compare the next two entries below.

Berkeley Heights (USA)

The **New Jersey** town was named after Lord John Berkeley (died 1678), who was one of the first proprietors of New Jersey, together with Sir George Carteret (see **Carteret**).

Berkeley Springs (USA)

The town and health resort in West **Virginia** has a name that could refer to one (or more) of a number of Berkeleys, as so many men of the name were administrators in colonial days. It could thus have been either Norborne Berkeley or Lord John Berkeley (see **Berkeley** and **Berkeley Heights**). Lord John's brother William was a governor of Virginia, and it could equally have referred to him. An earlier name for the town, still legally in use, was Bath, for the springs here (the second half of the present name).

Berks (USA)

Berks County, **Pennsylvania**, is named after the English county of Berkshire, conventionally abbreviated to Berks. Thomas and Richard Penn, sons of William Penn (see **Pennsylvania**), had purchased much of the land here from the Indians, and they named the region for the English county where their family still held large estates. Compare the next entry (especially for the pronunciation).

Berkshire (USA)

Berkshire County, Massachusetts, and the Berkshire Hills that mainly lie in it, take their name from the English county, with the connection with Penn present as mentioned in the entry above. The American pronunciation of this name and **Berks** (above) rhymes with 'perk', not 'park'. See also **Pittsfield**.

Bernardsville (USA)

The **New Jersey** borough was named for Sir Francis Bernard (1712–1779), colonial governor of New Jersey from 1758 to 1760 and subsequently of Massachusetts.

Berwick (Canada)

The town of Berwick in **Nova Scotia**, Canada, was settled by **New England** farmers in the early nineteenth century and probably named after the English port of Berwick-upon-Tweed, Northumberland. However, some sources claim that the name was a borrowing of that of Berwick, Maine, USA. The latter Berwick may not have been named after the Northumbrian port. But Berwick, **Pennsylvania**, was. It was founded in 1786 by one Evan Owen, who named it for his home town of Berwick-upon-Tweed. The North American Berwick is pronounced 'burr-wick', not 'berrick'.

Berwyn (USA)

The community near **West Chester, Pennsylvania**, was named (originally as a railway station) after the Berwyn Mountains in North Wales. Compare **Cynwyd**.

Bessemer (USA)

The name is that of at least three towns in the United States, and in each case is a tribute to Sir Henry Bessemer (1813–1898), the British inventor and engineer who pioneered the first method for manufacturing steel inexpensively, and who gave his name to the Bessemer converter and the Bessemer process. It is no surprise, therefore, to find that the towns themselves are associated with the steel industry, and Bessemer, Alabama, for example, founded in 1887, was developed by a local coal baron who built the first steel plant in the district. Bessemer, Michigan, too, prospered in the 1890s as the centre of an iron-mining district. Other towns of the name are Bessemer, **Pennsylvania**, and Bessemer City, North **Carolina**.

Beverly (USA)
Both Beverly, the city in Massachusetts, and the famous Beverly Hills, home of film and television personalities next to Hollywood, are named after the Yorkshire (now Humberside) town of Beverley. The former town was settled by emigrants from this part of Yorkshire in about 1626, but the latter city was not laid out and named until 1906. Beverly Hills thus has no direct or even indirect connection with the Yorkshire town, but was given a name that was regarded as typically English. The same applies to Beverly Hills in Michigan, another late development.

Bexley (USA, Canada)
The city of Bexley, Ohio, was originally known as Pleasantridge before it merged with the neighbouring community of Jeffery (named for a local manufacturer) and became Bexley Village in 1908 (subsequently simply Bexley). The name was given after Bexley, Kent (now a London borough), although the precise motivation for the name is uncertain. On the other hand, Cape Bexley, on the **Dolphin and Union Strait**, Northwest Territories, Canada, was named as a tribute to Nicholas Vansittart, 1st Baron Bexley (1766–1851), Chancellor of the Exchequer from 1812. Compare **Vansittart** Bay.

Biddeford (USA)
The industrial city in Maine was originally settled in 1630 by Englishmen led by the colonist captain Richard Vines. He wintered there, so that the first name of the port was Winter Harbour. But he was also born near Bideford, Devon, like other settlers, and this gave the present name of the city, with its slightly modified spelling. Compare the next entry below.

Bideford (Canada)
Like **Biddeford**, the area here in **Prince Edward Island** was settled by immigrants from Bideford, Devon, and was named after that town. The settlement dates from 1818.

Bigelow Mountain (USA)
The mountain, in western Maine, was named after Hosea Bigelow, a British officer in the French and Indian Wars of 1689–1783.

Billerica (USA)
The Massachusetts town was named after Billericay, Essex. (Billerica was an earlier spelling for the English town.) The American township was settled in 1637 and originally had the Indian name of Shawsheen.

Bingham (USA)
Many places of the name in the United States are named for American officers and officials, such as Binghamton, **New York**. However, Cape Bingham on Yakobi Island, Alaska, was named in 1794 by George Vancouver (see **Vancouver**) as a tribute to the amateur painter Margaret Bingham, Countess of Lucan (1740–1814).

Birchenough Bridge (Zimbabwe)
The community near Masvingo is named after the bridge built here over the Sabi River in 1935. This was funded by Sir Henry Birchenough (1853–1937), President of the British South Africa Company and Chairman of the **Rhodesia** and Mashonaland Railway Company, and was thus named in his honour. The ashes of Sir Henry and his wife Mabel are interred in one of the pillars of the bridge.

Birmingham (USA)
Just as **Bessemer** was adopted as a suitable name for a steel manufacturing town, so Birmingham, as the name of Britain's famous industrial and metal manufacturing city, was adopted for a new industrial settlement. Birmingham, the largest city in Alabama, was so named, and developed as the iron and steel centre of the South after its foundation in 1871. Similarly, Birmingham, Michigan, settled in 1817, was also named for the British city, although its main manufacturing today is concentrated on agricultural implements. Birmingham in **Pennsylvania** was founded in 1797 by John Cadwallader, who regarded the site at the

head of navigation on the Juniata River as suitable for a manufacturing town. Its iron industry developed early and thus gave its name.

Biscoe Islands (Antarctica)
The Biscoe Islands, west of **Graham** Land, are named after the English explorer and sealhunter John Biscoe, who discovered many new features in this part of Antarctica when he sailed here in the 1820s and 1830s.

Blackall (Australia)
The **Queensland** town was named after the colony's governor from 1868 to 1870, the Irishman Samuel Wensley Blackall (1809–1871).

Blackstone (USA)
Blackstone, Massachusetts, is named after the Blackstone River here, itself named for William Blackstone (1595–1675), the first white settler in what is now **Cumberland**, Rhode Island.

Blaketown (Canada)
The Newfoundland community is named after Sir Henry Arthur Blake (1840–1918), who was Governor of Newfoundland for two years from 1887.

Blantyre (Malawi)
Malawi's largest city was founded in 1876 as a Church of Scotland mission station, and was named after the Scottish birthplace of David Livingstone (see **Livingstone**), the town of Blantyre, Lanarkshire (now Strathclyde).

Blenheim (New Zealand)
The town is the administrative centre of **Marlborough** County, South Island, and its name commemorates the Battle of Blenheim in 1704 in which the Duke of Marlborough won a victory over the French in the Wars of the Spanish Succession.

Bligh Island (USA)
The island, in Alaska, was named after William Bligh (1754–1816), the captain of HMS *Resolution* on James Cook's third voyage. He is better remembered as 'Captain Bligh' of the *Bounty*, famous (or notorious) for the ship's mutiny in 1789. See also **Bounty Islands**.

Boalsburg (USA)
The village in **Pennsylvania** was settled in 1799 and named for Captain David Boal, from Co. Antrim in Ireland, who had emigrated to this region the previous year. Attempts were made by others to change the name to Springfield in the early years of the nineteenth century, with reference to the local springs, but Boalsburg remained as the official name, and was adopted by the Post Office in 1820.

Bolingbrook (USA)
The village of Bolingbrook, in Illinois, was named by (or for) settlers from Old or New Bolingbroke, Lincolnshire. The English villages are connected with the Bolingbroke family name and title, itself derived from them, and the fact that this name is pronounced 'Bolingbrook' probably resulted in the spelling of the American village.

Boothia (Canada)
The name is most familiar for the Gulf of Boothia and the Boothia Peninsula, both in the Northwest Territories (**Franklin** District). The latter was formerly known as Boothia Felix, and both geographical features are named after Sir Felix Booth (1775–1850), who had financed the Arctic expedition of James Ross (see **Ross Sea**) in 1829, with Ross making the actual discovery of the peninsula and giving the name. (Ross gave other names here in honour of his financier and his family, such as Felix Harbour, Cape **Felix**, Brown Island and Elizabeth Harbour, these last two for Sir Felix's sisters. Ross even named Brentford Bay and North Hendon here, after the then village of Hendon, Middlesex, where Sir Felix lived.) Sir Felix Booth was the son of Philip Booth, the founder of the company of gin distillers which still produces Booths Gin.

Boscawen (USA)
The town of Boscawen, **New Hampshire**,

was named after Admiral Sir Edward Boscawen (1711–1761), who led the British fleet in the capture of Fort Louisburg in Canada in 1758, thus blocking French preparations for an invasion of **New England**.

Boston (USA)
The name is that of one of the best-known transatlantic tranfers from the mother country. Boston was settled in 1630 by English Puritans of the Massachusetts Bay Company. Ostensibly for commercial reasons, but actually for religious reasons (the 'split' with the Church of England), the Massachesetts Bay Company transported its charter to the New World to establish a new settlement. They named it after the Lincolnshire town from which many of them had come, Boston. (It is said, however, that many Puritans were dismayed to find that the English name ultimately derives from 'Botulf's stone' as a Catholic 'saintly' name!)

Bothwell (Canada)
Bothwell, Ontario, was named in about 1856 by George Brown,of the Toronto *Globe* newspaper, after the Scottish town of Bothwell in Lanarkshire (now Strathclyde), from which his family had originated.

Bounty Islands (New Zealand)
The islands were discovered by Captain William Bligh (see **Bligh Island**) in 1788 on HMS *Bounty*, and were named after his ship. Bligh and his crew were thus the original 'Bounty hunters'. The following year, however, the crew mutinied, and the tale of this event, in many embroidered forms and reenactments, has gone down in legend as the 'Mutiny on the *Bounty*'. (The actual bounty which Captain Bligh and his men were seeking was in fact breadfruit trees in the South Sea Islands.) The Islands lie some distance east of New Zealand, but are under its administration. They are uninhabited.

Bourke (Australia)
The town of Bourke, on the **Darling** River in **New South Wales**, arose round a stockade erected in 1835 by Sir Thomas Mitchell as a defence against the Aborigines. It was named after the Irish-born colonial governor (mainly of New South Wales) Sir Richard Bourke (1777–1855).

Bowbells (USA)
The city of Bowbells, North Dakota, was named by an English railway stockholder, apparently a Londoner (even Cockney), after the famous bell peals of the church of St Mary-le-Bow, London.

Bowen (Australia)
The town and port in **Queensland** was named after the first Governor of Queensland, Sir George Ferguson Bowen (1821–1899). The colony had just been severed from its dependence on **New South Wales**, whose own government had earlier commissioned a Captain H.D. Sinclair to locate a new harbour. But an independent Queensland was then created before this could be carried out (in 1859).

Bowers Mountains (Antarctica)
The name is that of the British naval officer, Lieutenant H.R. Bowers, who accompanied Scott on his fateful Antarctic expedition in 1912, and was given to the mountains here on **Victoria** Land (discovered and named in 1911). The names of other members of this last expedition were similarly preserved here, as for the **Scott Coast** and the **Wilson** Hills.

Boxford (USA)
The Massachusetts town is named after Boxford, Suffolk, from which village one or more of the original settlers must have come.

Brackenfell (South Africa)
The village near Cape Town took the name of the farm on which it arose. The farm itself was acquired in 1901 by a Scotsman, George Henry Walton, who named it thus evocatively after his native land, but also because the terrain reminded him of the Scottish countryside.

Braddock (USA)
Braddock, in **Pennsylvania**, is tradition-

ally regarded as having been settled in 1742 by John Frazier, the first white man to build his cabin west of the Allegheny Mountains. However, the town is not named for him but for the British general Edward Braddock (1699–1755), who was fatally wounded near here in 1755 by the French and Indians, as they lay in ambush.

Braintree (USA)
The Massachusetts town was settled in 1634 and at first had the Indian name of Monoticut ('abundance'). It was part of early **Boston** until it was separated in 1640 and renamed after Braintree, Essex, doubtless because of local colonial ties with this town.

Brampton (Canada)
The town of Brampton, in southeast Ontario, was founded in about 1830 and was named after the birthplace of John Elliott, one of the first settlers, namely the town of Brampton, Cumberland (now Cumbria).

Branford (USA)
Branford, in Connecticut, was settled in 1644 and named (with variant spelling) after Brentford, Middlesex, with which its early settlers had links.

Bransfield Strait (Antarctica)
The strait, between the tip of **Graham** Land and the **South Shetland Islands**, was discovered in 1820 by the English naval officer Edward Bransfield (?1795–1852), and was named after him, as was Mount Bransfield on the Antarctic mainland.

Brentwood (USA)
The city of Brentwood in California was named by early settlers after their home town of Brentwood in Essex. Brentwood, **Maryland**, however, was probably named after an early settler, said to have been George Brent.

Bridgeport (Canada)
Bridgeport in **Nova Scotia** is named after the London firm of Rundell, Bridge and Rundell, who at one time supported the General Mining Association here. In the 1880s the community was actually known as Bridgeport Mines. The many places named Bridgeport elsewhere, however, are mostly descriptive, referring to a port with a prominent bridge.

Bridgewater (USA)
The Massachusetts town is named after Bridgwater, Somerset, from which town one or more of its original settlers had emigrated.

Bright (Australia)
The town in **Victoria** was founded in 1862 on the site of an alluvial gold deposit, and was named in honour of the British reform politician John Bright (1811–1889). At the same time, the name is in itself clearly propitious for a new settlement, especially one promising a 'bright future' for gold prospectors.

Brighton (USA)
The Colorado city is probably named not directly after the famous seaside resort of Brighton, East Sussex, but after **New Brighton, Pennsylvania**. This in turn was so named because it lay over the Beaver River from 'Old Brighton' (now called Beaver Falls), which *was* named directly after the resort. Old Brighton arose in about 1830 on land bought the year before.

Brisbane (Australia)
Both the famous city, the third largest in Australia, and the river on which it lies, the Brisbane, are named after the Scottish soldier, astronomer and science patron Sir Thomas Brisbane (1773–1860), who was governor of **New South Wales** from 1821 to 1825. The city, which originated as a penal colony named Edenglassie in 1824, was originally in New South Wales, but became the capital of **Queensland** in 1859, the year when this state became independent. The river was discovered in 1823 by three convicts escaping from the colony at Sydney, and was explored by Lieutanant John Oxley, who rescued

them. Sir Thomas gave his baby daughter the Christian names of Eleanor Australia.

Bristol (USA, Canada)
Bristol is quite common as a placename of many sizeable towns and cities (and counties) in North America, in each case bearing tribute to the English city that has long been an important port on the estuary of the river Severn. In many cases the United States or Canadian namesakes also became noted industrial settlements or ports (or both). Bristol, Connecticut, was settled in 1727 and was originally known as New Cambridge before being organised as a town in 1785 and renamed Bristol. It stands on the Pequabuck River. Bristol, **Pennsylvania**, is on the **Delaware** River, and when originally laid out in 1697 was known as Buckingham, becoming New Bristol about three years later and simply Bristol two years after that. The name is specially significant here, as William Penn's grandfather, Giles Penn, was a Bristol man, while his father, Sir William Penn, was buried in the church of St Mary Redcliffe, Bristol. Moreover, this Pennsylvania town arose on a site near William Penn's home, in what is now **Bucks** County. Another important place of the name is the Bristol that lies on the **Virginia**-Tennessee border, in an extension of the Shenandoah Valley. It arose as a trading post in 1771. Bristol Bay, however, is an arm of the Bering Sea, off Alaska, and was named in 1778 by Captain Cook in honour of Vice-Admiral Augustus John Hervey, 3rd Earl of Bristol (1724–1779), who had distinguished himself in many naval exploits. In Canada, Bristol in **New Brunswick** is named for the English port, although it was originally called Kent Station until the 1880s.

British Channel (USSR)
The channel, usually marked on modern maps by its Russian (translated) name of Britanskiy Kanal, lies between **George** Land and a number of other islands east of it in Franz Josef Land (Zemlya Frantsa Iosifa), north of the Arctic Circle. It was so named by the English explorer F.G. Jackson in his expedition of 1894–7 to this region ('The channel up which we have travelled, and which is as wide as the English Channel, I have named the British Channel', Frederick G. Jackson, *A Thousand Days in the Arctic*, 1899). See also **George** Land, **Salisbury** Island, **Queen Victoria Sea**, and Appendix II, pp. 208–12 for a detailed account of Jackson's naming processes here.

British Columbia (Canada)
The Canadian province of British Columbia was one of the last regions of North America to be explored and settled. When the Crown Colony was formed here in 1858, it was originally intended to have the name New Caledonia, from the Roman name for Scotland (see **New Caledonia**, now in quite a different part of the world). This name was already in use for what is now mainland British Columbia. However, in order to avoid confusion with the French island of New Caledonia, and also to honour Christopher Columbus (although he was no Englishman!), Queen Victoria suggested that the new province should be renamed British Columbia. Hence the name. (Columbia, moreover, had already been loosely used for the southern part of the colony, although this name was American in origin, from the Columbia River, which was in turn named by an Americal naval officer after his ship.)

British Empire Range (Canada)
The mountain range is at the northern extremity of **Ellesmere** Lane, Northwest Territories, where it lies just north of its American equivalent, the United States Range. The name was given by the Oxford University Exploration Club during its expedition to this part of the Arctic in 1934, a year when admittedly the British Empire was well past its heyday. But possibly it was felt desirable to 'match' the American mountain range. A member of the expedition was Edward Shackleton, son of the famous Shackleton who gave his name to the **Shackleton Glacier** down at the opposite end of the world.

Brockville (Canada)
The city, in Ontario on the St Lawrence River, was founded in about 1790, and was known by a succession of 'royal' names (Elizabethtown, Williamstown, Charlestown) until the War of 1812 (with Great Britain), when it was renamed in honour of the British soldier and subsequent Lieutenant-Governor of Canada, Sir Isaac Brock (1769–1812). He forced the surrender of General William Hull's forces at Detroit in 1812, but only a few months later was fatally wounded in the Battle of Queenston Heights on the Niagara frontier.

Bromptonville (Canada)
The village in Quebec was established in 1804 and was originally known as Brompton Falls. It was certainly named for an English Brompton, although precisely which is uncertain. Possibly the Brompton that is now a suburb of Northallerton, North Yorkshire, is the most likely, although there is another Brompton in modern North Yorkshire (a village not far from Scarborough), and Brompton in Kent, now a district of Gillingham, must not be overlooked. Brompton in southwest London seems a little less likely, but is not impossible by any means as the source of the name.

Broome (Australia)
The port of Broome, in the north of Western Australia, arose in 1883 in connection with the discovery of pearl-oyster beds off the coast here. The settlement was named after Sir Frederick Napier Broome (1842–1896), Governor of Western Australia from 1883 to 1891. See also **Wyndham**.

Broughton Island (Canada)
There are at least two islands of the name, both in Northwest Territories. Broughton Island lying east of **Baffin Island** was named by James Ross (see **Ross Sea**) for Commodore William Robert Broughton (1762–1821), who had carried out survey work along the northwest coast of North America in the 1790s, much of it together with George Vancouver (see **Vancouver**). Broughton Island in **Hudson** Bay, however, was named after W. K. Broughton, an employee of the Hudson's Bay Company.

Brown, Mount and **Point** (Australia)
Both Mount Brown and Point Brown, in South Australia, were named after the Scottish botanist Robert Brown (1773–1858), who accompanied the expedition to Australia led by Matthew Flinders in 1801 (see **Flinders**). For Brown Island, see **Boothia**.

Brunswick (USA)
Brunswick is not only the name of a historic duchy in northwest Germany (where it is known as Braunschweig), but the title of many British rulers, in particular the royal house of Hanover, which included all Georges from I to IV, William IV, and Queen Victoria. (The title represents the marriage connections with the British royal family.) In many place-names, therefore, the reference will normally be to a king or queen. Brunswick in Maine was incorporated as a township in 1717, when it was named for George I, who was Elector of Brunswick-Lüneburg. Brunswick in **Georgia**, however, was founded later, in 1771, and was named for George III. See also **New Brunswick** and the next entry below.

Brunswick Bay (Australia)
Brunswick Bay, in northern Western Australia, was so named in 1820 by the English surveyor Philip Parker King (see **King**) 'in honour of the illustrious House of Brunswick'. Specifically, this would have been a tribute to George III, then in the last year of his reign. See also **Prince Regent**.

Bryce, Mount (Canada)
Mount Bryce is in **British Columbia**, and was named for the Irish-born viscount (of Scottish ancestry) James Bryce (1838–1922), who among his other responsibilities, such as Ambassador to the United States, was at one time a

member of the London-based Alpine Club.

Bryn Mawr (USA)
Bryn Mawr is a residential community in **Pennsylvania**, and is well known for its Bryn Mawr College, founded in 1880. But although the name duplicates that of the former mining and steel centre in South Wales, itself also a nineteenth-century development, it appears to have a more descriptive relevance in this case, with the two Welsh words meaning 'big hill'.

Buccaneer Archipelago (Australia)
The archipelago lies off the northern coast of Western Australia at the entrance to **King** Sound, and it was named after the famous (or infamous) English buccaneer and circumnavigator William Dampier (1652–1715), who gave his name to other features in the area such as Dampier Land and the Dampier Archipelago (see **Dampier**).

Buckingham (USA, Canada)
A name typical of those that can derive equally from a duke or the town. If a duke, the reference will almost certainly be to either George Villiers, 1st Duke of Buckingham (1502–1628), who virtually ruled England in the latter part of James I's reign and the first years of Charles I's reign, or George Villiers, 2nd Duke of Buckingham (1628–1687), a member of the Cabal (see **Arlington**) in the reign of Charles II. Buckingham County, and its seat, identically named, in **Virginia**, probably honour the latter duke. In Canada, the town of Buckingham in Quebec has a more certain origin, as it was founded in 1827 by emigrants from its English counterpart. Compare the next entry below.

Bucks (USA)
Bucks County is in **Pennsylvania**, and derives its name from the regular abbreviated form of Buckinghamshire. The particular association is that William Penn's family had lived in the English county for many generations, and many of the Quakers that came over with him in 1682 had emigrated from there. At first the Pennsylvania county was named Buckingham, in full, but the shorter form gradually became more popular until it was finally adopted.

Bulwer (South Africa)
The town of Bulwer, in Natal, was established in 1890 and named for Sir Henry Bulwer (1836–1914), Governor of Natal from 1882 to 1885.

Bunbury (Australia)
The seaport in southwest Western Australia was founded in 1843 and named after Lieutenant Henry Bunbury, who explored the area.

Buntingville (South Africa)
Buntingville is a Methodist mission station in Transkei. It was called Old Bunting when first established (some distance from the present site) in 1830. The name honours Dr Jabez Bunting (1779–1858), the English Wesleyan leader.

Burke (USA)
There are several counties and communities of the name in the United States, many of them American in origin, not British. However, the statesman and philosopher Edmund Burke (1729–1797), who defended the American colonies in his speeches, is recorded as having given the name of Burke County, **Georgia**, and Burke Mountain, Vermont. Compare the next entry below.

Burketown (Australia)
Burketown lies in far northwestern **Queensland**, and was named for the Irish explorer Robert O'Hara Burke (1820–1861), who led the first expedition to cross Australia from south to north, but who died from exhaustion on the return journey.

Burlington (USA, Canada)
There are well over a dozen places of the name in the United States, in several instances borrowing it from one another (and in the case of Burlington, North

Carolina, selecting it from a postal guide). However, the town of the name in **New Jersey** was originally called Bridlington, and before that, New Beverly, showing its colonial (and Quaker) link with Beverley, in Yorkshire (see **Beverly**), and with Bridlington, also in Yorkshire (both English towns are now in Humberside). Here, therefore, Burlington was an 'Americanisation' of Bridlington, and thus incidentally preserves the local pronunciation of the name of the English town. The New Jersey town was settled in 1677. Burlington in Vermont was settled in 1763 and was named for the Burling family, who were pioneer landowners here. Many other Burlingtons, including the one in Ontario, Canada, were nineteenth-century foundations.

Burnaby (Canada)

The name is found noticeably in **British Columbia**, where it exists for Burnaby Island, Burnaby Lake, Mount Burnaby and the community of Burnaby itself. These are all named for Robert Burnaby (1828–1878), an English businessman who spent sixteen years in British Columbia from 1858, chiefly in connection with survey work. The lake was the first to be named.

Burnhamthorpe (Canada)

The community in Ontario was named after the village of Burnham Thorpe near Burnham Market, Norfolk. The village was the birthplace of Nelson (in 1758), and doubtless this particular connection prompted the name.

Burns (USA)

The Oregon town, built on a cattle ranch, was named in honour of the Scottish poet Robert Burns (1759–1796). Compare **New Scotland**.

Burnshill (South Africa)

The former mission station of the Glasgow Missionary Society, in Ciskei, was founded in 1831 and named after one of the Society's founders, the Rev. John Burns (1743–1839). The station was destroyed in 1851.

Bury (Canada)

The community of Bury, in Quebec, was named in 1803 after the English town of Bury, Lancashire (now Greater Manchester), presumably through direct colonial links there.

Butterworth (Malaysia, South Africa)

The coastal town of Butterworth, Malaysia, was named for William T. Butterworth, Governor of Singapore and Malacca from 1843 to 1855. In South Africa, Butterworth in Transkei was developed from a station of the Wesleyan Missionary Society founded in 1827, and itself named after a former treasurer of the Society, Joseph Butterworth.

Button Bay (Canada)

Button Bay, in Manitoba, was named after the English explorer and navigator Thomas Button (died 1634), who was sent to search for the Northwest Passage and who explored the coasts of **Hudson** Bay in 1612 and 1613. Button Bay is actually in Hudson Bay, just north of **Churchill**, and Button wintered there. See also **Nelson** River.

Buxton (USA, South Africa)

The town of Buxton, in Maine, was named after the Norfolk village near Aylsham, from which early settlers had come. The South African village of Buxton in Cape Province, though, where it is located near **Fort Beaufort**, was established in the early nineteenth century as part of the Kat River settlement here, and was named for the philanthropist Sir Thomas Fowell Buxton (1786–1845), who advocated the abolition of slavery in British colonial possessions and the repression of the African slave trade.

Byam Martin Island (Canada)

The island, in **Franklin** District, Northwest Territories, was discovered by Sir William Parry (see **Parry**) in 1819 and was named for Sir Thomas Byam Martin (1773–1854), Comptroller of the Royal Navy. Other features here are also named after him, such as Byam Martin Channel and Byam Martin's Mountains.

Byron (Australia, Gilbert Islands, Canada)
It was not the poet Lord Byron who gave his name to most of these places, but his grandfather, John Byron (1723–1786), the admiral and explorer who came to be nicknamed 'Foul Weather Jack' for having successfully survived an Atlantic storm. He commanded an expedition to explore the South Pacific in 1764, and was appointed Governor of Newfoundland in 1769. The best-known places that still bear his name are the town of Byron Bay in **New South Wales**, Australia, on the bay of the same name which was discovered by James Cook in 1770 and named by him after the admiral, and the island of Byron (now usually known by its local name of Nikunau) in the **Gilbert Islands** (now **Kiribati**), discovered by Byron himself in 1765. Byron in Ontario, Canada, however, was named after the poet, by way of a tribute. The community's original name here was Hall's Mills, after the local postmaster.

Bytown (Canada)
The name is no longer in use, but Bytown was what Ottawa was originally called, after Lieutenant-Colonel John By (1781–1836), who arrived here in 1826 as a member of the Royal Engineers to work on the canal. The capital city (so later designated officially by Queen Victoria) was not named Ottawa until 1854, when it was incorporated and rechristened.

C

Caird Coast (Antarctica)

The Caird Coast lies as the eastern sector of **Coats Land**, and was so named by Ernest Shackleton (see **Shackleton Glacier**) when surveying the coast here in 1915 on board the *Endurance*. He gave the name as a tribute to his financial sponsor, James Caird.

Cairns (Australia)

The **Queensland** seaport was founded in 1873 as a customs collection point on Trinity Bay, and was subsequently named after Sir William Cairns (1828–1888), Governor of Queensland from 1875 to 1877.

Calderwood (South Africa)

The settlement of Calderwood, Cape Province, was named after the Rev. Henry Calderwood of the London Missionary Society (and also author of *Caffres and Caffre Missions*).

Caledon (South Africa)

The town of Caledon, in the Cape Province, was originally settled in 1713 and known as Zwarte Berg ('black mountain'), after the Swartberg mountain by which it lies. In 1813 it was renamed Caledon, after the Earl of Caledon, Governor of the Cape from 1807 to 1811. The Caledon River, in Orange Free State, was at first named Prinses Wilhelminarivier when discovered in 1877, after Princess Wilhelmina of Prussia and of Orange. In 1809, however, it was renamed in honour of the same Earl of Caledon as gave the town its name. (By coincidence, the name is apt for the town with its hot springs, as Caledon suggests Latin *calidus*, 'hot'.)

Caledonia (USA)

The ancient Roman name of Scotland is found adopted in a few United States towns and counties, such as Caledonia County, Vermont, and Caledonia in Minnesota. See also **New Caledonia**.

Calgary (Canada)

The city in southern **Alberta** was originally called Fort Brisebois when it arose in 1875 as a post of the North West Mounted Police. The following year it was renamed Fort Calgary by Colonel James F. Macleod, of the Royal Canadian Mounted Police, for the Scottish village of Calgary on the Isle of Mull, where some of his ancestors and family lived.

Callander (Canada)

The Ontario village was probably named for the Scottish town of Callander in Perthshire (now Central), where the first postmaster of the village, George Morrison, was born.

Calvert (USA)

Calvert is the family name of the various Lords Baltimore who were proprietors of **Maryland** (and who gave their name to **Baltimore**). There are four that need to be considered here. The first was George Calvert, 1st Baron Baltimore (?1580–1632), a Yorkshire nobleman who became Secretary of State and who was granted territory in what is now Maryland in 1632, but who died before the charter could be issued. (He had earlier been granted Newfoundland, but objected to it because of its climate.) The first proprietor of Maryland was thus his son, Cecilius Calvert, 2nd Baron Baltimore (1605–1675). His other interests kept him in his native England, however, and he never visited America. Even so, he gave his Christian name to **Cecil** County, Maryland, and his wife gave her name to **Anne Arundel** County, also in this state. Their son, Charles Calvert, 3rd Baron Baltimore (1637–1715), was the second proprietor of the colony, and he gave his name to **Charles** County, Maryland. Finally, for our purposes, there was Frederick Calvert, 6th Baron Baltimore (1731–1771), the fifth and final proprietor of Maryland (as well as 'rake and writer', according to Hyamson (see Bibliography, p. 217). He tried to name his illegitimate son, Henry Harford, as his heir (see **Harford County**), but without success. He did succeed, however, in having his own Christian name adopted for **Frederick** County, and its seat of the same name. And after this biographical résumé, it is no surprise to find that **Calvert** County itself, Maryland, is named after the first of the lords mentioned above, as a tribute to George Calvert, who should have become the first proprietor of the colony, but who did not live to do so.

Cambria (USA)
Cambria was the Latin name for Wales, and Cambria County, **Pennsylvania**, takes its name from the original settlement of Cambria here, which was created in 1798 and peopled almost entirely by Welsh emigrants.

Cambridge (USA, Canada, Australia, New Zealand, South Africa)
It is hardly surprising that such a prestigious name should have been seized on for colonial purposes when establishing new settlements or territories. But, as so often with names of this type, the reference may be to a duke rather than to the famous university city. Cambridge, **Maryland**, was founded in 1684 and two years later named for the English city, and Cambridge, Massachusetts, was also named after it, although it was originally settled under the name of Old Towne in 1630, and renamed six years later. The latter Cambridge has a link with the founding of Harvard University as Harvard College by the English clergyman John Harvard (died 1638), a graduate of Emmanuel College, Cambridge. Cambridge in Ohio, however, was named after the Maryland city. In Canada, on the other hand, Cambridge Bay (both settlement and bay) on **Victoria** Island, Northwest Territories, was named after the 1st Duke of Cambridge (1774–1850), brother of William IV, as was Cambridge Gulf in northern Western Australia. The latter was named in 1819 by Philip Parker King, who gave his own name to **King** Sound. Again, the town of Cambridge in North Island, New Zealand, was named after the English river Cam by British officers in the Maori Wars of the mid-nineteenth century (compare the name of **Thames** to the north of it), and in South Africa, the suburb of **East London** named Cambridge was founded (as a village) in 1856 and named after the 2nd Duke of Cambridge (1819–1904), the 1st Duke's son.

Camden (USA, Australia)
Most United States counties and towns of the name were so designated after Sir Charles Pratt, 1st Earl of Camden (1714–1794), the statesman who campaigned against taxation of the American colonies and who denounced the Stamp Act of 1765. (This required all publications and legal documents in the colonies to bear a tax stamp, and was a cause of considerable unrest.) Probably the best known is the city of Camden in **New Jersey**, which was settled and named in 1773. However, the town of Camden in **New South Wales**, Australia, where it was originally known as Cowpastures, was renamed Camden Park in 1805 after the 1st Earl's son, John Jeffreys Pratt, 2nd Earl and 1st Marquess of Camden (1759–1840), who at that time was Secretary of State for War and the Colonies. (Also named after him is Camden Bay in Alaska, USA).

Campbell River (Canada)
Both the community and the river on which it stands, on **Vancouver** Island,

British Columbia, are named after Samuel Campbell, the British naval surgeon on board the *Plumper*, when she was stationed here from 1857 to 1861.

Campbellton (Canada)
The city, in northern **New Brunswick**, was originally called Martin's Point when it was founded by Scottish fishermen in about 1793. In 1833 it was renamed Campbellton, probably not after Campbeltown, Argyllshire (now Strathclyde), despite the Scottish connection, but most probably as a tribute to Sir Archibald Campbell (1769–1843), who was Lieutenant-Governor of New Brunswick from 1831 to 1837.

Campbelltown (Australia)
The **New South Wales** town was originally named Airds in 1810 by the British Governor of New South Wales, Lachlan Macquarie (see **Macquarie**). In 1820, however, he renamed the settlement as Campbell. Both names were a compliment to his second wife, née Elizabeth Campbell, who came from Airds, Scotland.

Camperdown (Australia, South Africa)
The Australian town of Camperdown, in **Victoria**, was founded in 1850 and named by Govenor Charles J. La Trobe to commemorate the British naval triumph over the Dutch in the Battle of Camperdown in 1797. (Camperdown, otherwise modern Camperduin, is a village in the Netherlands northwest of Amsterdam. The battle was fought in the North Sea off the coast here.) In South Africa, the town of the same name, in Natal, derived its name for identical reasons. It was laid out in 1865. The British victor at Camperdown was Admiral Duncan (see **Duncan Island**).

Camrose (Canada)
The city is in **Alberta**, and when originally founded in 1905 was named Sparling, after the Methodist clergyman Joseph Sparling. Two years later it was renamed after the Welsh village of Camrose, near Haverfordwest. The name was changed in order to avoid confusion with the Canadian towns of Sperling and **Stirling**.

Canning (USA, Canada)
Both Canning River, Alaska, and the community of Canning, **Nova Scotia**, are named for the British statesman George Canning (1770–1827), who was first Foreign Secretary, then Prime Minister, and who supported the independence of the Spanish-American colonies. The Canadian settlement was renamed by public vote to replace the earlier name of Apple Tree Landing.

Canterbury (New Zealand, USA, Canada)
The municipality of Canterbury, in South Island, New Zealand, was settled in the mid-nineteenth century by the so-called Canterbury Association, a Church of England colonising organisation established in 1848 to found an Anglican settlement in New Zealand. The Association had the Archbishop of Canterbury as its head. Hence the name, which not only honours him but pays tribute to the mother church. The Archbishop was John Sumner, who gave his own name to the town of **Sumner** in the present district of Canterbury. (The district is famous for its Canterbury Plains, on which graze the sheep who produce the meat known as Canterbury lamb.) The actual leader of the association was the man who founded **Christchurch**, now in the Canterbury district, and the original settlers in that place were therefore known as 'Canterbury Pilgrims'. The name is not all that common in the USA, but Canterbury, Connecticut, was probably named after the English city, while in **New Brunswick**, Canada, the name is not for the city at all, but for Thomas Manners-Sutton (1814–1877), later 3rd Viscount Canterbury, who was Lieutenant-Governor of New Brunswick from 1854 to 1861. See also **Wakefield**.

Cape Elizabeth (USA)
The town of this name in Maine, on the Atlantic coast, takes its name from the

cape here which honours Princess Elizabeth, eldest daughter of James I. The name was placed on John Smith's map of **New England** in 1616, together with others, by Elizabeth's brother, Prince Charles. See also **Elizabeth**.

Carberry (Canada)

The community of Carberry, Manitoba, was so named in 1882 after Carberry Tower near Musselburgh, Midlothian (now Lothian), the Scottish home of the then Lord Elphinstone, who was a director of the Canadian Pacific Railway.

Cardiff-by-the-Sea (USA)

The Californian resort is named after the Welsh city, itself also a seaport. The link may be national as well as geographical.

Cardigan (Canada)

Cardigan, on **Prince Edward Island**, was named after Cardigan Bay and Cardigan River in Wales, with their own names honouring George Brudenell, Earl of Cardigan (1712–1790).

Carleton (Canada)

The name is found in Carleton County and Mount Carleton, both in **New Brunswick**. It honours either Sir Guy Carleton (1724–1808) or Thomas Carleton (1735–1817), or even both. The former was the British statesman and administrator who was dominant in Canada in the first fifty years of British rule there; the latter was the first governor of New Brunswick. See also **Guysborough** and the next entry.

Carleton Place (Canada)

Carleton Place, Ontario, is not named for either Sir Guy Carleton or Thomas Carleton (see entry above), but is on record as having been so called by early settlers after a square in Glasgow, Scotland.

Carlisle (USA)

Many places of the name in the United States are so called after Carlisle in Cumberland (now Cumbria). Carlisle, **Pennsylvania**, in **Cumberland** County, is an example, laid out in 1751. In a few cases, however, towns or counties are named after prominent Americans of the name, such as Carlisle, Ohio, and Carlisle County, Kentucky.

Carlyle (Canada)

The community of Carlyle, Saskatchewan, was so named in 1882, probably by way of a compliment to the Scottish essayist and historian Thomas Carlyle, who had died the previous year.

Carnarvon (Australia, South Africa)

The town of Carnarvon in Western Australia was proclaimed in 1886, the site having been surveyed three years previously, and was named for Henry Herbert, 4th Earl of Carnarvon (1831–1890), who was twice Secretary of State for the Colonies, from 1866 to 1867, and from 1874 to 1878. Carnarvon in Cape Province, South Africa, was named after the same minister, although the town was founded somewhat earlier, in 1860, and it was known as Harmsfontein and Schietfontein before becoming Carnarvon in 1874.

Carnegie (USA)

The town (strictly, borough) of Carnegie, in **Pennsylvania**, was formed in 1894 by the merger of two other communities, Chartiers and Mansfield, and took its new name from the steel industrialist, Andrew Carnegie (1835–1919), who was born in Scotland but died in America, where he emigrated in 1848. Before the town was named, Andrew Carnegie had taken no interest in it, but once he learned of its compliment, he donated a richly stocked library to the borough.

Carolina (USA)

This is the famous name that today lies behind the two states of North Carolina and South Carolina, settled respectively in 1650 and 1670. The name pays tribute to Charles I of England (whose Latin name was Carolus), and he himself had named the territory occupied by the present states as 'Carolana' in his grant of 1629 made to Sir Robert Heath, his Attorney-General.

However, the name of 'Carolina' is on record as already existing for the territory at this time, having been given by the French navigator Jean Ribaut in 1562 in honour of his patron, the French king Charles IX. Moreover, the patent given by Charles I was revoked in 1663 by Charles II, and he made a new grant to eight patentees (so called 'Lords Proprietors') who changed 'Carolana' to 'Carolina', giving the compliment to their monarch. So three different kings named Charles lie behind the name.

Caroline (USA)

The name is found for two counties in the United States, respectively in **Maryland** and **Virginia**. Caroline County, Maryland, was named after Caroline Calvert, the sister of Frederick Calvert, 6th Lord Baltimore (1731–1771), who was the last proprietor of Maryland (see **Calvert**). Caroline County in Virginia, however, was named after Princess Wilhelmina Carolina of Anspach (1683–1737), wife of George II. The Caroline Islands, although part of the US Trust Territory, are not named after an Englishwoman at all, or even a woman, for the name honours Charles II of Spain, in whose reign they were annexed by his country.

Carrick (USA)

The community in **Pennsylvania** derives its name from Carrick-on-Suir, in Ireland. The name was proposed by an Irish doctor, John O'Brien, in honour of his native town. Dr O'Brien had settled in nearby Baldwin in 1846.

Carteret (USA)

The borough of Carteret in **New Jersey** is named for Sir George Carteret (?1610–1680), who had been granted what is now the state of New Jersey by Charles II in 1650. Carteret County in North **Carolina**, however, was named after his grandson, John Carteret, 1st Earl Granville (1690–1763), twice Secretary of State and a lord proprietor of North and South Carolina (see **Carolina**).

Cathcart (South Africa)

The town of Cathcart, in Cape Province, was developed from a military camp established in 1850, and was named for Sir George Cathcart (1794–1854), Governor of the Cape from 1852 to 1854.

Cathkin Peak (South Africa)

Cathkin Peak, a mountain in the Drakensberg range near the more interestingly named Champagne Castle, was named after Cathkin Braes, a hill ridge near Glasgow, by a David Gray, a Scot who settled in Natal in 1849. The mountain was itself named Champagne Castle at one time, until the name was transferred to the neighbouring peak. (David Gray was behind this other name, too, as it allegedly refers to a brawl he had with a climber colleague over a bottle of champagne, half of which had been consumed by one of them.)

Cecil (USA)

Cecil County, **Maryland**, was named after Cecilius Calvert, 2nd Lord Baltimore (1605–1675), the second proprietor of the colony of Maryland. See **Calvert**.

Cessnock (Australia)

The city, now part of Greater Cessnock, in **New South Wales**, arose as a coal-mining town in the 1880s. The name is usually attributed to the original land grantee here, the Scotsman James Campbell, who is said to have been inspired by Robert Burns's poem 'On Cessnock Banks'. However, the actual origin could have been the historic building that was itself named after the burn (stream) in this poem, Cessnock Castle, near Galston in Ayrshire (now Strathclyde).

Chalfont (USA)

The **Pennsylvania** community, in **Bucks** County, was named after the town of Chalfont St Giles, in Buckinghamshire, near where William Penn, the founder of Pennsylvania, is buried.

Challenger Deep (Pacific Ocean)

The Challenger Deep, the deepest part of

the Mariana Trench in the Pacific, is named for the ship HMS *Challenger*, on which, with the backing of the Admiralty and the Royal Society, a British oceanographical expedition was made to this part of the Pacific over the four years from 1872 to 1876.

Charles (USA)

Cape Charles is at the entrance to Chesapeake Bay, **Virginia**, opposite Cape **Henry**. It was so named in 1608 by Captain John Smith (see **Smith**), after Charles I, because it lay across the water from Cape Henry, named after Charles's eldest brother. For Charles County, **Maryland**, however, see **Calvert**.

Charleston (USA)

The name is a common one in the United States, although not all places so designated were named for a British Charles, and in some cases a Charleston adopted the name of an existing place in America. However, the well-known historic city of Charleston, South **Carolina**, where the jazz dance of that name originated, was named for Charles II (at first as Charles Towne) when it was founded by English colonists in 1670, and it is easily the oldest place of the name. Compare the next entry below.

Charlestown (USA, West Indies, South Africa)

Here it is a matter of getting the right Charles, king or not. Charlestown, Massachusetts, now a part of **Boston**, was first settled in 1628 and named after Charles I. It lies on the Charles River, which was itself placed on John Smith's map of **New England** by Prince Charles himself, the future king. Charlestown, **New Hampshire**, however, was named after Admiral Sir Charles Knowles (died 1777), a friend of the founder (and namer), Governor Benning Wentworth. (Knowles was governor of Jamaica at the time.) In the West Indies, Charlestown is the chief town and port on the island of Nevis, and was named after Charles II. (It became the chief town in 1680, in his reign, after the first settlement, **Jamestown**, had been flooded by a tidal wave.) In South Africa, the town of Charlestown in Natal was founded in 1889 and named for the new Governor of Natal from that year, Sir Charles Mitchell (died 1899). Compare the entry above.

Charleville (Australia)

The town of Charleville, in **Queensland**, was settled in 1842 and named after Charleville (now Ráth Luirc) in Ireland, the link being a national one for the early settlers. The Irish town, in Co. Cork, was named for Charles II.

Charlotte (USA, Canada)

Places having this name in North America will often turn out to be named after George III's queen, Charlotte Sophia of Mecklenburg-Strelitz (1744–1818), mother of George IV. This is so for the city of the name in North **Carolina**, which was settled in about 1750. (Charlotte was still a very young princess then, and she did not marry George until 1761. However, the town of Charlotte was not named until it was incorporated in 1768). Appropriately, Charlotte is the seat of **Mecklenburg** County. Charlotte County, **Virginia**, is also named after the queen, as is Charlotte County in **New Brunswick**, Canada. But, as always, not all places of the name have an identical origin, and Charlotte County, Florida, is not named after George II's wife but after the Spanish king Charles V, while Charlotte in Tennessee, for example, is named for the wife of an American soldier. See also the next two entries below.

Charlottesville (USA)

The city of this name in **Virginia** was originally settled in the 1730s but received its name in 1761 when it became the courthouse seat of **Albemarle** County. The tribute is to Queen Charlotte, wife of George III, as some of the places mentioned in the entry above. See also the entry below.

Charlottetown (Canada)

Charlottetown is not only the seat of **Queens** County but the capital of **Prince**

Edward Island. It originated in about 1720 as a French settlement called Port la Joie, but was renamed after the queen of George III in 1763, when the island passed to Britain. Compare the two entries above, which also centre on Queen Charlotte.

Charlton (USA)

The Massachusetts town is named after Sir Francis Charlton, who was a member of the Privy Council at the time of the naming.

Charters Towers (Australia)

The Australian town arose in 1871 as the result of a gold boom in this area of northeast **Queensland**. The first word of the name is the surname of a local colonial mining warden, while the second word refers to the local 'tors' (corrupted to Towers), or rocky hills.

Chatham (USA, Canada, Galápagos Islands, Pacific Ocean)

Although the town of Chatham, Kent, was long famous as a naval port, and therefore suggests itself as a suitable name for a group of emigrant settlers, it will be found that most places of the name honour not the town but the famous prime minister William Pitt, 1st Earl of Chatham (1708–1778). This applies for the towns and cities of the name in Massachusetts (settled in 1656), **New Jersey** (originally called John Day's Bridge but renamed in 1773), **New Brunswick**, Canada (founded in about 1800) and Ontario, Canada (also settled then). Pitt, whose surname is similarly represented (see **Pitt Island**, **Pittsburgh**, **Pittsfield**), was specially honoured in this way because he persuaded the French to give up their American possessions, and defended the American colonies before the War of American Independence (the American Revolution). It is possible that George Vancouver (see **Vancouver**) had the 2nd Earl of Chatham in mind, not the 1st, when he named Chatham Strait, southeast Alaska, in 1794, and Captain Charles Duncan may likewise have sought to honour the same earl when he named Chatham Sound, in **British Columbia**, Canada, in 1788. This earl was William Pitt's eldest son, Sir John Pitt (1756–1835), Lord Privy Seal for three years from 1794. Chatham Island, in the Galápagos Islands, where it is officially known by its Ecuadorian name of San Cristóbal, was also named after Sir John Pitt by Captain James Colnett in 1793. On the other hand, the Chatham Islands in the Pacific, east of New Zealand, were discovered by the British naval captain William Broughton in 1791, when on his way to Tahiti, and he named them after his ship, the *Chatham*. (Even so, the two main islands of the group are respectively Chatham Island and Pitt Island, showing the ultimate link with the statesman.)

Chatom (USA)

It is worth recording that this town, in Alaska, was named after William Pitt like many of the places called **Chatham** in the entry above. The spelling, however, was deliberately altered so that the place should not be confused with any of them.

Chatsworth (USA)

The city in **Georgia** is named after Chatsworth House, the mansion that is the seat of the Duke of Devonshire in Derbyshire. The name was suggested through the fanciful resemblance between this house and some Indian fortifications east of the city on Fort Mountain.

Chelmsford (USA, Canada)

Probably the best known place of the name in the United States is the town in Massachusetts. This was settled in 1633 and named for Chelmsford in Essex, from which some of the original immigrants had come. The link between Chelmsford in Ontario, Canada, and the English town is identical. The community was incorporated into Rayside-Balfour in 1973.

Chelsea (USA)

The city of Chelsea in Massachusetts, now a residential suburb of **Boston**, was originally settled in 1624 with the Indian name of Winnisimmet. It was renamed Chelsea, for purely 'cultural' rather than direct ancestral reasons, in 1739. Other places of the name, such as Chelsea in Maine, Michigan and Vermont, had a similar motivation for the choice of this particular designation. London's Chelsea has long had historic cultural associations, for example with such literary figures as Sir Thomas More, George Eliot, and Dickens.

Cheshire (USA)

It is likely that most instances of the name arose from family links with the English county. Examples are Cheshire County, **New Hampshire**, and the town of Cheshire in Connecticut.

Chester (USA)

Many of the settlers brought to America by William Penn came from this historic English city, although it should not be assumed that this is the origin of the name in every instance. In South **Carolina**, for example, the city of Chester was founded (in about 1755) by settlers from **Pennsylvania** who named it for their original settlement, which they had at first called Upland when William Penn arrived there. However, some records state that Penn renamed Upland not so much for the city but as a tribute to his friend Lord Chester. In Tennessee, Chester County is named for a Texan colonel.

Chesterfield (USA, Canada)

The allusion in most cases for the name is to the 4th Earl of Chesterfield, Philip Stanhope (1694–1773), the English statesman (and writer) who held many important posts, including that of Lord Lieutenant of Ireland and Secretary of State, both these in the 1740s. Places bearing the name include Chesterfield County, South **Carolina**, and its seat of the same name, Chesterfield County, Vermont (likewise), and, in Canada, the Chesterfield Inlet in **Hudson** Bay, Northwest Territories.

Cheviot (USA)

Cheviot, Ohio, was first settled by one Enoch Carson in 1804, but the name was given in 1818 by John Craig, who named it after the Cheviot Hills, his 'native heath' on the English–Scottish border. There is some evidence that he gave the name to a tavern in the town, originally, and that it then came to be adopted for the settlement as a whole.

Christchurch (New Zealand)

Although the city in South Island is on the **Avon** River, it is not named for the Hampshire town of Christchurch that is likewise on a river of this name. It was founded in 1848 by members of the Christchurch Association, a Church of England colonising group set up to establish a model Anglican settlement here (see **Canterbury** in this respect). The Association itself was so named because its leader, the Irish social reformer and politician John Robert Godley (1814–1861), had attended Christ Church college, Oxford. In fact, the original immigrants here, who arrived on five ships in 1850, called their founding settlement by the name of Canterbury. The present name was adopted, however, soon after. It is an appropriate (and doubtless deliberate) coincidence that Canterbury Cathedral, the Anglican 'mother church', is itself named Christ Church.

Churchill (Canada, USA)

The famous English name is found chiefly, but not exclusively, in Canada, where it usually honours John Churchill, 1st Duke of Marlborough (1650–1722), who was a governor of the Hudson's Bay Company from 1685 to 1691. The Manitoba seaport of the name, for example, is on the west coast of **Hudson** Bay, where it developed from the original Hudson's Bay Company's wooden fort, Fort Churchill, built here in 1688. The port is at the mouth of the Churchill River, which was named after this fort. At first, however, it was called English River, because it was the route into the Canadian interior for 'the English', i.e. for traders of the Hudson's Bay Company. But this river must not be confused with Canada's other Churchill River, in Labrador, Newfoundland. It was originally called the **Hamilton** River (which see for the origin of the name), and was renamed as recently as 1965, this time for Sir Winston Churchill (1874–1965), who died that year. In this same year the great British statesman's name was similarly assigned to the former Grand Falls on the latter river in Newfoundland, and to Mount Churchill and the Churchill Peaks, in Alaska, USA. The Churchill Falls form part of a series of impressive cataracts and rapids on the river as it flows through west Labrador. Churchill County, Nevada, however, is named after an American army officer, not a British Churchill.

Clanwilliam (South Africa)
Clanwilliam, the town in Cape Province, was originally known as Jan Disselsvlei, after the farm on which it was laid out. In 1814, however, it was renamed by Sir John Cradock (see **Cradock**), Governor of the Cape, after his father-in-law, the Earl of Clanwilliam.

Clare (Australia, USA)
The South Australia town of the name was founded in 1839 and named for the Irish county, in which one of its earliest settlers was born. Similar family ties link Clare County, Michigan, USA, and its seat of the same name (which was originally known by the Indian name of Kaykakee).

Claremont (USA, South Africa)
The original town of the name in the United States was Claremont, **New Hampshire**, first settled in 1762 and organised as a town two years later. The name itself honours the Holles family, either specifically John Holles, 1st Earl of Clare (?1564–1637), or John Holles, Duke of Newcastle (1662–1711), both of whom were indirectly related to Governor Benning Wentworth of New Hampshire. (The earlier John Holles's daughter Arabella, for example, married Sir Thomas Wentworth.) Claremont, California, was founded much later, in 1887, and was named after the New Hampshire city. In South Africa, Claremont, the suburb of Cape Town, was named after Claremont House in Surrey, which was the residence of the first Prime Minister of the Cape, Sir John Molteno (1814–1886). The house was itself named after Sir Thomas Pelham-Holles, Duke of Newcastle and Earl of Clare, who bought it in 1714. His uncle was John Holles, the Duke of Newcastle, mentioned above, so that here we have more or less turned a full family circle. (The Clare in this case is not the Irish county but the town in Suffolk.)

Clarence River (Australia)
The river is in **New South Wales**, where for many years it was simply known as the Big River. It was renamed after the last Duke of Clarence, Albert Victor (1864–1892), the eldest son of Edward VII.

Clarendon (USA)
Clarendon County, South **Carolina**, is named after Edward Hyde, 3rd Earl of Clarendon (1661–1723), the colonial governor of **New York** and **New Jersey**, among his other positions in the colonies. The city of Clarendon, Texas, could also have been named after this Lord Clarendon, or possibly a later one, as was the Clarendon River, Vermont. Compare the next entry.

Clarendon Hills (USA)
The village in Illinois is named after Clarendon near Salisbury, Wiltshire, famous for its Clarendon Park containing Clarendon House. It is not clear what the precise link was, but possibly an early settler had some connection with the place.

Clark Point (Canada)
The original name of the community was Clarkes Church, this in turn deriving from the name of William Clark, an immigrant from Edinburgh.

Clarkson (South Africa)
The Moravian mission village in Cape Province was founded in 1839 and named after Thomas Clarkson (1760–1846), the noted English slavery abolitionist.

Clipperton Island (South Pacific)
The Pacific island is named after the English mutineer and pirate John Clipperton, who made his base here in the

early eighteenth century. The island, which is uninhabited, was listed as American territory before being claimed by France in 1858 (and officially awarded to that country in 1930).

Clive (New Zealand)
The coastal settlement of Clive, between **Hastings** and **Napier**, North Island, was named after the British conqueror and military 'hero' Robert Clive (1725–1774), 'Clive of India'. The region around Hawke Bay here was settled at the time of the Indian Mutiny (late 1850s), when patriotic feeling was running high.

Cloncurry (Australia)
The town of Cloncurry, **Queensland**, was named after the river on which it stands, this in turn being named after the Irish village Cloncurry in Co. Kildare, from which an early settler had come.

Clutha River (New Zealand)
The river was given the early Celtic name of the River Clyde, in Scotland. See **Balclutha** for further detail, but also compare the next entry below.

Clyde (USA, Canada)
It is likely that the Clyde River, **New York**, was named for its Scottish counterpart, doubtless with an immigrant link. In Canada, Clyde on **Baffin** Island, Northwest Territories, where it is located on Clyde Inlet, was so named in 1818 by the Arctic explorer John Ross, uncle of James Ross (see **Ross Sea**), and doubtless the compliment was intended to be made to the Scottish river similarly, since Ross was a Scot.

Coalbrook (South Africa)
The colliery and settlement near Sasolburg, Orange Free State, was very likely named after Coalbrookvale, South Wales, in a coal-mining district, rather than for Coalbrookdale, the 'cradle of the iron industry' in Shropshire. But probably it was the first part of the name that was regarded as important, with any exact identification with a particular place being of secondary or even no relevance.

Coats Land (Antarctica)
Coats Land, which is on the southeast coast of **Weddell Sea**, was discovered in 1904 by the Scottish explorer William Speirs Bruce, and named by him after the financial backers of his expedition, the brothers James and Andrew Coats.

Cobden (Canada)
The community was named for the British statesman Richard Cobden (1804–1865), best known for his repealing of the Corn Laws and for his defence of free trade. The post office dates from 1851, within his lifetime.

Cobourg (Canada, Australia)
The town of Cobourg, Ontario, was originally known as Amherst when settled in 1798, and was later renamed Hamilton. In 1819 however, it was again renamed Cobourg in honour of the marriage of Princess Charlotte of England to Prince Leopold of Saxe-Cobourg that year. In Australia, the name of the **Coburg Peninsula** (see next entry) is sometimes spelt in this way.

Coburg Peninsula (Australia)
The Coburg Peninsula (sometimes spelt **Cobourg**, as in the entry above) is the northwest extremity of Arnhem Land, Northern Territory. It was discovered in 1818 by the British naval officer Philip Parker King (see **King**) and was named the following year for Prince Leopold of Saxe-Cobourg as a commemoration of his marriage to Princess Charlotte. (The prince was the uncle of Queen Victoria.)

Cockburn (Australia, Canada, Turks and Caicos Islands)
In almost every instance where the name occurs, the reference will be to Admiral Sir George Cockburn (1772–1853), who contributed to the capture of Martinique and who took part in the capture of Washington, D.C., in the United States in the War of 1812. The name is widely found in Australia, one of the better known instances being Cockburn Sound, in Western Australia, where it forms part of the harbour of **Fremantle**. But although

Cockburn Island in the St Lawrence River, Ontario, is named after the Admiral, Cockburn Island in Lake Huron, also Ontario, is named for Colonel Francis Cockburn (1779–1854), who accompanied Lord Dalhousie on a survey of the area here in 1821. However, it is the Admiral again who gave his name to Cockburn Harbour in the Turks and Caicos Islands, where it is the largest settlement, dating from 1850.

Colbeck, Cape (Antarctica)
The cape, on **Edward VII Peninsula**, Marie Byrd Land, was discovered (as was the peninsula itself) by Scott's first Antarctic expedition of 1901 to 1904. His ship, the *Discovery*, was accompanied by two smaller auxiliary vessels, the *Morning* and the *Terra Nova*. The first of these was captained by William Colbeck, a former Merchant Navy officer, and it was his name that was thus given to the cape. Compare **Pennell Coast**.

Colchester (USA)
The town of Colchester in Connecticut was named after Colchester, Essex, from where early settlers had come. Colchester in Vermont, however, is a town that was named for Viscount Tunbridge, Baron Enfield and Colchester, a political figure under George II. He features in few reference books today, but in his time he must have seemed significant to Governor Benning Wentworth, who gave his name not only to Colchester but to **Enfield** and **Tunbridge**!

Colenso (South Africa)
The town of Colenso, in Natal, was established in 1855 and was named after the Cornish-born Anglican bishop of Natal, William Colenso (1814–1883), a champion of the Zulus.

Colesberg (South Africa)
The town, in Cape Province, was established in 1830 and after initially being known as Toverberg was renamed for Sir Galbraith Lowry Cole (1772–1842), Governor of the Cape from 1828 to 1833. The '-berg' of both names refers to a nearby hill.

Collingwood (Australia, New Zealand, Canada)
In Australia, Collingwood is an inner suburb of **Melbourne**, **Victoria**. It arose as a mid-nineteenth-century settlement named for the British naval commander, Baron Cuthbert Collingwood (1748–1810), who was Nelson's second-in-command at the Battle of Trafalgar, later taking over command when Nelson was killed. And it is not surprising to find that other places also honour the admiral, such as the town of Collingwood in the north of South Island, New Zealand, where it arose in 1857 as a result of the gold rush, and the town of Collingwood in Ontario, Canada, which was first settled in the late 1830s. The New Zealand town is less than a hundred miles from the city of **Nelson**.

Colville, Cape (New Zealand, Canada, USA)
The cape, on the north coast of North Island, was named after Captain Lord Colville, under whom Cook had served when in Canadian waters, while in Canada and the USA, many places named Colville honour Andrew Colville, London governor of the Hudson's Bay Company. Examples include the city in Washington, the Colville River in Alaska, and Lake Colville northwest of Great Bear Lake, Northwest Territories. Andrew Colville was Governor of the Company from 1852 to 1856, and before that, Deputy Governor from 1839 to 1852.

Compton (Canada)
Compton County, Quebec, is on record as being named after the village of Compton near Guildford, Surrey, presumably through an emigrant connection.

Condamine River (Australia)
The long Condamine River is in **Queensland**, where it flows through the **Darling** Downs. It bears the name of the man who was Darling's secretary.

Conway (USA)
Some places of the name in the United States honour Henry Seymour Conway (1721–1795), the Member of Parliament who opposed the Stamp Act (see **Camden**) and who opposed any British policies that were disadvantageous to the colonies. They include the town of Conway and Conway Lake, both in **New Hampshire**. Other Conways, such as Conway County, Arkansas, are named after an American family of politicians and military men.

Cook (New Zealand, USA, South Pacific)
It is rare to find a place with the name that does not honour 'Captain Cook', James Cook (1728–1779), the Yorkshire-born naval captain who is one of the most renowned explorers in world history. Here one can only summarise the best-known places of the name: Mount Cook, New Zealand's highest mountain, in South Island, was sighted in 1641 by the Dutch navigator Abel Tasman and was known by the Maori name of Aorangi ('cloud piercer') before being renamed after Cook in 1851; Cook Strait, between North and South Islands, was also explored by Tasman in 1642, when he believed it to be a bay, and was renamed for Cook who discovered its true nature (as a strait) in 1770; Cook Inlet, in Alaska, USA, was entered by Cook in 1778 when he was searching for the Northwest Passage; the Cook Islands, in the South Pacific, were discovered by Cook in 1773 (when he originally named them **Hervey** Islands, after August John Hervey, a lord of the Admiralty). Cook was killed (in a scuffle with natives about a boat) in the Hawaiian Islands, where his name is preserved, among all the Polynesian names, in the settlement of Captain Cook. Cook had himself named the islands the Sandwich Islands (see **Sandwich**). See also the next two entries below.

Cook's Harbour (Canada)
The Newfoundland settlement commemorates the famous explorer and circumnavigator James Cook (see entry above), who charted much of the Newfoundland coast in the 1760s.

Cooktown (Australia)
The port of Cooktown, in **Queensland**, was named after the well-known explorer James Cook (see above), who beached his ship the *Endeavour* here for repairs in 1770. The present town was founded in the gold rush of 1873. See also **Endeavour**.

Cooper River (USA)
The river in South **Carolina** is named after Anthony Ashley Cooper, 1st Earl of Shaftesbury (1621–1683), who was one of the original Lords Proprietors of Carolina. Compare **Ashley River**, also in South Carolina.

Cornwall (Canada)
As often, we here have a 'titular place-name', which could derive from the county of Cornwall or a Duke (or other rank) of Cornwall. The city of Cornwall in Ontario was founded as New Johnstown in 1784, but in 1797 was renamed for the eldest son of George III, Prince George, Duke of Cornwall (1762–1830), the future George IV (from 1820). (The Duke also gave his name, under his other regal 'hat' as Prince of Wales, to **Prince of Wales** Island, on which there is a Cape Cornwall named after him by James Cook.) There is no doubt, however, that some of the places named Cornwall were so christened by emigrants from the English county.

Cornwallis Island (Canada)
The island is one of the **Parry** Islands, in the **Franklin** District, Northwest Territories, in **Barrow** Strait between **Devon** and **Bathurst** Islands. It was discovered in 1819 by Sir William Parry, who gave his name to the whole group, and was named by him after the naval officer Sir William Cornwallis (1744–1819), who died that year.

Coromandel (New Zealand)
The township in North Island, and the Coromandel Channel, between the southern end of Great Barrier Island and the mainland here, were named after the

ship HMS *Coromandel*, which frequently called in here for spars in the early 1800s. The finding of gold in the region in 1852 boosted the growth of the settlement. The ship was herself named after the Coromandel Coast, in southeast India.

Coronation (Canada)
With names like this the question is always '*Which* coronation?' There are two places of the name in **Alberta** alone. Mount Coronation, in the Rocky Mountains, commemorates the coronation of Edward VII and Queen Alexandra in 1902. The settlement of Coronation, nowhere near it, was designated by the Canadian Pacific Railway (on which it lies) to mark the coronation of George V and Queen Mary in 1911. The Coronation Gulf, in Northwest Territories, was discovered by John Franklin (see **Franklin**) in 1821, the year of the coronation of George IV.

Courtenay (Canada)
The city of Courtenay, southwest **British Columbia**, was named after the naval officer Captain G.W.C. Courtenay, master of HMS *Constance*, who was stationed here for five years in the 1840s. The city is directly named after the river here on which it stands, and the river after the captain.

Coventry (USA)
Both towns of Coventry, respectively in Connecticut and Rhode Island, are named after the Warwickshire city from which one or more of the original settlers had come.

Cradock (South Africa)
The town in Cape Province was proclaimed a township in 1814 and named after Sir John Cradock (1762–1839), Governor of the then Cape Colony from 1811 to 1814.

Cranbrook (Canada)
The city in **British Columbia** was first settled by gold prospectors in 1863. An early settler here, Colonel James Baker, named his farm here after his birthplace, Cranbrook in Kent, and this in turn gave the name of the town that developed.

Craven (USA)
Craven County, in North **Carolina**, was probably named after William Craven, 2nd Earl of Craven (1668–1711), at least according to the records. But an equally good candidate for the name would be the 1st Earl Craven (1606–1697), who was one of the original proprietors of Carolina.

Creighton (South Africa)
The village of Creighton, Natal, was laid out in 1865 and named after Lady McCallum, née Creighton, the wife of Sir Henry McCallum (1852–1919), Governor of Natal from 1901 to 1907.

Croker (Australia)
Both Croker Island, and its headland of Cape Croker, immediately northeast of **Coburg Peninsula**, Northern Territory, are named after John Wilson Croker (1780–1857). He was chief secretary to the Admiralty from 1810 to 1830, during which period Captain Philip Parker King visited the island (in about 1818) and named it after him. Captain King's name is preserved in that of **King** Sound.

Cromwell (USA, New Zealand)
Oliver Cromwell (1599–1658), the famous (self-styled) Lord Protector of England, gave his name to the town of Cromwell, Connecticut, as he did to the community of Cromwell in southeast South Island, New Zealand. The latter name, according to one story, was deliberately given to the site by a Roman Catholic surveyor 'to annoy some Irishmen'. The New Zealand Cromwell is less than 50 miles (as the crow flies) from **Naseby**, whose name marks Cromwell's battle victory of 1645.

Croydon (USA, South Africa)
It is Croydon, Surrey that gave its name to Croydon Peak, **New Hampshire**, and in South Africa the origin is the same. The Swaziland settlement was laid out in 1824 on a farm of the name owned by a man who came from Croydon, Surrey.

Crozier Channel (Canada)
The channel, between Patrick Island and **Melville** Island at the western end of the **Parry** Islands, Northwest Territories, was named after Francis Rawdon Moira Crozier (?1796–1848), a naval captain who served in ships with a succession of 'exploratory' names. He was first appointed to the *Fury*, the 'discovery ship' commanded by Parry (of the **Parry** Islands), subsequently accompanying Parry on his Arctic expeditions on the *Hecla*, then he joined the *Cove*, captained by Ross (of the **Ross Sea**). Afterwards the famous *Terror* was also under him, then finally he accompanied Franklin (of **Franklin** District) on the same *Terror*, with both men tragically perishing in the Arctic. See also **Fury and Hecla Strait**, Mount **Terror**.

Cudworth (Canada)
The community of this name in Saskatchewan derives as a tribute to Ralph Cudworth (1617–1688), the English theologian and philosopher who was first master of Clare Hall, Cambridge, then of Christ's College.

Cumberland (USA, Canada, Australia)
The name is found fairly frequently in the New World, and in many instances it honours the third son of George II, William Augustus, Duke of Cumberland (1721–1765), nicknamed 'Butcher Cumberland' for his harsh treatment of Jacobite rebels in 1745. His name (or title, from the former English county) lies behind that of the Cumberland Plateau with its famous pass, the Cumberland Gap, near the point where Kentucky, **Virginia** and Tennessee meet, that of the Cumberland River on this plateau, and Cumberland County, **Pennsylvania**. But Cumberland Sound, an inlet of **Davis** Strait and the Atlantic in Northwest Territories, Canada, was named after an earlier lord, the naval commander George Clifford, 3rd Earl of Cumberland (1558–1605), who was a personal friend of Davis. Again, the Cumberland Islands, off the east coast of **Queensland**, Australia, were named after another lord of the title. The group was discovered in 1770 by James Cook and named for the brother of George III, Henry Frederick, Duke of Cumberland and Strathearn (1745–1790). There is little doubt, though, that several places of the name derive directly from the county, marking emigrant ties with England. Compare the next entry below.

Cumberland House (Canada)
The community in Saskatchewan arose on the site of the first inland trading post of the Hudson's Bay Company, and was established in 1774. It was probably named after the royalist general and administrator Prince Rupert, Duke of Cumberland (1619–1682), nephew of Charles I. This same man gave his name to **Prince Rupert** (and Prince Rupert's Land).

Curtis (Australia)
The name is found for the Curtis Group, small islands in the **Bass Strait** between Tasmania and mainland Australia, and for Curtis Island and Curtis Channel off the east coast of **Queensland** (as well as the settlement of Port Curtis on the coast itself). They were all named after Admiral Sir Roger Curtis (1746–1816), who served under Howe (see **Howe**) and who presided at the court martial which tried and acquitted his friend Lord Gambier (see **Gambier Islands**).

Cynwyd (USA)
The **Pennsylvania** community was named in the nineteenth century by a man of Welsh ancestry after the Welsh village of Cynwyd in the valley of the river Dee (now in Clwyd).

Dalby (Australia)
The **Queensland** town, near the **Condamine River**, was founded as Myall Creek Station (after the creek it is actually on) in 1841, but was soon after renamed for Dalby in the Isle of Man, through an emigrant connected with that village.

Dalhousie (India, Canada)
In India, Dalhousie is a hill station in Himachal Pradesh state, in the northwest of the country, where it was named after James Ramsay, 1st Marquess of Dalhousie (1812–1860), Governor General of India from 1847 to 1856. Another lord of the title gave his name to the Canadian town of Dalhousie, **New Brunswick**, settled by Scots in the early years of the nineteenth century but actually named in 1826. The honour in this case was paid to James Ramsay's father, George Ramsay, 9th Earl of Dalhousie (1770–1838), Governor General of Canada at the time of the naming. The Scottish family took their title from their (former) seat of Dalhousie Castle, near Newtongrange, Midlothian (now Lothian).

Dalrymple, Mount (Australia)
The mountain, near the eastern coast of **Queensland**, was named after the Scottish hydrographer and Indian official Alexander Dalrymple (1737–1808). Other places of the name are likely to commemorate the same man, who was not only the first hydrographer to the Admiralty (from 1795 to 1808) but the author of discoveries in the South Pacific, where he named an illusory territory as 'Great South Land'.

Dalton (South Africa)
The village in Natal, south of **Greytown**, was named after the village of North Dalton, Yorkshire (now Humberside), as it was from this village that one Henry Boast came in 1850 to organise an emigration of Yorkshire people to South Africa.

Daly River (Australia)
The river, in northwest Northern Territory, was discovered in 1865 by one Boyle Finniss, first governor of the proposed new territory here, and named by him after Sir Dominick Daly (1798–1868), Governor of South Australia at the time.

Dampier (Australia, Papua New Guinea)
There are three major places of the name in Australia, all honouring the same man. The locations concerned are: Dampier, the port in northwest Western Australia; the Dampier Archipelago, a group of small islands off the coast here; Dampier Land, a peninsula here. There are also the two straits of the name: Dampier Strait between **New Britain** Island and Umboi Island, in the Bismarck Achipelago, in the west Pacific, and Dampier Strait between New Guinea and Waigeo Island, Indonesia. All of these are named after the great buccaneer and naval officer William Dampier (1652–1715), who explored the coasts of Australia, New Guinea and **New Britain** for the Admiralty. The port of Dampier takes its name from the archipelago, visited by Dampier in 1688 and again in 1699. See also **Buccaneer Archipelago**, **Rooke Island**.

Danbury (USA)
The Connecticut city was settled in 1685 and named two years later after the village

of Danbury near Chelmsford, Essex, from which one or more of the original emigrants had come.

Darby (USA)
The borough of Darby, in **Delaware** County, **Pennsylvania**, was originally called Derbytown when its name was first recorded, in 1698, and this gives the more readily recognisable (to British eyes) source in the city of Derby, from which early settlers had come.

Dare (USA)
Although, in general, names are not included in this book for people who were born outside their native country, perhaps we can make one exception for Virginia Dare, who was born on Roanoke Island in 1587. The little girl who gave her name to what is now Dare County, North **Carolina**, is accorded this special treatment because she was the first child of English parents to be born in the American continent. And do not overlook her Christian name (or even the coincidentally 'pioneering' surname)!

Darien (USA)
There are two towns of note of the name – Darien in Connecticut, and Darien, the county seat of McIntosh County, both in South **Carolina**. The county name will supply the essentially Scottish clue. In fact the names were given not for any person or place in Scotland, but for the Isthmus of Darien (now in Panama), to which a luckless Scottish expedition ventured in 1697. The American places were thus named by Scottish Highland settlers.

Darling (Australia, South Africa)
If one were unaware of the true source of the name, one might be half-deceived into assuming it had been given by romantically minded settlers. But the Darling River that flows through **Queensland** and **New South Wales**, the Darling Downs in the former state, and the Darling Range of mountains in Western Australia were all named for Sir Ralph Darling (1775–1858), the governor of New South Wales who endowed the new Australian landowners with vast land grants. The headwaters of the Darling River were gradually discovered by settlers from about 1815. In 1828, however, Sir Ralph sent the explorer Charles Sturt (see **Sturt Desert**) to investigate not this river but the **Macquarie**. Making his survey, Sturt by chance came across the mainstream of the Darling early the following year, and named it for his governor. But this was not the first use of his name in the country, for the Darling Downs had been discovered by the Scottish botanist Allan Cunningham in 1827, the year before Sturt's exploration. Darling was Governor from 1825 to 1831. The town of Darling in Cape Province, South Africa, however, was named after another man. This was Sir Charles Henry Darling (1809–1870), Lieutenant-Governor of the Cape from 1851 to 1854, with the town laid out in 1853. Sir Charles was the nephew of Sir Ralph, and indeed was his private secretary for a time.

Darlington (USA)
Darlington County and its seat of the same name in South **Carolina**, the latter settled in the 1780s, were both named for Darlington in Co. Durham. The link was not a manufacturing one, but for an emigrant connection with the town.

Dartmouth (USA, Canada)
The town of Dartmouth in Massachusetts was settled by English Quakers in the 1650s and named for the English port in Devon, as was the city of Dartmouth in **Nova Scotia**, although this was founded almost exactly a century later. The English port has a special significance for early settlers in North America, as it was just off Dartmouth that the ships *Speedwell* and *Mayflower* lay in 1620 on their way to America. However, some sources claim that the Canadian Dartmouth was primarily named after William Legge, 1st Earl of Dartmouth (1672–1750), whose death occurred in the year the place was settled. (While mentioning such earls, one can note that the privately controlled Dartmouth College, in **Hanover**, **New Hampshire**, was not named for its

English naval counterpart, but for the 1st Earl's grandson, of identical name, who as 2nd Earl of Dartmouth was president of the trustees of the English funds and thus gave his name to the College when it was chartered in 1769.)

Darwin (Australia, USA, Falkland Islands, Antarctica)
It is of course the great naturalist and writer Charles Darwin who gave his name to most of the localities quoted here. Darwin set off in 1831 on board the *Beagle* commanded by Robert Fitzroy (see **Fitzroy**) to survey the wildlife of the west coast of South America and a number of the Pacific islands. During his five-year voyage he developed his famous theory about the gradual evolution of species, and began to write his pioneering work on the subject immediately after his return. Darwin, the capital and chief port of Northern Territory, Australia, derives its name from Port Darwin, the harbour that was found here by John Stokes, surveyor on board the *Beagle*, in 1839, and that he named after Charles Darwin. However, the actual settlement here was not initiated until 1869, when it was at first called **Palmerston** (see entry for other places of the name). Only in 1911 was the town renamed after the harbour (first as Port Darwin, then as Darwin). Darwin Peak, the mountain in Wyoming, USA, was also named for Darwin, as was the settlement of Darwin in the **Falkland Islands**. The scientist visited the Falklands twice in the *Beagle*, in 1833 and 1834, and spent a night near the site of the present community. But in the Antarctic, Mount Darwin, in the **Queen Alexandra Range**, was named not after Charles Darwin but after his son, Leonard Darwin (1850–1943), a noted engineer, economist and traveller, and a president of the Royal Geographical Society.

Davis (Canada/Greenland, Antarctica)
Probably the best known location of this name is Davis Strait, between **Baffin** Island, Northwest Territories, Canada, and Greenland. The strait was discovered in 1585 by the navigator John Davis (?1550–1605) in the course of his voyage in search of the Northwest Passage (through the Canadian Arctic to the Pacific). He himself named many Arctic locations, including **Cumberland** Sound and Cape **Walsingham**. In the southern polar regions, Davis Sea, north of Wilhelm II Coast, was named after a much later explorer, however. This was J.C. Davis, the Australian captain of the ship *Aurora* on which Douglas Mawson (see **Mawson**) led his Antarctic expedition of 1911–14.

Dawson-Lambton Glacier
(Antarctica)
The glacier is on the coast of the **Weddell Sea**, and was so named by Ernest Shackleton (see **Shackleton Glacier**) after one of two ladies, the Misses Dawson-Lambton, who had helped finance his second expedition of 1914–16. This was Elizabeth Dawson-Lambton. Both sisters also had their Christian names given individually to two mountains in the **Queen Alexandra Range**, Mount Elizabeth and Mount Anne. Shackleton actually named the glacier in 1915.

Dedham (USA)
The town of Massachusetts is one of the oldest inland settlements of the Massachusetts Bay Colony. It was established in 1635 and was named for Dedham, the Essex village from which some of the original settlers had come.

De Grey River (Australia)
The river, in Western Australia, was visited by the English-Australian explorer Francis Gregory in 1861 and named by him after the then President of the Royal Geographical Society, George Robinson, 3rd Earl de Grey (1827–1909). See also **Greytown**.

Delaware (USA)
The name of the American state derives directly from that of Thomas West, 3rd Baron De La Warr, known as Lord Delaware (1577–1618), the first British governor of **Virginia** (from 1610). The name did not become official for the state until 1776, although it had been given to

Delaware Bay as early as 1610 by Captain Samuel Argall, the Deputy Governor of Virginia, who had discovered it that year when making his way from England to Virginia. The majority of other places of the name in the United States, such as the many Delaware Counties, will also have honoured the baron. The name (or title) is ultimately Norman-French in origin, serving as a nickname for a warrior. The first holder of the barony was Roger La Warre, who died in 1320, and a descendant of the baron, George John West (died 1869), married a Sackville and took the name Sackville-West, now familiar, mainly, through the writer and gardener Victoria ('Vita') Sackville-West, who died in 1962. See also the next entry below.

Delmarva Peninsula (USA)

The peninsula, on the Atlantic coast, between Chesapeake and **Delaware** Bays, includes parts of the states of Delaware, **Maryland** and **Virginia**. Hence its name, which in typical American innovative fashion combines letters from each of these three state names.

Deloraine (Australia)

The town of Deloraine, Tasmania, takes its name either from William of Deloraine, a fictional knight in Scott's *The Lay of the Last Minstrel*, or directly from the place (or burn) of this name (which Scott used for the knight), near Selkirk, Scotland. The former is possible because the town's surveyor was related to Scott, and the name could thus have been an imaginative tribute to him. The Tasmanian town was founded in the 1840s.

Denton (USA)

The **Maryland** town was originally known as Eden Town, with this then 'smoothed' to the present spelling. The name honours Sir Robert Eden (1741–1784), Governor of Maryland from 1769 to 1776. Denton in Texas is named for an American officer.

Derby (Australia, USA, South Africa)

The port of Derby in northern Western Australia was declared a town in 1883 and named for Edward Stanley, 15th Earl of Derby (1826–1893), then Secretary of State for the Colonies. The city of Derby in Connecticut, USA, however, was founded much earlier. It arose as a trading settlement in 1642 and was at first known as Paugasset, after the Indian tribe from whom the land here was bought. In 1675 it became a town and was named after the English city, presumably for original emigrant links. In South Africa, the village of Derby in Transvaal was apparently named after the same lord as the one who gave his title to the Australian port. The name of the American city is pronounced to rhyme with 'Kirby', unlike the English.

Derry (USA)

The **New Hampshire** town was first settled in the early eighteenth century by a group of Scottish immigrants who had settled in or near Londonderry (also known as Derry) in Ireland before continuing across the Atlantic to make their homes in the New World. It was set off from **Londonderry** in 1827, and the two places are now distinct.

Derwent (Australia)

The Derwent River in Tasmania was named in the late eighteenth century after one of the English rivers Derwent, but precisely which is not certain. The best known is probably the one in Derbyshire.

Devon (Canada, South Africa)

Devon Island, the largest of the **Parry** Islands, Northwest Territories, was discovered by William Baffin (see **Baffin**) in 1616 and was originally known as North Devon. The name was not given by Baffin, however, but by Parry, who was thus honouring the native county of a member of his crew, Lieutenant Liddon. The same kind of link applies for the village of Devon in Transvaal, South Africa, where the Devonshire man was the surveyor who laid it out.

Didsbury (Canada)

The community of this name in **Alberta** preserves an original colonial link with Didsbury in England, where it is now a district of Manchester.

Digby (Canada)
The town in **Nova Scotia** was founded in 1783 by the British admiral Robert Digby (1732–1814), and is named after him.

Dinwiddie (USA)
Both Dinwiddie County, **Virginia**, and its seat of the same name honour Robert Dinwiddie (1693–1770), the colonial Governor of Virginia from 1751 to 1758.

Discovery (Australia, Antarctica)
Discovery Bay, an inlet of the Indian Ocean on the southern coast of Australia, is named after the ship *Discovery* that the Scottish explorer Thomas Mitchell found waiting for him on the coast here after he had descended (and named) the **Glenelg** River in his overland journey from the **Murray River** in 1836. (See also **Mitchell River**.) Mount Discovery, in **Victoria** Land, Antarctica, was likewise named after a ship, the better-known *Discovery* on which Robert Falcon Scott made his expedition to the Antarctic in 1901.

Disraeli (Canada)
The village of Disraeli, in Quebec, was named after Benjamin Disraeli (1804–1881), the famous British prime minister and author. Disraeli's title was 1st Earl of Beaconsfield, and this was given to another community in Quebec (see **Beaconsfield**).

Dixon Entrance (USA/Canada)
The Dixon Entrance is a strait in the eastern North Pacific, between the Alexander Archipelago of Alaska, USA, to the north, and the **Queen Charlotte** Islands of **British Columbia**, Canada, to the south. It was so named in 1788 by Sir Joseph Banks (see **Banks**) after Captain George Dixon (?1755–?1800), the English navigator who had sailed his ship *Queen Charlotte* through it the previous year.

Dolphin and Union Strait (Canada)
The strait lies between **Victoria** Island and the Canadian mainland in Northwest Territories. Its name marks the two small boats, the *Dolphin* and the *Union*, used by Sir John Richardson to traverse and explore it in 1825, when he was acting as surgeon and naturalist in Franklin's second overland expedition to the Canadian Arctic coast in 1824–7.

Donnybrook (South Africa)
The village in Natal was named after Donnybrook, the district of Dublin, Ireland, from which came Robert Comrie, the owner of the farm where the village was laid out.

Doonside (South Africa)
The holiday resort in Natal, southwest of **Durban**, was originally known as Middleton, after the man who built the first railway siding here. In order to avoid confusion with Middleton in Cape Province, however, the name was changed in 1910 to Doonside, after a house called Lorna Doone that overlooked the siding. (And the house, directly or not, has a name taken from the title of R.D. Blackmore's famous novel, published in 1869.)

Dorchester (USA, Canada)
Dorchester, now a district of **Boston**, Massachusetts, was founded in 1630 and named for the Dorset town, since famous for its connection with Thomas Hardy. The particular link here is with the English clergyman and religious writer John White (1575–1648), who was rector of Holy Trinity Church, Dorchester, while at the same time organising groups of Dorset men to emigrate to Massachusetts. (This soon led to the formation of the Massachusetts Bay Company.) As a result of his activity, White became known as the 'Patriarch of Dorchester', although he never visited America himself. The name thus directly derives from the home town of many of the original settlers, while indirectly honouring White and his work. Dorchester County, South **Carolina**, is named after the Massachusetts Dorchester, but Dorchester County, **Maryland**, was named for Richard Saville, 5th Earl of Dorset (1622–1677), a friend of the Calvert family who gave their name to **Calvert** County in this state. In Canada, Dorchester County, Quebec, the town of

Dorchester in **New Brunswick**, and Cape Dorchester on **Baffin** Island, Northwest Territories, are all named for Sir Guy Carleton, 1st Lord Dorchester (see **Carleton**), who was Governor General of Canada from 1786 to 1796. The Boston district is directly associated with a hill here named Dorchester Heights, the fortifying of which resulted in the departure of the English from Boston in 1776. See also **Stoughton**.

Dorset (Canada)
The name is found in the Northwest Territories for both Cape Dorset, the southern tip of **Foxe** Peninsula on **Baffin** Island, and Dorset Island here. The name was given (first to the cape, then to the island) by Captain Luke Foxe in 1631, thus honouring Edward Sackville, 4th Earl of Dorset (1591–1652), the statesman who was interested in colonising the Bermuda Islands and **Virginia**.

Douglas (USA, Canada)
Cape Douglas, at the mouth of **Cook** Inlet, Alaska, was named by James Cook after Dr John Douglas (1721–1807), then Canon of Windsor and later Bishop of Salisbury. (Mount Douglas, Alaska, was named after the cape.) In Canada, many places of the name, such as Douglas, Manitoba, and Douglas, Ontario, pay tribute to the Scottish coloniser Thomas Douglas, 5th Earl of Selkirk (1771–1820), who settled eight hundred emigrants from the Scottish Highlands on **Prince Edward Island** in 1803. (See also **Selkirk**.)

Douglastown (Canada)
The community of this name in **New Brunswick** was originally known as Gretna Green. After the fire of 1825, however, its name was changed to honour Sir Howard Douglas (1776–1861), the then Lieutenant-Governor of New Brunswick. In Quebec, however, Douglastown was probably named for Rear-Admiral Sir Charles Douglas (died 1789), who organised the relief of Quebec in 1776.

Dover (USA)
Many places of the name can be traced back to Dover, the well-known port in Kent, such as the city of Dover (the seat of **Kent** county) in **Delaware**, which was personally named in 1683 by William Penn (see **Pennsylvania**). But Dover in **New Hampshire**, originally named **Bristol**, may have been named after an English lawyer called Robert Dover (1575–1641), who opposed the harsh laws of the Puritans, while Dover, Tennessee, is said to have derived its name from the trade name of the iron produced locally. But even this would come ultimately from the English town.

Drake (USA, Atlantic/Pacific)
The name of Francis Drake (1540–1596), the great circumnavigator, is represented in several places in the world, but most obviously in Drake's Bay, an inlet of the Pacific in California, and in Drake Passage, linking the Atlantic and Pacific Oceans to the south of South America. The former place commemorates the landing here of Sir Francis Drake from the *Golden Hind* in 1579, during his voyage round the world. The latter strait, however, was not actually sailed through by Drake, for he passed through the Straits of Magellan, north of Tierra del Fuego, when making his way from the Atlantic to the Pacific. But his ship, the self-same *Hind*, was blown back into the northern regions of the passage by a storm, and this is the reason for naming it after him.

Drayton (Canada)
Drayton, Ontario, was named after the English residence of Sir Robert Peel, Drayton Manor, built by him near Tamworth, Staffordshire. The town of Drayton Valley in **Alberta**, however, was named after one of the English Draytons, possibly the village near Abingdon, Berkshire (now Oxfordshire). (It was earlier known as Power House, for a power dam that was planned here, but that in the event was never completed.)

Drummond (Canada)
Drummond County, Quebec, with its seat of the same name, honours Sir Gordon Drummond (1771–1854), the British gen-

eral who became administrator of the former province of Upper Canada (corresponding to southern Ontario) for three years from 1813, and then of Canada for two more years after that. Compare the next entry below.

Drummondville (Canada)
The Quebec city, incorporated as a town in 1888, was named after the British soldier Sir Gordon Drummond, similarly honoured by other places named **Drummond** (see entry above).

Dublin (USA)
Most places of the name were so designated after the Irish capital, either through direct emigrant links with Dublin, or more generally because many original settlers were Irishmen (not necessarily from Dublin itself). The city of Dublin, Texas, had its streets laid out by a civil engineer named O'Neill, who must certainly have been Irish. Moreover, many of the streets have Irish names still.

Dufferin (Canada)
The Ontario county is named after Frederick Temple Blackwood, 1st Marquess of Dufferin and Ava (1826–1902), who was Governor General of Canada from 1872 to 1878. His title derives from Dufferin in Co. Down, Ireland, where his (originally Scottish) family settled near the end of the seventeenth century.

Duff Islands (Santa Cruz Islands)
The islands are a small group in the Santa Cruz Islands, themselves in the southwest Pacific. Their name is said to derive from a missionary ship, the *Duff*, that visited them in 1797.

Duke of York (Canada, Papua New Guinea)
The Duke of York Archipelago, in **Coronation** Gulf, at the mouth of the Coppermine River, Northwest Territories, was discovered by Sir John Franklin (see **Franklin**) in 1812 and named after the then Duke of York, the son of George III and the future King George IV (1762–1830). The Duke of York Islands (originally called Neu-Lauenburg), in the Bismarck Archipelago, Papua New Guinea, were discovered by the English navigator Philip Carteret (see **Carteret**) in 1767 and were subsequently similarly named.

Duncan Island (Galápagos Islands)
The island, whose official Ecuadorian name is Pinzón Island, was originally named for Sir Anthony Deane (1638–1721) an English shipbuilder. In the eighteenth century, however, the name was changed to honour the British admiral, Sir Adam Duncan (1731–1804). See also **Albemarle** for more on the names generally here, and **Camperdown** for the name bestowed in honour of Admiral Duncan's famous battle victory.

Dundalk (Canada)
The community in Ontario was named after the Irish port of Dundalk, Co. Louth, from which an early settler, one Elias Gray, had emigrated.

Dundas (Australia, Canada)
Dundas Strait, between **Coburg Peninsula** and **Melville** Island, Northern Territory, Australia, and Dundas Peninsula, in the Melville Islands, Northwest Territories, Canada, both owe their names to Henry Dundas, 1st Viscount Melville (1742–1811), First Lord of the Admiralty, as does also the town of Dundas in southern Ontario, which was laid out in 1801 (originally as Coote's Paradise).

Dundee (South Africa)
The town in Natal near **Glencoe** was laid out in 1882 and named after the Scottish city, the birthplace of its founder, Thomas Paterson Smith.

Dunedin (New Zealand, USA)
The South Island city was founded in 1848 as a Scottish Free Church settlement, one of the settlers being William Cargill (see **Invercargill**), and at first was named New Edinburgh. The Gaelic name of Edinburgh (properly Din Eydin, 'fortress of Eydin') was then substituted as more

original and historic. In the United States, the city of Dunedin in western Florida was originally called Jonesboro in 1860, when it was first settled, after a local store owner. In 1882, however, two Scotsmen, J.O. Douglas and James Summerville, made an official request for a post office and proposed the same historic name of Edinburgh for it.

Dungarvan River (Canada)
The river is in **New Brunswick**, and is named after Dungarvan, the town in Co. Waterford, Ireland, from where the original namer is said to have come. (He is named as Michael Murphy.)

Dunk (Australia, Canada)
Dunk Island, off **Queensland**, Australia, was named by James Cook after George Montagu Dunk, 2nd Earl of Halifax (1716–1771), who aided the founding of **Nova Scotia** (where the chief town is named **Halifax** after him). The Dunk River in **Prince Edward Island** is also named after him, the namer being the Dutch-Canadian surveyor-general, Captain Samuel Holland.

Dunmaglass (Canada)
The community in **Nova Scotia** was founded by Scottish settlers from Dunmaglass, an estate near Foyers, Inverness-shire (now Highland), and was named after it.

Dunmore (USA)
The best known town of the name in the United States is probably Dunmore, **Pennsylvania**. This was settled in about 1783 and was at first known as Bucktown, for the large number of deer here. In 1840, however, the settlement was renamed Dunmore, after Charles Augustus Murray (1806–1895), second son of George Murray, 5th Earl of Dunmore, in the hope that this wealthy young Englishman would succeed in raising funds to build a new railroad here. However, Charles Augustus was more interested in hunting and fishing (when in America), and in cultivated leisure (when back in England). The project was thus never realised, but his father's title optimistically remains for the town. Lake Dunmore, Vermont, was named after (and by) an earlier member of this same family, John Murray, 4th Earl of Dunmore (1732–1809), who 'practically baptized himself in the water' in the process, according to Harder (see Bibliography, p. 218). This same lord, who became Governor of **New York** in 1770, and of **Virginia** the following year, also gave his name to the community in West Virginia. However, on this occasion he himself was not the namer, who was Major Jacob Warwick, an officer who had earlier served under him when he (Dunmore) sought to suppress unrest in the colony (and was obliged to flee back to England in 1776).

Dunvegan (Canada)
The community in **Nova Scotia** was originally known as Broad Cove Marsh. This descriptive name was superseded in 1885 by Dunvegan, as a Scottish link with Dunvegan, and especially its castle, on the Isle of Skye.

Durban (South Africa)
Natal's largest city and South Africa's chief seaport was first settled in 1824 by a group of pioneers. The present community proper was established in 1835, however, originally as Port Natal. This name was then changed to D'Urban in honour of Sir Benjamin D'Urban (1777–1849), who was Governor of the Cape from 1834 to 1838. Finally, in about 1870 the name was 'smoothed' to its present spelling. Sir Benjamin's somewhat unusual surname is of Norman-French origin, meaning 'son of Urban', the latter being the saint's name Urbanus used as a family name. See also the next entry.

Durbanville (South Africa)
The town in Cape Province was originally called Pampoenkraal ('pumpkin kraal') when it arose as an outspan in 1824. In 1836 it was renamed D'Urban after Sir Benjamin D'Urban (see **Durban**, above). However, as this name became confused with the Natal seaport, it was altered to

its present form, adding '-ville' for 'town', in 1886.

Durham (USA, Canada)
The name frequently, but not always, derives from that of the English city, or the county of which it is the county town. Durham, **New Hampshire**, was first known as Oyster River when settled in 1635. When incorporated in 1732, however, it was renamed after Richard Barnes (1532–1587), a former bishop of Durham who was well known for his Puritan leanings. Durham, North **Carolina**, where it is the seat of Durham County, also had a different earlier name, which was Prattsburg, after a local landowner, one William Pratt. But when Pratt refused to donate land for a new railroad station to be built, the name was changed to honour the man who would, who was Bartlett S. Durham (1822–1858). The name was used in the form of Durhamville or Durham Station before becoming Durham, as now. Meanwhile Durham in Ontario, Canada, where it was originally named Bentinck, changed its name to Durham in 1866, presumably as a direct compliment to the English city rather than paying tribute to a person from there.

Dutchess County (USA)
The **New York** county was named, with the spelling of the day, for Mary of Modena (1658–1718), wife of James, Duke of York and Albany (i.e. as the Duchess of York), who later became James II of England.

Duxbury (USA)
The town in Massachusetts, on Duxbury Bay, was settled in about 1628, with its founders including Myles Standish (of Longfellow's poem 'The Courtship of Miles Standish'), Elder William Brewster and John Alden. It was named after Duxbury Hall, near Chorley, Lancashire, which was the seat of the Standish family.

Dyer, Cape (Canada)
The cape is on the **Cumberland** Peninsula on **Baffin** Island, Northwest Territories, where it was named in 1585 by the English explorer John Davis (see **Davis**) for his friend Sir Edward Dyer (1540–1607), the courtier and poet.

E

Eardley (Canada)
The community in Quebec was apparently named after a village of Eardley in England, possibly Eardley End near Newcastle-under-Lyme, Staffordshire. The link was presumably with an emigrant from here.

East Liverpool (USA)
The city was founded in 1798 by an Irish Quaker named Thomas Fawcett, and was originally called St Clair and then Fawcettstown, after him. After it became a village in 1834 it was renamed after the English city, with 'East' for its location in the east of the state. Liverpool developed important trading links with America in the seventeenth century.

East London (South Africa)
The port in Cape Province arose as a landing place for troops in the Kaffir War of 1847, although it had been visited by the British around ten years earlier. At first it was named Port Rex, after the rather mysterious George Rex, who was said (as his false name hints) to be the illegitimate son of George III. He and his son, John Rex, played an important part in developing the port for shipping. In 1848, however, the presumably embarrassing name was altered to the innocuous one of East London. 'East' seems not very appropriate, and one wonders why 'South' was not preferred. But one could argue that the port is on the east coast of Cape Province, not the west, and that it is actually east of London, England, in terms of geographical longitude.

Easton (USA)
Several places of the name are simply directional in origin, to refer to an eastern location or to contrast with another settlement that was the original one or to the west. But the city of Easton in **Pennsylvania**, which was founded in 1752 at the request of Thomas Penn, was so named for the English estate, Easton Neston, Northamptonshire, of Penn's father-in-law, Thomas Fermor, 2nd Baron Leominster and Earl of Pomfret. See also **Northampton**.

Ebensburg (USA)
Ebensburg is the seat of **Cambria** County, **Pennsylvania**, and arose in about 1796 as a settlement peopled mainly by Welsh emigrants. The town was laid out by a Welsh minister, the Rev. Rees Lloyd, and was named after his eldest son Eben, who died in infancy.

Edenburg (South Africa)
The town was laid out in 1862, and although it may have been given a name of biblical origin, referring to a new 'Garden of Eden' that would arise here, it is possible that the name is a version of Edinburgh, which was the native city of the only minister here in the Orange Free State, the Rev. Andrew Murray (1828–1917).

Edgartown (USA)
The Massachusetts town, originally called Great Harbor, was renamed after Edgar, one of the sons of the Duke of York, the future James II of England.

Edgecombe County (USA)
The county, in North **Carolina**, was named after Richard Edgecumbe, 1st Baron Edgecumbe (1680–1758), Chan-

cellor of the Duchy of Lancaster from 1743 to 1758.

Edina (USA)
Both the village in Minnesota and the city in Missouri derive their name from Edinburgh, Scotland, with the former place developing round the Edina Flour Mill (itself named after Edinburgh). The name marks a Scottish emigrant connection. Compare the next two entries below.

Edinboro (USA)
Edinboro, **Pennsylvania**, has a name derived from the Scottish city of Edinburgh, with the '-boro' a common shortening of longer names in '-burgh' or '-borough' (compare **Marlboro**).

Edinburg (USA)
The Texan city was originally founded (on a nearby site) as Old Edinburgh, so named after the native Scottish city of the founder, one John Young. In 1908, by referendum, the city (now as the seat of Hidalgo County) was moved to what was then called Chapin, a settlement established the previous year. Finally, in 1911, this name was changed to Edinburg (without the final 'h') to mark the original connection with the Scottish city.

Edmonton (Canada)
The city that is the capital of **Alberta** was named directly after Fort Edmonton, a Hudson's Bay Company fur-trading post that was twenty miles down the North Saskatchewan River when itself built in 1795. When the post was destroyed by Indians in 1807, a new fort was built on the present site, and today's city developed round it. The original fort was built by a member of the Hudson's Bay Company, George Sutherland, and he named it after Edmonton (now a district of London), from which his clerk, John Prudens, had come.

Edward, Lake (Zaire/Uganda)
Many places of this name relate to Prince Edward Augustus, Duke of Kent, as in **Prince Edward Island**, Canada. But here in Africa the name honours a later Edward. The lake that is half in Zaire and half in Uganda was visited by Stanley (see **Stanley**) in 1889, when he named it in honour of the then Prince of Wales, Albert Edward, the future King Edward VII (1841–1910). At first the lake was known as Lake Albert Edward (or Albert Edward Nyanza), but then became Lake Edward, with this name being locally usurped for some time in the 1970s by that of Lake Idi Amin Dada, for the Ugandan dictator who held power then. See also the next entry.

Edward VII Peninsula (Antarctica)
The peninsula, in Marie Byrd Land, on the eastern coast of the **Ross Sea**, was originally known as King Edward VII Land. It was claimed for Britain by Captain Scott (see **Scott Coast**) during his expedition of 1901–4, when he discovered it and named it for the newly enthroned King Edward VII (reigned 1901–10). See also the previous entry above.

Edwardsville (USA)
The coal-mining borough in **Pennsylvania** was incorporated from the parts of other townships in 1884, when it was named after one Daniel Edwards (died 1901), a Welshman who was superintendent of the Kingston Coal Company here from 1868 to his death. The naming was a tribute by the local residents for the contribution Mr Edwards had made to the industrial development of the town.

Effingham (USA)
Effingham County, Illinois, and its seat of the same name, were probably named after Thomas Howard, Earl of Effingham, who was known to be a 'pro-colonial' army officer. But if not named for him, the Effingham may have been a local railroad promoter of the name.

Egmont (New Zealand, Canada)
North Island, New Zealand, has both Cape Egmont and Mount Egmont, with the former lying to the west of the latter. They were both discovered by James Cook in 1770, and named by him after Sir John Perceval, 2nd Earl of Egmont (1711–

1770), who had been First Lord of the Admiralty from 1763 to 1766. The name is suitable, as it happens, for this volcanic peak, since it can be understood, from the French, as meaning 'sharp peak' (as the name Montague can). It was the same earl who gave his name to Egmont Bay in **Prince Edward Island**, Canada, in this case because he had an extravagant settlement scheme for the island, which was in the event never realised. The namer here was not Cook but Samuel Holland, who also named **Dunk** River.

Eildon (Australia)
The town in central **Victoria** was originally called Eildon Weir, the latter word referring to the dam ('weir') that was built over the **Goulburn** River here to create a reservoir. The main part of the name was transferred from the Eildon Hills near Melrose in southern Scotland, presumably for an emigrant Scottish link.

Elgin (USA, Canada)
With a name like this, one has several possibilities, including the Scottish town of Elgin or one of the Earls of Elgin who took their title from it. And for the city of Elgin in Illinois there is a third possibility, which is that the name derives from a hymn tune! The traditional account is thus that one of the founders, a devout Scotsman named James T. Gifford, gave the name after his favourite hymn, known as 'The Song of Elgin'. The actual founding took place in 1835. In Canada, Elgin County, Ontario, Elgin, **New Brunswick**, and Elgin Ontario are all probably named after James Bruce, 8th Earl of Elgin, (1811–1863) who was Governor General of Canada from 1847 to 1854.

Elizabeth (USA, Australia, Chile)
Although a fairly common place-name, Elizabeth will not necessarily honour either of the English queens. In **New Jersey**, for example, the city of the name bears tribute to Lady Elizabeth Carteret, wife of Sir George Carteret (see **Carteret**), who shared with her husband the royal grant that gave him much of **New England** and **New York** and all of what is today New Jersey. The Elizabeth Islands, Massachusetts, too, are named for a princess rather than a queen. This was Princess Elizabeth (1596–1662), daughter of James I of England. But in Australia, the city of Elizabeth in South Australia was founded in 1955 and named after Queen Elizabeth II, crowned only two years earlier. And to complete the royal circle, Elizabeth Island (or as it now is, Isla Isabela) in the Strait of Magellan, extreme South America, was named by Francis Drake in 1578 after Queen Elizabeth I when he sailed through here on his circumnavigation of the world (see **Drake** for more on this). See also the next entry below.

Elizabethtown (USA)
There are various places of the name that bear tribute to the wives or daughters of early settlers and founders. Elizabethtown, New York, for example, was actually named after two identically named women, both Elizabeth Gilliland, respectively the wife and daughter of William Gilliland (1734–1796), a pioneer settler in the Champlain valley here. But some of the Elizabeths will have been American, not English or Scottish (or Welsh or Irish), so do not properly belong in this book.

Ellesmere (Canada, New Zealand)
Look at a map of northern Canada and you cannot fail to see Ellesmere Island, the northernmost island of any size in the Northwest Territories. It was discovered in 1616 by William Baffin (see **Baffin**), but was not named until 1852, after Francis Egerton, Earl of Ellesmere (1800–1857), the statesman and poet whose original surname was Leveson-Gower. The occasion of the naming was the expedition to this part of Canada that year led by Sir Edward Inglefield. It was the same earl who gave his name (or rather, his title) to Lake Ellesmere in South Island, New Zealand.

Elliot (South Africa)
The town of Elliot in Cape Province was founded in 1885 and was named after Sir George Henry Elliot (1826–1912), Chief Magistrate of the Transkeian Territories

from 1891 to 1902 (and before this, Magistrate of Tembuland). Compare the next entry.

Elliotdale (South Africa)
The town, in Transkei, was named after the same official who gave his name to **Elliot**. The official name of the town is now Xhora (since 1976), this being an indigenous name perhaps meaning 'chosen one'.

Elsinore (USA)
The city in California was named by one Donald Graham after the Danish castle that features in Shakespeare's *Hamlet*, by way of a literary tribute.But why did he choose the name of gloomy, ghostly Elsinore for this city in sunny California?

Emmet County (USA)
The two Emmet Counties, respectively in Iowa and Michigan, were named for the Irish patriot Robert W. Emmet (1778–1803), executed by the English for his revolutionary activities. The name was given at a time when revolutionary leaders were held in high regard by Americans, in the years after the Revolution (War of American Independence), which began in 1775 and lasted for most of the next decade. Compare the next entry below.

Emmetsburg (USA)
The city of Emmetsburg, Iowa, is named after the same eighteenth-century Irish revolutionary leader who gave his name to **Emmet County**.

Emo (Canada)
The community in Ontario was named after the village of Emo in Co. Laois, Ireland, with Emo River named after the small river that runs by the latter place, south of Portarlington.

Endeavour (Australia)
The Endeavour River in northeast **Queensland**, and the Endeavour Reef that lies off the coast here, were named after James Cook's ship *Endeavour*, on board which he set out in 1768 to make his voyage of exploration and scientific discovery to Tahiti, New Zealand and Australia. Cook beached his ship at the spot where **Cooktown** now stands.

Enderbury Atoll (Pacific Ocean)
The atoll is in the Phoenix Islands, where it was discovered in 1823 by the British naval officer J. J. Coffin, who named it after an English merchant, a Mr Enderbury.

Enderby (Antarctica, Pacific Ocean, Australia)
The largest feature of the name geographically speaking is Enderby Land, a semicircular projection in the Antarctic, south of Madagascar. It was discovered in 1831 by the English navigator John Briscoe, who named it after the whaling firm of Enderby Brothers who owned the ship, the *Tula*, on which they had sent him on his voyage of exploration and commercial exploitation. Also named after the firm are Enderby Island in the **Auckland** Islands, south of New Zealand, and Enderby Island lying just west of the coast near **Dampier**, Western Australia. The Antarctic territory of the name is currently claimed by Australia.

Enfield (USA)
The town of Enfield, Connecticut, was the first community to be so named, in 1683, with the link presumably an emigrant one with what was then the village of Enfield in Middlesex (now a town and London borough). Enfield in **New Hampshire**, however, was named in 1761, and was named for the same Baron Enfield and Colchester that gave his name(s) to **Colchester** and **Tunbridge**, in Vermont.

English Bazar (India)
The town in the state of West Bengal, where it is also known as Angrezabad, has a name that really means what it says. The community was selected as the site for the silk factories (effectively, trading stations) of the British East India Company in 1676. The town is still an important silk centre. Compare the next entry below.

English Company's Islands (Australia)

The islands (properly *The* English Company's Islands), which lie to the north of Arnhem Land, Northern Territory, were discovered by Matthew Flinders (see **Flinders**) in 1803, and named by him as a compliment to the East India Company, which had promoted his voyage. The islands in the group were named after individual directors of the Company, and include Wigram, Cotton, Inglis, Bosanquet and Astell Islands. Compare the entry above.

Enid (USA)

The Oklahoma city was founded literally overnight in 1893 as a tented community round a US Land office when the Cherokee Strip was opened by 'runs' of settlers. It was given a literary name, after 'the fair Enid', Geraint's wife in Tennyson's *Idylls of the King*.

Erebus (Antarctica, Canada)

In Antarctica, Mount Erebus is an active volcano on Ross Island, in the **Ross Sea**, where it stands near Mount **Terror**. Both mountains were discovered by Ross (see **Ross Sea**) in 1841, and were named after his ships, the *Erebus* and the *Terror*. The ship's name is that of the personification of darkness in classical mythology. Similarly, Erebus Bay on **King William** Island, Northwest Territories, Canada, also has an adjacent Terror Bay. In 1847 the *Erebus* and the *Terror* were abandoned here, after being used by Franklin (see **Franklin**) in his final, fatal Arctic expedition. See also **Terror**.

Erewhon (New Zealand)

Erewhon is a high sheep station above the **Canterbury** Plains in South Island. It takes its name from Samuel Butler's famous novel *Erewhon* (whose title is roughly 'Nowhere' backwards), which was published in 1872 and which was based on Butler's own experiences as a sheep farmer in New Zealand. The essential plot of the novel is based on the book by Butler's father, *A First Year in Canterbury Settlement*, published in 1863 and compiled from Samuel's letters.

Essex (USA, Canada)

There are five Essex Counties in the United States, and one in Canada (in Ontario), as well as several towns of the name. They all honour the English county, regarded both as an essentially 'English' name and county, and as the part of England from which many early settlers had come (see, for example, **Chelmsford** and **Colchester**).

Estcourt (South Africa)

The town of Estcourt, in Natal, was originally known as Bushmans River Post (or simply Bushmans Drift) when it was laid out in 1848. In 1863 its name was changed to Estcourt, apparently as a mark of respect to the British Member of Parliament, Thomas H.S. Estcourt (1801–1876), MP for Devizes, Wiltshire, from 1835 to 1844, and after that for North Wiltshire until 1865. He was a friend of one of the early settlers, J.W. Wilks.

Eston (Canada)

Eston in Saskatchewan is named after the Yorkshire (now Cleveland) town, presumably for emigrant connections there.

Evans Glacier (Antarctica)

Edgar Evans was one of the four companions of Robert Falcon Scott on his final, fated expedition to the South Pole in 1911, from which none would return alive. Like the other four men, Evans has had his name commemorated in the Antarctic, where there are actually two glaciers named for him: the Evans Glacier on the edge of the **Ross Sea**, and another Evans Glacier at the foot of the **Beardmore Glacier**, where he met his fate on the return journey in 1912. See also **Bowers Mountains**, **Oates Coast**, **Scott Coast**, **Wilson** Hills.

Everest, Mount (Nepal/Tibet)

The famous Mount Everest, in the Himalayas, where it is the highest mountain in the world, was originally designated simply as Peak XV, when its unique status was first realised in 1852, its altitude having been determined that year by the governmental Survey of India. In 1865 the mountain was given its present name for Sir George Everest (1790–1866), the British official who was Surveyor-General of India from 1823 to 1843, and who completed the first general survey of this region in 1841. In one sense, his was a suitable name for a lofty mountain, one that 'ever rests', but in another sense, was it appropriate to name such a unique peak after a man who had more to do with maps than with mountains? The Tibetan name of Everest is Chomolungma, said to mean 'goddess mother of the world'. That sounds much more fitting!

Exeter (USA)

The town of Exeter in **New Hampshire** was settled in 1638 and named by the Rev. John Wheelwright, a member of the so-called Exeter Combination, a group of exiles from the original Massachusetts Bay Colony. His group took their name from the English city in Devon from which many of them had come. Other places of the name, such as Exeter, **Pennsylvania**, and Exeter, Rhode Island, similarly derive their names from this city. For once, therefore, we have a name that did not originate from a 'Lord Exeter', although the city's name commonly occurs in royal and aristocratic titles, such as the well-known Cecil family, who have been earls of Exeter from the sixteenth century (and marquises from the early nineteenth).

Exmouth Gulf (Australia)

The gulf, between North West Cape and the mainland of Western Australia, was named for Admiral Edward Pellew, 1st Viscount Exmouth (1757–1833) by Lieutenant Philip Parker King (see **King**), who in 1818 surveyed the coast here in HMS *Mermaid*. The specific tribute was to Admiral Pellew's command of the Anglo-Dutch force during the bombardment of Algiers two years previously.

Eyre (Australia)

Australia has two noted sites of the name, both in South Australia. These are Lake Eyre and the Eyre Peninsula to the south of it (and some distance from it). The lake, the largest salt lake in Australia, was first sighted in 1840 by the Yorkshire-born explorer Edward Eyre (1815–1901), during his hazardous journey round the Great Australian Bight. It is thus named after him, as is the Eyre Peninsula, which had similarly been investigated by him (although first sighted in 1802 by Eyre's fellow-countryman, Matthew Flinders, who gave his name to the **Flinders** Range, among other Australian features). Taylor (see Bibliography, p. 217), records the name of the peninsula as Eyria, a rather witty designation, and presumably intentionally so.

F

Fairfax (USA)

The city in **Virginia**, in Fairfax County, of which it is the seat (although administratively independent of it), developed soon after 1800 and was originally known as Earp's Corner. In 1805 it was incorporated in the town of Providence and renamed after Thomas Fairfax, 6th Baron Fairfax of Cameron (1692–1780), who had inherited the so-called 'Fairfax Proprietary', large estates in northern Virginia, from his maternal grandfather, Lord Thomas Culpeper. He settled permanently in Virginia in 1747 as the only resident peer in the colonies. Fairfax, California, is also believed to have been named after one of the Barons Fairfax, and although it could have been this same man, this has not been reliably determined. Fairfax, Alabama, is said to have been given the name simply for the euphony. (As a personal name, it actually means 'fair-haired'.) See also **Romney**.

Fairfield (USA)

As mentioned for **Fairfax**, Fairfield is a name that is simply attractive (or descriptive) in its own right. In the case of the town in Connecticut, however, Fairfield was named after the hamlet of Fairfield in Kent, near Rye, from which one of the early settlers had come when the community was founded in 1639. Fairfield, California, is named after the Connecticut town, from where the namer had come.

Falkland Islands (South Atlantic)

When news broke in 1982 that Argentina had invaded the Falkland Islands, many Britons at first supposed that, for some inexplicable reason, certain Scottish islands were the subject of the claim. In a sense the error was justifiable, as Falkland is a fairly well-known Scottish town in Fife, and Scotland is familiar for her many islands. (There may also have been some confusion with the doubtless even better known town of Falkirk, also in Scotland.) But the Falkland Islands are hundreds of miles from Britain, close to the Antarctic, where Captain John Strong, an English sailor, made the first recorded landing in 1690 and named the sound between the two main islands Falkland Sound, after Anthony Cary, 5th Viscount Falkland (1656–1694), Treasurer of the Navy from 1681 to 1689, and First Lord of the Admiralty subsequently. The name 'Falkland's Lane' is first recorded in the log of Captain Woodes Rogers, who visited the island in 1708, and the name 'Falkland's Islands' was given by John Byron (see **Byron**) when he took possession of the group in 1765. (Byron later renamed Falkland Sound as 'Carlisle Sound', probably for Charles Howard, 3rd Earl of Carlisle, who was First Lord of the Treasury in 1701 and again in 1715, but the name did not last.) Viscount Falkland's title does come from the Scottish borough, however, and was granted to the Cary family in 1620 by James VI of Scotland (James I of England).

Falmouth (USA)

The town of Falmouth in Massachusetts was settled in 1661 by a group of Quakers led by one Isaac Robinson, and was originally known by its Indian name of Succanessett. Three years later it was incorporated and renamed after Falmouth in Cornwall, from where some of the Quaker settlers had come.

Fanettsburg (USA)
The Pennsylvania community was settled in the second half of the eighteenth century by Irishmen originally from Scotland, and they named it after the peninsula with a lighthouse (now Fanad Head) in northern Co. Donegal, Ireland.

Farnham (Canada)
The Quebec city is named after Farnham, Surrey, from which town the original settlers must have come.

Fauquier County (USA)
The **Virginia** county is named after Francis Fauquier (?1704–1768), the English statesman who was Lieutenant-Governor of Virginia from 1758 to 1768.

Featherston (New Zealand)
The small town in southeast North Island was named in 1854 after the Scotsman, Dr Isaac Featherston (1813–1876), who was Superintendent of the **Wellington** District from 1853 to 1871, and Agent General for New Zealand subsequently.

Felix, Cape (Canada)
Cape Felix forms the northern point of **King William** Island, in the Northwest Territories, where it was so named by James Ross (see **Ross Sea**) after Sir Felix Booth (see **Boothia**).

Fergus (USA, Canada)
Fergus County, Montana, was named after the Scottish legislator, James Fergus (1813–1897), who emigrated to the United States in 1835 and took up a legal practice in Montana. The town of Fergus in Ontario, Canada, however, is named after another Scotsman, Adam Ferguson, who founded the settlement in 1834.

Fitz-James (France)
A small village north of Paris, it was known as Warty until 1710, when it was renamed on being elevated to the status of a duchy in honour of the British soldier James Fitzjames, Duke of Berwick (1670–1734), the illegitimate son of the Duke of York, later James II. In 1706 he earned the title of Marshal of France by capturing Nice from Eugene of Savoy. In 1710, the year that the village was renamed for him, Louis XIV created him Duc de Fitz-James for his prowess as the king's commander in the War of the Spanish Succession (1701–14). The Duke was actually born in France, at Moulins, near Bourges.

Fitzroy (Australia, Falkland Islands)
There are two Fitzroy Rivers in Australia, each named after a different man. The **Queensland** river, formed by the confluence of the Dawson and **Mackenzie** rivers, is named after Sir Charles Fitzroy (1796–1858), who was Governor of **New South Wales** from 1846 to 1850, when he became Governor of Australia. Fitzroy River in Western Australia, however, which enters the sea at **King** Sound, was explored in 1838 by Lieutenant John Lort Stokes (see Mount **Stokes**) of HMS *Beagle*, who named it after Captain Robert Fitzroy (1805–1865), a former commander of the ship and later a noted hydrographer and meteorologist. Fitzroy Island east of **Cairns**, Queensland, is also named after the captain, as is Fitzroy, the settlement in the **Falkland Islands**, which Captain Fitzroy visited in the *Beagle* when surveying there between 1828 and 1836. For related Australian namings, see **Grafton**.

Fleetwood (USA)
The town in **Pennsylvania** was originally known as Coxtown, after an early settler. This name lasted for some sixty years until 1859, when the railroad reached the settlement and industrial development began. Construction of the railroad had been encouraged by Sir Peter Hesketh Fleetwood (1801–1866), and the community was thus named after him, as indeed in his home county the Lancashire port of Fleetwood had been just over twenty years previously.

Flinders (Australia)
The name of Matthew Flinders (1774–1814), the Lincolnshire hydrographer and mariner, is found in many parts of Australia and in some locations off it. This is

perhaps not surprising, for he made two voyages to the continent, in 1795 and 1801, exploring and surveying the southeast coast and Tasmania during his first expedition, and surveying the entire southern coast during the second, after which he sailed from **Port Jackson** (now **Sydney**) to chart the eastern coast. The result was that he circumnavigated the whole country and returned to Port Jackson in 1803. So named after him are: The Flinders Range of mountains in South Australia, Flinders River in **Queensland**, Flinders Bay in Western Australia, and Flinders Island in the **Furneaux Islands**, Tasmania. Flinders himself was a great namer, as is reflected in his obituary in the *Dictionary of National Biography* (1882–1900), where the following extract concerns his exploration of the southern coast in the *Investigator* in 1801, as he made his way round the **Eyre** Peninsula:

> The greater part of this was new ground, seen for the first time, and the names given by Flinders to the different bays, gulfs, headlands, and islands still call attention to the names of the officers of the *Investigator*, to some of the incidents of the voyage, and to the fact that the captain, his brother, the second lieutenant, and a midshipman named John Franklin were natives of Lincolnshire. Cape Catastrophe commemorates the loss of the cutter with her crew and two officers, whose names, Thistle and Taylor, live in two neighbouring islands. Hard by is Memory Cove, and a few miles further are Port Lincoln, Cape Donington, Boston Island, Spalding Cove, Grantham Island, and Spilsby Island, one of the Sir Joseph Banks group.

A large-scale map will reveal further Lincolshire names here, such as Sleaford Bay, Louth Bay and Stamford Hill. **Port Lincoln** itself has a Flinders Monument. The 'midshipman named John Franklin', at this time a mere 15-year-old, grew up to become the famous Arctic explorer who gave his own name to many territories and features (see **Franklin**). See also **Investigator Group**.

Florenceville (Canada)

The **New Brunswick** community was named at the time of the Crimean War (1855) to honour the pioneering medical work undertaken by Florence Nightingale (1820–1910) in that War. (Compare the mention of Nightingale Sound in Appendix II, p. 211.)

Footscray (Australia)

Now an inner suburb of **Melbourne**, **Victoria**, Footscray was proclaimed a city in 1891 and named after Foots Cray in Kent (now in the borough of Bexley, Greater London), with which one or more settlers here must have had a link.

Forbes (Australia, Canada)

The town in **New South Wales**, proclaimed in 1861, is named after Sir Francis Forbes (1784–1841), the Bermuda-born Chief Justice of New South Wales. Mount Forbes in **Alberta**, Canada, however, was named for the Scottish scientist James David Forbes (1809–1868), Professor of Natural History at Edinburgh University and later its Principal. He made a special study of glaciers and climate, and was interested in the history of discovery.

Fort Albany (Canada)

Fort Albany is a trading post in eastern Ontario, where it stands on **James** Bay at the mouth of **Albany** River. It was founded in about 1684 by the Hudson's Bay Company, and gave its name to the river (whose own name see for the origin).

Fort Beaufort (South Africa)

The town in Cape Province was established in 1837 round a fort of the same name, itself built in 1822 by Lieutenant-Colonel H. Maurice Scott as a defence against the Xhosas and named after the Duke of Beaufort, father of Lord Charles Henry Somerset (1768–1831), Governor of the Cape. See also **Beaufort** and **Somerset**.

Fort Frances (Canada)

The town of Fort Frances, in Ontario, originated as a fur-trading post built in 1731 near the present location and at first known as Fort-Saint-Pierre. In 1830 it was renamed in honour of the wife of Sir George Simpson (1792–1860), the Scottish General Superintendent of the Hudson's Bay Company. His wife, whom he had married three years before this, was also named Simpson before her marriage, and died in 1853. See also **Fort Simpson**.

Fort Garry (Canada)

Fort Garry was the original name of Winnipeg, the capital of Manitoba. The first fort here was Fort Rouge, built in 1738 by the French on the Red River, the river's present name being an English translation of the French. The fort was then renamed Fort Douglas, after the family name of Lord Selkirk, one of the directors of the Hudson's Bay Company. Then in 1804 a nearby trading post named Fort Gibraltar was built by the North West Company, with the two posts being fiercely competing (and warring) rivals. Later, in 1821, the Hudson's Bay Company built a third post here, Fort Garry, this being a general Scottish highland name (see **Garry**). Eventually, a sort of compromise or truce was reached, together with yet another post named the Red River Settlement, founded by Scottish colonists, and in the 1860s the village of Winnipeg evolved, taking its Indian name from the nearby lake. The Indian name means simply 'muddy water'.

Fort George (Canada)

The river and community of the name in Quebec honour King George IV. The settlement of Fort George was founded in 1804 by the Hudson's Bay Company.

Fort James (Zambia)

The present town, named Chipata since 1964, when Zambia gained her independence, was founded in 1899 as the capital of North Eastern **Rhodesia**. It was named Fort James after the Scottish-born South African and Rhodesian Statesman Sir L. S. Jameson (1853–1917), who carried out the 'Jameson Raid' when he organised an armed invasion of the Transvaal in 1895. The town's present African name means 'gateway'.

Fort Johnston (Malawi)

This is the former name of the town that is now called Mangoche. It arose in the 1890s as a defence post founded by the British explorer and colonial administrator Sir Harry Johnston (1858–1927), changing its name to Mangoche soon after 1966 when Malawi became an independent republic.

Fort Loudon (USA)

Fort Loudon is a historic site in Tennessee, where it commemorates the fort built by the British at the request of the Cherokee. The fort, which was occupied to 1760 (and has now been restored), was named after the Earl of Loudon (see **Loudon**), who commanded the British forces in the early stages of the French and Indian Wars.

Fort Prince of Wales (Canada)

The fort was constructed at the entrance to **Churchill** Harbour, Manitoba, in 1734, and was named after the then Prince of Wales, Prince George William Frederick, the future George III. Although destroyed by the French in 1782, the fort has been partially restored as a tourist attraction. See also **Prince of Wales**; **Georgetown**.

Fort Raleigh (USA)

Fort Raleigh National Historical Site, in North **Carolina**, was established to mark the site where Sir Walter Raleigh (see **Raleigh**) endeavoured to build an English colony in America. The site, on Roanoke Island, is also the birthplace of the 'pioneer baby' Virginia Dare (see **Dare**).

Fort Sandeman (Pakistan)

The town, in Baluchistan Province, was founded in 1889 by the Scottish-born Sir Robert Sandeman (1835–1892), officer and colonial administrator in India, and is named after him. The town's local name is Apozai. Fort Sandeman was renamed Zhob in the 1970s.

Fort Simpson (Canada)

Fort Simpson, also known simply as Simpson, is a town in the **Mackenzie** District, Northwest Territories, that was originally known as Fort of the Forks, for its location at the confluence of the Mackenzie and Liard Rivers. It had this name from 1804 to 1820, when it was renamed in honour of Sir George Simpson (1792–1860), one of the governors of the Hudson's Bay Company from 1822 to 1860. See also **Fort Frances**.

Fort Smith (Canada)
The town, in the **Mackenzie** District, Northwest Territories, at the **Alberta** border, arose from a site that was originally known as either Fort York or Rapids of the Drowned, the latter name referring to the Slave River on which it stood, with the rapids upstream from it. The present name derives from the Hudson's Bay Company post set up here in 1864, so designated to honour Donald A. Smith, Baron Strathcona (1820–1914), who was not only Governor of the Company but President of the Canadian Pacific Railway.

Fort Victoria (Southern Rhodesia)
This is the original name of the Zimbabwean town Masvingo, which arose as an earthwork fort built in 1890 by the Pioneer Column, the British force set up by Rhodes to occupy Mashonaland (where they founded **Salisbury**). The tribute is to Queen Victoria. The name lasted until the independence of Zimbabwe in 1980 out of the former Southern **Rhodesia**, when it was changed first to Nyanda, then two years later to Masvingo.

Foxborough (USA)
The Massachusetts town, also spelt Foxboro, honours the English politician Charles James Fox (1749–1806), who was Foreign Secretary under Lord Grenville (the first foreign secretary in English history), and who earlier had opposed Lord North's American policies and called for an improvement in the treatment of the rebellious colonies there.

Foxe (Canada)
The Foxe Basin, Foxe Channel and Foxe Peninsula, all on or near **Baffin** Island, Northwest Territories, preserve the name of the early Arctic explorer Luke Foxe (1586–1635), who came from Hull. His name was formerly often spelt Fox, as were these three Canadian eponyms. See also **Roes Welcome**.

Fox Glacier (New Zealand)
The glacier, which falls from the Southern Alps in South Island, was named after Sir William Fox, the English-born Prime Minister of New Zealand who also gave his name to **Foxton**.

Foxton (New Zealand)
The town, in southwest North Island, was founded in 1855 and for many years was the biggest township between **Wellington** and Wanganui. It was named after the English-born statesman Sir William Fox (1812–1893), who came to New Zealand in 1842 and was four times Prime Minister.

Framlingham (USA)
The Massachusetts town, west of **Boston**, was settled in 1650 and derived its name from the small Suffolk town of Framlingham, from where doubtless one or more of the original settlers had come.

Frankford (Canada)
The Ontario community, whose name was formerly frequently spelt Frankfort, is believed to compliment Sir Francis Bond Head (1793–1875), the English soldier who became Lieutenant-Governor of Upper Canada in 1835 and who the following year visited this area.

Franklin (Canada, USA, Australia)
The name is very popular in North America. But the places called Franklin in the United States are nine times out of ten not for us, alas, as they honour the great patriotic American president, Benjamin Franklin. We will thus do rather better in Canada, where the tribute will almost always be to the Lincolnshire-born Rear-Admiral and Arctic explorer, Sir John Franklin (1786–1847), whose life ended so tragically when searching for the Northwest Passage. The best-known territory named after him is that of Franklin District, Northwest Territories, which was

created in 1895, and which includes **Boothia** and **Melville** peninsulas and all the Arctic islands in the Territories. Franklin Bay, in the north of **Mackenzie** District, is also named after him, as is Lake Franklin in Keewatin District. In Alaska, USA, Point Franklin is similarly named in his honour. And in Australia, Franklin Sound in the **Furneaux Islands**, off Tasmania, bears his name, as do the small Franklin Islands in the St Francis group, South Australia, up the western coast of **Eyre** Peninsula. It was round this same peninsula, after all, that Franklin had sailed in the *Investigator* as a young midshipman under Matthew Flinders (see **Flinders**) in 1801. In this respect, see also **Investigator Group**.

Fraser (Canada, Australia)

The Fraser River, one of the most important in North America, in **British Columbia**, was discovered by Alexander Mackenzie (see **Mackenzie**) in 1793. It takes its name, however, from the first European known to have explored it. This was the Scots fur trader Simon Fraser (?1776–1862), of the North West Company, who travelled up it by canoe from **Fort George** in 1808. Fraser Island off the coast of **Queensland**, Australia, was named for another man, though. This was Captain James Fraser, who was killed here by Aborigines in 1836, together with other members of his party. (The island is also known as Great Sandy Island.)

Frederick (USA)

In British royal history, probably the best-known Frederick will be the eldest son of George II, Frederick Louis (1707–1751), if only because of his bad relations with his father. He gave his name to Frederick County, **Virginia** and possibly also to Frederick County in **Maryland**, whose seat of the same name was settled in 1733 and laid out in 1745 as Frederick Town. Some sources claim, however, that the Maryland county and city have a name that honours Frederick Calvert, 6th Baron Baltimore, the last proprietor of Maryland. (See **Calvert** for more about him.) Frederick Louis was the father of George III, and George III's second son was Frederick Augustus, Duke of York and Albany (1763–1827). It was this Frederick who gave the name of Frederick Sound in Alaska. The channel between **Chatham** and Dry Straits was so named in 1794 by George Vancouver (see **Vancouver**). Frederick, Oklahoma, however, was named after an American railroad executive, not an English prince. See also the next two entries below.

Fredericksburg (USA)

Fredericksburg, **Virginia**, famous (or infamous) for its bloody battle of 1862 in the Civil War, was named after Prince Frederick Louis, eldest son of George II (see **Frederick**). The city was settled in 1671 and laid out in 1727, developing as a port with an active English trade. On the other hand, Fredericksburg in Texas was named after a Prussian prince, so does not belong here, despite the British royal family's German connections.

Fredericton (Canada)

Which Frederick do we have here, compared to the ones involved in **Frederick** and **Fredericksburg**? The city, which has been the capital of **New Brunswick** since 1785, was laid out by United Empire Loyalists (i.e. Tories) in that year and named after Frederick Augustus, son of George III. This is perfectly appropriate for the town that is the capital city of a state whose name honours George III himself. (See also **Brunswick** in this respect.)

Fremantle (Australia)

Fremantle, the principal port of Western Australia, bears the name of Captain Sir Charles Fremantle (1800–1869), the British naval officer who took possession of the region round the mouth of the Swan River here to prevent incursions by the French or the Americans. The town itself was laid out in 1829, and the name was given to it by James Stirling (later Admiral Sir James Stirling), who was the first Governor of Western Australia. Stirling, who was a Scot, also named **Perth**. (And for more about him, see **Stirling**.) Perhaps fortuitously, Fremantle seems an aptly suggestive name for a newly founded city in a newly colonised area, one that has been given a kind of administrative 'free mantle'. But on the other hand it is not so appropriate for the original Swan River Settlement here, which became a penal colony for nearly forty years from 1850.

Frere, Mount (South Africa)

The mountain in Transkei was named after Sir Bartle Frere (1815–1880), Governor of the Cape Colony from 1877 to 1880. It in turn gave the name of the town of Mount Frere, founded at its foot in 1876. See also Mount **Bartle Frere**.

Frobisher Bay (Canada)

The bay, on **Baffin** Island, was discovered in 1576 by the navigator and early explorer of the Canadian coast, Sir Martin Frobisher (?1535–1594), who believed it to be a strait. For this reason, it was known as 'Frobisher's Strait' for nearly three hundred years, and it was only in 1860 that it was found to be a bay. The error is understandable, for the bay is in fact an inlet about 150 miles in length. There is now a settlement of Frobisher Bay here, established as a trading post in 1914 and today the largest community in the eastern Arctic.

Furneaux Islands (Australia)

The Furneaux Islands, or Furneaux Group, are in the **Bass Strait** off northeast Tasmania, where the largest of the group is **Flinders** Island. They are named after their discoverer, Tobias Furneaux (1735–1781), a naval officer and explorer who came across them here in HMS *Adventure* in 1773. The group was surveyed by Matthew Flinders in 1798.

Fury and Hecla Strait (Canada)

The strait lies between **Melville** and **Baffin** Island, Northwest Territories. It was discovered in 1822 by William Parry (see **Parry**) on his second voyage, and is named after his two ships, the *Fury* and the *Hecla*. (The latter takes her name from a volcano in Iceland.) Compare **Hecla and Griper Bay**.

G

Gagetown (Canada)

The **New Brunswick** town takes its name from General Thomas Gage (1721–1787), commander-in-chief of the British forces at the Battle of Bunker Hill (1775). Gage had received a grant of the township, earlier named Grimross, in 1765.

Galt (Canada)

The city in southeast Ontario was founded in about 1816 with the original name of Shade's Mills, after a local builder. In 1827 it was renamed after the Scottish novelist John Galt (1779–1839), who after travelling to many countries came to Canada in 1826 and founded the city of **Guelph** in what was then Upper Canada (now Ontario) the following year. Galt was a friend of the Hon. William Dickson, who founded the town that now bears his name.

Gambier Islands (South Pacific, Australia)

The islands, in French Polynesia, were discovered by Captain James Wilson, master of the missionary ship *Duff*, in 1797, and were named by him after the British naval commander, James Gambier, 1st Baron Gambier (1756–1833), who led the British fleet in the bombardment of Copenhagen in 1807. The small Gambier Islands at the mouth of Spencer Gulf, South Australia, were named by Matthew Flinders in 1802 (see **Flinders** for his feats and namings in this area). The Pacific island group are also known by their local name of Mangareva Islands, and most of the names are similarly Polynesian. See also **Duff Islands**.

Garry (Canada)

Lake Garry, on the **Back River** in Keewatin District, Northwest Territories, was so named by Back himself in 1834 after Nicholas Garry, Deputy Chairman of the Hudson's Bay Company, and the same man's name was similarly given to Cape Garry in **Prince Regent** Inlet (between **Somerset** and **Baffin** Islands) by William Parry (see **Parry**) in 1825, and that same year by John Franklin (see **Franklin**) to Garry Island in the delta of the **Mackenzie** River. There is also a Garry River in the **Boothia** Peninsula, named by James Ross (see **Ross Sea**). But the name of **Fort Garry** was not given for the official, but generally for the Scottish name, familiar not only from the surname but from the river Garry, Loch Garry, and Glengarry.

Gawler (Australia)

Both the town of Gawler and the Gawler Range of mountains in South Australia are named for George Gawler (1795–1869), Governor of South Australia from 1838 to 1841. Gawler was recalled to England in the latter year when the home government became concerned about his financial trustworthiness, and 'by a mishap his recall was first announced to him by his successor' (*DNB*). This was George Grey (later Sir George Grey), who gave his name to **Greytown** and other colonial places (see **Grey**).

George (USA, Canada, Australia, South Africa, Uganda, Indian Ocean, Antarctica, USSR)

A worldwide name! The reason is not hard to see, for Britain's colonial past extends over the reigns of more than one king of the name, and the lifetime of more than one prince. The kings, in particular, include George I (1660–1727), George II (1683–1760), George III (1738–1820), George IV (1762–1830), George V (1865–1936) and even, in post-colonial days, George VI (1895–1952). In the United States, Lake George, in eastern **New York**, originally had the Indian name of Andaitarocte ('place where the lake contracts'). In 1646 a French Jesuit missionary then christened it as Lac du Saint-Sacrement. Finally, in 1755, General Sir William Johnson, who oversaw Indian affairs in America, especially those of the so-called 'Six Nations', renamed it in honour of George II, who had come to the throne in 1727. In Canada, Cape George in **Nova Scotia**, however, was named after the archetypal English George, that is, St George, England's patron saint. (The French knew this headland at Cap St Louis.) In Australia, Lake George, in **New South Wales**, was discovered and explored in 1820 by an ex-convict settler named Joseph Wild. He did not name the lake, though, for this honour fell to Lachlan Macquarie (see **Macquarie**), Governor of New South Wales, who thus paid tribute to George IV. (The lake's aboriginal name is Werrima.) But, again, Georges River that flows into Botany Bay, **Sydney** was named after George Bass (see **Bass Strait**), who discovered it. In South Africa, the town of George in Cape Province was the first to be established after the British occupation of 1806, and in 1811 it was proclaimed as George Town, in honour of George III (who donated a Bible to the church here). Travelling north through Africa, one then finds Lake George in Uganda. The lake was visited by Stanley (see **Stanley**) in 1875, and he somewhat mistakenly named it Beatrice Gulf – mistakenly, as it is not a gulf at all, but he supposed that it was part of Lake **Albert**, which lies to the north. Beatrice honours the daughter of Queen Victoria and Prince Albert, Princess Beatrice (1857–1944), who ten years after Stanley's visit married Prince Henry of Battenburg. The lake was subsequently renamed after George V, who came to the throne in 1910. And so out of Africa southwest to the Kerguelen Islands, in the Indian Ocean, where Cape George was named by Cook in 1775. The islands are French territory, but several English names remain, including this one, which honours George III. (That same year Cook visited **South Georgia**, now in the **Falkland Islands** Dependencies, where he similarly named Cape George after the same king.) While down in this part of the world we should consider George V Coast and George VI Sound, both in the Antarctic. Their names spell out their particular allegiance, but do not reveal that the former was named by Douglas Mawson (see **Mawson**) during his expedition of 1911–14. The latter, of course, was a much later naming. George VI came to the throne in 1936, and this region of the Antarctic Peninsula, in what is now Palmer Land, was named by the British **Graham** Land Expedition of 1934–7 led by John Rymill. (It is not really a sound at all, but an ice shelf, and in recent years there have been proposals to redesignate such misleading 'watery' names more accurately, so that Ross Island becomes the Ross Peninsula, and Alexander Island, which lies immediately to the west of George VI Sound, is Alexander Land.) Finally, at least for this present Georgian sampling, we must go to the opposite end of the world, where George Land can be found as an island in Franz Josef Land. The island (today frequently appearing on maps in its Russian version of Zemlya Georga, for the archipelago here is in Soviet territory) was named by the explorer F. G. Jackson, who was here in his expedition of 1894–7. As he recorded in his account of the expedition, *A Thousand Days in the Arctic*, published in 1899, Prince George's Land (as he first called it) was 'so named by me after H.R.H. Prince George of Wales'. This was in 1897, when the prince had thirteen years to wait before he would become George V. See Appendix II, p. 208, for a detailed survey of other namings by Jackson. And see the next four entries below, **King George** and the associated patriotic **St George**.

Georgetown (USA, Canada, Guyana, Gambia, Malaysia)
Most, but not all, of these towns were named for a King George. In the United States, however, where there are at least a dozen Georgetowns, the name is not so likely to be royal in origin. But in South **Carolina** it is, where Georgetown County and its seat of the same name honour George II. The first English settlement arose here in about 1700, and the community was formally established in 1734. Georgetown, now a section of the city of Washington, D.C., was also named for George II when it was settled in 1751. And similarly Georgetown in **Georgia** pays tribute to the same king, as does the very name of the state itself (see below). But many other places of the name commemorate American citizens, among them, naturally enough, George Washington. In Canada, Georgetown in **Prince Edward Island** honours George III. The town was so named in 1765 by the English surveyor Samuel Holland. And although the name of Georgetown in Ontario ultimately derives from an early settler here, one George Kennedy, there could also have been an indirect compliment to George III, as this king died in 1820, the year when Kennedy settled in the area. The capital city of Guyana, Georgetown, was founded by the British in 1781 and named for George III. And although under the Dutch occupation it was renamed Stabroek ('standing pool'), it was renamed Georgetown again when the British gained control in 1812. The port of Georgetown in Gambia was founded in 1823 by Captain Alexander Grant, as a settlement for liberated slaves. In that particular year, the name could be a compliment only to George IV, who had succeeded to the throne three years earlier. In Malaysia, Georgetown was the original name of Pinang (Penang) when it was founded in 1786 by Captain Francis Light of the British East India Company. But although George III was on the throne in this year, it seems likely that the name honours not the king, but his son. Prince George Augustus Frederick, who was born in 1762 and who became George IV in 1820. As with the British **George** names in the previous entry, there is always a suggestion of St George behind the kingly or princely origin, and some towns called George or Georgetown will have a St George's church or cathedral to illustrate the connection. Pinang, for example, has its St George's Church, built in 1817. See also the next three entries below.

Georgia (USA)
The American state was founded in 1732, when James Oglethorpe (see **Oglethorpe**) was granted a royal charter by George II to settle the land here. Its name derivation is therefore certain and well documented. This is not the case for what is now the Soviet republic of Georgia, whose name origin has been under dispute for many years. It certainly does not honour any English George, but it may, at least popularly, have an association with St George.

Georgian Bay (Canada)
Georgian Bay is the northeast arm of Lake Huron, in Ontario, and although the first Europeans to explore it were the French, its name is English enough. It was given by the British naval officer Captain Henry Bayfield when he made an Admiralty survey here in 1819–22, and it thus honours the reigning king, George IV.

Georgina (Australia)
Georgina is an intermittent river in the Simpson Desert, extending across the border between Northern Territory and **Queensland**. The attractive variation on George, however, is a not a compliment to a king, but to the first Governor of Queensland, Sir George Bowen (1821–1899), who gave his surname to **Bowen**.

Geraldine (New Zealand)
By coincidence (and not before time) we have two feminine names together at this point in the listing. But just as Georgina turns out not to honour a woman at all, so Geraldine is similarly revealed to pay a male compliment. Here it is to the Irish Prime Minister of New Zealand, James Edward Fitzgerald (1818–1896), who came to the country in 1850 with the

'Canterbury Pilgrims' (see **Canterbury**) and led a distinguished life as a politician, administrator and journalist. (He founded *The Press* in 1861, which remains to this day one of the country's leading daily newpapers, published in **Christchurch**.)

Germiston (South Africa)
The city of Germiston, Transvaal, was founded in 1887 and originally had the name of Elandsfontein, after the farm on which it was laid out. In 1904 it was renamed Germiston, after a farm near Glasgow, Scotland, where a goldmining pioneer, one John Jack, had been born. The name appeared on large-scale maps and plans of Glasgow until fairly recently, but is now no longer found because of industrial and housing developments.

Giant's Castle (South Africa)
This is the name of a mountain in the Drakensberg, not far from Champagne Castle. It was so named by one Captain Allen Gardiner in 1835, allegedly because it suggested the outline of Edinburgh Castle to him when seen from certain angles. But possibly the name really refers simply to the size of the mountain, for 'Giant's' is a common descriptive for large or impressive natural features (such as Giant's Causeway in Northern Ireland).

Gilbert Islands (Pacific Ocean)
The islands are part of a former British colony in the western Pacific, where they were known as the Gilbert and Ellice Islands. The Gilbert Islands, the larger of the two groups, were discovered in 1765 by the navigator John Byron (see **Byron**), and were named subsequently for Thomas Gilbert, who arrived here in 1788 after helping to convey the first shipload of convicts to Australia. (Captain John Marshall came here with him: see **Marshall Islands**). The Gilbert and Ellice Islands separated as two independent groups in 1976, when the Ellice Islands became known by their local name of Tuvalu. In 1979 the Gilbert Islands similarly achieved independence, and changed their name to **Kiribati**. This name is actually a local rendering of 'Gilbert' (in the indigenous pronunciation), so is not such a sea change as it might seem. (Other islands in the group underwent a similar localisation. For example, Christmas Island, now part of Kiribati, became Kiritimati.)

Gilford Island (Canada)
The island, in **British Columbia**, was named after Richard James Meade, Viscount Gilford (1832–1907), the Irish peer and admiral who commanded HMS *Tribune* when on duty on the Pacific station, west of here, in 1864.

Gillitts-Emberton (South Africa)
The community is an amalgamation of townships in Natal, established in 1939. It is named after an early English pioneer here, one William Gillitt, and his birthplace, the village of Emberton, near Olney, Buckinghamshire. The name is usually shortened to Gillitts.

Gilroy (USA)
The city of Gilroy, California, was named after John Cameron Gilroy (1794–1869), a Scottish sailor and landowner who was influential in the neighbourhood.

Gippsland (Australia)
The region of southeast **Victoria** known as Gippsland was originally called **Caledonia** Australia by the Scot who made the first exploration here in 1839, Angus McMillan. It was renamed by the Polish explorer Count Paul Edmund de Strzelecki as a tribute to the former Governor of **New South Wales**, Sir George Gipps (1791–1847). The first settlers came here in the 1850s, lured by gold finds.

Gisborne (New Zealand)
Gisborne, the seaport city in North Island, was first permanently settled by Europeans in 1852, with the town site surveyed in 1870. It is named after Sir William Gisborne, who was Secretary for the Colonies in this latter year. The city is on Poverty Bay, so named by Cook when he landed here in 1769 and failed to obtain any provisions from the hostile Maoris. He chose the name by contrast with the

neighbouring Bay of Plenty, which he so named because the Maoris seemed well supplied and were generous. Gisborne is the chief city of Cook County (see **Cook**) and as the area was Cook's first landing place in New Zealand (see **Young Nick's Head**), there is a monument to him here, as well as a cannon said to be from his ship, the *Endeavour* (see **Endeavour**).

Gladstone (Australia, USA, Canada)
All the places of the name mentioned here honour the great British statesman, William Ewart Gladstone (1809–1898), four times Prime Minister. The Australian town of Gladstone, in **Queensland**, was originally settled in 1847 but then abandoned the following year only to be resettled in 1853. It became a municipality in 1863. The three cities of Gladstone in the respective American states of Michigan, Missouri and Oregon also pay tribute to the statesman, with the last of these said to have been so named by a local citizen who admired him. In Manitoba, Canada, the community of Gladstone was incorporated as a town in 1882 and was similarly named for the Prime Minister, who coincidentally was first nicknamed 'G.O.M.' ('Grand Old Man') by journalists that year. See also **Hawarden**.

Gladwin (USA)
Gladwin County, Michigan, and the city of the same name that is its seat honour Henry Gladwin (1729–1791), the British soldier who commanded the post at Detroit in 1763 when the Indian chief Pontiac led his rebellion against the British. Gladwin was successful; Pontiac made peace three years later and remained friendly with the British.

Glasgow (USA)
The city in Montana was named for the city in Scotland, doubtless through emigrant connections there. Glasgow in Kentucky was settled later (in 1799) and was probably named after it. Glasco in Kansas was named by Scots settlers in 1886, but the first postmaster spelt the name incorrectly and it has never been altered since.

Glassville (Canada)
Glassville, in **New Brunswick**, was founded in 1861 by the Rev. Charles Gordon Glass, from the Scottish village of Birse, Aberdeenshire (now Grampian), and so preserves his name.

Glastonbury (USA)
The Connecticut town, originally an Indian settlement, was first opened to white residents in 1635. It developed as a district of **Wethersfield**, but when the householders petitioned to secede, was named Glastonbury, after the town in Somerset, when this came about in 1693. There must have been colonial links with the ancient market town, now famous for its mystic associations.

Glencoe (USA, Canada, South Africa)
The Scottish glen is famous for the so-called Massacre of Glencoe, when in 1692 the Macdonalds were murdered by the Campbells and English troops. But the glen is equally famous in its own right as a picturesque location, and names derived from it may reflect this attractive aspect rather than the treacherous clan massacre. It is known, however, that Glencoe, Minnesota, does commemorate the killing, which Martin McLeod, the namer, wished to mark. It is likely, however, that Glencoe, Illinois, does not derive from the Scottish glen, but refers to a surname (Coe). In Canada, the reference could also have been historical, especially as the namer of the Ontario community was its surveyor, A.P. Macdonald. In South Africa, on the other hand, the town of Glencoe in Natal, west of **Dundee**, was probably named simply for the valley when it was founded in 1921. (The Scottish glen is nowhere near Dundee, however.)

Glenelg (Australia)
The two chief features of the name in Australia are the suburb of **Adelaide**, South Australia, and the Glenelg River, **Victoria**. The present suburb arose as a

settlement in 1836, when it was named after Charles Grant, Lord Glenelg (1778–1866), the Secretary of State for the Colonies at the time. (That same year, South Australia was first declared a British colony.) Also in 1836, the Glenelg River was discovered. At first it was called Nangeela, but was later renamed to honour the same minister. Charles Grant took his title from his estate in his native Scotland.

Glocester (USA)

The Rhode Island town has a name that is a variant of **Gloucester** (see the next entry), and probably has the same kind of link, to the prince not the place.

Gloucester (USA, Canada, Australia)

Gloucester County, **Virginia**, with its identically named seat, and Gloucester County, **New Jersey**, almost certainly pay tribute to Henry, Duke of Gloucester (1639–1660), the third son of Charles I and brother of Charles II and James II. But Gloucester, Massachusetts, is likely to have had direct colonial links with the English city, despite the fact that it was actually settled in 1623 by emigrants from Dorchester. Gloucester City in New Jersey (now in **Camden** County but originally the seat of Gloucester County) was certainly named for the English city (or county). The Gloucester County in **New Brunswick**, Canada, was not named for a prince but for a princess, and this was Mary, Duchess of Gloucester (1776–1857), the daughter of George III who married William Frederick, 2nd Duke of Gloucester. In Australia, Gloucester Island, **Queensland**, was so named by Cook in 1770, with the honour due to William Henry, 1st Duke of Gloucester (1743–1805), younger brother of George III.

Glynn (USA)

Glynn County, **Georgia**, has a name that derives from that of John Glynn (1772–1779), the English politician and lawyer who was known for his sympathies with the colonists in their struggle for independence.

Goderich (Canada)

The Ontario town, which originated as the western terminus of the Huron Road from **Guelph** to Lake Huron in 1827, was laid out the following year by William Dunlop and named after Frederick John Robinson, Viscount Goderich (and 1st Earl of Ripon) (1782–1859), then Chancellor of the Exchequer. It was at this time that the British government sold the land in the Huron territory here to the Canada Company, the organisation set up to colonise the western part of what was then known as Upper Canada (modern Ontario).

Godley Head (New Zealand)

Godley Head forms the northern headland of **Lyttelton** Harbour, south of **Christchurch**, South Island. It takes its name from John Robert Godley (1814–1861), the Irish politician and social reformer who gave the name of his Oxford college, Christ Church, to Christchurch. He was the local leader of the colonising Christchurch Association. (See the name of the town for more on this.)

Godwin Austen, Mount (Pakistan)

Mount Godwin Austen (now usually called by its much more characterless designation of K2) is the second highest mountain in the world, in the Karakoram Range. (The 'K' of this brief name stands for 'Karakoram', although the '2' does not refer to its altitude but to the fact that it was the second to be measured in this range.) The longer name is that of the peak's first surveyor, the English explorer and geologist, Colonel Henry Haversham Godwin-Austen (1834–1923), who began his survey work here in 1856. The name itself was proposed in 1888 by General J. T. Walker, a former Surveyor-General of India, but at first the Indian government did not adopt his suggestion on the rather strange grounds that personal names were unsuitable for Himalayan summits. This is how 'K2' arose as an alternative, with the name locally pronounced something like 'Kechu'.

Goochland (USA)
Goochland County, **Virginia**, and its seat of this name pay compliment to Sir William Gooch (1681–1751), the English statesman who was the Governor of Virginia from 1727 to 1749 and who defended the interests of the colonists.

Goodenough Island (Pacific Ocean)
The island is in the D'Entrecasteaux group, east of New Guinea. It was visited in 1873 by the British captain John Moresby (see **Port Moresby**) who named it after Commodore James Graham Goodenough (1830–1875), naval attaché to several foreign embassies and an active seafaring officer. (He died when shot by a poisoned arrow in Santa Cruz (Solomon Islands) when 'engaged in what seemed friendly intercourse with the natives' (*DNB*).) His name is represented elsewhere on the island in the form of Mount Goodenough, its central peak, and in Goodenough Bay, New Guinea. The local name of the island is Morata.

Goodsir, Mount (Canada)
Mount Goodsir, in the Rocky Mountains, near the border with **Alberta**, was so named in 1858 by James Hector, a member of the expedition led by John Palliser to determine the boundary between the USA and Canada. He seems to have intended the tribute to be made either to John Goodsir (1814–1867), Professor of Anatomy at Edinburgh University, or to his brother, Harry Goodsir, who was a member of Franklin's expedition to the Arctic (see **Franklin**) and who perished there with him in 1847. The name was officially approved in 1904.

Goodwood (South Africa)
The town in Cape Province was established in 1905 and was intended to be a racing centre. It was therefore named after the famous English racecourse in Sussex. However, after only one race, the plan was abandoned, and the South African town became a respectable manufacturing and residential community instead, not a noted horseracing venue.

Gore (New Zealand)
The town of Gore, in southwest South Island, was at first known as Longford when surveyed in 1862. Later, however, it was renamed after Sir Thomas Gore Browne (1807–1887), Governor of New Zealand from 1855 to 1862, when he was succeeded by Sir George Grey, who gave his name to **Greytown**, among other places. (For a less happy succession by this same man, see **Gawler**.)

Gosford (Australia)
Gosford, **New South Wales**, was surveyed in 1839 and founded that same year, when it was named after Archibald Acheson, 2nd Earl of Gosford (1776–1849), the Irish Governor-in-Chief of British North America from 1835 to 1837. In view of the controversial nature, and failure, of his conciliation policy towards the French-Canadians, which resulted in his resignation, it seems strange that his name was nevertheless adopted for the town. But doubtless the namers were still too close to the matter to appreciate the damage Gosford had caused.

Goulburn (Australia)
The name is found in several parts of Australia, such as the Goulburn River, **Victoria**, as a tributary of the **Murray River**, the city of Goulburn in **New South Wales**, and the Goulburn Islands off the coast of Arnhem Land, Northern Territory. These all compliment one man, Henry Goulburn (1784–1856), Under-Secretary for the colonies from 1813 to 1821, and, later in his career, Chancellor of the Exchequer and Home Secretary. It is the first of these posts that is significant here, however. The river was discovered by bush explorers Hamilton Hume and William Hovell in 1824, after Goulburn had completed his colonial duties. But the city arose in 1818 (on a site chosen by Hume) when he still held the post, and the islands were named after the Under-Secretary this same year by Captain Philip Parker King (who gave his own name to **King** Sound).

Grafton (USA, Australia)
Grafton, Massachusetts, and Grafton, North Dakota, were both named after a Duke of Grafton – but not the same one! The Massachusetts town was originally known by the Indian name of Hassanisco when it was founded in 1654. The English settlement here dates from 1718, when it was renamed after Charles Fitzroy, 2nd Duke of Grafton (1683–1722), a member of the Privy Council. The North Dakota city was settled much later, in 1877, and was named after Grafton County in **New Hampshire**, because that was where the pioneers had begun their journey to the west. The county was thus named after Augustus Henry Fitzroy, 3rd Duke of Grafton, who was Secretary of State for the Northern Department from 1765 to 1766, and Prime Minister for three years from 1768. (He was the grandson of the 2nd Duke.) Grafton, West **Virginia**, however, appears to have been named after a local family, not after either duke. In Australia, the city and port of Grafton in **New South Wales** was formed in 1856 as a merger of the two municipalities of Grafton and South Grafton, both named for the 3rd Duke. And Cape Grafton, East of **Cairns**, **Queensland**, was named by Cook for this same duke, who was Prime Minister by then. Off Cape Grafton lies **Fitzroy** Island, named after the 3rd Duke's grandson, Robert Fitzroy (himself no duke). So the family are well represented in their several generations, with or without titles.

Graham (South Africa, Antarctica, Canada)
Two men named Graham lie behind these places. In South Africa, the city of Grahamstown (originally Graham's Town) in Cape Province was established on the basis of military headquarters here in 1812 and was named after Colonel John Graham, its founder, who had required a frontier post in Kaffir territory. (It was thus not named, as some sources claim, after General Thomas Graham, Lord Lynedoch, who died in 1843 and who had no connection with South Africa.) In the Antarctic, Graham Land (formerly Graham Coast) was at one time the name of the whole of the Antarctic Peninsula, and was claimed by Britain. The Americans, however, preferred to name it after one of their explorers, Nathaniel Palmer, and called it Palmer Peninsula. Only in 1964 did place-name committees in both countries agree to 'split' the peninsula, so that the northern half is now Graham Land, and the southern Palmer Land. The English name honours Sir James Graham (1792–1861), twice First Lord of the Admiralty. His first term extended from 1830 to 1834 during which, in 1832, the peninsula was discovered by the English explorer John Biscoe (see **Biscoe Islands**). In Canada, Graham Island, the largest and most northern in the **Queen Charlotte** group, **British Columbia**, was named in 1853 for the same Sir James Graham.

Grampian (USA)
The community of Grampian, **Pennsylvania**, was named by one Dr Samuel Coleman in 1809 after the Grampian Hills in Scotland. Not only did the locality remind him of them, but he had actually come from there. What could be more obvious?

Granby (USA, Canada)
The usual 'title versus place' problem confronts us here. John Manners, Marquis of Granby (1721–1770), politician and soldier (he commanded the Leicestershire 'Blues'), gave his title to the towns of Granby in Connecticut and Massachusetts, respectively. Granby itself, however, is a village in Nottinghamshire, and it gave the name of the Canadian city of Granby, Quebec, which was established in 1803 by settlers who had ties with the English place. It is perhaps surprising that the name is not more frequent, in view of its suggestion of 'grand'. Compare all the New World places (not in this book) whose names actually begin with 'Grand', such as Grand Falls, Grand Lake, Grand River, Grand Rapids and so on, even where these are translations from the French.

Granville (USA)
All the following places took their names from John Carteret, Earl of Granville (1690–1763), the English orator and statesman who was also a landowner in North **Carolina**: Granville County, North Carolina; Granville, Massachusetts; Granville, Ohio (named after the last); Granville, **Pennsylvania**. Earl Granville was the grandson of Sir George Carteret (see **Carteret**).

Great Barrington (USA)
Great Barrington is the name of an English village in Gloucestershire, near the Oxfordshire town of Burford. But alas, this is not the origin of the name of the town of Great Barrington in southwest Massachusetts. The town is almost certainly named for William Wildman, 2nd Viscount Barrington (1717–1793), a leading British politician and – more importantly - a nephew of the namer of the town, the Massachusetts Governor, Samuel Shute. The town itself was incorporated in 1761. The name may have added 'Great' in order to distinguish it from **Barrington**, Rhode Island.

Great Victoria Desert (Australia)
The desert extends across much of Western and South Australia, and was given its name, after Queen Victoria, by the explorer Ernest Giles, who crossed it from east to west in 1875. See also **Victoria** for a still impressive range of regal namings.

Greenwich (USA)
The town of Greenwich in Connecticut was founded in 1640 by two **New Haven** Colony agents, Robert Feaks and Captain Daniel Partick, who purchased land from the Indians here for the barter price of twenty-five English coats. The original name of the settlement appears to have been Elizabeth's Neck, perhaps for the wife of one of the settlers. The name then became Greenwich for the village that is now a borough of London. The famous Greenwich Village, the residential area of **New York** that is now well known as a cultural and artistic centre, is also named after the London village. The 'Village' originally indicated that the settlement was distinct from New York itself. Doubtless the 'green' element of the name made it specially attractive, apart from any colonial links.

Gregory, Lake (Australia)
The lake lies almost east of Lake **Eyre**, in South Australia. It is named after the English explorer and geologist John Walter Gregory (1864–1932), who led an expedition to Lake Eyre in 1901.

Grenfell (Canada)
The community of Grenfell, Saskatchewan, is named after Pascoe de P. Grenfell, a London merchant and a shareholder and director of the Canadian Pacific Railway.

Grenville County (Canada)
Grenville County, Ontario, is named after William Wyndham Grenville, Baron Grenville (1759–1834), who was Foreign Secretary from 1791 to 1801 at the time when the county was declared (in 1792).

Gretna (USA, Canada)
The Louisiana city of Gretna was originally known as Mechanickham when it was founded in the early 1800s. It was renamed after the famous Gretna Green in Scotland, because an early justice of the peace here performed marriages twenty-four hours a day without the need for a legal certificate, rather in the manner that eloping English couples could get married without a licence in the Scottish village (until 1856). The Canadian Gretna is a port of entry on the Manitoba–North Dakota border and it was so named by the Canadian Pacific Railway in 1883 because the Scottish Gretna Green is similarly near the border (with England).

Grey (Australia, New Zealand, Canada)
The places are not all named for the same man. Cape Grey, on the western shore of the Gulf of Carpentaria, Northern Territory, was named by Matthew Flinders (see **Flinders**) after Charles Grey, 1st Earl Grey (1729–1807), the soldier in the

American Revolution who almost became Commander-in-Chief in America. The Grey River in New Zealand, however, was named in 1846 after the colonial governor Sir George Grey (1812–1898), who became Governor of New Zealand (having been Governor of South Australia) in 1845. This river then gave its name to **Greymouth** (see below). In Canada, Grey County, Ontario, was named after Charles Grey's son Henry George Grey, 3rd Earl Grey (1802–1894), who was Secretary for the Colonies from 1846 to 1852. See also **Greyton**, **Greytown**, **Howick**, **Lady Grey**.

Greymouth (New Zealand)

The town and port of Greymouth, in South Island, was established as a government depot in 1863 at the mouth of the **Grey** River. This was not its original name, however, which was Crescent City. It was then twice renamed, as Blaketown and Greytown, before becoming Greymouth in 1864. Compare the next two entries below.

Greyton (South Africa)

Greyton, in Cape Province, was established in 1854 and was named after the distinguished colonial governor Sir George Grey (see **Grey**, above), who was Governor of the Cape (having been twice Governor of New Zealand) from 1854 to 1859 and from 1860 to 1861 (after which he again became Governor of New Zealand). Compare the next entry below, for more of his colonial range.

Greytown (New Zealand, South Africa, Nicaragua)

Greytown was one of the original names of **Greymouth**, New Zealand, where it originally honoured the colonial governor Sir George Grey (see **Grey**). The name was changed, however, because there was (and still is) another Greytown, in North Island. This Greytown was founded in 1854, so is older. Even so, it is still named after the same governor. After twice being Governor of New Zealand, Sir George became Governor of South Africa, where he gave his name to both **Greyton** (see above) and Greytown, the latter in Natal, where it was laid out in 1850. In Central America, the Nicaraguan seaport that is now known as San Juan del Norte was also formerly known as Greytown. It was not named for Sir George, however, but for his grandfather, Sir Charles Grey, who gave his name to Cape Grey (see **Grey**) and who distinguished himself in the American Revolution. The English name was given because this area of Nicaragua, the Mosquito Coast, was claimed by the British in 1841, with the port occupied in 1848. Only in 1860 did Britain give up control of the coastal region here.

Grimsby (Canada)

The Ontario town was originally known as The Forty when settled in 1783, presumably for the number of settlers. It was soon renamed after Grimsby (Great Grimsby) in England, however, with which port one or more of the settlers must have had home ties.

Groton (USA)

The Connecticut town lies on the east bank of the **Thames** River, opposite **New London**. A trading post was established here in 1649 (as part of New London), but in 1705 was incorporated as a separate town, taking its name from the Suffolk village of Groton, near Hadleigh. This village was the birthplace of John Winthrop (see **Winthrop**), an early governor of Connecticut. The name of the English village is pronounced like 'grow', but the American town is pronounced like 'grot' (causing British sailors who visit it to nickname it unfairly, as sailors will, as 'grotty Groton').

Guelph (Canada)

The city in Ontario was founded in 1827 by the Scottish novelist and Canadian coloniser John Galt (see **Galt**), who in literary fashion named it after the Guelphs (Welfs), a German princely family from whom the British royal family (the House of Windsor) are descended. (The Guelph dynasty ruled in Hanover until 1866.)

Guernsey County (USA)
Guernsey County, Ohio, takes its name from the second largest of the Channel Islands, famous for its Guernsey cattle. There must have been emigrant ties with the island.

Guildhall (USA)
The town of Guildhall, in northeast Vermont, may possibly have been named for a person with the surname Guild. But equally, there could have been some link with the Guildhall in London, the centre of government of the City of London.

Guilford (USA)
Guilford County, North **Carolina**, was named for Francis North, 1st Baron Guilford (1637–1685), who became Lord Chancellor in 1682 and participated in the coronation of James II. The town of Guilford in Connecticut, however, was named after the Surrey town of Guildford, no doubt for emigrant ties there.

Guysborough (Canada)
Guysborough County, **Nova Scotia**, and its seat of the same name honour Sir Guy Carleton, 1st Baron Dorchester (1724–1808), the Irish-born soldier and administrator who was Governor of Quebec and Commander of the British forces in Canada from 1775 to 1777, when he defended Quebec against the Americans, thus being instrumental in preserving Canada for Britain. See also **Carleton**.

H

Haddonfield (USA)
The **New Jersey** borough of Haddonfield takes its name from Elizabeth Haddon, an English Quaker girl who settled here in about 1701. Longfellow's series of narrative poems entitled *Tales of a Wayside Inn*, published between 1863 and 1874, recounts the story of her romance with a Quaker missionary, John Estaugh. She lived to the age of 80, and her personal possessions are on display here in the headquarters of the Haddonfield Historical Society.

Hadley (USA)
The town of Hadley, Massachusetts, settled in 1659, takes its name from one of the Hadleys in the United Kingdom, possibly the Hadley that is now in the borough of Barnet, or Hadley Wood in the borough of Enfield, both in Greater London. The connection was doubtless an emigrant one.

Haileybury (Canada)
The residential town of Haileybury, in Ontario, was founded in about 1873 and was named by its founder, C.C. Farr, after the public school he had attended in England, Haileybury College, near Hoddesdon in Hertfordshire. He must have been one of the first pupils at the school, which was itself founded in 1862.

Haldimand (Canada)
Haldimand County, Ontario, and its town of the same name (which is not its seat) are named after Sir Frederick Haldimand (1718–1791), the British soldier who was Governor-in-Chief of Canada from 1778 to 1786. The town of Haldimand was formed only in 1974 from a number of other towns, villages and townships.

Halifax (Canada, USA, Australia)
Halifax, the city that is the capital of **Nova Scotia**, was originally the site of a French fishing station in the first years of the eighteenth century. In 1749, however, it was settled by the English, and the founder, Edward Cornwallis, named it after George Montagu Dunk, 2nd Earl of Halifax (1716–1771), who was President of the Board of Trade at the time. (Later, Lord North, his nephew, was Prime Minister during the American Revolution.) Other places named after him in the United States are Halifax County, North **Carolina**, and its seat of the same name, Halifax County, **Virginia**, and *its* identically named seat, and Halifax, **Pennsylvania**. This last derived its name from Fort Halifax, built in about 1756 by Colonel William Clapham about half a mile north of the present town. The fort name itself honours the same earl. The town here was laid out in 1784. In Australia, Halifax Bay is an inlet of the Pacific in **Queensland**, where it was so named by James Cook in 1770, either directly after Lord Halifax or possibly because the bay resembled Halifax Bay, Nova Scotia, which he had previously visited and surveyed. The former seems likely, especially as Cook also named **Rockingham** Bay (after Lord Rockingham), immediately to the north of it. See also **Dunk**.

Halley (Antarctica)
The research station of Halley on the Brunt Ice Shelf, north of **Coats Land**, was opened by a British Antarctic expedition

in 1955 with the original name of Halley Bay, the name honouring the famous English astronomer Edmund Halley who had been born three hundred years previously (in 1656). In 1977 the name was shortened to its present form.

Hamden (USA)
Hamden, the town in Connecticut, was first settled in 1664 and named after the English parliamentarian John Hampden (1594–1643) (see **Hampden**).

Hamilton (USA, Canada, New Zealand, Bermuda)
Many of the places of the name in the United States pay tribute to Alexander Hamilton, who although usually regarded as American, was actually the illegitimate son of a Scottish father (himself the son of Alexander Hamilton, Laird of Cambuskeith) and a French Huguenot mother (herself married to a German or Dutch merchant named John Michael Lavine). Hamilton, therefore, was of Scottish blood and proud of it – he himself once said, 'My blood is as good as that of those who plume themselves upon their ancestry' – so that he qualifies for this book. He was born in the West Indies in 1755, and became aide-de-camp to Washington in the American Revolution and the first United States Secretary of the Treasury. He died in 1804, killed in a duel. There are ten counties named after him in the USA, as well as several cities, such as Hamilton, Ohio, which developed as a town (originally called Fairfield) round Fort Hamilton in the 1790s. In Canada, however, the city of Hamilton in Ontario was not named for him but for its founder in 1813, George Hamilton (1787–1835), the landowner here, while the Hamilton River in Labrador (now the **Churchill** River), was named in 1821 after Sir Charles Hamilton (1767–1849), the British admiral who was the first colonial governor of Newfoundland (from 1818 to 1824). Meanwhile the city of Hamilton in North Island, New Zealand, founded in 1877 from an existing military settlement, was named after another Hamilton. This was Captain John Hamilton, an officer of the Royal Navy who was killed while fighting the Maoris. Finally (for this selection), the Hamilton that is the capital of Bermuda was named for yet another Hamilton. This was Henry Hamilton, who was Governor of Bermuda when the town was incorporated in 1790.

Hammonds Plains (Canada)
The **Nova Scotia** community was named after Sir Anthony Hammond (1738–1828), Lieutenant-Governor of Nova Scotia from 1780 to 1782. The post office here had the name of English Corner for some time.

Hampden (USA)
Hampden County, Massachusetts, with its town (not its seat) of Hampden, and also Hampden, Maine, are all named after the English statesman and opponent of Charles I, John Hampden (1594–1643). The particular connection here is that he was influential in establishing Puritan colonies in North America. See also **Hamden**.

Hampshire (USA)
There are two counties of the name in the United States, respectively in Massachusetts and West **Virginia**. They take their name after the English county. For the connection, see **New Hampshire**.

Hampstead (Canada)
The residential town in south Quebec takes its name from the residential district of northwest London.

Hampton (USA, Canada)
The city in **Virginia** originated round Fort Algernourne (now Fort Monroe), which had been built in 1609 to protect the James River canal to **Jamestown**. A permanent English settlement arose in about 1610, and when this was organised as a town in 1705, it was named after Henry Wriothesley, 3rd Earl of Southampton (1573–1624), who was not only Shakespeare's patron but, more relevantly here, a backer of the expedition to Virginia in 1605, and subsequently a member of the council of the Virginia Company. Hampton, Iowa, was named after

Hampton Roads, which itself, like the Virginia city, had been named after the 3rd Earl of Southampton. (See also **Southampton**.) Hampton in **New Hampshire**, however, was named after the London Hampton (of Hampton Court fame) by the Rev. Stephen Bachiler, who had preached there. In Canada, Hampton, **New Brunswick**, which was originally known by the Indian name of Ossekeag, was also probably named after this Hampton, although some sources claim that it was named after one of the United States Hamptons. Compare **Rockhampton**.

Ham South (Canada)

Ham South (or Ham-Sud) in Quebec is a village that probably takes its name from an English village Ham, but which one is not certain.

Hankey (South Africa)

The town of this name in Cape Province was established in 1825 as a station of the London Missionary Society and was named after its treasurer, William Alers Hankey.

Hannastown (USA)

Hannastown, **Pennsylvania**, is named after the Irishman Robert Hanna, one of the commissioners appointed to find a suitable site for the new seat of the recently created **Westmoreland** County. It was decided that Hanna's own residence was the best place, and the settlement here duly became the county seat from 1773 to 1782. In the latter year, the last of the American Revolution, the settlement was burned down by the Indians and the Tories (the Americans who supported the British cause), and Hannastown was thus wiped off the map, except for the present post office, which is now about a mile away from the original settlement.

Hanover (USA)

Almost all places of the name in the United States are named for the British royal house of Hanover, whose line began with George I (as Duke of Hanover). In some cases a place will be named after an existing settlement Hanover, as happened with Hanover, **New Hampshire**, which was named for Hanover, Connecticut, where many of its early residents had lived previously.

Hantsport (Canada)

The **Nova Scotia** community has a name that is intended to suggest 'Hampshire port', using the abbreviated name of the English county. Directly, it took its name from the county in which it is located, Hants County, likewise named for the English Hampshire.

Harford County (USA)

The county is in **Maryland**, and takes its name from Henry Harford, an illegitimate son of Frederick Calvert, 6th Lord Baltimore (see **Calvert**).

Harrisburg (USA)

Many places of the name commemorate an American called Harris, so do not belong here. Harrisburg, the capital of **Pennsylvania**, is different, however. It was established in about 1718 as a trading post and ferry point on the Susquehanna River by John Harris, an Englishman who had obtained a licence to trade with the Indians here in 1705. It was thus originally known as Harris' Ferry (compare similar names, such as the famous Harpers Ferry), but was then called Louisburg (in honour of Louis XVI) when it was officially laid out for John Harris's son, also John Harris, in 1785. The name Harrisburg was already in use on some maps, however, and this was the name that prevailed.

Harrismith (South Africa)

The Orange Free State town was originally laid out in 1849 at the site now known as Majoorsdrif. Owing to lack of water, however, it had to be moved the following year to its present location, when it was named after Sir Harry Smith (1787–1860), Governor of the Cape from 1847 to 1852. (Compare **Ladismith** and **Ladysmith**.) As Sir Harry and his wife were a devoted couple, it seems reasonable to interpret the name as half his (Sir Harry) and half hers (Lady Smith).

Harrow (Canada)
The name of the Ontario community was given not so much for the famous English school as for the town (now London borough) of Harrow where it is located. The name seems to have been given by the Postmaster General here, John O'Connor, during his two-year term of office (from 1880).

Hartford (USA)
The best-known place of the name is the city that is the capital of Connecticut. Dutch traders from New Amsterdam (see **New York**) built a fort here in 1633, but the first settlement proper arose two years later, when sixty English pioneers came from Old Towne (modern **Cambridge**, Massachusetts). Two church leaders who followed later here from Old Towne were Thomas Hooker and Samuel Stone. The latter came from Hertford, the English town, and this became the settlement's name in 1637. The spelling with 'a' reflects the pronunciation. Other towns and counties of the name mostly derived from the Massachusetts settlement, although the origin of Hartford, Kentucky, is uncertain, and Hartford, Michigan, was merely a renaming from Hartland, to avoid confusion with another place of this name. Hartford City, Indiana, was named after a prominent local farmer. See also **Hertford**.

Hartington (USA)
The Nebraska city is named after one of the Marquises of Hartington who visited the settlement at the time of its naming. This could have been William Cavendish, 1st Duke of Devonshire (1640–1707), who was created Marquis of Hartington in 1694.

Harwich (USA)
The town in Massachusetts is named for the English port of Harwich, in Essex, taking the name in 1684, no doubt through emigrant connections there.

Hastings (New Zealand, USA, Canada)
The New Zealand city, in North Island, was first settled in 1864 on land leased from the Maoris. It was subsequently named after Warren Hastings (1732–1818), the first Governor General of British India. The apparent time-lag was due to the fact that the region round **Hawke** Bay, where Hastings is, was settled at the time of the Indian Mutiny (late 1850s), and there was then much patriotic interest in British India. Compare the names of other towns here, such as **Clive**, **Napier** and **Havelock**. In the United States, virtually every place of the name was derived from an American, so does not concern us here. In Canada, however, Hastings County in Ontario was named for Francis Rawdon-Hastings, 1st Marquis of Hastings (1754–1826), who was aide-de-camp to General Clinton in the American Revolution (War of American Independence).

Havelock (New Zealand, Canada, South Africa)
The earlier places of the name pay tribute to Sir Henry Havelock (1795–1857), the British soldier who distinguished himself in the Indian Mutiny of 1857 and who effected the relief of Lucknow (where he died). There are two noted places of the name in New Zealand: Havelock, in the north of South Island, and the larger Havelock North just south of **Hawke** Bay in North Island (with 'North' distinguishing it from its namesake). Havelock North, only three miles from **Hastings**, was founded soon after the time of the Indian Mutiny, so acknowledges Sir Henry's feat in this way. The southern Havelock similarly pays its tribute to the 'Saviour of Lucknow'. And so too does the **New Brunswick** community of Havelock in Canada. In South Africa, however, Havelock in Swaziland commemorates another man of the name. This was Sir Arthur Havelock (1844–1908), Governor of Natal from 1886 to 1889. It is now usually known by its indigenous name of Bulembu.

Haverford (USA)
The **Pennysylvania** township, which was in existence by 1722, was so named by Welsh settlers who had emigrated from (or near) Haverfordwest, Pembrokeshire (modern Dyfed). The Welsh town was actually known simply as 'Haverford' (or some form of this) until the seventeenth century (the 'west' being added to distinguish it from Hereford), so the settlers were perhaps not being original in adopting the shortened form of the present name.

Haverhill (USA)
The city in Massachusetts was founded by the Rev. John Ward in 1640, and he named it after his birthplace in England, the market town of Haverhill, Suffolk. Both the American and the English places are pronounced identically (like 'waver', not 'have a'). An earlier Indian name here was Pentucket.

Hawarden (USA)
The Iowa city was named after the Welsh village (formerly Flintshire, now Clwyd) of Hawarden, near Chester, as a tribute to the Prime Minister, W. E. Gladstone, who long had his home there. See also **Gladstone**.

Hawke (New Zealand, Australia)
Hawke Bay (or Hawkes Bay), the oval inlet of the Pacific in North Island, was visited in the late eighteenth century by James Cook, who named it after Sir Edward Hawke (1705–1781), First Lord of the Admirality from 1766 to 1771. (Properly speaking, Hawke Bay is the name of the bay, and Hawkes Bay, or Hawke's Bay, the name of the inland region to the west of it.) There is a Cape Hawke that similarly honours him in Australia, where it lies roughly halfway between **Port Macquarie** and **Newcastle**. This was also visited and named by Cook.

Hawkesbury (Canada, Australia)
Both the Canadian town, in Ontario, and the Australian river, in **New South Wales**, are named after the same man. This was Charles Jenkinson, 1st Earl of Liverpool and 1st Baron Hawkesbury (1727–1808), who was President of the Board of Trade and Chancellor of the Duchy of Lancaster from 1768 to 1801. It was during this period that the town of the name was founded (in 1798) and the river discovered (in 1789, by Captain Arthur Phillip, later Governor of New South Wales: see **Phillip Island**).

Hayes River (Canada)
The river, in northeast Manitoba, enters the **Hudson** Bay at **York Factory**, and is named after an official of the Hudson's Bay Company, Sir James Hayes.

Healdtown (South Africa)
Healdtown is a Methodist missionary station in Ciskei. It was established in 1853 and named after the treasurer of the Wesleyan Methodist Missionary Society, James Heald, who two years later provided the finance for a new school of industries here founded by Sir George Grey (see **Grey**).

Healesville (Australia)
The town of Healesville, **Victoria**, was founded in 1860 and named for Sir Richard Heales (1823–1864), then Premier of Victoria.

Heaphy Track (New Zealand)
Heaphy Track arose as a trail blazed in 1862 by goldminers for about forty miles through the bush to the west coast of northern South Island, where it serves today as a tourists' track. It is named after the English colonial official (and V.C.) and artist, Charles Heaphy (?1821–1881), who was appointed Chief Surveyor to the New Zealand government. For his bravery in defending a party of troops (who were bathing at the time) against a Maori attack in 1864, he was commended in despatches by Sir Henry Havelock (see **Havelock**) and was consequently awarded his Victoria Cross in 1867.

Hearne, Cape (Canada)
Cape Hearne, near the mouth of the Coppermine River, **Mackenzie** District, Northwest Territories, is named after Samuel Hearne (1745–1792), an English

explorer and agent of the Hudson's Bay Company who surveyed this region for the Company in 1771. (On reaching it, he believed he had come to the northern coast of North America, and that he then stood on the shore of the 'Hyperborean Sea'. Little did he realise that all the islands comprising the present-day **Franklin** District lay to the north of him.)

Hecate Strait (Canada)
Hecate Strait is a channel in **British Columbia** extending from **Dixon Entrance** to **Queen Charlotte** Sound. It is named after the *Hecate*, the ship in which the British admiral Sir George Henry Richards (1832–1896) made his survey of the coast here in 1861–2.

Hecla and Griper Bay (Canada)
The bay of this name is on **Melville** Island, Northwest Territories. It was so designated by William Parry (see **Parry**) in his first exploratory voyage here in 1819–20, after his ships, the *Hecla* and the *Griper*. It was in his second voyage, with the *Fury* and the *Hecla* (again), that two years later he discovered and named the **Fury and Hecla Strait**. (In his third voyage, with these same two ships, in 1824–5, the *Fury* was lost here.)

Helen Furnace (USA)
The rather unusual name of the community in **Pennsylvania** is believed to be a corruption of 'Hieland Furnace', and was probably given by an early Scottish settler here, one Alexander McNaughton, who boasted that he was a 'Hielander', i.e. a Highlander. (In eastern states, 'Furnace' in a place-name denotes a place where iron was worked at a furnace.) See also **Highland**.

Helensville (New Zealand)
The small town in northern North Island was founded in 1862 and was named after the wife of the first European settler here.

Hellam (USA)
The name of this **Pennsylvania** community is a corruption of 'Hallam'. It was given by Samuel Blunston, one of the founders of **York** County in which it is located, after his native village of Upper Hallam, Yorkshire (now a western suburb of Sheffield).

Hemmingford (Canada)
The name is given for one or other (or both) of the villages of Hemingford Abbotts and Hemingford Grey, less than a mile apart near Huntingdon (now in Cambridgeshire). An early settler must have had links here. See also **Huntingdon**.

Hempstead (USA)
The town of Hempstead, **New York**, arose on land purchased from the Indians in 1643 by John Carman and the Rev. Robert Fordham, who both came here from Stamford, Connecticut, but who earlier had emigrated to America from Hemel Hempstead, Hertfordshire. Other places of the name in the United States were mostly derived from personal names (surnames).

Henley-on-Klip (South Africa)
The village and resort in the Transvaal is directly named for its location on the Klip River here, but indirectly seems to have based its name on the well-known English town and resort of Henley-on-Thames, Oxfordshire.

Henrico County (USA)
The **Virginia** county somewhat unexpectedly reveals the name of Prince Henry Frederick (1594–1612), the Prince of Wales and young son of James I who died, possibly poisoned, when still only 18 years old. (If he had lived, he would have succeeded to the throne as Henry IX, as he was James's eldest son.) The place-name was originally applied to a settlement called Henricopolis, the last part of which represented Greek *polis*, 'town' (i.e. 'city of Henry'). In the event the final syllables were dropped, and the shorter version of the name was the one that prevailed. See also Cape **Henry**.

Henrietta Maria, Cape (Canada)
The cape lies at the entrance to **James**

Bay, Ontario, and it was so named in 1631 by the explorer Captain Thomas James (1593–?1635), after the ship on which he made his survey, the *Henrietta Maria*, itself named after the queen consort of Charles I. She had actually named his ship as the *Maria*. See also **Maryland**.

Henry, Cape (USA)

Cape Henry, at the entry to Chesapeake Bay, **Virginia**, where it is opposite Cape **Charles**, was named after the eldest son of James I, Prince Henry Frederick (see **Henrico**, above, and also Cape **Charles**, named for another of his sons).

Hensall (Canada)

The Ontario community was named by its two founders, George and James Petty, after their native village of Hensall, near Snaith, Yorkshire.

Hepburn Island (Canada)

Hepburn Island is in **Coronation** Gulf south of **Victoria** Island, Northwest Territories, where it is named as a tribute to the heroism of John Hepburn, a sailor in John Franklin's Arctic expedition of 1819–22 (see **Franklin**), who in difficult conditions did much to preserve the lives of many of his fellow explorers when they were suffering with extreme cold, hunger and fatigue.

Herald Island (USSR)

The small island, today formally known by its Russian name of Ostrov Geral'd, lies east of Wrangel Island (Ostrov Vrangelya) in the Chukchi Sea, off northeast Siberian Russia, inside the Arctic Circle. It was named after the *Herald*, the ship in which the British admiral Sir Henry Kellet sailed in search of the explorer Franklin (see **Franklin**), when he went missing in the Arctic in 1845. The island was discovered in 1849.

Herbert (Australia, South Africa, Canada, Antarctica)

The Herbert River, in northeast **Queensland**, was discovered in 1864 by the explorer George Dalrymple, who named it after Sir Robert George Wyndham Herbert (1831–1905), the first Premier of Queensland (from 1860 to 1865). In South Africa, the district of Herbert, Cape Province, was named after Henry Howard Molyneux Herbert, 4th Earl of Carnarvon (1831–1890), twice Colonial Secretary (1866–7 and 1874–8). In Canada, the community of Herbert, Saskatchewan, was named after Sir Michael Henry Herbert, British ambassador to the United States from 1902 to 1903. And in the Antarctic, Herbert Bay, in the **South Shetland Islands**, was named by James Ross (see **Ross Sea**) in 1843 after Sidney Herbert, 1st Baron Herbert of Lea (1810–1861), who at the time was Secretary to the Admiralty. See also **Herberton**.

Herberton (Australia)

The town in northeast **Queensland** stands in the upper valley of the **Herbert** River (see previous entry), and is named after it.

Hereford (USA)

The city of Hereford, Texas, is named after the Hereford breed of cattle that was introduced here in the 1890s. The town itself was settled in 1898. The cattle have been a distinctive breed of the West of England county since at least the eighteenth century. Hereford, **Pennsylvania**, however, although also named after the English county, derives from the ironmasters from Herefordshire who emigrated to prospect here.

Hermes, Cape (South Africa)

Cape Hermes, on the coast of Transkei, was named after HMS *Hermes*, an English sloop that surveyed here in the mid-nineteenth century.

Hermiston (USA)

The community of Hermiston, Oregon, is said to be named after R. L. Stevenson's novel, *Weir of Hermiston*, published in 1896, simply because one of the founders liked the name. Perhaps he was a Scot, for Hermiston is a village in Midlothian (now Lothian). (The 'Weir' of the novel is the name of the main character, Archie Weir, son of Adam Weir, Lord Hermiston.)

Herschel (Canada, South Africa)
The names respectively honour the famous astronomers, father and son. Herschel Island, in **Mackenzie** Bay, Northwest Territories, was given its name in 1825 by Sir John Franklin (see **Franklin**) as a tribute to the German-born astronomer working in England, Sir William Herschel (1738–1822). In South Africa, however, the village of Herschel in Transkei was founded in 1879 and named after Sir William's son, Sir John Frederick William Herschel (1792–1871), who worked at the Cape for two years from 1834, among other projects studying Halley's Comet there. Compare the name of **Maclear**, which also honours an astronomer.

Hertford (USA)
Rather perversely, the town of Hertford, North **Carolina**, is not the seat of Hertford County. Moreover, each place seems to have been named after a different Hertford. The town was founded in 1758, and is named after Francis Seymour-Conway, 1st Marquis of Hertford (1719–1794), and English supporter of the colonies. Hertford County, on the other hand, is named after the English town, with which early settlers had a link. Compare **Hartford**.

Hervey (Australia, South Pacific)
Hervey Bay, an inlet of the Pacific in southeast **Queensland**, was discovered by Cook in 1770 and named after Admiral Augustus John Hervey, 3rd Earl of Bristol (1724–1779), active in many naval campaigns, while the Hervey Islands, now known as the **Cook** Islands, in the South Pacific, were discovered by Cook in 1773 and similarly named after the admiral.

Hicks (Australia, New Zealand)
Point Hicks, in eastern **Victoria**, was discovered by Cook in 1769 and was named by him after the member of his crew who had sighted it, Lieutenant Hicks of the *Endeavour*, and this same officer also gave his name to Hicks Bay in eastern North Island, New Zealand, discovered by Cook the following year.

Highland (USA)
Many of the places of this name in the United States are simply descriptive, referring to the 'high land' of a location. But the city of Highland in Illinois was named specifically after the Highlands of Scotland, and was so called by Scottish settlers, while the community of Highland in Clarion County, **Pennsylvania**, was named after the same Scot that gave the name of **Helen Furnace**.

Hillsboro (USA)
One or two places of the name relate not to a hill or a person named Hill but to the earldom or viscountcy of Hillsborough. This is certainly so for Hillsboro, Ohio, which was named after Wills Hill, 1st Earl and 2nd Viscount of Hillsborough (1718–1793), who was Secretary of State for the Colonies from 1768 to 1772 and for the Northern Department from 1779 to 1782. This same man also gave his name to the Hillsboro Canal, Florida, running from Lake Okeechobee to the Atlantic. Lord Hillsborough held a large grant of land here. Compare the next entry below.

Hillsborough (USA, Canada)
Hillsborough River, Florida, is named after Lord Hillsborough, who held a land grant here during the English occupation of Florida (compare **Hillsboro**, above). The township of Hillsborough in **New Brunswick**, Canada, is similarly named for the same man. The township was founded in 1765.

Hilton (South Africa)
The town of Hilton in Natal is believed to have been named after an English village, with the name originally given to the farm bought here in 1853 by one Joseph Henderson. Precisely which English Hilton is involved here is uncertain, and there are at least a dozen places of the name in Britain.

Hilton Head Island (USA)
The Atlantic island, in South **Carolina**, is

named after the English sea captain and adventurer William Hilton, who explored it in 1663. (His name was first given to a headland here, then from that to the whole island.)

Hinchinbrook (Australia, USA)
Hinchinbrook Island, off the northeast coast of **Queensland**, was named by Cook in 1770 after the family seat, Hinchinbrooke House, near Huntingdon, of his patron, George Montagu Dunk, 2nd Earl of Halifax (see **Dunk, Halifax** and **Sandwich**). (It was not actually identified as an island until 1819, however, by Philip Parker King, who gave his name to **King** Sound.) The identically named island in Alaska was also named by Cook, in 1778, for the same man.

Hindmarsh (Australia)
Lake Hindmarsh, **Victoria**, and Hindmarsh, the district of **Adelaide**, South Australia, as well as other places of the name, honour Sir John Hindmarsh (1784–1860), the first Governor of South Australia, from 1836 to 1838, when he was succeeded by George Gawler (see **Gawler**).

Hingham (USA)
The Massachusetts town was settled in 1633, and was originally known as Barecove Common. Two years later it was incorporated, and was named after the Norfolk village of Hingham, near Wymondham, from which several of the early settlers had come. The bay on which the town lies is similarly named Hingham Bay.

Hobart (Australia)
The capital city of Tasmania, Australia's most southerly city, lies on the estuary of the **Derwent** River, which was explored by George Bass (see **Bass Strait**) in 1798. He noted that the land site here was ideal for a settlement. Five years later Philip Gidley King (see **King**) sent a lieutenant to establish a settlement at what is now Risdon Cove, on the estuary. Finally, in 1804 the settlement was moved to Sullivan Cove, the site of the present city, and was named Hobart after Robert Hobart, 4th Earl of Buckingham (1760–1816), who at this time was Secretary for War and the Colonies.

Hobhouse (South Africa)
The town of Hobhouse, in the Orange Free State, was laid out in 1912 and was named after Emily Hobhouse (1860–1926), the Cornish-born woman whose humanitarian work in South Africa among Boer women and children earned her the nickname of the 'Angel of Love'.

Hollidaysburg (USA)
The **Pennsylvania** borough was founded in 1768 by two cousins from Northern Ireland, Adam and William Holliday, who had emigrated from their homeland in about 1750. As Adam drove the first stake into the ground, he is alleged to have said to William, 'Whoever is alive one hundred years hence will find a considerable town here.' Now, some two hundred years hence, the small town has a population of over 6000.

Hollis (USA)
The town of Hollis, **New Hampshire**, was named after the soldier and politician John Holles, 1st Earl of Clare (?1564–1637) (see **Claremont**).

Holliston (USA)
Holliston, the Massachusetts town, was named after Thomas Hollis, a London merchant who was a patron of Harvard College (now Harvard University). Other places of the name are designated for Americans, not Britons.

Hood (USA, Canada, Australia)
The Hood River, Oregon, was named after the English admiral Samuel Hood, 1st Viscount Hood of Whitley (1724–1816), who saw extensive service in the American Revolution (War of American Independence), and who subsequently organised the expedition led by George Vancouver (see **Vancouver**) to Australia, New Zealand, and the Pacific coast of North America. The river almost certainly gave its name to Hood River County here, and

to its seat, the city of Hood River, settled in 1854, although it is possible that Samuel Hood's name may have blended by then with that of another British admiral, Arthur William Acland Hood (1824–1901). Mount Hood, however, the highest peak in Oregon, is certainly named for Samuel Hood. It was first sighted in 1792 by the English navigator William Broughton (see **Broughton Island**). (Coincidentally, the name happens to be apt for a mountain, actually an extinct volcano, that has a permanent snowcap or 'hood'.) The Canadian Hood River that flows into **Coronation** Gulf, Northwest Territories, however, is named after Robert Hood, the member of Franklin's expedition to the Copper Mine River in 1821 (see **Franklin**) who was murdered by an Indian hunter. In Western Australia, Hood Point, east of **Albany**, was named after Samuel Hood, like the American river. See also **Port Hood**.

Hooker (USA, USSR)

Hooker Mountain, Wyoming, was named after the English author and explorer Sir Joseph Dalton Hooker (1817–1911), as also was Hooker Island (Ostrov Gukera) in Franz Josef Land, USSR, in the Arctic Circle. The latter was on maps of the archipelago before Jackson made his exploratory journey there (see Appendix II, p. 215).

Hope Point (Canada)

The headland is on **Dolphin and Union Strait** in **Mackenzie** District, Northwest Territories, where it was named after the British admiral, Sir William Johnstone Hope (1766–1831), a member of the Board of the Lord High Admiral in the 1820s. Most places named Hope are usually for the sentiment (such as the Cape of Good Hope), which in many instances remained unfulfilled.

Hoppner River (Canada)

The river, which lies northwest of Coppermine, Northwest Territories, where it flows into the **Dolphin and Union Gulf**, is named after Lieutenant Henry Parkins Hoppner (1793–1833), the English explorer who was a member of Parry's expedition to the Arctic (see **Parry**).

Horsham (Australia)

The city of Horsham, **Victoria**, was named after Horsham, West Sussex, the home town of its first settler in 1841, James Darlot.

Horton River (Canada)

The river is in the Northwest Territories, between the Coppermine and the **Mackenzie** Rivers. It was discovered in 1826 and was named after Wilmot Horton, Under-Secretary of State for the Colonies.

Hotham Heights (Australia)

The resort of this name in **Victoria** bears tribute to Sir Charles Hotham (1806–1855), the naval commander who was appointed Lieutenant-Governor of Victoria in 1854 and full Governor the following year. The stress and responsibility of the difficult post were too much for him, and caused his breakdown and premature death that year, when he was still under 50. Compare the next entry below.

Hotham Inlet (USA)

The Hotham Inlet, in Alaska, was discovered in 1826 and named after Sir Henry Hotham (1777–1833), the British admiral who was twice a Lord of the Admiralty between 1818 and 1830.

Howard (USA)

Most places of this name in the United States honour American soldiers and officials. Howard, **Pennsylvania**, however, was given its name as a compliment to the English philanthropist and prison reformer, John Howard (?1726–1790), who made many journeys to European prisons and other institutions, including military hospitals in Russia, but who never crossed the Atlantic.

Howe (Australia, Indian Ocean)

Cape Howe is the most extreme southeastern point of Australia, on the border between **Victoria** and **New South Wales**.

It was sighted by James Cook in 1770 and named after the British admiral Richard Howe, Earl Howe (1726–1799), who at the time was Treasurer of the Royal Navy. Howe Island in the Kerguelen Islands, in the southern Indian Ocean, was discovered by Cook six years later, and was similarly named after the admiral, who that year became engaged in the American Revolution (War of American Independence). See also **Lord Howe Islands**.

Howick (South Africa)
The town in Natal was established in 1850 and was named after Sir Henry George Grey, Viscount Howick and 3rd Earl Grey (1802–1894), who was Secretary of State for the Colonies from 1846 to 1852. See also **Grey**.

Hudson (USA, Canada)
One of the best known geographical names in North America, if only through the Hudson River, on which **New York** stands, and the famous Hudson Bay in Canada. They, and other places of the name, all ultimately derive from the English navigator and explorer Henry Hudson (died 1611), who endeavoured to discover a short route from Europe to Asia through the Arctic Ocean, i.e. the famous Northwest Passage. The Hudson River was explored by Hudson in 1609, and Canada's Hudson Bay the following year, when he passed into the bay through what is now known as the Hudson Strait, between **Baffin** Island and Quebec. This became a main route for the famous Hudson's Bay Company, named after the bay (and thus indirectly after Hudson). The company was set up in 1670 to seek a Northwest Passage, as Hudson had tried to do, to the Pacific, while occupying the lands round Hudson Bay and carrying on any commerce that might be favourable there. (This was primarily fur trading.) The company thus played a very important role in the economic and political development of Canada, and many names of its officers have been preserved in place-names. Hudson's crew mutinied in the bitter winter of his second voyage in search of the Northwest Passage, and set him adrift on the bay that now bears his name. The exact date and place of his death are still not known, and even his year of birth is uncertain. It was perhaps some time in the 1560s. Many other Hudsons in North America are not named after him at all, but honour local citizens.

Hughenden (Australia)
The town in **Queensland** was surveyed in 1877 and proclaimed a town ten years later. It was given a name that was intended to honour the British Prime Minister of the day, Benjamin Disraeli, 1st Earl of Beaconsfield (1804–1881), whose residence was at Hughenden Manor, near High Wycombe (and Beaconsfield), Buckinghamshire. See also **Beaconsfield**, **Disraeli**, **Lothair**.

Hull (Canada, USA)
Hull County, Quebec, and its seat of the same name both pay tribute to the English city from where the parents of the Canadian city's founder, Philemon Wright, had emigrated. The Canadian city was founded in about 1800. In the United States, the town of Hull in Massachusetts was also named for the English port and city, and was founded in 1644 by emigrants from there.

Humber River (Canada)
The Newfoundland river was named in more a general than a specific way after the English river Humber, one of the best known in the country.

Hunter (Australia, New Caledonia)
The Hunter River, **New South Wales**, was originally discovered in 1791 by convicts, who called it the Coal River. It was subsequently renamed for John Hunter (1738–1821), the vice-admiral who was Governor of New South Wales from 1795 to 1800, when he was relieved by Philip Gidley King (see **King**), who had previously been Lieutenant-Governor. Hunter Island, on the other hand, in **New Caledonia**, was discovered in 1798 by an English sailor, Captain John Fearn of the *Hunter*, who thus named it after his ship. (The island is still sometimes referred to

as Fearn Island, or, as it is now in French territory, Île Fearn.) The island is uninhabited. This island should not be confused with the next entry!

Hunters Islands (Australia)
The Hunters Islands lie off northwest Tasmania, where they were discovered by Matthew Flinders (see **Flinders**) in 1798. He named them after John Hunter, the Governor of **New South Wales** (see the previous entry).

Huntingdon (USA, Canada)
Both Huntingdon County, **Pennsylvania**, and its identically named seat were designated as a compliment to Selina Hastings, Countess of Huntingdon (1707–1791), renowned for her missionary zeal and for her generosity and charitable works. The present town was laid out by a Doctor Smith in 1767, and he had given the name for the countess because she had donated liberally to a college he had founded in Philadelphia. The original name of the site here was Standing Stone. The county, which was formed in 1787, took the name of the town. In Canada, Huntingdon County in Quebec and *its* seat of the same name derive from the English town of Huntingdon, with which settlers must have had a connection. This Huntingdon dates from 1826. (Compare **Hemmingford**, which derives from the names of two villages near the English town.) Huntingdon, Tennessee, honours a native resident, not a Briton. See also the next entry below.

Huntington (USA)
The town of Huntington, **New York**, honours the English town of Huntingdon, where Oliver Cromwell was born. The site was settled in 1653, within Cromwell's lifetime. Other places of this name are usually tributes to local citizens. See also above.

Huntly (New Zealand)
The town in North Island was named by an early settler after his native town in Scotland (then in Aberdeenshire, now in Grampian). The Maori name of the town is Rahuipukeko, said to mean 'sanctuary of swampbirds'.

Hurd, Cape (Canada)
Cape Hurd, in southeast Ontario, was named after Captain Thomas Hurd (1757–1823), who had been appointed Hydrographer to the Admiralty in 1808.

Hurley (USA)
The **New York** community was named after Hurley, Berkshire, the village on the river Thames where Francis Lovelace (?1618-?1675), Governor of New York, had his estate. See also **Kingston**.

Hutchinson (South Africa)
The Cape Province village, near **Victoria**, West, was founded in 1885 and was originally known as Victoria West Road. In 1901, however, it was renamed after the Governor of Natal from 1893 to 1901 and of the Cape Colony from the latter year to 1910, Sir Walter Hely-Hutchinson (1849–1913).

Hutt (New Zealand)
The urban area in North Island, near **Wellington**, was pioneered by the New Zealand Company in 1910 and is named for one of the original shareholders in this company, William Hutt.

Hyde County (USA)
Hyde County, North **Carolina**, was named for Edward Hyde, 1st Earl of Clarendon (1661–1723), a somewhat controversial governor of **New Jersey** and **New York**. Some places of this name derive from London's Hyde Park, however, such as in the next entry.

Hyde Park (USA)
The town and village in **New York** are named indirectly after London's Hyde Park, but more directly after a local estate which was itself called after Edward Hyde, Viscount Cornbury (1710–1752), colonial governor of New York from 1702 to 1708.

I

Imperial (Canada)
The community of this name in Saskatchewan was settled mainly by Britons, and this is reflected in the name which therefore alludes to the British Empire.

Inman River (Canada)
The Inman River, northwest of Coppermine, Northwest Territories, was named after the nautical scientist and architect, James Inman (1776–1859), Professor of Mathematics (and effectively principal) of the Royal Naval College, Portsmouth, from 1808 to 1839, when the college was reorganised and he retired.

Innisfail (Australia)
The **Queensland** town, between the coast and Mount **Bartle Frere**, was settled in 1880 by an Irishman, Thomas Fitzgerald, who pioneered the state's sugar industry. When the community became a shire in 1910, it was named Geraldton, after its founder's surname, but the following year was renamed Innisfail, after the poetic name of Ireland.

Invercargill (New Zealand)
The city in South Island arose on a site bought from the Maoris in 1853. Two years later the first settlers arrived, and one of them gave his name to the new settlement as Kelly's Point. In 1857 the name was changed to Invercargill, to honour Captain William Cargill (1784–1860), the Scottish colonist who was instrumental in founding **Dunedin**. The Scottish prefix 'Inver-' means 'river-mouth', so is not inappropriate for the city, which lies on the Waihopai River near the point where it flows into the New River Estuary, an inlet of Foveaux Strait. The name sounds genuinely Scottish, too, even though it was artificially devised. (Taylor, see Bibliography, p. 217, calls it 'an absurd compound'.) But in general Invercargill is a name that blends well with the many other Scottish names in this part of southern South Island, such as Dunedin, **Balclutha**, **Stirling**, and **Stewart Island** to the south. The streets of central Invercargill, too, are mostly named after Scottish rivers, such as Tay Street, Dee Street, Spey Street and Forth Street. Compare also the next three entries.

Inverell (Australia)
Inverell, the **New South Wales** town, lies at the confluence of Swanbrook and Macintyre Rivers. It was established in 1848 and declared a town ten years later. Its rather ingeniously contrived Scottish name means 'confluence of the swans', alluding to the meeting of the two rivers (and the name of the first mentioned). Compare the previous entry above, with its equally artificial name and the two below.

Invermere (Canada)
The community in **British Columbia** was at first known as Copper City. In 1912, however, its name was changed to Invermere, a Scottish-style name intended to indicate its location at the 'mouth of (Windermere) lake'. Compare the previous two entries above and the next entry.

Inverness (Canada)
The town of Inverness, **Nova Scotia**, where it is in the county of the same name (although not its seat), was originally known as Broad Cove Mines, referring to the local coal mines. When a number of

Scotsmen settled near the mines in 1865, however, and coal-mining began in earnest, the name was changed to Inverness, for the Scottish city. The name was given to the county on the suggestion of Sir William Young, the Scottish-born Chief Justice of Canada. The town is on the west coast of Cape Breton Island, so in a sense the 'Inver-' is reasonably appropriate for a place by the water (compare the three entries above).

Investigator Group (Australia)

The group of islands, off the west coast of **Eyre** Peninsula, South Australia, were discovered by Matthew Flinders (see **Flinders**) in 1802 and are named after his ship, the *Investigator*. That same year, and this same ship, also gave the name of the well-known Investigator Strait, to the east, where the channel forms one of the main approaches to **Adelaide**.

Ipswich (USA, Australia)

The Massachusetts town, on the river of the same name, was settled in 1634 and originally had the Indian name of Agawan. The following year it was renamed Ipswich, for the town in Suffolk, because colonists bound for Massachusetts Bay were given hospitality there. In Australia, the city of Ipswich in **Queensland** was founded in 1827, originally as Limestone Hills, a penal settlement where lime was burned and stone quarried for **Brisbane**, which lies some twenty miles away. In 1842 it was declared a village and renamed for the same Suffolk town, with which early settlers had had domestic ties.

Isle of Wight (USA)

Isle of Wight County, **Virginia**, and its identically named seat take their name from the island off the south coast of England. The county has a coastline on the estuary of the **James** River, and is not far west of **Portsmouth**, like its English counterpart.

Islip (USA)

The **New York** town was named after the Oxfordshire village of Islip, from which the first settler had come.

Ivanhoe (USA)

The village of Ivanhoe, southwest Minnesota, is named for Walter Scott's novel, published in 1819. The name does not necessarily indicate a Scottish connection, and the reference may be a purely 'romantic literary' one. The names of other well-known novels by Scott also appear on the map, among them **Kenilworth**, **Montrose**, **Waverly** and **Woodstock**.

J

Jackson Island (USSR)

Jackson Island is one of the islands in Franz Josef Land, within the Arctic territory of the Soviet Union, where its official Russian name, as found on modern maps, is Ostrov Dzheksona. Its eponym is the subject of Appendix II, pp. 208–15, as the English explorer Frederick G. Jackson (1860–1938), who spent almost three years in the Arctic exploring and surveying Franz Josef Land, from 1894 to 1897. Suffice it to say here that although he bestowed many names himself there (hence the Appendix), he did not devise this one, which was given to the island, in the north of the group, by the Norwegian explorer Fridtjof Nansen, who met him there. (Nansen and his party were returning from the North Pole and were aiming for Spitsbergen.) See also **British Channel**; **Queen Victoria Sea**; **Salisbury**.

Jacobabad (Pakistan)

The city in the Sind province of southern Pakistan was founded in 1851 by Brigadier-General John Jacob (1812–1858), an English cavalry officer who was respected for his bravery and swordsmanship as well as for his interest in public administration and the promotion of irrigation development. He died here and was buried here, together with his favourite horse. As with **Abbottabad**, the final '-abad' of the name means 'town'.

James (USA, Canada, Galápagos Islands)

Many people of the name, as first name or surname, have passed on their particular James to a number of places, whether in 'neat' form or in combination, such as **Jamestown**. In several instances, the reference will be to St James. In others, which will interest us here, the nominee will have been a king or prince James, and there it will be a matter of determining which. Again, a Briton may lie behind the name. James River, **Virginia**, formed by the confluence of Jackson and Cowpasture Rivers, was originally known as King River. The king in question is James I of England (James VI of Scotland) (1566–1625), who happened to be on the throne at the time of the first English colonisation of America. The river's name was reinforced by the fact that Jamestown (see below) was founded on it. James Bay in Canada, however, where it lies as a southern extension of **Hudson** Bay between Ontario and Quebec, was discovered in 1610 by Hudson himself and later named not for the king but for the explorer Captain Thomas James (?1593-?1632), who led an expedition in 1631 for 'the discovery of the northwest passage into the South Sea', like others before him and after him. His ship was the *Henrietta Maria*, which gave her name to Cape **Henrietta Maria** at the entrance to the bay. (James's account of his Arctic voyage was regarded by some as forming the basis for Coleridge's famous poem, *The Rime of the Ancient Mariner*, with the South Pole substituted for the North.) In the Galápagos Islands, where James Island is officially known by its Ecuadorian name of San Salvador, the reference is to James II. The island had also been known in the past as Duke of York Island, from the king's former title. (See also the names of other islands in the group: **Albemarle**, **Chatham**, **Duncan Island**.) For other names directly linked with James II or his brother Charles II, see **Albany**, **Dutchess County**, **Kings**, **Kingston**, **Queens County**, **Richmond**, and also the entries below.

Jamesburg (USA)

The name of this borough in **New Jersey** honours James I of England (James VI of Scotland). See the entry above.

James Ross Island (Antarctic)

James Ross Island (formerly Ross Island) is in the **Weddell Sea**, east of **Graham** Land, with its name honouring the Scottish polar explorer, James Ross (see **Ross Sea**), who led an Antarctic expedition here from 1839 to 1843.

Jamestown (USA, St Helena, West Indies)

Not all United States places of the name honour a British James. But Jamestown, Rhode Island, and Jamestown, **Virginia**, do. The former town was settled in 1672 and later named for James II. The latter, now a ruined village in Virginia, where it lies on the **James** River as the site of the first permanent British settlement in North America (1607), pays tribute to James I of England. Although rebuilt after more than one fire, Jamestown, Virginia, fell into decay in 1699 when the seat of government of Virginia was moved to what is now **Williamsburg**. Jamestown, the capital of the South Atlantic island of St Helena, was founded in 1659, when the British East India Company built a fort here and named it after Prince James, then Duke of York and subsequently James II. In the West Indies, Jamestown was the former chief town on the island of Nevis (now superseded by **Charlestown**).

Jenkintown (USA)

The residential borough in **Pennsylvania**, in **Montgomery** County, was named after an early Welsh settler here in the late seventeenth century, William Jenkins.

Jermyn (USA)

The **Pennsylvania** borough of Jermyn was originally named Gibsonburg, after the original proprietor, John Gibson. In 1874, however, the settlement was renamed Jermyn, after a well-to-do English settler named John Jermyn, who gave the place much of its present prosperity.

Jersey City (USA)

Jersey City, the seat of **Hudson** County, **New Jersey**, was first visited when an unsettled site by Hudson in 1609. It was then settled by Dutch trappers, who named it Paulus Hook. In 1836 it was given its present name, which derives directly from that of the state, earlier known simply as Jersey.

Jerseyside (Canada)

The community in Newfoundland derives its name from Jersey, in the Channel Islands, with which Newfoundland has long had an association. (Hermitage Bay on the south coast for example, was a place of refuge for fishermen from the Channel Islands, who named it after an island in the bay which suggested to them the similar island of Hermitage off St Helier, Jersey. See also **Bay Roberts**.)

Jervis Bay (Australia)

The inlet called Jervis Bay, in **New South Wales**, was originally named as Long Nose by James Cook when he discovered it in 1770. (He was usually more original than this.) In 1791, however, it was renamed as now, in honour of the English naval commander, Admiral John Jervis, Earl of St Vincent (1735–1823), who received his earldom for his victory over the Spanish off Cape St Vincent (Madagascar) in 1797. And although this event occurred after the naming of the bay, his exploits were already sufficiently renowned in 1791 for him to be accorded the tribute. (He had by then captured two famous French ships, in 1778 and 1782.) The community of Jervis Bay on the coast here was named after the bay.

Jesselton (Malaysia)

This was the former name of what is now Kota Kinabalu, the capital of Sabah, Malaysia, on the island of Borneo. The original settlement on the island of Pulau Gaya nearby was burned down in 1897 by an anti-British Muslim rebel, which explains the capital's native name of Api-Api ('place of fire'). The settlement was re-established on its present site in 1899 under the name of Jesselton, in honour of Sir Charles Jessel, a director of the British North Borneo Company. The capital was renamed Kota Kinabalu (meaning 'Fort of [Mount] Kinabalu') in 1968.

Johnston Island (Pacific Ocean)

This is the name of the largest of the Johnston and Sand Islands, in the central Pacific, where they are incorporated United States territory. The island was named after an English sea captain, Charles James Johnston, who discovered the group in 1807. See also **Smith**.

Johnstown (USA)

Both Johnstown, **New York**, and Johnstown, Ohio, take their names from Sir William Johnson (1715–1774), an Irish-born superintendent of Indian affairs in the Mohawk Valley, New York, where he managed to keep the Iroquois neutral, even friendly, towards the British. The present New York city was founded by him in 1762, and his baronial home, Johnson Hall, is still preserved here. The Ohio village was probably named after Johnstown, New York. Johnstown, **Pennsylvania**, although larger than either, does not take its name from a Briton but a Swiss, so we cannot legitimately include it here.

Jones Sound (Canada)

Jones Sound is between **Ellesmere** Island and **Devon** Island, at the head of **Baffin** Bay, where it was discovered by Baffin in 1616. He named it after Alderman Sir Francis Jones, who was one of the London merchants who had equipped Baffin's ship *Discovery* for one of his Arctic voyages of exploration (see **London Coast**).

K2 See **Godwin Austen, Mount**.

Katherine (Australia)
The town of Katherine, on the river of the same name in Northern Territory, takes its name from this river, which was discovered in 1862 by the Scottish explorer in Australia, John McDouall Stuart (1815–1866), who named it after the daughter of an acquaintance. Other places named by Stuart include the Hanson Range of mountains, with Mounts Younghusband and Kingston, Mount Stuart in the John Range, the Strangways River, and Sturt Plain to the south of it, all these in Northern Territory and all named after acquaintances (with Mount Stuart named after himself). Sturt Plain was named by him after Charles Sturt, whose expedition to central Australia he had joined in 1844 (see **Sturt Desert**).

Kearsney (South Africa)
The village of Kearsney, in Natal, arose round the house built in the 1880s by Sir James Liege Hulett (1838–1928), the English-born industrialist and Minister of Native Affairs in Natal. He named his house after his birthplace, the small village of Kearsney near Dover, Kent (now virtually a northwest suburb of Dover).

Keeling Islands (Indian Ocean)
The Keeling Islands, also known as the Cocos Islands, in the Indian Ocean south of Sumatra, are an external territory of Australia and were discovered in 1609 by William Keeling (died 1620), a British mariner of the East India Company, who gave them his name. At the time of discovery Keeling was on his way back to England from the Moluccas.

Keene (USA)
The city of Keene, in southwest **New Hampshire**, was originally settled at another nearby site (that of modern Upper Ashuelot) in 1733. This was then abandoned because of hostile Indians, and was resettled on its present site in 1753 and was named by Governor Benning Wentworth after Sir Benjamin Keene (1697–1757), the British consul to Madrid (from 1724 to 1739) and subsequently Envoy Extraordinary and Plenipoteniary to Portugal (from 1746).

Kelso (USA)
The city of Kelso, Washington, was settled in 1847 by a Scottish surveyor, Peter Crawford, who named it after his native town of Kelso, Roxburghshire (now Borders).

Kelvington (Canada)
The community in Saskatchewan was named in 1905 by a Mrs John McQuarrie. She had lived as a child near the estate of Sir William Thomson, 1st Baron Kelvin (1824–1907), at Largs in Ayrshire, and so devised the name of the settlement by way of a compliment to the famous mathematician and physicist.

Kemp (Antarctica)
The name exists in the Antarctic for the Kemp Coast (former Kemp Land), south of the Kerguelen Islands, and for Kemp Peninsula there. It comes from that of the English captain of a whaling ship who discovered it in 1833, Peter Kemp.

Kempsey (Australia)
The town of Kempsey, **New South Wales**, was established in 1834 and

named after the village of Kempsey, south of Worcester, from which one or more of the original settlers had come.

Kenilworth (USA)
The village of Kenilworth, Illinois, and the borough of Kenilworth, **New Jersey** are both named after Walter Scott's novel, published in 1821. Kenilworth itself is a castle in the town of the same name in Warwickshire.

Kensington (USA, Canada)
Both Kensington, California, and Kensington, **Pennsylvania**, are named after the fashionable London district, whose suggestion of 'king' may have helped in the choice. The Pennsylvania community of the name was founded in about 1735. In Canada, Kensington in **Prince Edward Island** was originally known as Barretts Cross, after an early tavernkeeper. The new name was adopted at a public meeting in the early 1870s.

Kent (USA, Canada)
In many instances, the name will be a family name or will derive from the county of Kent. But equally, the name may honour the Duke of Kent. Where it does, this will almost always be Prince Edward Augustus (1767–1820), the fourth son of George III and the father of Queen Victoria. However, it seems likely that counties of the name will at least partially imply a reference to the English county, as for Kent County in Delaware, **Maryland**, Rhode Island and (in Canada) **New Brunswick**. Kent, Washington, is certainly named after the county, for this region cultivated hops, as did (and does) the English county. Kent County, Michigan, however, is named after an American. Compare the next entry.

Kentville (Canada)
The town in **Nova Scotia** was originally known as Horton Corner when settled in about 1760. In 1826 it was renamed in honour of the Duke of Kent (see entry above).

Keppel (Australia, Pacific Ocean)
Keppel Bay, **Queensland**, was discovered by James Cook in 1770 and named by him after Rear-Admiral Augustus Keppel, 1st Viscount Keppel (1725–1786), who had commanded ships in several victories and who was promoted to vice-admiral that year. In the Pacific, Keppel's Island (now known by its indigenous name of Niuatoputapu), is an island in Tonga (Friendly Islands). It, too, is named after the British naval officer, with the namer this time being Samuel Wallis (see **Wallis Islands**), who discovered it in 1767.

Kildonan (Canada)
Kildonan is now a suburban area of Winnipeg, Manitoba, where its districts either side of the Red River are known as East Kildonan and West Kildonan, and its rural districts are Old Kildonan and North Kildonan. The original colony here was founded by the Scottish philanthropist Thomas Douglas, 5th Earl of Selkirk, in 1817, when he named it after the village of Kildonan, Sutherland (now Highland), from where a number of the settlers had emigrated.

Killaloe (Canada)
The community of Killaloe, Ontario, is named after the Irish town in Co. Clare, from which early settlers had come.

Killingly (USA)
The town of Killingly, Connecticut, was first settled in about 1700 and was named for Kellingly Manor, near Knottingley, Yorkshire, the ancestral home of the Governor of Connecticut, Gurdon Saltonstall (1667–1724).

Kilsyth (USA)
The community of Kilsyth, West **Virginia**, was named after the Scottish town in Stirlingshire (now Strathclyde), from where some of the original settlers had come.

Kimberley (South Africa, Australia, Canada)
The city of Kimberley, in Cape Province, South Africa, developed from a diamond-

mining camp known by different names (for its different parts), and was declared a township in 1873 under its present name, which was given in honour of John Wodehouse, 1st Earl of Kimberley (1826–1902), the British Colonial Secretary. In Australia, the plateau region of Kimberley (or Kimberleys, as it is often called, for its different sections), in Western Australia, was similarly named for the earl. The Canadian city of Kimberley, **British Columbia**, was named in 1896 as a borrowing of the South African town's name, the link being that both places are mining centres. The earl took his title from his family seat, Kimberley House, near Wymondham, Norfolk.

King (USA, Canada, Australia)
There are several places of the name, and each time one is faced with the decision: surname or monarch? However, the places are mostly natural features such as islands rather than towns or counties, which will tend to give the name of a discoverer rather than a ruler. Thus King Island, in the Bering Strait off Alaska, USA, was discovered in 1778 and named for James King, one of the officers of Cook's expedition, and this same Captain King gave his name to King Island, **British Columbia**, Canada. The latter name was given by George Vancouver (see **Vancouver**), and both he and King had been midshipmen together under Cook's command in HMS *Discovery*. In Australia, however, King Island in **Bass Strait**, off northwest Tasmania, was named in 1801 for Philip Gidley King (1758–1808), third governor of **New South Wales** (from 1800 to 1806), while somewhat confusingly from our point of view, King Sound, an inlet of the Indian Ocean in Western Australia, was named after his son, the naval officer and surveyor Philip Parker King (1793–1856). The sound was explored and named in 1838 by John Stokes (see Mount **Stokes**) and John Wickham, captains of the *Beagle*. See also the next entries below, some of which indicate specific kings.

King and Queen (USA)
King and Queen County, **Virginia**, and its seat, King and Queen Courthouse, are somewhat wordily named after the best known dual British monarchy, William and Mary, in whose reign (1689–1694) the village was settled.

King Edward, Mount (Canada)
Mount King Edward, in **Alberta**, was named for Edward VII (1841–1910), who came to the throne in 1901.

King George (USA, Canada, Australia)
Both King George County, **Virginia**, and its seat of the same name honour George I of England, who reigned from 1714 to his death in 1727. It was during this period that the village was settled. In Canada, Mount King George, in **British Columbia**, pays tribute to George V, who reigned from 1910 to 1936. (The mountain is in the Rockies, near the frontier with **Alberta**, and seven neighbouring mountains are named for members of the king's family.) In Australia, King George Sound, an inlet and natural harbour on the south coast of Western Australia, was formerly known as King George III Sound, thus revealing which king is honoured here. The inlet was charted in 1791 by George Vancouver (see **Vancouver**), who named it after the reigning monarch. George III came to the throne in 1760 and was on the throne until 1811 (when he became mentally deranged and his son, the future George IV, acted as regent until his death in 1820). So three different King Georges here in as many names. See also **George** for further variety, as well as the next two entries below.

King George IV Lake (Canada)
The Newfoundland lake was named for George IV (reigned 1820 to 1830) by William Epps Cormack (1796–1868) the first white man to cross Newfoundland from east to west (in 1822). A community here is named for him, also.

King George's Islands (Pacific Ocean)
The islands are a group in the Tuamotu Archipelago, French Polynesia, where

they were discovered and named after George III (reigned 1760 to 1811) by John Byron (see **Byron**) in 1765.

Kings (USA, Canada)
There are two Kings Counties in the United States, and three in Canada. But not all of them were named after a king, or even for a Briton surnamed King. Kings County, **New York**, was, however, as it was formed in 1683 and named for Charles II (reigned 1660 to 1685). The namer was the Duke of York himself, the future James II (1633–1701), who gave his title to New York. Kings County in **Prince Edward Island**, too, was named for a king, in this case George III (reigned 1760 to 1811). But Kings County, California, was named after the river there, which was named after the biblical 'Holy Kings' (the Three Wise Men).

Kingsey Falls (Canada)
Kingsey Falls, Quebec, is a community with a name said to derive from the village of Kingsey in Buckinghamshire, near Thame. Presumably an early settler came from there.

Kingston (USA, Canada, Australia, New Zealand, Jamaica)
A very popular name, implying a royal settlement, a 'king's town'. Many Kingstons are large and important places, as one might expect with such a 'prestige' name. But the particular king (or King) is not always easy to determine. For the city of Kingston, **New York**, for example, there is evidence that the name was that of the English estate of the governor of the state, Francis Lovelace (see **Hurley**). (Was it a coincidence that he had married a Mary King?) Then the town of Kingston, Massachusetts, could have been named for King William III, who reigned from 1689 to 1702. However, some sources claim the name honours Evelyn Pierrepont, 1st Duke of Kingston (?1665–1726), the statesman and society leader. But the New York city, which was earlier named successively Esopus, Wiltwyck and King's Town, could equally well have been named after Charles II (reigned 1660 to 1685), as Kingston, Rhode Island, probably was. Post-Revolutionary United States names (i.e. after 1775) will not be royal honorifics, however, but will have taken the family names of local citizens. In Canada, Kingston, Ontario, was originally a French foundation of 1673. It was resettled by the British, however, in 1783 and named in honour of George III (reigned 1760 to 1811). But Kingston in South Australia, founded in 1858, was not named for a king but for Sir George Strickland Kingston (1807–1880), who was an early Irish settler. The smallish town of Kingston in New Zealand, in the south of South Island, appears to have been named simply to match its larger neighbour to the north, **Queenstown**. Both places are on the same Lake Wakatipu. And Kingston, the capital of Jamaica, founded in 1692, was named in compliment to William III, like its namesake in Massachusetts. Compare the next entry.

Kingstown (West Indies)
A name that is more obviously 'king's town' than **Kingston**, and that is also more recent and less frequent. Kingstown, the capital of the island of St Vincent, in the West Indies, has in effect a general 'royal' name to indicate the allegiance of St Vincent to Britain historically. But if a specific king is sought for, then it must be George III, for it was in his reign (1760 to 1811) that the island was ceded to Britain. Associations with Britain, however, go back before this to the early seventeenth century, when Charles II included the island in a grant made to the Earl of Carlisle, and in 1668 Francis Lord Willoughby made a treaty with the native Caribs by which they acknowledged that they were the subjects of the English king (i.e. Charles II).

King William (USA, Canada)
King William County, **Virginia**, and its seat of the same name pay honour to William II (reigned 1689 to 1702), as it was in his reign that the present village was settled. In Canada, King William Island, in **Franklin** District, Northwest Territories, was discovered by James Ross

(see **Ross Sea**) in 1830, so has a name that honours William IV (reigned 1830 to his death in 1837). Compare the next entry below. Compare also **Williamsburg, Williamstown**.

King William's Town (South Africa)
The Cape Province town, whose name is locally shortened to King, was founded in 1835 on the site of a mission station set up ten years previously, and was thus named in honour of William IV (compare the entry above).

Kinloch (USA)
The city of Kinloch, Missouri, was settled by a Scottish family, who had an estate of this name in **Virginia**, and who thus named both the estate and the settlement after their native village of Kinloch, possibly the one near Blairgowrie, Perthshire (now Tayside), although there are other Scottish places (including rivers and family seats) of this name.

Kinnaird (Canada)
The village in **British Columbia** was so named by the Canadian Pacific Railway in 1904 as a tribute to Arthur Fitzgerald Kinnaird, 11th Baron Kinnaird, who was a shareholder in the company.

Kinross (South Africa)
The village of Kinross, in the Transvaal, was founded in 1910 and named after the Scottish town of Kinross (now in Tayside) from which many of the engineers who constructed the railway here had come.

Kinston (USA)
A rather interesting name. Originally the city here in North **Carolina** was named Kingston or Kingstown, to honour the name of the reigning monarch at the time of settlement, who was George III. After the American Revolution (War of American Independence), however, the 'g' was omitted to eliminate any royal reference. (The name was even changed altogether for a while, first to Atkins Bank, then to Caswell, respectively for local dignitaries, but finally reverted to Kinston.)

Kipling (Canada)
The community of this name in Saskatchewan was so called to honour the writer Rudyard Kipling (1865–1936), originally as Kipling Station. Kipling is only about fifty miles from Ituna, which is also a name referring to this writer, who names the Solway Firth Ituna in one of his books.

Kiribati (Pacific Ocean)
The name is the indigenous rendering of the **Gilbert Islands**, as the group were formerly known before their independence in 1979. See this name for further details.

Kitchener (Canada)
Kitchener, the industrial city in southeast Ontario, was first settled in 1806 by Dutchmen from **Pennsylvania**, who named it Sand Hill, then Ebytown (after the Mennonite bishop, Benjamin Eby). In 1824 the name was changed patriotically to Berlin, alluding to the large number of German residents that were now here. Finally, in the First World War the name was changed yet again (equally patriotically) to pay tribute to Lord Kitchener (1850–1916), the British soldier who had distinguished himself in Egypt (as 'Kitchener of Khartoum') and who organised the British forces for war from 1914. The name was given in the year of his death (which occurred when the ship on which he was proceeding to Russia sank in a storm off the Orkney Islands).

Kittery (USA)
The town in Maine was settled in 1623 and was subsequently named Piscataqua Plantation. It was later renamed after Kittery Court, the family seat of the Champernownes, near Kingswear in Devon, as they were represented in the early settlers here.

Kyle, Lake (Zimbabwe)
The lake southeast of Masvingo was formed in 1961, when a dam was built, and it was given the Scottish word for 'channel' as a name (as in Kyles of Bute or Kyle of Lochalsh).

L

Lac-Brôme (Canada)
There are a number of lakes (sometimes merely a widening in a river) that have given their names to various communities in Quebec, with the second part of the name that of the lake proper, and often deriving from a family or place-name. This is the first of just two to be included here, with the second word of the name of this town deriving from the village of Brome, near Eye, Suffolk, from which early settlers must have come. See also **Lac-Kempt**.

Lachlan River (Australia)
The Lachlan River, the main tributary of the Murrumbidgee, in **New South Wales**, was discovered in 1815 by the English explorer and surveyor, George William Evans, who named it for Lachlan Macquarie (1761–1824), Governor of New South Wales from 1810 to 1821. See also **Macquarie**.

Lac-Kempt (Canada)
The lake and the community in Quebec are named after Sir James Kempt (1764–1854), Governor of Quebec from 1828 to 1830. See also **Lac-Brôme** (above).

Ladismith (South Africa)
The town in Cape Province was laid out on a farm in 1852 and was originally named Lady Smith, after the wife of Sir Harry Smith (1787–1860), Governor of the Cape Colony (as it then was) from 1847 to 1852. In order to avoid confusion with **Ladysmith** in Natal, however, the name was changed to its present form in 1879. See also **Aliwal North**, **Harrismith**, **Whittlesea**. The bald title and ordinary surname of Smith's wife do not reveal that she was a Spanish lady, Juana Maria de los Dolores de León, who had sought Smith's protection (as only a young girl of 14) during the Peninsular War of 1808–14, when Smith was in Spain on army service.

Lady Frere (South Africa)
Lady Frere, the town in Transkei, was established in 1879 and was named after the wife of Sir Bartle Frere (1815–1884), Governor of the Cape Colony from 1877 to 1880. See also Mount **Bartle Frere**, Mount **Frere**.

Lady Grey (South Africa)
The town in Cape Province was founded in 1858 and was named after the wife of Sir George Grey (1812–1898), Governor of the Cape from 1854 to 1859. See also **Grey**, **Greymouth**, **Greyton**, **Greytown**. Sir George's wife was Harriet Spencer, an admiral's daughter. Their marriage was not a happy one, and they were separated for many years, unlike the devoted marriage of Sir Harry Smith (see **Ladismith**, **Ladysmith**).

Ladysmith (South Africa)
The town in Natal, famous for its siege in the Boer War, was founded in 1847 and was originally known as Windsor, after a local trader, one George Windsor. Subsequently it was renamed as now after the wife of Sir Harry Smith (1787–1860), Governor of the Cape from 1847 to 1852. The present town of **Ladismith**, Cape Province, was also originally named Ladysmith, but was renamed to avoid any confusion with its Natal namesake. See also **Aliwal North**, **Harrismith**, **Whittlesea**.

Lake Arthur (South Africa)
Lake Arthur is a storage dam in the Tarka

River, southeast of **Cradock**, Cape Province. Construction was begun in 1921 and completed the following year, when it was named after Prince Arthur of Connaught (1883–1938), Governor General of the Union of South Africa from 1920 to 1924. Prince Arthur, the third son of Queen Victoria, had earlier been Governor General of Canada (from 1911 to 1916).

Lake George (USA)

The village of Lake George, **New York**, is directly named after the lake where it is located, with the lake taking its name from George II (1683–1760), in whose reign (from 1727 to 1760) it was first given its name.

Lake Louise (Canada)

The village of this name in **Alberta**, in **Banff** National Park, was originally known as Holt City when settled as a construction camp for employees of the Canadian Pacific Railway. It was then named Laggan for a while, and finally as today, in honour of Princess Louise, the daughter of Queen Victoria and wife of the Marquis of Lorne, who was Governor General of Canada from 1878 to 1892. The direct source of the village's name is from the lake near which it is located.

Lambert, Cape (Australia)

Cape Lambert, due east of **Dampier**, Western Australia, was so named after the English botanist, Aylmer Bourke Lambert (1761–1842), Vice-President of the Linnean Society, who identified various species of Australian plants, including the *Lambertia* genus of the Proteaciae family of shrubs, named after him.

Lambeth (Canada)

The community in Ontario is named after the London borough, probably not so much for any emigrant links as for its proximity to the industrial city of the same name here. See **London** for further place-name associations.

Lambton County (Canada)

Lambton County, Ontario, was named for John George Lambton, 1st Earl of Durham (1792–1840), who was Governor General of Canada in 1838 (resigning that same year), when the county was created.

Lanark (USA, Canada)

The community of Lanark, West **Virginia**, was named for the town (or county, Lanarkshire) in Scotland, from which early settlers had emigrated. Lanark County, Ontario, was similarly named and settled (in 1820). Its seat is **Perth**.

Lancaster (USA, Canada)

There are many counties and communities of the name in the United States, all named for the English city in Lancashire, although in some cases named after each other. In certain instances, the link was a colonial one, with original settlers having emigrated from there. This is so for Lancaster, Massachusetts, for example, whose founder, John Prescott, was born in the English city. But in other cases it seems the name was adopted simply as a suitable one. However, Lancaster County, **Pennsylvania**, is another example of a 'home tie', for it was named by an early settler, John Wright, who had come from Lancashire. The county seat was then named after the county, and the urban area of Lancaster in California was named after this Pennsylvania town, as was the city of Lancaster in Wisconsin. (The Pennsylvania city, founded in 1730, was originally known as Hickory Town, before adopting the name of its county, then much more extensive in area than it is today.) In Canada, however, Lancaster Sound, in **Baffin** Bay, **Franklin** District, Northwest Territories, was discovered by Baffin in 1616 and named after the financial backer of his expedition, Sir James Lancaster (?1550–1618), the English navigator. For once we have no earls of Lancaster responsible for the place-name, which is rather surprising in view of its popularity. (But many such earls lived well before colonial times!)

Lanesborough (USA)

The Massachusetts town was named for the Earl or Countess (or both) of Lanesborough (their ancestral home in the town of the same name in Co. Longford, Ireland). Early settlers had come from this part of Ireland.

Lark Harbour (Canada)
The community of Lark Harbour, on the west coast of Newfoundland, was named after the *Lark*, a ship used by James Cook in his coastal surveys here in the 1760s. Lark Island here has a name of identical origin.

Latrobe (Australia)
The town of Latrobe, in north Tasmania, was founded in 1850 and eleven years later named for Charles Joseph Latrobe (1801–1875), the London-born administrator of Tasmania (for two years from 1846). Also named after him is the La Trobe River, in **Victoria**, which was originally known as the Glengarry. It was renamed to honour Latrobe in his other role as the first Lieutenant-Governor of Victoria (from 1851 to 1854, when he retired).

Launceston (Australia)
Launceston is the chief city and port of northern Tasmania. It developed upstream on the River **Tamar** here from the settlement of George Town, which was founded at its mouth in 1804, and it was named for the Cornish birthplace of the third Governor of **New South Wales** (from 1800 to 1806), Philip Gidley King (see **King**). (George Town will have been named after George III: see **George** and **Georgetown**.)

Lawford Islands (Canada)
The islands are in **Coronation** Gulf, Northwest Territories, where they were so named in 1821, at the mouth of the Coppermine River, by John Franklin (see **Franklin**), as a compliment to Captain John Lawford, under whom he had served in the *Polyphemus* at the Battle of Copenhagen in 1801.

Lawley (South Africa)
The Transvaal township of Lawley takes its name from Sir Arthur Lawley, 6th Lord Wenlock (1860–1932), who was Lieutenant-Governor of Transvaal from 1902 to 1906.

Lawrence (New Zealand)
The town in southern South Island was originally known by the Maori name of Tuapeka, when it arose in 1861 as a gold-rush settlement. It was soon renamed after Sir Henry Montgomery Lawrence (1806–1857), the British general who was the defender of Lucknow at the time of the Indian Mutiny. The name thus falls into the same 'patriotic' group as already noted for the North Island city of **Hastings** and other towns in that region.

Lawrencetown (Canada)
There are two communities of the name in **Nova Scotia**, respectively in **Annapolis** and **Halifax** Counties. Both names honour the same man, Charles Lawrence (1709–1760), the British general who was Governor of Nova Scotia from 1753 to 1760.

Leacock, Mount (Canada)
The mountain in Yukon Territory was named as recently as 1970 after the humorist Stephen Leacock (1876–1944). Although thought of as a Canadian writer (a politician economist as well as a humorist), Leacock was actually born in Hampshire, England, so qualifies for this entry. One must admit it is good to have a mountain named after a humorist, as distinct from the more familiar run of cartographers, statesmen and 'heavy heroes'.

Leamington (Canada)
The town in Ontario was probably named for the Warwickshire town and spa (Royal Leamington Spa), presumably for a colonial tie there.

Leeds (USA, Canada)
The city of Leeds in Alabama is known for its steel-wire industry, and was given its name after the English city because that, too, is a mainly industrial centre. It may well be no coincidence, either, that the American city is just northeast of **Birmingham**, another city with an 'indus-

trial' name. In Canada, however, Leeds County, Ontario, was named by way of a tribute to Francis Godolphin Osborne, 5th Duke of Leeds (1751–1799), the British Secretary of State for the Home Department.

Leicester (USA)
The Massachusetts town was named after the English city (or its county, Leicestershire), from which early settlers must have come.

Lennox and Addington County (Canada)
There were originally two separate counties here in Ontario. Lennox County was named for Charles Lennox, 4th Duke of Richmond (1764–1819), appointed Governor General of British North America in 1818 (although dying the following year from a fox bite). His predecessor had been John Simcoe (see **Simcoe**). Addington County was named for Henry Addington, 1st Viscount Sidmouth (1757–1844), First Lord of the Treasury and Chancellor of the Exchequer (from 1801 to 1804) and subsequently Home Secretary (1812 to 1821). The two counties were united in 1860 to enable the single county to be represented in the Legislative Assembly of Upper Canada (modern south Ontario). See also the next two entries.

Lennoxville (Canada)
The Quebec town is named after the same man who gave his name to the original Lennox County, Ontario (see the entry above). Compare the next entry below.

Lenox (USA)
The town in Massachusetts is probably named after the Lennox who was the uncle of the man who gave his name to **Lennox** County, Canada, and the town of **Lennoxville** (see the two entries above). This was Charles Lennox, 3rd Duke of Richmond (1735–1806), Secretary of State for the Southern Department (for two years from 1766) and a denouncer of ministerial policy towards the American colonies. (He is on record as declaring, during the parliamentary debate on the American Prohibitory Bill of 1775, that the resistance of the colonists [against the Americans, in the War of American Independence that began that year] was 'neither treason nor rebellion, but is perfectly justifiable in every possible political and moral sense'.)

Leominster (USA)
The Massachusetts city arose on land purchased from the Indians in 1701, and was originally part of **Lancaster**. In 1740 it was incorporated as a separate town and was named after the English town of Leominster, Herefordshire, with which early settlers must have had family ties.

Leonardtown (USA)
Leonardtown, **Maryland**, was named after Leonard Calvert (1606–1647), the first colonial governor of Maryland, and the son of George Calvert, 1st Lord Baltimore. See **Calvert**, **Baltimore**.

Leslie (South Africa)
The village of Leslie in the Transvaal was proclaimed in 1939 and is believed to be named after one or other of the Scottish places of the name (either the town in Fife or the village near Huntly, Aberdeenshire, modern Grampian). Settlers could well have come from either.

Lewes (USA)
The **Delaware** city was founded in 1631 by Dutch colonists as the first white settlement on the Delaware River. Its original name was Swanendael, but in about 1685 it was renamed after the Sussex town in order to show that it was the seat of **Sussex** County, just as the English Lewes is the county town of (East) Sussex.

Lewisporte (Canada)
The Newfoundland town was originally known as Big Burnt Bay, after the inlet on which it stands. It was then renamed Marshallville, and finally Lewisporte, after Lewis Miller and Co, a Scottish company that engaged in lumbering locally in the 1900s. Compare **Millertown**.

Lexington (USA)

There are at least a dozen places of the name in the United States, and they all began with the town of Lexington in Massachusetts, which was settled in 1640. It was originally known as Cambridge Farms when organised as a parish in 1691, but was renamed Lexington in 1713 on becoming an independent township. The name is that of the Nottinghamshire village now known as Laxton (near Ollerby), but called Lexington in the seventeen century and even as recently as the nineteenth century. (An Ordnance Survey map of 1824 names it as 'Laxton alias Lexington'.) The link was a colonial one, with an early settler coming from the village. But the reason why there are so many other Lexingtons is that the Massachusetts town became famous as the site of the first skirmish of the American Revolution (War of American Independence), on 19 April 1775, when seventy-seven local minutemen (colonial militiamen pledged to fight with one minute's notice) took up their position here to resist the British troops sent to seize American arms at Concord. This event went down in history as the Battle of Lexington and Concord. (The name of the latter town, some six miles west of Lexington, refers to its peaceful settlement, and thus belies the fact that it contained an arms depot destined to feature crucially in the Revolution.) Lexington has thus become one of the most significant place-names for Americans, and has been adopted for various other objects, from racehorses to aircraft carriers.

Ligonier (USA)

The borough and mountain resort of Legonier in **Pennsylvania** took its name from Fort Ligonier built here in 1758 and itself named for Jean Louis (or John) Ligonier, 1st Earl Ligonier (1680–1770), a British officer of Huguenot descent who became a field marshal in 1766, in which year he received his earldom. The town was laid out in 1817.

Lincoln (USA, Canada)

Very many places of the name in the United States will have been so designated to honour Abraham Lincoln, or if not him, the famous Massachusetts soldier and statesman Benjamin Lincoln. But in a few instances the name will derive from the English city, or the county of Lincolnshire. The town in **Middlesex** County (but not Franklin County), Massachusetts, is one such, with an emigrant connection, while in Canada, Lincoln County in Ontario was named for Lincolnshire in 1792.

Lismore (Australia)

The city of Lismore, in **New South Wales**, was settled in 1845 and was probably named not for the Irish town but for the Scottish island in Loch Linnhe, now in Strathclyde, for the original settler, William Wilson, was a Scot.

Litchfield (USA)

The town in Connecticut, the seat of the county of the same name, was settled in 1719 and named for the cathedral town of Lichfield, Staffordshire, with which early settlers had links.

Livermore (USA)

California city is named after Robert Livermore (1799–1858), the English sailor who was the first white settler here.

Liverpool (Australia, Canada, USA)

The Liverpool that is now a southwest suburb of **Sydney**, **New South Wales**, was founded in 1810 and although originally a port was not named for the English city and port of Liverpool but for Robert Banks Jenkinson, 2nd Earl of Liverpool (1770–1828), who was Secretary for War and the Colonies from 1809 to 1812 and after that Prime Minister until 1827. The town of Liverpool in **Nova Scotia**, Canada, however, was named after the city. It was originally an Indian settlement named Ogumkiqueok, then, when colonised by the French, Port Rossignol. When New England settlers eventually arrived here in 1759, however, it was named after that city and port. Appropriately, the Canadian town is at the mouth of the **Mersey River**. There are not many places of the name in the

United States, but the community of Liverpool in West **Virginia** was so named in 1890 when a British company bought woodland nearby and shipped the timber back to Liverpool in England. (Earlier names for this settlement had been Green's Corner and Le Roy.)

Livingston (USA)
Most United States Livingstons are named for American statesmen or officials, such as Edward Livingston, Mayor of **New York** City, and Robert R. Livingston, Chancellor of New York. However, Livingston, California, is a city named after David Livingstone, the famous explorer, for details of whom see the next entry below.

Livingstone (Zambia, Zaire, Tanzania)
Although many African place-names have reverted or altered to an indigenous form, the name of the famous Scottish explorer David Livingstone (1813–1873) still remains on the map in the last quarter of the twentieth century, even if it will eventually be superseded by a quite different name. The city of Livingstone, Zambia, where it is the capital of Southern Province, arose in the 1890s as a development from a settlement somewhat further up the Zambezi River than the present site, under the name of Old Drift Ferry Station. In 1905 the present location was occupied and was named after Livingstone, who had discovered (and named) the **Victoria** Falls near here in 1855. The city does have an African name as well, however, which is Maramba, and equally there have been plans in recent years to rename it with the African name of the falls, which is Mosi-oa-Tunya (in English, 'the smoke that thunders'). This brings us to the Livingstone Falls themselves, which are on the Congo River, Zaire, between Kinshasa and Matadi in that country. (The river itself is now frequently also known as the Zaire.) The falls, which consist of a series of rapids extending for more than 200 miles, were crossed by the explorer Henry Morton Stanley (see **Stanley**) in 1877, and were named by him after Livingstone. The Livingstone Mountains in Tanzania are similarly named for him. See also **Blantyre**, **Livingston**, and the next entry below.

Livingstonia (Malawi)
The first memorial mission to the explorer David Livingstone (see **Livingstone**, above) was set up in 1875 at Cape **Maclear**, on the south coast of Lake Malawi (formerly known as Lake Nyasa). It was named for the explorer but was subsequently moved twice because of the hot and humid climate: first to Bandawe, on the east coast of the lake, then to its present site further north and some distance inland from the lake. Livingstone had reached and explored Lake Nyasa from the south in 1859.

Llandudno (South Africa)
Llandudno is a seaside settlement in Cape Province, on the west coast of the Cape Peninsula, southwest of Cape Town. It is named after the seaside resort in North Wales, and the connection may be no more than one of identity in this respect.

Lloydminster (Canada)
The city of Lloydminster, on the border between **Alberta** and Saskatchewan, was settled in 1903 by a group known as the Barr Colonists, a community of some two hundred churchpeople recruited in London by a Church of England clergyman, the Rev. I. M. Barr. Their leader was the Rev. George E. Lloyd, the future Anglican bishop of Saskatchewan, and he gave his name to the new settlement. (Note that the settlers chose the suffix '-minster', with its ecclesiastical associations, rather than the more common '-ville' or '-ton'.)

Lochaber (Canada)
It must have been Scottish emigrants here in **Nova Scotia** who chose the name of the Scottish Highland district and loch for the Canadian lake, and for the settlement that subsequently arose by it.

Lochgelly (USA)
The community in West **Virginia** was

originally known as Stuart, a name given by Samuel Dixon, a coal operator, in honour of the royal house of Scotland. After a tragic mining accident in 1907, however, in which 84 men lost their lives, he changed the name to Lochgelly, after the Lochgelly Coal and Iron Company at the town of this name in Fife, which was owned by an associate of his. Dixon had experienced difficulties hiring new miners after the disaster, and so felt that a change of name might help to rid the settlement of its former tragic associations. See also **Longacre**.

Loddon River (Australia)
The river of this name in central **Victoria** was discovered in 1836 by Thomas Mitchell (see **Mitchell River**), and he named it after the river Loddon, in Hampshire.

Logan (Australia, Canada)
The Logan River, **Queensland**, is named after an explorer here, one Captain Logan, who was killed by the Aborigines. Mount Logan, Canada's highest mountain, in Yukon Territory, was named after Sir William Logan (1798–1875), a geologist born to Scottish parents in Montreal, who was Director of the Geological Survey of Canada from 1842 to 1870. (Before this, he was the manager of a copper-smelting works in Swansea, South Wales, and he died in Wales.)

Loggieville (Canada)
The site of this community in **New Brunswick** was first settled in the 1790s by a Scottish family named Loggie (or Logie). Initially, the settlement was known as Black Brook, after a John Black who had also emigrated here at about the same time, possibly a few years earlier. In 1895, however, the present name was established.

Londina (South Africa)
Although the region of this name in the Transvaal was established by one Alexander McCorkindale as a settlement for Scottish emigrants, the name itself appears to derive from that of London. Compare the next entry.

London (USA, Canada)
As schoolchildren, obligatorily (or even voluntarily) studying a map of Canada, we have almost all of us, at least in Britain, been surprised and pleased to find London on the **Thames** in Ontario, with **Windsor** not too far away on the same river. Why, here too, if on the 'wrong' side, are **Lambeth**, **Chatham** and **Tilbury**. Certainly, London is found several times on the map of North America, and the reason is self-evident. What more obvious than for newly arrived emigrants to name their settlement after their capital city? It may seem surprising that the name is not even more frequently encountered than it is. In most instances, the borrowing was simply a tribute, not implying necessarily that the settlers were actually Londoners. For the Kentucky city, for example, it is known that the name was chosen after a heated argument in which rival Scottish and Irish settlers respectively demanded Edinburgh and Dublin for the new community. And the perhaps better known Canadian London has a similar, if more peaceful, attribution. In 1793, John Simcoe (see **Simcoe**) proposed that the future provincial capital be known as 'the Forks of the Thames', while in 1799 'London' was the name given to the newly organised district here. In 1826 the present location was selected for the new settlement, and was initially named New London. (The Thames River was known as the Tranche at this time.) The name then finally became established in its present form, despite an attempt to rename the community as 'Georgina on the Thames' (after George III). See also the next entry.

London Coast (Greenland)
The name is no longer in existence, but it is worth recording that this was the designation used by William Baffin (see **Baffin**) for a section of the west coast of Greenland explored by him in 1616 on board the *Discovery*. He gave the name in honour of the London merchants who had backed

his expedition: Sir Thomas Smith, Sir Francis Jones, Sir Dudley Digges and Sir John Wolstenholme. For modern-day derivate Londons, see the entry above.

Londonderry (USA, Canada)
Londonderry, **New Hampshire**, was settled in 1719 by around one hundred Presbyterian families from Northern Ireland, who named it after one of their best-known cities. The community of Londonderry, **Nova Scotia**, was named after the New Hampshire town, from which Ulster Scots emigrants had come to settle in Canada. See also **Derry** (USA), set off from Londonderry in 1827.

Londres (Argentina)
The community of Londres, in west central Argentina, was founded by Philip II of Spain at the time of his marriage in London in 1554 to Mary I ('Bloody Mary') of England. The name has survived, despite Anglo-Argentine disputes and the conflict in 1982 over the rival claim to the **Falkland Islands**.

Longacre (USA)
The community of this name in West **Virginia** was founded by Samuel Dixon, the coal operator who also gave **Lochgelly** its name. Dixon founded the Longacre Colliery Company of West Virginia here, and named the settlement after his native home of Longacre, near Castleford, Yorkshire.

Lord Hill (South Africa)
Lord Hill is the highest peak in the Great Karas Mountains, Namibia (southwest Africa), where it was so named in about 1836 by Sir James Alexander, the British general and military writer, after Lord Hill, otherwise Rowland Hill, 1st Viscount Hill (1772–1842), the officer who distinguished himself in the Peninsular War and at Waterloo and who in 1828 succeeded Wellington as Commander-in-Chief of the British Army. But 'Lord Hill' is an apt name in its own right for a mountain that is a sort of 'lordly hill'!

Lord Howe Islands (Pacific Ocean)
The island group, in the Solomon Islands, is today more usually known by its indigenous (Melanesian) name of Ontong Java. The earlier name honours the naval exploits of the British admiral Lord Howe (see **Howe**), and the islands were so named in in 1791 by John Hunter (see **Hunter**). Various other Lord Howe Islands still exist individually in different parts of the world, and they will have been similarly named after the admiral.

Lorne (Australia)
The town in southwest **Victoria** was founded in 1871 as a coastal resort and was named by its Scottish settlers after the Firth of Lorn, western Scotland, or the area of Lorn that lies to the east of it in Argyll (now in Strathclyde).

Lorneville (Canada)
The name of Lorneville, **New Brunswick**, honours John Sutherland Douglas Campbell, 9th Duke of Argyll and Marquis of Lorne (1845–1914), who was Governor General of Canada from 1878 to 1883. His title comes from the Lorn of the entry above.

Lothair (South Africa)
The Transvaal village is in an area settled by Scottish emigrants. When it was surveyed in 1878 it was given the literary name of Lothair, after the novel with this title by Disraeli, published in 1870. The eponymous hero of the novel is a young English nobleman, brought up in Scotland under the guardianship of a Scottish nobleman, Lord Culloden, and a clergyman, before coming of age and receiving a great fortune, for which the Anglican Church, the Roman Catholic Church, and the revolutionary societies of Italy all vie.

Loudon (USA)
Loudon County and its seat of the same name in Tennessee are named after John Campbell, 4th Earl of Loudon (1705–1782), the Scottish Commander-in-Chief of British forces in the early years of the French and Indian Wars. See also **Fort**

Loudon. Loudon County, **Virginia**, is also named after the earl.

Louisa (USA)

Louisa County, **Virginia**, and its identically named seat take their names from Princess Louisa (1724–1751), the youngest daughter of George II who married Frederick V of Denmark. The same queen's name lies behind that of Louisa County, Iowa, despite a local romantic legend telling of one Louisa Massey who avenged the death of her brother by killing the man who had murdered him.

Louise (Canada)

Lake Louise, **Alberta**, was originally known as Emerald. The name was then changed to honour Princess Louise Caroline Alberta, the fourth daughter of Queen Victoria who married the Marquess of Lorne, the Governor General. Louise Island in the **Queen Charlotte Islands**, **British Columbia** was also named after this same lady. See also **Alberta**, **Lorn**, **Lorneville**, **Regina** and the entry below.

Louiseville (Canada)

The town of Louiseville in Quebec was named after the same Princess Louise who gave her name to Lake **Louise**, **Alberta** and Louise Island, **British Columbia**. See entry above, and also **Alberta**, **Lorn**, **Lorneville**, **Regina**.

Lovelock (USA)

The city of Lovelock, Nevada, was originally settled in 1861 as Big Meadows. Five years later, George Lovelock, an Englishman, arrived at the settlement and purchased the properties there, which duly became known as Lovelock's Ranch. The name then became shortened to Lovelocks, and eventually lost its final 's', as today.

Lucan (Canada)

The name of the community in Ontario had a link with Irish settlers, who named it after the village (now small town) of Lucan, west of Dublin.

Ludlow (USA)

The town of Ludlow, Massachusetts, was settled in about 1751 and originally known as Stony Hill. Four years later it was renamed Ludlow, probably for the Shropshire town, and presumably because one or more of the early settlers had emigrated from there.

Lunenburg (Canada)

The **Nova Scotia** town, the seat of the county of the same name, was originally an Indian settlement before being acquired by the French. In 1656, Oliver Cromwell granted it to Charles de Saint-Étienne de la Tour, Governor of Acadia, but there was no permanent settlement until Hanoverians from the German town of Lüneburg, together with Swiss emigrants, arrived in the 1750s. They named their community in honour of the royal house of Brunswick-Lüneburg, for George I, who as the Elector of Hanover and Duke of Brunswick-Lüneburg came to the English throne in 1714.

Lyallpur (Pakistan)

The city of Lyallpur, in Punjab Province, was founded in 1892 and named after Sir Charles James Lyall (1845–1920), then Lieutenant-Governor of the Punjab. In 1975, however, the town was officially renamed Faisalabad, to honour the Saudi monarch, King Faisal, who died that year and who had been widely respected in Pakistan.

Lyndhurst (USA)

The **New Jersey** town was originally known as Union. In 1917, however, it was renamed as a tribute to John Singleton Copley, 1st Baron Lyndhurst (1772–1863), Lord Chancellor of England from 1827. Lord Lyndhurst, it is true, was born in **Boston**, Massachusetts, as his father had been (although *his* father was an Irishman, of a family who came originally from Yorkshire!). But his father came to Europe when he was only two, and his mother brought him to England a year later, so perhaps he can qualify for admittance here, especially as most of his long public life was led in England.

Lynn (USA)

The Massachusetts town was originally settled in 1629 under the name of Saugus. In 1637, however, it was renamed after Lynn Regis (as the Norfolk town of King's Lynn was then known). The first minister of the American settlement, the Rev. Samuel Whiting, had been a curate in that town.

Lyttelton (New Zealand)

The borough and port of Lyttelton, on the harbour of the same name in South Island, was originally known as Port Cooper and Port Victoria when used as a port in the late eighteenth century by sealers and whalers. (Many of them began to come here from Australia, soon after **Sydney** had been founded there in 1788.) The actual town of Lyttelton, however, was not laid out until 1849, when it was named after Lord George Lyttelton (1817–1876), the Chairman of the Canterbury Association which sent Church of England colonists to New Zealand. Lyttelton is now a southern suburb of **Christchurch** (which name see in this connection), and is in the province of **Canterbury** (likewise). See also **Sumner**.

Lytton (Canada)

The **British Columbia** community was named in 1858 as a compliment to Sir Edward Bulwer-Lytton (1803–1873), who became Secretary of State for the Colonies that year, having already made his name as a novelist and playwright several years earlier.

M

Macadam Range (Australia)

The Macadam Range of mountains, southwest of **Darwin** in Northern Territory, was so named by John Stokes (see Mount **Stokes**) because the pudding-stone conglomerate of which the hills are chiefly composed reminded him of the macadamised road surface invented by the Scottish engineer, John McAdam (1756–1846), whose name also lies behind that of Tarmac (a proprietary name for a special surface of this type). Taylor (see Bibliography, p. 217) regards it as 'an absurd name'. But isn't it actually rather imaginative?

McAllen (USA)

The Texan town of this name was founded in 1905 by John McAllen, a Scottish settler who had a ranch here and who donated a sizeable portion of his land to the railroad. (He also built a depot to enable the railroad to terminate near a hotel that he owned.)

MacCarthy Island (Gambia)

MacCarthy Island, now usually known by its African name of Jangjangbure, is upstream from the country's capital, Banjul (formerly **Bathurst**), in the Gambia River. It was originally called Lemain Island, and was ceded in 1823 to Captain Alexander Grant of the African Corps, who was acting on behalf of the British Crown. The intention was to exploit the island as a centre for liberated slaves. Subsequently, however, it was renamed after Sir Charles MacCarthy (1770–1824), Governor of Sierra Leone, to which the territory of Gambia was then subordinate, from 1812 to his premature death in 1824. (He was fatally wounded in a dispute with the Ashantis, who then took his head as a war trophy.)

M'Clintock Channel (Canada)

The channel, between **Victoria** Island and **Prince of Wales** Island, Northwest Territories, was named after the Irish-born naval officer and explorer, Sir Francis Leopold McClintock (1819–1907), who in 1859 discovered the tragic fate of Sir John Franklin and members of his expedition of 1845 to the Canadian Arctic. (See **Franklin**.) McClintock found the graves of some of Franklin's crew on **King William** Island, to the south of the channel that now bears his name. In 1987, BBC television transmitted a documentary showing the opening of two similar graves discovered on the much smaller Beechey Island, the unfortunate subjects being John Hartnell, a sailor, and William Brain, a marine. (Beechey Island was named after Frederick William Beechey (1796–1856), the British admiral, geographer and Arctic explorer.) See also the next entry below.

M'Clure Strait (Canada)

The strait is in Northwest Territories, between **Banks** and **Melville** Islands. It is named for Sir Robert McClure (1807–1873), the Irish naval officer who completed the first crossing of the Northwest Passage by this route, and who in 1850 took command of the *Investigator* (see **Investigator Group**) to try to find the missing British explorer John Franklin (see **Franklin**), of whom no news had been heard since 1845. Icy conditions obliged him to abandon the ship, and when two rescue ships were in turn abandoned near Melville Island, McClure and his party had to proceed on foot to Beechey Island (see entry above) before a ship could take them back to England.

Macdonnell Ranges (Australia)
The ranges of mountains and hills lie in south central Northern Territory, where they were discovered in 1860 by the Scottish explorer John Stuart. They are named after Sir Richard MacDonnell (1814–1881), the Irish-born Governor of South Australia from 1855 to 1862. The namer was Lachlan Macquarie, Governor of New South Wales, who was a keen name-giver (see **Macquarie**).

McGregor (South Africa, Canada)
The village of McGregor, in Cape Province, was established in 1861 and was originally named Lady Grey, after the wife of Sir George Grey (see **Grey**, **Greymouth**, **Greytown**). It was subsequently renamed, however, to avoid confusion with the existing **Lady Grey** near **Aliwal North**. The new tribute was thus paid to Andrew McGregor (1829–1918), minister of the Dutch Reformed Church at the nearby town of **Robertson** from 1862 to 1902. In Canada, the community of Macgregor in Manitoba was so named by the Marquess of Lorne (see **Lorneville**), Governor General of Canada, as a compliment to his chaplain, Dr James Macgregor (1832–1910), the first minister of St Cuthbert's Church, Edinburgh (from 1873). Although frail, Macgregor accompanied the Marquess to the Northwest Provinces in 1881 to inspect progress in the construction of the Canadian Pacific Railway. The present town that bears his name has a main church appropriately named St Cuthbert's, and a portrait of Macgregor is preserved there.

McKeesport (USA)
The industrial city of McKeesport, **Pennsylvania**, was settled in about 1755 by David McKee, an Irish ferry operator on the Monongahela River here. The town was laid out in 1795 by his son John, who named it after him.

Mackenzie (Canada, Australia)
The name is prominent in Canada, chiefly for the long Mackenzie River, which flows northwards from the Great Slave Lake, Northwest Territories, to the **Beaufort** Sea in the Arctic Ocean, and for the Mackenzie District, which was formed in 1895 in the Territories and named after the river that flows through it. Also prominent are the Mackenzie Mountains, a northern extension of the Rockies in the Yukon and Mackenzie District. All three are thus directly or indirectly named after Sir Alexander Mackenzie (?1755–1820), a Scottish trader and explorer who discovered and followed the river that bears his name in 1789, pursuing a course for the whole of its length of over two thousand miles from the Great Slave Lake to the Arctic Ocean. Four years later he crossed the Rocky Mountains from Fort Chipewyan to the Pacific coast of what is now **British Columbia**. (Earlier unsuccessful attempts to explore and exploit the river had resulted in the name of Disappointment River for it, or for the part that could not be followed.) In Australia, the seasonal Mackenzie River in **Queensland**, where it is a tributary of the **Fitzroy**, was discovered in 1844 by the German explorer Ludwig Leichhardt and named for Sir Evan Mackenzie, an early settler.

Macleantown (South Africa)
The village in Cape Town, northwest of **East London**, was named in 1881 after Colonel John Maclean (1810–1874), Lieutenant-Governor of British Caffraria from 1860.

Maclear (South Africa)
The name is familiar for the Cape Province town, north of **East London**, and for Cape Maclear, the promontory at the southern end of the Cape Peninsula, near the Cape of Good Hope. Both places honour the famous astronomer, Sir Thomas Maclear (1794–1879), who worked at the Cape from 1834 to 1870 and who made an important trigonometrical survey while there, as well as studying comets and nebulae. Semi-seriously, the name can be regarded as an apt one for

an astronomical site where there are 'clear' conditions for observing the southern celestial hemisphere. (The Royal Observatory, Cape Town, where Maclear worked, was founded in 1820 and is still controlled by the British Admiralty.) The town of Maclear was founded in 1876 as a military camp. For another astronomer who worked at the Cape and gave his name to a settlement, see **Herschel**.

Mac-Mac (South Africa)

The Transvaal gold-mining village is said to be so named either (more probably) because the first diggers here included Scottish brothers named MacClaughton or (less probably) because a list of diggers handed to the South African President, Thomas F. Burgers, contained so many Scottish names that he called the place Mac-Mac. But nothing is impossible in the world of naming, as this book shows! The village gave its name to the nearby Mac-Mac Falls on the Waterval River.

McPherson Range (Australia)

The shortish mountain range, which forms the east end of the border between **New South Wales** and **Queensland**, was sighted by James Cook in 1770, when he named the prominent peak he saw Mount Warning. In 1827, the first European to explore the interior of the range was Captain Patrick Logan, who named it as a whole for a colleague of his, Major Duncan McPherson.

Macquarie (Australia, South Pacific)

The name of Lachlan Macquarie abounds in Australia! He was a Scotsman, born in 1761, who joined the English Army as a boy and served in many countries of the world before being appointed Governor of **New South Wales** in 1809. He served in this post until 1821, when he was recalled by the home government who were displeased with his 'emancipist' agricultural policies. He died three years later. He gave his name to the following, among others: Lake Macquarie, New South Wales; Macquarie Harbour, western Tasmania; Macquarie Island, in the South Pacific, southwest of New Zealand; two Macquarie Rivers, in New South Wales and Tasmania respectively; the Macquarie Ridge, submarine mountains in the South Pacific. Macquarie was himself a keen name-giver – it amounted almost to a craze with him – and many of the Scottish names in Tasmania are his creations, especially those of rivers, such as the Clyde, Leven, Esk, Forth and Gordon. The **Lachlan River** in New South Wales is also named after him (but not by him).

Magnet Bay (Antarctica)

Magnet Bay, in **Enderby** Land, was named after the *Magnet*, the ship captained by Peter Kemp (see **Kemp**) who explored the Antarctic in the 1830s. The backer of his expedition had been the same firm of Enderby Brothers who gave the name to the land area here. Magnet Bay was itself named by Douglas Mawson as leader of the **Banzare** expedition to this area of the Antarctic in 1929–31 (see **Mawson**).

Maidstone (USA, Canada)

The town of Maidstone, Vermont, and also Lake Maidstone in this state were named for the English town in Kent, no doubt through an emigrant link. Rather unusually, the town gave the name to the lake, not the other way round. (A natural feature usually gives its name to a later, manmade one.) In Canada, Maidstone, Saskatchewan is similarly named after the English town.

Maitland (South Africa)

The eastern suburb of Cape Town is named after Sir Peregrine Maitland (1777–1854), Governor of the Cape Colony from 1844. His name was nearly also given to the town now known as Burgersdorp, southwest of **Aliwal North**. Sir Peregrine visited the area in 1845, and several of the residents asked him if they could rename their settlement of Klipdrift in his honour. He refused, however (no doubt most diplomatically), so the inhabitants named the place after themselves (as 'burghers'), as they had initiated the naming procedure.

Malden (USA, Pacific Ocean)
The city of Malden, Massachusetts, was settled in 1640 and became an area of **Charlestown** under the name of Mystic Side (the river here is the Mystic). In 1649 it was incorporated as a town and named after Maldon, in Essex. The honour to this town was in effect to one of its natives, Joseph Hills, who was Speaker of the Massachusetts House of Deputies (from 1647). In the southwest Pacific, Malden Island is one of the Line Islands, and was originally known as Independence Island. It was discovered in 1825 by John Byron (see **Byron**), and he named it after a surveyor who was with him on his ship the *Blonde*. Compare the next entry below.

Maldon (Australia)
The town in central **Victoria** was founded in 1853 after gold had been discovered in the area, and it was named after the town of Maldon, Essex, from which some of the early settlers or goldseekers must have come. See also above.

Malmesbury (South Africa)
The Cape Province town, northeast of Cape Town, was established in 1829 and named by Sir Lowry Cole, Governor of the Cape from that year, after his father-in-law, Sir James Harris, 1st Earl of Malmesbury (1746–1820). He had had little to do with South Africa, however, and the naming was thus really a posthumous tribute. Malmesbury became well known for its so called 'Malmesbury accent', otherwise the characteristic rolled 'r' of Afrikaner speech. (General Smuts came from the Malmesbury area and always rolled his letter 'r' in this way.)

Malone (USA)
The village of Malone, **New York**, is named after Edward Malone (1741–1812), the Irish Shakespeare scholar and critic who was a personal friend of the founder.

Malton (Canada)
Malton, Ontario, now part of the city of Mississauga, has a name that apparently derives from the Yorkshire town of Malton, although emigrant connections seem to be hard to prove.

Malvern (USA)
The city of Malvern, Arkansas, is probably named for a Malvern in **Virginia** which was itself named by way of an emigrant link after the English town, now Great Malvern in Hereford and Worcester. Compare the next entry.

Malvérnia (Mozambique)
This is the former name of the village now known (from the 1980s) as Chicualacuala. It was given by way of a tribute to Sir Godfrey Huggins, Viscount Malvern (1883–1971), who was Prime Minister of Southern **Rhodesia** and also of the Central African Federation. See also above.

Man, Isle of (Papua New Guinea)
The Isle of Man is a small island (one of about two hundred here) in the Bismarck Archipelago, east of Papua New Guinea in the western Pacific. The island lies between the two largest islands, **New Britain** and **New Ireland**, and was so named for its position (like the British Isle of Man between England and Ireland) by the English navigator Philip Carteret, who discovered it in 1767. (This Philip Carteret should not be confused with the Carterets of New Jersey: see **Carteret**.) See **New Ireland** for some more of Carteret's namings here.

Manchester (USA)
There are well over a dozen places of the name in the United States, many of them noted industrial centres, as one might expect, for it was with regard to Britain's great manufacturing city that they were named in the first place. Manchester, Connecticut, had sawmills and papermills even before the American Revolution (i.e. earlier than 1775), and the name of Manchester, **New Hampshire**, originally known as Old Harry's Town when first settled in 1722, was renamed in 1810 by one Samuel Blodget, a local merchant, after the barge canals he had seen in the English city. He went on to construct the first canal round the Amoskeag Falls here,

which together with the **Middlesex** Canal in Massachusetts thus opened a barge route to **Boston**. In some cases, of course, the name was given by way of a future intention, in the hope that the place would prosper through its industry. This was so for Manchester, Tennessee, although the community now there is not notably a manufacturing one.

Mandeville (Jamaica)
The town of Mandeville, west of **Kingston**, was named after the courtesy title, Viscount Mandeville, of William Montagu, 5th Duke of Manchester (1768–1843), who was Governor of Jamaica from 1808 to 1827.

Manning Strait (Solomon Islands)
Manning Strait, in the Solomon islands, east of Papua New Guinea, lies between Choiseul and Santa Isabel Islands. It is so named after the captain of a ship, the *Pitt*, that passed through it in 1792.

Mansfield (USA)
The city of Mansfield, Louisiana, was named after William Murray, 4th Earl of Mansfield (1705–1793), Lord Chief Justice from 1756 to 1788. He was much admired by Thomas Abbington, the founder of the settlement, for his support for the American colonies and for his influence on Anglo-American mercantile law. He also gave his name to Mansfield, Massachusetts, which town was so named after him by his personal friend, the Loyalist Governor of Massachusetts, Thomas Hutchinson. Other places of the name may in some instances have been named after early settlers (Mansfield, Texas, was named after two such, a Mr Mann and a Mr Field), but this should not be assumed for all Mansfields.

Margate (USA, South Africa)
Both Margate, Florida, and Margate City, **New Jersey**, are named after the English coastal town and resort of Margate in Kent. The former is only around five miles from the coast, and the latter is actually on it. It therefore seems likely that the association is more a geographical one rather than an emigrant link. The same applies in South Africa, where moreover Margate, in Natal, is a seaside resort immediately to the north of **Ramsgate**, just like its English namesake. All three overseas Margates, too, are on or near an east coast, like the English resort.

Maria (Canada)
The Quebec community and the bay of the same name (as part of the Baie des Chaleurs) on which it is located honour Lady Maria Effingham, wife of the Governor of Quebec, Guy Carleton, 1st Lord Dorchester (1724–1808). Sir Guy married Lady Maria, who was the daughter of Thomas, 2nd Earl of Effingham, in 1772, and she long outlived him, dying in 1836 at the age of 82.

Markham (Canada, Papua New Guinea, Antarctica)
The town of Markham, in **York** County, Ontario, was named after William Markham (1720–1806), Archbishop of York from 1777. The settlement was founded in 1794 by a German colonist, William Berczy, who had come here from **New York** with his compatriots. York is thus an influential name here. In Papua New Guinea, the Markham River is named for Sir Clements Markham (1830–1916), the English geographer and historical writer, who had been Secretary of the Royal Geographical Society and who had recommended that the National Antarctic Expedition of 1901 should be led by Captain Scott, as well as travelling widely himself. Scott thus repaid the compliment by naming Mount Markham, in **Victoria** Land, Antarctica, after him, and **Minna Bluff**, also in the Antarctic, after his wife. The two families were close friends, so the tribute was a personal one, not a mere formal compliment.

Marlboro (USA)
The Massachusetts city, whose name is also spelt in full as Marlborough, was incorporated as a town in 1660 and so named after the town in Wiltshire, from which early settlers probably came. Marlboro County, South **Carolina**, was

named after John Churchill, Duke of Marlborough, however, for details of whom see the next entry below.

Marlborough (USA, New Zealand)
The Connecticut town of Marlborough was probably named after John Churchill, 1st Duke of Marlborough (1650–1722), the British soldier who was the victor at the Battle of Blenheim in 1704. In New Zealand, the same man gave his name to the statistical area (former province) of Marlborough in the north of South Island. The name accords with the many other 'heroic' names here, including **Havelock**, **Nelson** and **Blenheim** itself. (Mrs Matthews, however, feels that to name a whole province after a military hero is to carry the fashion for such names rather too far! See the Bibliography, p. 217.) See also the previous entry above.

Marshall Islands (Pacific Ocean)
The Marshall Islands, in eastern Micronesia, were originally discovered by the Spanish in the first half of the sixteenth century. They were subsequently partially explored in 1788 by the British naval officer, Captain John Marshall, and were named after him (although much of the proper exploration and mapping here was carried out by two Russians in the early nineteenth century, Kruzenshtern and Kotzebue). Marshall was here in the merchant vessel *Scarborough*, and accompanying him in the *Charlotte* was Thomas Gilbert, who gave his name to the **Gilbert Islands**. The two had been conveying convicts to Australia, and so were in a sense only incidentally explorers.

Martha's Vineyard (USA)
There is still some dispute about the precise origin of the name of this island off Cape Cod, Massachusetts. One account does relate, however, that the name was given by the Cornish sea captain Bartholomew Gosnold, when sailing up the coast here from **Virginia** in 1602, with Martha the name of his daughter and the 'Vineyard' a description of the wild vines he saw here. But other sources say the name actually commemorates a Dutch seaman, perhaps named Martin Wyngaard, or that the namer was not Gosnold at all, but one Gabriel Archer. Be that as it may, an English connection is possible, and Gosnold certainly named Cape Cod here, where on 15 May that year he 'took great store of cod fish'. In general, too, so many Massachusetts names have originated in the 'Old Country', that the likelihood of this one being British is quite considerable.

Marton (New Zealand)
The borough of Marton, in the south of North Island, was established in 1866 by four settlers who divided up their large holdings into acre lots by way of speculation. They named the place after Captain Cook's birthplace in Yorkshire (now Cleveland), the village of Marton southeast of Middlesbrough, and now virtually one of its suburbs.

Maryborough (Australia)
There are two cities of the name in Australia. Maryborough in **Queensland**, on the **Mary River**, was proclaimed a town (originally as Maryborough Port) in 1861 and was named after the late wife, Lady Mary Fitzroy, of the Governor of Australia (see entry above). Maryborough, **Victoria**, on the other hand, arose in 1831 as a sheeprun called Simson's Plains (or according to other sources, Charlotte Plains), and when founded as a town in the gold rush of 1854 was renamed either after the wife, Mary, of the local police commissioner, or after his native town of Maryborough (modern Port Laoise) in Ireland.

Maryland (USA)
Maryland was one of the original thirteen colonies of the United States, settled in 1634, when Leonard Calvert (see **Calvert**), younger brother of Lord Baltimore (see **Baltimore**) landed the founding expedition on what is now Blakistone Island (then Clement's Island) in the lower Potomac River. The first settlement and capital here was the present village of St Marys City. (The capital was moved to **Annapolis** only in 1694.) But despite the

allusion to St Mary, an association that must have pleased the Catholic founders of the colony, the actual name was intended as a royal compliment to Henrietta Maria (1609–1699), the queen and wife of Charles I. Compare Cape **Henrietta Maria**.

Mary River (Australia)
The **Queensland** river was named as a memorial to Lady Mary Fitzroy, the wife of Sir Charles Fitzroy (see **Fitzroy**), Governor of Australia for the five years from 1846. Lady Mary, whom he had married in 1820 as Lady Mary Lennox, daughter of the 4th Duke of Richmond, was tragically killed in a carriage accident in 1847, and the naming was thus a posthumous tribute to her. Her father had also met an untimely death (see **Lennox and Addington County**). See also the relevant next entry below.

Mason and Dixon Line (USA)
The Mason and Dixon Line originally arose as the United States boundary between **Maryland** and **Pennsylvania**, and was intended to settle a dispute between the proprietors of these states, respectively the Penns and the Baltimores. It was laid down between 1763 and 1767 by two English astronomers, Charles Mason (1730–1787) and Jeremiah Dixon (dates uncertain). The line became famous subsequently in 1820 at the time of the so-called Missouri Compromise (the compromise worked out between North and South to allow the admission of Missouri as the twenty-fourth state), and ever since that date has served as the generally understood political and social dividing line between the North (implying the free states) and the South (the slave states). Its name is sometimes shortened to Mason-Dixon Line. In their actual surveying work, Messrs Mason and Dixon set up rocks at five-mile intervals, with William Penn's coat of arms on one side, and Lord Baltimore's on the other. At one-mile intervals between these rocks they placed smaller stones as markers, with 'P' on one side and 'M' on the other, these being the initials letters of the states. The line runs absolutely straight along the southern boundary of Pennsylvania for a distance of 233 miles at a latitude of 39°40′. (This does not include the last 36-mile section at the western end, which was added later, in 1784.)

Matthew Island (New Caledonia)
Matthew Island, in the French overseas territory (disputed since 1984) of **New Caledonia**, in the southwest Pacific, was discovered in 1788 by the English sailor Thomas Gilbert (see **Gilbert Islands**) and named after a close associate of his.

Maugerville (Canada)
The **New Brunswick** community is named after one of the original grantees in the area here, Joshua Mauger (died 1790), a Jerseyman who settled in **Halifax** as a merchant and smuggler.

Mawson (Antarctica)
The name of Sir Douglas Mawson (1882–1958) can be found in more than one point of the Antarctic, such as the Mawson Coast in MacRobertson Land (and the Australian research station of Mawson there), the Mawson Peninsula on the **Oates Coast**, and the Mawson Escarpment that runs down to the **Amery Ice Shelf**. One of the latest additions to the Antarctic map made in his honour is that of the Mawson Sea, placed on the outer edge of Wilkes Land by Soviet scientists in 1964. Douglas Mawson was a Yorkshireman who made his reputation as an explorer and geologist, and who first worked as a member of Shackleton's Antarctic expedition of 1907–9 (see **Shackleton Glacier**), then led two notable expeditions of his own, the Australian one of 1911–14, which discovered and explored George V Coast (see **George**) and **Queen Mary Land** (as it now is), and the so-called **Banzare** one of 1929–31 which discovered MacRobertson Coast (or Land) (named after an Australian businessman who had backed the expedition).

Mecklenburg (USA)
There are two counties of the name in

the United States, respectively in North **Carolina** and **Virginia**. The name honours Charlotte Sophia, Princess of Mecklenburg-Strelitz (1744–1818), wife of George III. Her Christian name gave the name of the seat of the former county, which is **Charlotte**.

Melbourne (Australia)
Unlike the capitals of the other Australian states, Melbourne, the capital city of **Victoria**, was founded by private enterprise. Its site was discovered in 1803, but it was not first settled until 1835, when the pioneer John Batman and his colleagues purchased a large portion of land on **Port Phillip** Bay from the Aborigines. He came from Tasmania, and a second party from there, led by a land speculator, John Fawkner, arrived a couple of months later and began to build houses and other establishments. Two years later, in 1837, the new settlement between the Yarra River and the Maribyrnong was named after William Lamb, 2nd Viscount Melbourne (1779–1848), Prime Minister of Britain from 1835 to 1841. The Australian city was capital of Australia as a whole from 1901 to 1927. Lord Melbourne took his title from the family's seat, Melbourne Hall, at the village (now town) of this name in Derbyshire. (His wife was the eccentric Lady Caroline Lamb, the subject of Robert Bolt's film of this name produced in 1972.)

Melfort (Canada)
The Saskatchewan town was originally known as Stoney Creek. In 1904 its name was changed to Melford, after the Scottish birthplace, Melford House south of Oban (now Strathclyde), of an early settler, Mary Melford Campbell (married name, Mrs Beatty).

Melmoth (South Africa)
The Natal town was named after Sir Melmoth Osborn, the British Resident who was in charge of the district from 1879, when the annexation of Zululand took place.

Melrose (USA)
The city of Melrose, Massachusetts, was settled in 1633, originally as part of **Charlestown**. After two further changes of name (North Malden, Pond Feilde), it became Melrose, after the Scottish town in Roxburghshire (modern Borders) that through Melrose Abbey has come to be closely associated with Walter Scott. No doubt Scottish settlers chose the name for these various links.

Melsetter (Southern Rhodesia)
The town of this name is now known as Chimanimani, and is in Zimbabwe. It was founded in 1893 by two Scottish trekkers from the Orange Free State, South Africa, whose names were Thomas and Dunbar Moodie and who came from an estate called Melsetter in the Orkneys. On the independence of Zimbabwe in 1980, the name was changed to Mandidzuzure. Two years later it was further changed to Chimanimani, as mentioned.

Melville (Australia, Canada)
The name abounds in both countries. In Australia it is found in Cape Melville, **Queensland**, and in Melville Island north of Northern Territory, to name but two places. In Canada there is also a Melville Island, in the **Queen Elizabeth Islands**, Northwest Territories, and a Melville Sound between the **Kent** Peninsula and the mainland in that region. Between Melville Island and **Victoria** Island, too, lies the **Viscount Melville Sound** (originally the Melville Sound). All these places honour the same man. This was Robert Saunders Dundas, 2nd Viscount Melville (1771–1851), who was First Lord of the Admiralty from 1812 to 1827 and who was keenly interested in Arctic exploration. The Australian Melville Island was named in 1818 by Philip Parker King (see **King**). Lord Melville took his title from his ancestral home in Scotland, Melville Castle, southeast of Edinburgh (now in Lothian).

Mercer (New Zealand, USA)
The town in western North Island was named after a British officer who was

killed at Rangiriri near here in the second Maori War of 1860–70. In the United States, most places of the name honour the Scottish-born soldier, General Hugh Mercer (1721–1777), who served as a surgeon at the Battle of Culloden (1746) and who two years later emigrated to **Pennsylvania**, where he served with General Braddock in the French and Indian Wars. He was killed in the Battle of **Princeton** in the American Revolution (War of American Independence). There are at least a dozen counties of the name, and several communities, with one of the best known being the Pennsylvania borough, founded in 1803.

Meredith (USA)

The **New Hampshire** town is named after Sir William Meredith (died 1790), the British politician and Lord of the Admiralty who supported the demands of the colonies that they should not be taxed without representation. ('If I were an American, I would not submit to them', he said in a speech on the subject of the imposts.) Meredith was a personal friend of Governor Benning Wentworth (see **Wentworth**).

Meriden (USA)

The city in Connecticut was settled in 1661 by one Jonathan Gilbert, who named it after his birthplace in Surrey, Meriden Farm, near Dorking.

Mersey River (Australia, Canada)

The Mersey River, Tasmania, was named after the well-known English Mersey, as was the Canadian river of the same name in **Novia Scotia**. The adoption of the name seems to have been on general geographical grounds, without any specific reference (although the Canadian river is also known as the Liverpool).

Methuen (USA)

The town in Massachusetts was settled in 1642 as part of **Haverhill**. In 1725 it was incorporated as a separate town and was named after the English diplomat, Sir Paul Methuen (1672–1757), a Lord of the Admiralty. He was a friend of the namer of the town, Massachusetts Governor Dummer.

Middlesboro (USA)

Many places with a name beginning 'Middle-' were so designated for their location, midway between one point and another. The Kentucky city of Middlesboro (officially, Middlesborough), however, was named after the English town of Middlesbrough, now in Teesside. The site was settled in 1889 and was developed by English investors as an iron and steel centre. They therefore named it after the English town that itself is well known for its iron and steel works.

Middlesex (USA, Canada)

There are four counties of the name in the United States, and one in Canada. In each case, they are named after the English county of Middlesex, for its important association with London. Middlesex County, **New Jersey**, has a seat of the same name, and Middlesex County, Ontario, has **London** as its seat.

Middleton Island (USA)

The island, in the Gulf of Alaska, was named by George Vancouver (see **Vancouver**) in 1794 in honour of Sir Charles Middleton, 1st Baron Barham (1726–1813), who was Comptroller of the Navy from 1778 to 1790.

Midlothian (USA)

The village of this name in Illinois was so designated not so much for the (former) Scottish county but as a literary tribute to Sir Walter Scott, and in particular his novel *The Heart of Midlothian*, published in 1818.

Milford (USA, New Zealand)

Some places of the name are really descriptive in origin, denoting a mill by a ford. The Connecticut city of Milford, however, which was settled in 1639 as part of the **New Haven** colony, was named the following year for an English Milford, or even the Welsh one of Milford Haven. It is not likely to be named after Milford-on-Sea, Hampshire, as stated by Harder (see

Bibliography, p. 218), as that resort did not develop until the present century. Milford Sound, New Zealand, however, which is an inlet of the Tasman Sea, was so named by whalers here in the 1820s for its resemblance to the drowned valley ('The Haven') that forms the harbour entrance at Milford Haven, the Welsh port. Milford Sound was similarly created when the sea flooded a valley here that had become unusually deep as a result of glacial action.

Millertown (Canada)

The community of Millertown, Newfoundland, was so named for the same Scottish firm, Lewis Miller and Co., that gave the name of **Lewisporte**.

Milne Bay (Papua New Guinea)

Milne Bay, an inlet on the coast of New Guinea, was so named in 1873 by the navigator Captain John Moresby (who gave the name of **Port Moresby**) after Admiral Sir Alexander Milne (1806–1896), First Lord of the Admiralty from 1872 to 1876 (for the second time in his long career).

Milnerton (South Africa)

The town of Milnerton, immediately northeast of Cape Town, was founded in 1902 and named after Sir Alfred Milner (1854–1925), Governor of the Cape from 1897 to 1901, in which year he was raised to the peerage as Baron Milner, of St James's, London and Cape Town.

Milton (USA, New Zealand)

We are on rather uncertain ground here, but it is very likely that more than a few places of the name, in the United States or elsewhere, were named after an English Milton, of which there are several. In some instances, a tribute to the poet John Milton (1608–1674) may have been intended, for he lived at the very time of colonial settlement and expansion in North America. For Milton, Vermont, the naming seems to have been a compliment to William Wentworth, Viscount Milton (1748–1833), who was an associate of William Pitt (see **Pittsburgh**) and a relative of John Wentworth, Governor of **New Hampshire**. The New Zealand town of Milton, in South Island, began its career as Milltown, a purely descriptive name. When later settlers began naming streets after famous poets, however, the spelling of the name was altered to conform with this poetic licence, and was designed to compliment the poet similarly.

Ministers Island (Canada)

The island of this name in **New Brunswick** was so called to honour a minister of religion, the Church of England clergyman, Rev. Samuel Andrews (died 1817), who had his home on the island from 1791 until his death.

Minna Bluff (Antarctica)

The name of this headland on the Ross Ice Shelf (see **Ross Sea**) was given by Scott as a compliment to the wife, Minna, of his close friend, the geographer and historical writer, Sir Clements Markham (see **Markham**). Minna was the daughter of a Devonshire clergyman, the Rev. James Chichester. The two married in 1857 and Lady Markham, herself a linguist and lover of literature, did much to contribute to her husband's work.

Minto (Canada)

Although now no more than 'an abandoned riverboat landing' (Hamilton, see Bibliography, p. 219) in the Yukon, it is worth recording that the place was given a fairly lofty name, that of Gilbert John Elliot-Murray-Kynynmound, 4th Earl of Minto (1845–1914), who was Governor General of Canada from 1898 to 1904 (and before that, Viceroy of India). The earl gets his title from his family seat, Minto House, at the Scottish village of this name near Jedburgh.

Mirabel (Canada)

Although quite possibly simply a pleasant name, devised for its euphony and ease of pronunciation, it may have originated from the names of two daughters of a Scottish settler here, Miriam and Isabel. But the first explanation is the more likely, for Mirabel is Quebec's new international airport, officially designated by this name in 1972. The name's French flavour suits the province.

Miranda (New Zealand)
The small settlement of Miranda, in North Island, was named after a British gunboat that took part in the skirmishes along the Waikato River between the British and the Maoris in the second Maori War (1860–70).

Mirror (Canada)
What sort of British name is this? Unexpectedly, the **Alberta** settlement is named after the London newspaper, the *Daily Mirror*. The name was given in 1911, in which year the Grand Trunk Pacific Railway advertised in this newspaper. The name happens to be equally appropriate for a community located not far from Buffalo Lake, whose sometimes stormy waters can at other times be 'mirror smooth'.

Mitchell River (Australia)
The Mitchell River, **Queensland**, was discovered in 1845 by the German explorer Ludwig Leichhardt, and was named after Sir Thomas Mitchell (1792–1855), the Scottish explorer who became Deputy Surveyor General for **New South Wales** in 1828.

Molteno (South Africa)
The Cape Province town was founded in 1873, when coal was discovered locally, and the new settlement was named after Sir John Molteno (1814–1886), the first Prime Minister of the Cape Colony (from 1872–78), when he resigned over differences with the Governor, Sir Bartle Frere: see Mount **Bartle Frere**). See also **Claremont**.

Moncton (Canada)
The **New Brunswick** city and port was originally known as The Bend, for its location on a bend of the Petitcodiac River. In 1855 it was renamed after Sir Robert Monckton (1726–1782), the British general sent to **Nova Scotia** in 1752 to become its Lieutenant Governor four years later (until 1761). The name is thus in effect a centenary tribute to this appointment. The present spelling without the 'k' was authorised in 1860 by the European and North American Railway.

Monmouth (USA)
The **New Jersey** county takes its name from the (former) Welsh county of Monmouthshire, at the border with England. There may have been an emigrant link with this county, or the name may have been selected simply to blend in with the names of many of the other New Jersey counties, which also have British county names (such as **Cumberland**, **Gloucester**, **Middlesex**, **Somerset**, **Sussex**). The city of Monmouth, Illinois, is named after the Battle of Monmouth, New Jersey, when in 1778 the British under Sir Henry Clinton fought the Americans under Washington.

Monson (USA)
The Massachusetts town of Monson is named after Sir John Monson (1693–1748), who was President of the Board of Trade and a personal friend of Thomas Pownall, Governor of Massachusetts.

Montagu (South Africa)
The town in Cape Province was founded in 1851 and was named that year after John Montagu (1797–1853), Colonial Secretary at the Cape from 1843 to his death. He should not be confused with the better known John Montagu in the next entry!

Montague (USA)
The name is found in Alaska for Montague Island and the Montague Strait. Both were named in 1778 by Captain Cook as a compliment to John Montagu, 4th Earl of Sandwich (1718–1792), three times First Lord of the Admiralty. This is the man who is popularly credited with having invented the sandwich (after his title), since when at the gaming table, and loth to leave it, he ate slices of ham between two pieces of bread. Cook also named the **Sandwich** Islands after him. (See also the **South Sandwich Islands**). The spelling

of the Alaskan name with a final 'e' seems to have been deliberate.

Montgomery (USA)
The very many Mongomery Counties in the United States – eighteen of them – all honour one and the same man. This was the Irish-born American Revolutionary general, Richard Montgomery (1737–1775), who was second-in-command to General Schuyler in the Canadian campaign and who was killed at the battle of Quebec. Many communities, such as Montgomery, the state capital of Alabama, and Montgomery City, the seat of Montgomery County, Missouri, are also named after him.

Montrose (USA)
The city of Montrose, Colorado, was settled in 1881 and named by an early romantically inclined resident and literary lover after Walter Scott's novel *A Legend of Montrose*, published in 1819. The attractive natural surroundings may have had something to do with it, as well as the pleasant sound of the name itself. Montrose is a town and port in eastern Scotland, up the coast from Dundee.

Moresby Island (Canada)
Moresby Island, in the **Queen Charlotte** Islands, **British Columbia**, was named after Admiral of the Fleet Sir Fairfax Moresby (1786–1877), the English naval commander who suppressed the slave trade at Mauritius in the 1820s and who, more relevantly here, was Commander-in-Chief of the Pacific station from 1850 to 1853. (He was only a Rear-Admiral at that stage.)

Moreton Bay (Australia)
The bay is an inlet of the Pacific, in southeast **Queensland**. In 1770 James Cook discovered a passage (now known as South Passage) between the main islands off the coast here that lead to the bay, and he named the bay itself after James Douglas, 14th Earl of Morton (1702–1768), President of the Royal Society. The name also originally applied to the mainland area of Australia that eventually became Queensland. Cook also named Moreton Island, across the bay, after the same man. (He at first thought it was a peninsula, so named the headland he saw at the northwest end Cape Moreton. It was left to Matthew Flinders (see **Flinders**) to establish that it was actually an island, in 1799.)

Morning, Mount (Antarctic)
Mount Morning is in **Victoria** Land, not far from Mount **Discovery**. It was so named by Scott during his expedition of 1901–4, after the *Morning*, one of the two auxiliary ships that accompanied the *Discovery*, the other being the *Terra Nova* (see **Terra Nova Bay**).

Mornington (Australia)
The name is found in at least two places in Australia. The Mornington Peninsula, south of **Melbourne**, **Victoria**, and also the seaside resort of Mornington on its west coast, were named after the Irish town in Co. Meath, which is also (perhaps not coincidentally) a seaside resort. But Mornington Island, largest of the **Wellesley** Islands, in the Gulf of Carpentaria, **Queensland**, was so named in 1802 by Matthew Flinders (see **Flinders**) after Richard Wellesley (who gave his name to the group), 1st Baron Mornington (?1690–1758). For more about him, see the name of the island group.

Mosgiel (New Zealand)
The town of Mosgiel, in South Island, was given the name of the Scottish farm (properly, Mossgiel) on which the Scottish poet Robert Burns lived for four years (see entry below). The giver of the name was an early settler here, a colleague of William Cargill (who gave his name to **Invercargill**), and who like him was a leading member of the Scottish Free Church and of the colonising community here.

Mossbank (Canada)
The Saskatchewan community was so named by two Scottish brothers, Robert and Alexander Jolly, who settled here in 1907. The name is their adaptation of that

of Mossgiel, the farm near Mauchline, Ayrshire (now Strathclyde) where Robert Burns lived with his brother for four years in the 1780s. This entry happens to steal most of the thunder, but not quite all, of the previous entry.

Mount Ayr (USA)
The Iowa town is named after the Scottish town of Ayr, perhaps by an emigrant from there, with the first word of the name referring to the high location of the place between the Missouri and Mississippi Rivers at this point.

Mount Fletcher (South Africa)
The Transkei town was founded in 1882 and directly named after the mountain nearby. This in turn was probably named after the Rev. John Fletcher, the vicar of Madeley, Staffordshire, and a friend of John Wesley. Other sources claim, however, that the mountain's name comes from a Captain Fletcher who was stationed in the area.

Mount Frere See **Frere, Mount**

Mount Gambier (Australia)
The city in South Australia lies at the foot of Mount Gambier, and takes its name from it. The mountain, an extinct volcano, was sighted in 1800 by the British naval officer Lieutenant James Grant, who named it after Admiral James Gambier, later 1st Baron Gambier (1756–1833), who had led the way to many naval victories. He also gave his name to the **Gambier Islands**.

Mount Pearl (Canada)
The town of this name in Newfoundland arose on a site originally granted by the British government to Sir John Pearl in 1834, and it thus takes its name from his. Mount Pearl is now a suburb of St John's.

Mount Pleasant (Canada)
The name is a fairly popular one in North America, if only for its agreeable associations (cool air, pleasant surroundings). The community of Mount Pleasant in Ontario was so named by one of the early settlers, Henry Ellis, after his native Welsh village of the same name. (There are more than one, such as the Mount Pleasant south of Merthyr Tydfil.) For some time in the 1860s and 1870s the settlement was known as Mohawk, but this was not the name that prevailed.

Mount Rainier (USA)
It is best to trace this name systematically back to its source. The city of Mount Rainier in **Maryland** was so designated by army officers from Seattle, who named the tract of land they bought here after Mount Rainier, the mountain, in Washington. The present Mount Rainier National Park in Washington, created in 1899, centres on this mountain, which was so named in 1792 by George Vancouver (see **Vancouver**) after his friend Peter Rainier (1742–1808), a British admiral.

Mount Sterling (USA)
The city of this name in Kentucky was settled in about 1790 and originally known as Little Mountain Town, from the Indian burial mound on the site. In 1792 its name was changed to Mount Stirling, after the Scottish town (and possibly by a Scottish settler), with the spelling later modified as at present.

Mount Vernon (USA)
Mount Vernon, as every American schoolchild knows, is the former home and burial place of George Washington, in **Virginia**. The original name of the estate here was Little Hunting Creek Plantation, and it descended by inheritance down to George Washington from John Washington, the first of the family in America. In 1743, Lawrence Washington, George's elder half-brother, renamed the plantation Mount Vernon after his former commander, Admiral Edward Vernon (1723–1794), under whom he had served in the Caribbean. George Washington took up residence here in 1759 on marrying, and lived here until his death in 1799, with interruptions and absences for public service (including that of becoming the first President of the United States). The

'Mount' is the hill by the Potomac River on which the estate stands.

Mowbray (South Africa)
Mowbray, the southern suburb of Cape Town, was originally known as Driekoppen ('three cups'), after the tavern here. In 1850 the *Government Gazette* announced the new name, commencing: 'His Excellency the Governor having been pleased to comply with the request made to him by the inhabitants of the village of Three Cups to change the name to Mowbray. . .'. No doubt His Excellency was told the reason for the new choice of name, which was taken from an estate here formerly owned (mostly) by an English settler from Melton Mowbray, Leicestershire.

Mudge, Mount (Australia)
The peak of Mount Mudge, in the Great Dividing Range, **Queensland**, was named for Lieutenant Colonel Richard Mudge (1790–1854), a surveyor in the Royal Engineers, who carried out a variety of survey work in Britain and abroad, notably in North America, where he helped arbitrate in the fixing of the boundary between Maine (USA) and **New Brunswick** (Canada). His partner in this important assignment was a Mr Featherstonehaugh. For a similar boundary-settling partnership, see **Mason and Dixon Line**.

Muir (USA)
Both the Muir Glacier, Alaska, and the national monument of Muir Woods, California, are named after John Muir (1838–1914), a Scottish-born geologist and explorer. He actually discovered the Alaskan glacier and worked for many years in the Arctic regions of North America in forestry and the establishment of national reservations and parks.

Mulgrave (Australia, Canada)
Mulgrave Island, in the Torres Strait, north of **Queensland**, was named after Constantine Phipps, 2nd Baron Mulgrave (1744–1792), a polar explorer and First Lord of the Admiralty. In Canada, the community of Mulgrave (originally Port Mulgrave) in **Nova Scotia** was named after a descendant, George Augustus Constantine Phipps, 2nd Marquis of Normanby (1819–1890), Lieutenant-Governor of Nova Scotia from 1858 to 1863. (He was known as Viscount Normanby from 1831 to 1838, and then as Earl of Musgrave until his father's death in 1863, when he returned to England on actually succeeding to the title: see also **Normanby Island**.)

Murchison (Australia, New Zealand, South Africa, Uganda, Malawi)
All the places featuring here, and many that do not, pay tribute to one man, the pioneering Scottish geologist, Sir Roderick Murchison (1792–1871), President of the Geological Society from 1831 to 1836 and Director of the Geological Survey from 1855. At its most obvious, geology is to do with rocks in mountains and rivers, so these are the features that predominate. The include the following: the Murchison River, Western Australia, and Mount Murchison in that province; the two Mount Murchisons in South Island, New Zealand; the Murchison Range of mountains in South Africa, and the Transvaal mining village of Murchison, in the area where Murchison himself prospected; the Murchison Falls (now usually known as the Kabalega Falls) on the Nile in Uganda; the Murchison Falls on the Shire River, Malawi. Many of these names were given in Murchison's lifetime, such as the Australian river, named in 1839 by the explorer Sir George Grey (see **Grey**), or the Ugandan falls, discovered by the English explorer Sir Samuel Baker in the mid–1860s.

Murray River (Australia)
The Murray is Australia's principal river, flowing for over a thousand miles across the southeast of the country into the Indian Ocean. Its downward course was explored by Charles Sturt (see **Sturt Desert**) in 1831, three years after he had discovered the **Darling**, and he named the river after the then Colonial Secretary, Sir George Murray (1772–1846).

Musgrave Ranges (Australia)
The series of granite hills in South Australia were discovered in 1873 by the English explorer William Gosse and were named after Sir Anthony Musgrave (1828–1888), then Lieutenant-Governor of South Australia. Compare the next entry.

Musgravetown (Canada)
The community of Musgravetown, in eastern Newfoundland, was named after Sir Anthony Musgrave (see the entry above), who served as Governor of Newfoundland from 1864 to 1869. The settlement was originally known as Goose Bay.

N

Napier (New Zealand, South Africa)
The New Zealand port, in eastern North Island, was laid out in 1856 and named after Sir Charles Napier (1782–1853), the British general who gained fame as the conqueror of Sind, India (now Pakistan), in 1843 and as the Governor of that province when it was subsequently annexed to British India as part of the Bombay presidency. This was therefore one of the names that reflected British patriotism at the time of the Indian Mutiny (late 1850s), others being for example **Clive**, **Hastings**, and **Havelock**. The South African town of Napier in Cape Province was named for Sir Charles's younger brother. He was Sir George Thomas Napier (1784–1855), Governor of the Cape Colony from 1837 to 1844. The town was laid out in 1838 and named two years later.

Naseby (New Zealand)
The isolated township of Naseby in southeast South Island arose in the goldrush days of the early 1860s, and was given a topically popular 'battle' name to mark its high British patriotic feeling after the Indian Mutiny a few years earlier (see **Napier**, above). Naseby, now a village in Northamptonshire, was the scene of Oliver Cromwell's victory over Charles I and Prince Rupert's Royalist forces in 1645.

Nassau (USA, Bahamas, Pacific Ocean)
Historically, Nassau was the German duchy that would give the titles of several royal houses in western Europe, among them the House of Orange. In so far as this concerns William III ('William of Orange'), king of Great Britain and Ireland from 1689 to 1702, we can regard the use of the name for place-names as legitimate here. The reference to William is thus implied for Nassau County, **New York**, which was formed in 1899 from **Queens County**. (For another American name relating to this same monarch, see **Williamsburg**.) It is also implicit for Nassau, the capital of the Bahamas, which took its name in the 1690s as a compliment to William III, but which was not actually laid out until 1729. The island of Nassau in the **Cook** Islands, however, has a more indirect link, for it is said to have been named after the ship belonging to an American whaling captain who discovered it in 1835. But his ship must surely have been named for the royal houses, so that the name belongs here. For further background to the name, see **Orange**.

Needham (USA)
The town of Needham in **Norfolk** County, Massachusetts, was named in about 1711 after the village of Needham, near Harleston, in the English county of Norfolk. There were doubtless emigrant connections there for one or more early settlers.

Nelson (New Zealand, Canada, Australia)
The town and port of Nelson, in the north of South Island, New Zealand, was settled by the New Zealand Company in 1841 and was named after the British naval hero, Lord Nelson (1758–1805), victor (and martyr) of the Battle of Trafalgar (1805). The town had already been planned in London as a model settlement 'to carve future independence and distinction', and the actual founder was the man who organised and managed the colonising New Zealand Company, Edward Gibbon Wakefield, who gave his

name to **Wakefield**. Nelson's streets and parks are full of naval names such as Trafalgar, Nile, Hardy, Collingwood, Vanguard and Victory. (And for towns with similar 'hero' names compare **Marlborough**, **Napier** and **Wellington**). The two best-known Canadian Nelsons, however, honour different men. The city of Nelson in **British Columbia** was originally known as either Stanley (see **Stanley**) or Salisbury (see **Salisbury**) when it was founded in 1887. The following year it was named after Hugh Nelson (1830–1893), the Irish-born Lieutenant-Governor of British Columbia. And the Nelson River, in Manitoba, was discovered in 1612 by the English explorer Sir Thomas Button (see **Button Bay**), who named it after the pilot of his ship, the *Resolution*, who died there. **Port Nelson**, at the mouth of the Nelson River, was the first post of the Hudson's Bay Company. Cape Nelson in Australia, south of **Portland** in **Victoria**, was probably named after the famous Horatio Nelson, like the New Zealand city. Compare the next entry.

Nelson-Miramichi (Canada)

The community of this name in **New Brunswick** was originally South Nelson before it combined with the Indian river name to become Nelson-Miramichi in 1968. The first part of the name honours the famous Admiral Lord Nelson.

New Albion (America)

We here begin a run of 'New' names, with many of the second words of the names also to be found individually in the book in their appropriate alphabetical place. This is so for New Albion, which is, however, a historic name. It was the name that Francis Drake gave to the point where he landed on the coast of what is now California (perhaps near modern San Francisco) in 1579, choosing this particular name 'in respect of the white banks and cliffs which lie toward the sea', according to the nineteenth-century antiquary William Vaux, who described his circumnavigation. But the name did not last, and it is possible that Drake did not even include the initial 'New'. But we do know that he actually wrote the name somewhere there on a wooden post. See **Albion** for the significance of the name.

New Annan (Canada)

There are at least two places of the name in Canada. New Annan, **Nova Scotia** is a community that was founded in about 1820 by a Scottish emigrant from Annandale (the central area of the valley of the river Annan), Dumfriesshire (modern Dumfries and Galloway). New Annan, **Prince Edward Island** was similarly settled and named, also in the 1820s, but this time by an emigrant from the town of Annan. Compare **Annandale**.

Newark (USA)

The **New Jersey** city was founded in 1666 on land purchased here from the Indians by Puritans who had emigrated from Connecticut. At first the settlement was known as Pesayak Towne. Later it was renamed New Milford, after **Milford**, Connecticut. Finally it became Newark. One account tells how the name honours the native town, Newark-on-Trent, of the local minister of religion, the Rev. Abraham Pierson. Other accounts claim that much of the land here was owned by one of the Lords Newark, or that one of the prominent citizens, James Bartle, simply liked the name. Again, there have been those who prefer to give a religious interpretation to the name, seeing it as a sort of symbolic 'New Ark'. Or could it be 'New Work', to signify a new settlement? These theories are in decreasing order of probability, and the link with the English Newark seems the most likely.

New Bedford (USA)

The Massachusetts city was settled in 1652 as part of **Dartmouth**. When separately incorporated in 1787 it was renamed Bedford, then subsequently New Bedford, to distinguish it from the **Bedford** in **Middlesex** County. The name is more likely to refer to the English town than to a Duke of Bedford, at least judging by other 'New' names.

New Brighton (New Zealand, USA)
New Brighton is a coastal suburb of **Christchurch**, South Island, and was undoubtedly named after the famous Sussex resort, as many other New Brightons are round the world, including others in Britain itself. The **Pennsylvania** borough of the name was founded in 1789 and so named because it lay across the river from 'old' **Brighton**.

New Britain (Papua New Guinea)
What more obvious colonial name (except perhaps **New England**)? New Britain is the largest island of the Bismark Archipelago – and *that* name reveals that the group has had German connections as well as British. The name was actually given to the island by William Dampier (see **Dampier**), who was here in 1699 and who confirmed its insular nature. The German connection was made in 1884 when the archipelago became part of a German protectorate and New Britain was renamed Neu-Pommern. (Same sort of idea, but this time 'New Pomerania'.) Its name reverted to New Britain after the First World War, when the territory was mandated to Australia. Dampier may have been a buccaneer, but he was also a patriot.

New Brunswick (Canada, USA)
The Canadian province was originally (before its foundation) territory that was included in **Nova Scotia**. As a result of the American Revolution (War of American Independence) of 1775–83, however, there was such an influx of Loyalist settlers in the region that demands were made for a new province to be created. Partition took place in 1784 and the 'name was chosen as a compliment to King George III (1760–1820) who was descended from the House of Brunswick' (quoted by Hamilton, see Bibliography, p. 219). Other suggestions of names for the new province were New Ireland (rejected because Ireland was not exactly in the royal favour at the time) and the more original Pittsylvania (by William Pitt out of **Pennsylvania**). In the United States, New Brunswick, the **New Jersey** city, was originally known as Prigmore's Swamp when it was settled in 1681 by one John Inian, who started up a ferry service on the Raritan River here. Later it was renamed (hardly surprisingly) Inian's Ferry. Finally, it was renamed further in honour of George I (1660–1727), who was also Duke of Brunswick. Compare **Brunswick**, and see also **Pittsburgh**.

Newburgh (USA)
The city of Newburgh, in **New York**, was originally settled by Germans in 1709 but then became a parish in 1752 and was named after the Scottish town of Newburgh, Fife. There may well have been emigrant Scottish connections, but of course the name does mean 'new borough' in its own right.

New Caledonia (Pacific Ocean)
It may seem strange that a French overseas territory should have a Scottish name. Why is it not 'Nouvelle France' by now? The half-English, half-Latin name, as it actually is, was given to the main island here in 1774 by that great namer and discoverer, James Cook. He chose the Roman name of Scotland as a compliment (and also a complement) to the nearby **New Hebrides** (now Vanuatu) which he had also named not so long before. The name also accorded well with the already named **New Britain** and **New Ireland**, further to the north in what later came to be called the Bismark Archipelago. Why no New Wales? The answer is that Cook had already used this name for **New South Wales**, where he had been similarly creative. So all four main constituents of the British Isles were now represented in new ('New') form on the map. Cook knew what he was doing! As to why the French did not change the name, the reason was probably simply that the islands were remote from the mother country, they were very much *outre-mer*, not *métropole*. And although the French arrived here in the late eighteenth century, their hold over the islands has never been very strong, and in recent years (especially since 1984) there have been increasing demands by the indigenous Melanesian population for

self-government. See also **Caledon**, **Caledonia**.

New Carlisle (Canada)
The Quebec village of New Carlisle was founded in 1887 and named for the English town, now in Cumbria, rather than a Duke of Carlisle. See **Carlisle**.

Newcastle (Australia, USA, Canada, South Africa)
The New World positively bristles with Newcastles, Australia having at least five places of the name, and the United States also having at least half a dozen fairly important ones (some as **New Castle**, see the next entry). The usual reference is to one or other of the English Newcastles, usually Newcastle-upon-Tyne, but the name in itself is appropriate for a new settlement that had to be raised under military conditions, as was often the case. Australia thus has the city of Newcastle, **New South Wales**, Newcastle Bay, **Queensland**, the settlement of Newcastle Waters, Northern Territory, and others besides. The particular link with the English city may be coal, of course ('coals to Newcastle'), and it certainly was for the Australian city, which arose as the Coal River Penal Settlement in 1801. It was renamed when the port became an outlet for coal from the nearby Newcastle-**Cessnock** field. On the other hand, it is probable that the bay, near Cape **York**, was named after Thomas Pelham-Holles, 1st Duke of Newcastle (1693–1768), twice Prime Minister (1754–6, 1757–62), when it was discovered by Cook in 1770. And Newcastle Waters, discovered in 1861 when its permanent waterholes were found by the Scottish explorer John Stuart, was named for the 5th Duke of Newcastle, then Secretary of State for the Colonies. In the United States, Newcastle, Wyoming was founded in 1889 and was originally a coal-mining town, so exploited this particular association of the name. In Canada, the **New Brunswick** town of Newcastle was founded in 1785 and so, at this date, was probably named for the 1st Duke of Newcastle, the Prime Minister (see above), but in South Africa, the coal-mining town in Natal was named, despite its industry, not directly after the English coal port but for the nineteenth-century Colonial Secretary, like Newcastle Waters.

New Castle (USA)
This name is in effect the same as **Newcastle** (see previous entry), so will have the same type of origin. New Castle, Indiana, is a city that was named for the English Newcastle-upon-Tyne when it was founded in 1819, and New Castle, **Pennsylvania** took the name even earlier, when in about 1798 it was settled by one John Stewart, who built an iron furnace here and chose the name for its industrial links.

New England (USA, Australia, South Africa)
The most famous New England of all is the United States region in the northeast, including the six states of Maine, **New Hampshire**, Vermont, Massachusetts, Rhode Island and Connecticut, the states, in fact, that are geographically the nearest to England. This is the New England of the Pilgrim Fathers, who crossed the Atlantic from Plymouth, England, and founded the new colony of **Plymouth** here. The name New England was actually given to the region by the Lincolnshire-born colonist, Captain John Smith, when he was exploring the coast here in 1614 on behalf of some London merchants. And what more English name than his? The name was confirmed by James I in 1620. The choice of name was an obvious one, of course, but it was timely also, for other European powers had already bestowed their own native names, such as New Netherlands, New Spain, New France, and so on, although these names are no longer on the map. In Australia, the New England Range, effectively a large plateau in **New South Wales**, was first settled in 1832 and was so named because the natural features of the plateau suggested an English landscape to the new residents. In South Africa, New England in the Cape Province is a region in the **Lady Grey** district that was so named because it was settled in 1860 by descend-

ants of the so-called 1820 Settlers, the group of British pioneers who emigrated to the eastern Cape in 1820.

Newenham, Cape (USA)
Cape Newenham, in Alaska, was named by one of Cook's officers in an expedition he made here in 1778. The name may have been taken from one or other of the Hampshire villages called Enham, such as Upper Enham or Knight's Enham (now Enham Alamein), near Andover.

New Glasgow (Canada)
The **Nova Scotia** town was founded in 1809 after the discovery of coal deposits locally some ten years earlier. It was named after the Scottish city by Scots settlers, and in particular by one William Fraser, who surveyed the site and foresaw 'another Clyde and another Glasgow'. (The 'Clyde' is actually called the East River here.) The coal connection is important here, as it is for some of the places above named **Newcastle**. Compare **Glasgow**.

New Hampshire (USA)
New Hampshire is the only US state that is named after an English county. How did this come about? The answer lies with Captain John Mason (1586–1635). Although born in King's Lynn, Norfolk, he later made his home in Portsmouth, Hampshire, and when he received a grant to a part of the territory that was later occupied by the colony (settled in 1623), he named it after his home county. Prior to this he had been Governor of Newfoundland (in 1615), so he was already familiar with transatlantic life and prospects. The company he organised to found an agricultural community in what became New Hampshire was known as the Laconia Company, after the ancient Greek kingdom whose capital was Sparta, and Laconia was originally considered as a name for the new American colony. See also **Hampshire**, **Portsmouth**.

New Hanover (Papua New Guinea)
New Hanover is an island in the Bismark Archipelago, at the western end of **New Ireland**. Its name has the same British royal connections that **Hanover** has, and it was given as a compliment to the royal house by the English navigator Philip Carteret in 1767. It so happens that the name was equally suitable for the island (as Neu-Hannover) when the group came under German rule in 1884.

New Haven (USA)
This name is both old and new in North America. Historically, it was a general name for any port that was a 'new haven', although in giving such a name, English settlers must have been aware of the Sussex port and harbour of Newhaven, even if they did not specifically intend the transference of this name. They did, however, for the Connecticut city, which was originally settled in 1638 by English Puritans who called it Quinnipiac, after the river here. Two years later this Indian name was abandoned in favour of New Haven, after the Sussex town, the particular reference being to the harbour at both places. (The American city's harbour is now tautologically named as New Haven Harbour.) New Haven is the seat of the county of the same name.

New Hebrides (Pacific Ocean)
The New Hebrides are a chain (or group) of islands in the southwest Pacific, west of Fiji, where they are currently jointly administered by France and Britain. They were initially discovered by the Portuguese in 1606, were rediscovered by the French in 1768, and six years later were charted and named by James Cook after the Scottish islands. He felt that the appearance of the jagged rocks and crags on the islands were similar to those of the Hebrides in his native land. See also **New Caledonia**, not so much for the French connection but for what Cook named next, and why.

Newington (USA)
Newington, the residential town in Connecticut, was first settled in 1670 as part of **Wethersfield**. When the community was organised as a parish in 1721 it was named after an English Newington,

perhaps the Kent village or what is now the London district of Stoke Newington. But again, possibly the name is near-arbitrary, and simply meant to suggest a new community?

New Ireland (Papua New Guinea)
New Britain is the largest island in the Bismark Archipelago, and New Ireland is the second largest. It was sighted, but not named, by a Dutchman in 1616, who thought it was part of a general landmass extending from New Britain to New Guinea. The English navigator Philip Carteret arrived here in 1767 and discovered that this was not so, enjoying a naming spree in the process:

> Arriving at New Britain, he found that an inlet, supposed to be only a bay, was a strait dividing the island into two, and to the second island he gave the name of New Ireland, distinguishing the intersecting channel as St George's. After discovering and naming the islands of Sandwich, Byron, New Hanover, the Duke of Portland's, the Admiralty, Denven's, Matty's, Stephen's and Freewill, he proceeded along the coast to Mindanao . . . (*DNB*).

Records show that he may have actually named New Ireland by its Latin name of Nova Hibernia (compare **New Caledonia**). Under German rule, from 1884 until after the First World War, it was known as Neu-Mecklenburg. See also **St George's Channel**.

New Jersey (USA)
The name of the US state, settled in 1664, is directly derived from that of the largest of the Channel Islands. On this island, Sir George Carteret was the head of the principal family, and after he had made a gallant effort to defend his native island for the king, Charles II, in the Civil War, he was granted territory in America as a reward by the king's brother the Duke of York (the future James II), who had in turn been granted it by the king. It had been acquired by the British from the Dutch in 1664. In the official conveyance, the name of the territory appeared in Latin as Nova Caesarea. The state itself was also known simply as Jersey (see **Jersey City**) before adding 'New'. See also **New York** for further relevant details.

New Kensington (USA)
The city in **Pennsylvania** was established in 1891 by a group of merchants from **Pittsburgh**. They named it after Kensington in London, perhaps simply for the association rather than for a specific reason. At first the name was the single word, but when it was found that there already existed a Kensington in Pennsylvania, the 'New' was added. For this other one, see **Kensington**.

New Liskeard (Canada)
The town in Ontario was originally known as Thornloe when first opened for settlement in 1822. It was then renamed for the Cornish town of Liskeard, the birthplace of John Armstrong, the founder of the town.

New London (USA)
The city in Connecticut was at first known by the name of Pequid, when founded in 1646. In 1658 it was renamed after the English capital. The city stands at the mouth of the **Thames** River, which was named later than the city, however.

Newmarket (USA, Canada)
Both Newmarket, **New Hampshire**, and Newmarket, Ontario, are named after the English town in Suffolk, not necessarily for any emigrant connections but simply because the name sounds typically 'English', as well as suggesting new commercial possibilities.

New Plymouth (New Zealand)
The city and port in western North Island was founded in 1841 by the New Plymouth Company under the auspices of the New Zealand Company. Many of the early settlers were emigrants from Devon and Cornwall, hence the name, for the significance of which see **Plymouth**.

Newport (USA)

In a way this is a name like **New Haven**, suggesting simply a new harbour or port, or being purely descriptive of one. But in some instances the name could have derived from a British Newport, such as the town and port in Monmouthshire (now in Gwent). In the case of Newport, **New Hampshire**, however, the name was probably for the British politician Richard Newport (1587–1651) or his son, Francis Newport, 1st Earl of Bradford (1619–1708), and for Newport, Kentucky, the name was a compliment to Christopher Newport, captain of the first ship to reach **Jamestown**, **Virginia**, in 1607. See also the next entry below.

Newport News (USA)

The site of this city and port was settled in 1621 by Irish colonists. The name already existed then – it was recorded in 1619 as Newports Newes – but the origin is still uncertain. It may, however, be a tribute to Christopher Newport, who commanded five expeditions to **Jamestown** over the six years from 1606. (See the entry above.) Some sources derive the second word of the name from an associate of his, one William Newce. This at least prevents the name being mistaken for that of a newspaper.

New Richmond (Canada)

The name of this Quebec community has the same origin as that of **Richmond**, also in Quebec, that is, it compliments the Duke of Richmond who was Governor General of the province.

Newry (USA)

The community of Newry, **Pennsylvania**, was founded in about 1793 by an Irishman named Patrick Cassidy, who named it after his native town in Co. Down.

New Scotland (USA, South Africa)

The **New York** community was settled and named by Scotsmen, so the name is self-explanatory. In South Africa, the present region of New Scotland in the Transvaal was similarly settled by Scottish immigrants. The head settlement was later named Roburnia, after the Scottish national poet, Robert Burns, although this name was soon changed to Amsterdam, with Dutch loyalties gaining the upper hand over the Scottish. Compare **Burns**.

New South Wales (Australia, Canada)

This was the name selected for the whole of the eastern coast of Australia by Captain Cook, who was here in 1770 and who saw a resemblance between this coastline and that of South Wales. In fact, the actual territory of this name was similarly much more extensive than it now is, and included the whole of Australia except Western Australia. The territory was then gradually reduced as the new colonies of South Australia, **Victoria**, **Queensland** and Northen Territory were set up in the nineteenth century, and in its new form it became part of the Commonwealth of Australia in 1901. In Canada, the same name was given in 1631 by Thomas James (see **James**) to the western shore of **Hudson** Bay, the honour thus being paid to the Prince of Wales, the future Charles II, who had been born the previous year. The 'South' is explained here because he similarly named the region to the northwest of Hudson Bay as New North Wales. However, these names have now long disappeared from the map. See also **Port Phillip**.

Newton (USA)

In most instances, the name will simply mean 'new town', so will be descriptive. (In some cases the original name will have actually been New Town). But Newton County, Mississippi, was named after Isaac Newton (1642–1727), the famous mathematician who discovered the law of gravity.

New Waterford (Canada)

The **Nova Scotia** town was founded in 1908 and at the suggestion of an early settler, one J.J. Hinchey, was named after his native Irish town of Waterford, in the county of the same name.

New Westminster (Canada)
New Westminster, the city in **British Columbia**, was founded in 1859 and was originally called Queensborough, as a compliment to Queen Victoria. Queen Victoria herself then proposed the name of New Westminster, presumably out of due modesty. The name was regarded as important for the town that would be the capital of British Columbia from 1860 to 1886. Hence the involvement of Her Majesty. See also **Port Moody**, and compare **Westminster**.

New York (USA)
The discoverer of New York is generally recognised as being Henry Hudson (see **Hudson**), who sailed into the harbour here in 1609 in search of a passage to India on behalf of the Dutch West India Company. His highly favourable report on the site to his superiors then led to the first big European bite proper at the future 'Big Apple', when the Dutch founded a colony here in 1625, naming it New Amsterdam, after their capital city. The Dutch 'reign' ended in 1664 when the English, sent by the Duke of York as part of the English–Dutch war in Europe, seized the city (without much resistance, since the Dutch were not too fond of their governor, Peter Stuyvesant) and renamed it New York, after the Duke. The history of the state of New York ties in at this point. When the British acquired the Dutch territories here, they were granted by Charles II to his brother, the Duke of York and Albany (the future James II). The territory west of the Hudson River was for a time called Albania, after the Duke's second title, while the area east of the Hudson was known as Yorkshire, after his first title. James then in turn granted his western territories to Lord John Berkeley (see **Berkeley Heights**) and Sir George Carteret (see **New Jersey**) and it became known as New Jersey while 'Yorkshire' became New York. There was a short hiatus in English rule in 1673, when the Dutch sprang a surprise invasion and renamed the territory as New Orange, after William III ('William of Orange'), who was Stadholder of the Netherlands at that time (and who would become king of Great Britain and Ireland subsequently: see **Nassau**, **Orange**, **Williamsburg**). But the city reverted to English rule and the former English name the following year. New York County, coextensive with Manhattan in the state of New York, and itself a borough in New York City, was similarly named for the Duke when it was formed in 1683. See also **Frederick**, **York**.

Nigel (South Africa)
Nigel is a gold mining town in the Transvaal, where it was established in 1909. It is said to be named after Walter Scott's novel *The Fortunes of Nigel* (published in 1822) which the surveyor who found gold here in 1886 happened to be reading at the time. Or perhaps his own name was Nigel? Either way, there is an implicit literary pun, for 'gold' equals 'fortune', and the 'fortunes' of the novel are an actual large sum of money.

Nimrod Glacier (Antarctica)
'Nimrod' itself is not of course a specifically English name. In this instance it was actually under Norwegian exploitation as the name of the small Norwegian whaler in which Shackleton sailed (see **Shackleton Glacier**) when he led an expedition to the South Pole in 1907. He gave the name of the ship to a small peak in the Dominion Range (**Victoria** Land), and subsequently the name was given to a large glacier that descended from the Transantarctic Mountains, near Mount **Markham**. So as the name was given by a Briton (Irish-born), there are reasonable grounds for including it here, one feels. Nimrod is familiar to many Britons as a name with hunting associations, and some British writers have even adopted it as a pen name (notably the nineteenth-century sporting writer C.J. Apperley).

Nith River (Canada)
The Nith River, Ontario was so named after the Scottish river in Dumfriesshire (now Dumfries and Galloway) by James Jackson, one of the founders of **Ayr** in the same province.

Norfolk (USA, South Pacific)

Duke or County? As always a name of this type can be either. The best known United States city of the name is Norfolk, **Virginia**, which is part of an urban complex at the mouth of Chesapeake Bay that includes the cities of **Portsmouth**, Chesapeake, Virginia Beach, **Newport News** and **Hampton**. The town was laid out in 1682 and was named for the English county, from which early settlers had emigrated. This was not the earliest American Norfolk, however, which was Norfolk County, Massachusetts, formed in 1643 and likewise named for the county. The county was abolished, though, and the present Massachusetts county dates from 1793. The city of Norfolk, on the other hand, derives from neither duke nor county, for it was originally North Fork, and its present name is a 'smoothing' of this. In the southwest Pacific, Norfolk Island, now Australian territory, was discovered by James Cook in 1774 and named by him after Charles Howard, 9th Duke of Norfolk.

Normanby Island (Papua New Guinea)

The island, in the D'Entrecasteaux group southeast of New Guinea was visited by the British sailor John Moresby (who gave his name to **Port Moresby**) in 1873 and was named by him after Sir George Augustus Constantine Phipps, 2nd Marquis of Normanby (1819–1890), who was Governor of **Queensland** from 1871 to 1874. See **Mulgrave** for the use of his other title as a place-name.

Norristown (USA)

The manufacturing borough of Norristown, **Pennsylvania** was founded in 1704 and is named after Isaac Norris (1671–1736), a Londoner who emigrated to Philadelphia in 1693 to lead an active public life there.

Northam (Australia)

The town in Western Australia was founded in 1830 as one of the state's oldest settlements and was named by Sir James Stirling (see **Stirling**), the colony's governor, after Northam, the Devon town, presumably for local emigrant links there, for he himself was a Scot.

Northampton (USA)

Another name where it is a question of town (or county) or earl (or marquess). Of the three counties of the name, Northampton County, North **Carolina** was named after James Compton, Earl of Northampton (1687–1754), while Northampton County, **Virginia**, was probably named for his ancestor, Spencer Compton, 2nd Earl of Northampton (1601–1643), who had supported the forces of Charles I and who was killed in the Civil War. Northampton County, **Pennsylvania**, however, was named for the English county, in which the village of Easton Neston is situated. It was at this village that Sir Thomas Fermor, 2nd Baron Leominster, otherwise the Earl of Pomfret, had his seat, and his fourth daughter, Juliana, married Thomas Penn, son of William Penn, the founder of Pennsylvania. For the other half of this story, see **Easton**.

North Hatley (Canada)

The Quebec community was originally known as Charleston, after the local minister of religion, the Rev. Charles Stewart. It was later renamed after the village of East Hatley (or possibly Hatley St George), Cambridgeshire, with which either the minister or other settlers had home links.

North Kent Island (Canada)

North Kent Island, between **Devon** Island and **Ellesmere** Island, Northwest Territories, was named after Edward Augustus, Duke of Kent (1767–1820), the father of Queen Victoria. Compare **Kent**.

Northumberland (USA, Canada, Australia)

Once more, the decision must be made between duke or county. It is very likely that the two United States counties of the name, in **Virginia** and **Pennsylvania**, were named after the English county, if only because one county is frequently named after another. In Canada, however, the Northumberland Strait, between **Prince Edward Island** and the two provinces of **Nova Scotia** and **New Brunswick**, was named after neither county nor duke. It was named after a ship, HMS *Northumberland*, the flagship of Admiral Lord Colville of Culross. It was on this ship that Joseph Frederick Wallet Desbarres (1722–1824) (*sic*), later Lieutenant-Governor of Cape Breton and, after that, of Prince Edward Island, surveyed the Nova Scotian and Cape Breton coasts over the ten years from 1763. The Northumberland Islands off the east coast of **Queensland**, Australia, were discovered by Cook in 1770 and named by him after Sir Hugh Percy, 1st Duke of Northumberland (1715–1786).

Norton (USA)

The name may in many cases be descriptive for a northern settlement (i.e. one to the north of an existing place), or it may derive from one of the many British places named Norton, and it is not always easy to say which. But Norton Sound, Alaska, has a well documented origin. The inlet was discovered by Cook in 1778 and named by him after Sir Fletcher Norton (1716–1789), Speaker of the House of Commons from 1770 to 1780.

Norwich (USA)

In some instances the name will have been given for the English cathedral city that is the county town of Norfolk, and this is certainly so for the city of Norwich, Connecticut, founded in 1659. However, this place may have given the names to other settlements named Norwich, as happened in the **New York** city. This was founded in 1788 and named by a settler who had come from the Connecticut namesake, as many settlers had.

Nottingham Road (South Africa)

The town in Natal was founded in 1905 and named after the Nottingham regiment who had been based here at a time when possible trouble was expected from the Basotho in the nineteenth century.

Nova Scotia (Canada)

The Canadian province began its colonial life as a territory settled by the French in 1604, when they named it Acadia, which is probably a name of Indian origin. The territory was then granted by James I in 1621 to Sir William Alexander Earl of Stirling (?1567–1640), a Scottish poet who was a tutor to the royal family (including the future Charles I). The conveyance included words referring to 'the lands lying between New England and Newfoundland [. . .] to be known as Nova Scotia, or New Scotland', and it was the Latin version of the name that prevailed. It did not appear on the map, however, until 1713, when after years of dispute and wrangling between the French and the English, the French finally built the powerful fortress of Louisbourg on the eastern coast of Cape Breton Island and the ownership was finally settled: the French retained this island and certain other areas, while most of the territory was ceded to the English. Or rather, the Scottish, for many Scottish names can still be found in the province today, such as **New Glasgow**, **Inverness** and **Waverley**. It is perhaps unusual that the Latin name was preferred to 'New Scotland', for other similar Latin names were always translated into English, as for **New Ireland** and **New Jersey**. But there is a **New Scotland** elsewhere (which see). See also **Scotia Sea**.

Oates Coast (Antarctica)

Oates Coast is an extensive area in **Victoria** Land. Lawrence Oates (1880–1912) was a member of Scott's expedition to the South Pole begun in 1910, and reaching it in 1912. On the return journey, when sickness threatened to delay the whole expedition's progress, he deliberately elected to walk out of his tent to his death in a blizzard in an attempt to ease the harsh conditions experienced by his colleagues. His sacrifice was in vain, for Scott and his remaining three companions all perished in the Antarctic. The name was given to the region by Harry Pennell (see **Pennell Coast**), the explorer who had been the captain of the ship, the *Terra Nova*, that had brought Scott to the Antarctic.

Oban (New Zealand)

The resort on **Stewart Island**, south of South Island, was given after the Scottish town and resort in Argyllshire (now Strathclyde). It is possible that Sir William Stewart, who gave his name to the island, came from Oban, but little is known about him, although he was certainly a Scot. Even if he did not, at least the Scottish connection is there, and both places are coastal resorts.

Oglethorpe (USA)

The name is found at least three times in **Georgia**, for Oglethorpe County, the city of Oglethorpe (not in this county), and Mount Oglethorpe. The name honours James Edward Oglethorpe (1696–1785), the English general and philanthropist who founded Georgia. He was interested in prison reform, and had proposed that the new colony should be settled by unemployed men released from debtor's prison.

Onslow County (USA)

The county in North **Carolina** was named after Arthur Onslow (1691–1768), Speaker of the House of Commons from 1728 to 1761.

Orange (USA, Australia)

Some places of this name in the United States are purely descriptive, referring to orange groves, especially in the hotter states such as California and Texas. But there are also many places where the name will refer to the royal house of Orange, and specifically to 'William of Orange', that is, William III, who came to the throne in 1689. Among counties of this type of Orange are those in Indiana, **New York**, North **Carolina**, Vermont and **Virginia**, some of these having seats named Orange. Both this name and **Nassau** originally had Dutch contexts, as the names were imported by the Dutch to refer to their own ruling house of Orange. Then when William came to the throne the names assumed a British context! In Australia, the city of Orange in **New South Wales** does not really belong here, but can be included because the reference is in effect to the namer, Sir Thomas Mitchell, (see **Mitchell River**). He bestowed the name after his commander in the Peninsular War, who was William I, Prince of Orange, king of the Netherlands. (The well-known South African Orange River and Orange Free State are entirely Dutch.) See also the next entry and **Williamsburg**.

Orangeburg (USA)

The county in South **Carolina**, with its seat of the same name, may be thought to honour the most familiar royal 'Orange', otherwise William III, as in many of the **Orange** names above. But here there is a difference, albeit with a certain English connection. The city was founded in 1735 (too late for 'William of Orange') by German, Swiss and Dutch settlers, and they named it after the Dutch count William IV (1711–1751), whose former name was Charles Henry Friso. He belonged not to the main house of Orange but to the second line of Orange-Nassau. However, he did marry the daughter of George II, and he was the grandson of a cousin of William III, so he just about qualifies for inclusion here. See also **Nassau**.

Orbost (Australia)

The coastal town in **Victoria** does not on the face of it appear to have a name of British origin. But it does, for it was named after a small village on the Scottish island of Skye, with which a settler must have had particular links. The town was proclaimed in 1885.

Orcadia (Canada)

A British name? Yes, for Orcadia was the classical name for the Orkney Islands. The area of this settlement in Saskatchewan was chosen by Scottish emigrants from the islands, and they preferred the Latin name to the English. Perhaps they were influenced by the similar name of **Nova Scotia**? Compare the next entry.

Orkney (South Africa)

Orkney is a goldmining town in the Transvaal, on the Vaal River. It was directly named after a goldmine just here, which was on a farm owned by a certain Scot named Mr Jackson, who came from the Orkney Islands. The town was proclaimed in 1940, although Jackson's farm had been here much earlier, some time in the 1880s.

Otway (Chile)

Otway Bay (Bahía Otway) and Otway Gulf (Seno Otway) are just two (or one) of the many British names to be found down the southern coast of Chile. Several of these will have been given by Charles Darwin (see **Darwin**) and Robert Fitzroy (see **Fitzroy**) when they surveyed the coast here in the *Beagle* in the period from 1831 to 1836. The name pays a compliment to Sir Robert Waller Otway (1770–1846), the British admiral who was appointed Commander-in-Chief on the South American station from 1828 to the following year.

Owen Sound (Canada)

The city of Owen Sound, Ontario, takes its name from the inlet (of Georgian Bay, Lake Huron) on which it is located. The inlet is named after the British naval officer who charted the Great Lake in 1815, Captain William Fitzwilliam Owen (1774–1857). The settlement was originally called Sydenham when it was first settled in 1841, after Charles Thomson, Baron Sydenham, Governor General of Canada, who died that year. Its name was changed to Owen Sound in 1857.

Owen Stanley Range (Papua New Guinea)

The highland range, in New Guinea, is named after Owen Stanley (1811–1850), the British naval officer and hydrographer who explored the coast of the island from 1845 to the year of his premature death.

Oxford (USA, Canada)

The name often denotes a 'status' (but not actual) link with Oxford University, and many United States universities and colleges have utilised the name in a similar fashion. But there could also be an emigrant link with the city of Oxford or with the county of Oxfordshire in some cases. A good example of the 'status' use of the name is that of the city of Oxford in Mississippi, which was incorporated in 1837. The townsfolk wished to found a university, and did so seven years later, when the University of Mississippi ('Ole Miss') was chartered in 1844. Similarly Oxford Township in Ohio was ceded by Congress to the State in 1803 to be held in trust for 'the endowment of an academy and other seminaries of learning'. The result: the foundation of Miami University here seven years later. In Canada's Northwest Territories, Mount Oxford on **Ellesmere** Island was so named in 1934 by the Oxford University Exploration Club, so the link in this barren land is paradoxically more real than for many high power American university and college seats. (One member of the Arctic expedition was Edward Shackleton, son of the famous explorer: see **Shackleton Glacier**.)

P

Palk Strait (India/Sri Lanka)
The strait between northern Sri Lanka and southeast India is named after Sir Robert Palk (1717–1798), Governor of Madras from 1763 to 1767. The same man gave his name to Palk Bay, an inlet on the northwest coast of Sri Lanka.

Palliser (New Zealand, South Pacific)
Cape Palliser, at the southern tip of North Island, was discovered by Cook in 1774 and named by him after his 'worthy friend', Sir Hugh Palliser (1723–1796), Comptroller of the Navy, and this same admiral gave his name to the Palliser Island, now the Tuamoto Archipelago, in French Polynesia, east of the **Cook** Islands in the South Pacific.

Palmerston (New Zealand, Australia, South Pacific)
All the places mentioned here are named after Lord Palmerston, otherwise Henry John Temple, 3rd Viscount Palmerston, (1784–1865), three times Foreign Minister and twice Prime Minister, the latter in the ten-year period from 1855. The New Zealand city of Palmerston North, North Island, was founded in 1866 (and is 'North' by contrast with the much smaller Palmerston in South Islands). Cape Palmerston, in **Queensland**, Australia, and the former island of Palmerston (now Avarau) in the **Cook** Islands, in the South Pacific, are also named after him, and in Australia again, Palmerston was also the first name of **Darwin**. Lord Palmerston's title came from the small Irish village of the name to the west of Dublin.

Palmerville (Australia)
The community of Palmerville, northern **Queensland**, is named after the Irish-born Premier of Queensland, Sir Arthur Palmer (1819–1898). (Palmer Land in the Antarctic, however, is named after an American explorer, so cannot be included here apart from this brief statement.)

Parkes (Australia)
The town of Parkes in **New South Wales** was originally known as Bushman's when founded in 1862 as an alluvial gold centre. In 1883 it was renamed after Sir Henry Parkes (1815–1896), five times Premier of New South Wales between 1872 and 1891.

Parrsboro (Canada)
The **Nova Scotia** town honours the name of John Parr (1725–1791), the Irish-born Governor of Nova Scotia from 1782 to 1791.

Parry (Canada)
There are three places of prominence in Canada that bear this name: the Parry Islands, Northwest Territories, Parry Peninsula (with Cape Parry), also there on the mainland in **Mackenzie** District, and Parry Sound, Ontario, as both town and district on Georgian Bay, Lake Huron. All were named after the Arctic explorer Sir William Parry (1790–1855), who made three attempts between 1819 and 1825 to locate a Northwest Passage in this part of the Arctic.

Paterson (South Africa)
The Cape District village was laid out in 1879 and named after John Paterson (1822–1880), the Scottish politician and merchant who founded it.

Paxton (USA)
The Illinois city was named after Sir John Paxton (1801–1865), the English architect who planned to settle here and found a colony. In the event he did not, but the name remained all the same.

Peard Bay (USA)
The bay, in northwest Alaska, is named after George Peard, the naval officer who was First Lieutenant to Frederick Beechey (who gave his name to Beechey Island: see **M'Clintock Channel**).

Peddie (South Africa)
The town in Ciskei was originally a frontier post named Fort Peddie. This was established in 1835 and took its name from Lieutenant-Colonel John Peddie (died 1840) who led his Highland regiment against the Xhosa.

Peel (Canada, Australia, New Zealand)
The Peel River, a tributary of the **Mackenzie** in northern Canada, and the Peel River in **New South Wales**, Australia, are both named for the well-known statesman and founder of the Metropolitan Police, Sir Robert Peel (1788–1850). Mount Peel, near **Geraldine** in South Island, New Zealand, is also named after him, as is the holiday resort of Peel Forest at its foot.

Pelham (USA)
The **New Hampshire** town is named after Henry Pelham (?1695–1754), Prime Minister of Britain from 1743 to 1754. He was a relation of Benning Wentworth, Governor of New Hampshire (see **Wentworth**).

Pellew Islands (Australia)
The island group, in the Gulf of Carpentaria, were named by Matthew Flinders (see **Flinders**) in 1802 as a tribute to Sir Edward Pellew, later 1st Viscount Exmouth (1757–1833), the English naval officer who had won several victories over the French. In many modern maps the islands are shown as the **Sir Edward Pellew Group**, spelling the name out like this in order to distinguish the islands from the Caroline Islands group called Palau (formerly Pelew). It is not often that similar geographical names are purposely distinguished like this.

Pelly (Canada)
Pelly River, in the Yukon, Lake Pelly, on the border between **Mackenzie** and Keewatin Districts, Pelly Island, off the mouth of the Mackenzie River and Pelly Bay, an inlet of the Gulf of **Boothia**, all these last in Northwest Territories, are all named after Sir John Henry Pelly (1772–1852), Governor of the Hudson's Bay Company (see **Hudson**) from 1822 to 1852. The river was discovered in 1840.

Pembroke (USA, Canada)
Most places of the name honour one of the many Earls of Pembroke, rather than the town (or former county) in Wales. The **New Hampshire** town pays a tribute to Henry Herbert, 9th Earl of Pembroke (1689–1750), who was Lord Chief Justice and a relative by marriage of the Governor of New Hampshire, Benning Wentworth. Pembroke, Ontario, however, founded in 1828, was named after the Hon. Sidney Herbert (1810–1861), War Secretary under Peel (see **Peel**) and later under Palmerston (see **Palmerston**), and he was the second son of the 11th Earl of Pembroke.

Penge (South Africa)
The Transvaal mining village was established after the mineral amosite (itself named after the Asbestos Mine of South Africa) was discovered here in 1907, and was named after the London suburb (now district) of Penge. Presumably a settler or miner had come from there.

Pennell Coast (Antarctica)
The Pennell Coast, part of **Victoria** Land, was so named in 1961 after Lieutenant Harry Pennell, captain of the *Terra Nova*, which had brought Scott and his party to the Antarctic for their fateful expedition of 1910–12. See also **Oates Coast**.

Pennfield Ridge (Canada)
The **New Brunswick** parish was founded by Quakers in 1786 and named for the

famous William Penn, founder of **Pennsylvania**. See the next entry below.

Pennsylvania (USA)

This is one of the most interesting of the English (as opposed to Indian) state names. There are some surprises for the unaware! First, although the state was founded in 1682 by William Penn (1644–1718), it was not named for him but for his father, Admiral Sir William Penn (1621–1670). Second, the name was not given by Penn, but by Charles II. And third, the name has a quite separate meaning! It is best to consult Penn's own words on the subject. Once the king had granted him the territory here (in 1681), William Penn wrote a letter on the subject to his friend. Robert Turner, as follows:

> After many waitings, watchings, solicitings, and disputes in Council, this day [14 March 1681] my country was confirmed to me under the great seal of England, with large powers and privileges, by the name of *Pennsylvania* [actually spelt 'Pennsilvania' in the charter]; a name the king would give it in honour of my father. I chose New Wales, [that] being, as this, a pretty hilly country; but Penn being Welsh for *head* (as Penmanmoire [modern Penmaenmawr] in Wales, and Penrith in Cumberland, and Penn in Buckinghamshire, the highest land in England), [they] called this Pennsylvania, which is the high head or woodlands; for I proposed when the Secretary, a Welshman, refused to have it called New Wales, *Sylvania*, and they added *Penn* to it; and though I much opposed it, and went to the king to have it struck out and altered, he said it was past, and would take it upon him; nor could twenty guineas move the under-secretary to vary the name; for I feared lest it should be looked on as a vanity in me, and not as a respect in the king, as it truly was, to my father, whom he often mentions with praise.
> [Quoted by Espenshade, pp. 24–5; see Bibliography, p. 218]

Penn helpfully spells out much here, although he could have added that his proposed 'Sylvania' is based on Latin *silva* 'wood'. The name thus means both head woodlands, (i.e. 'high woodlands') and 'Penn's woodlands'. (Nor did Penn mention another curiosity: that his own surname was believed to derive from the Buckinghamshire village of Penn that he mentions, and that this is where his ancestral home was said to be. Moreover, although Penn was himself buried at the nearby village of Jordans, where the Quaker meeting house had been that he had attended, many of his descendants lie buried in Penn parish church, and there are brasses there to members of the Penn family.) As a Quaker leader, Penn wished to found a colony for his fellow Quakers, and in naming the territory after his father, Charles II wished to compliment the admiral for his success in the wars against the Dutch.

Penrhyn (South Pacific)

Penrhyn is the most northerly of the **Cook** Islands, and when discovered in 1788 it was named for a British ship taking convicts to Australia, the *Lady Penrhyn*. Its indigenous name is Tongareva ('Tonga in the heavens').

Penrith (Australia)

The city of Penrith, in **New South Wales**, was founded in 1815 and was known as Evan and Castlereagh before being named after the town of Penrith in Cumberland (modern Cumbria). Doubtless an early resident had come from there.

Percy Islands (Australia)

The Percy Islands, off the east **Queensland** coast, were named by Matthew Flinders (see **Flinders**) in 1802 as a tribute to Sir Hugh Percy, 2nd Duke of Northumberland (1742–1817), who had fought in the American Revolution (War of American Independence). The islands are an outlying group of the **Northumberland** Islands, named after the Duke's father.

Perth (Australia, Canada)

Perth, the capital of Western Australia,

was founded as a colony in 1829, with Charles Fremantle (see **Fremantle**) having taken possession of the area the previous year and James Stirling (see **Stirling**) having arrived here the year before that to found a town site. The colony was named after Perthshire, the native Scottish county of the then Colonial Secretary, Sir George Murray (see **Murray**). In Canada, Perth County, Ontario, and the industrial town of Perth in that province (although not the county seat) were similarly named by (or for) Scottish emigrants from Perthshire. The town was founded in 1816.

Perth Amboy (USA)
The **New Jersey** city and port was settled in the late seventeenth century, originally with the Indian name of Amboy. Later, Perth was added in recognition of James Drummond, 4th Earl of Perth (1648–1716), who permitted a large number of persecuted Scots to emigrate to **Middlesex** County, New Jersey, in 1683.

Peterborough (Canada, USA)
The Ontario city was not named after the English cathedral city in Northamptonshire (now Cambridgeshire), as might be supposed. It was at first known as Scott's Plains, after one Adam Scott who had founded a sawmill here in 1821. In 1825 some two thousand Irish emigrants settled here, and the colony was renamed after their Irish leader, Colonel the Hon. Peter Robinson (1785–1838). The name thus implies 'Peter [Robinson]'s borough'. Nor was the United States city of the same name, in **New Hampshire**, named for the English city. It was settled in 1749 and named in honour of Charles Mordaunt, 3rd Earl of Peterborough (1685–1735), a naval hero in the wars against France and Spain, and also First Lord of the Treasury.

Philippolis (South Africa)
The town, in the Orange Free State, was founded as a station of the London Missionary Society in 1823 and named after the Society's Superintendent, Dr John Philip (1775–1851), who had selected the site. The name is mock Greek, meaning 'Philip's town', and also appropriately suggests the biblical town of Philippi, whose name has an identical meaning (after Philip II, king of Macedon).

Philipsburg (USA)
The **Pennsylvania** borough is named after the two Englishmen who laid it out in 1797, Henry and James Philips.

Philipstown (South Africa)
Philipstown, in Cape Province, was established in 1863 and was named after Sir Philip Edmond Wodehouse (1811–1887), Governor of the Cape Colony from 1861 to 1870. (But would not 'Wodehouse' have been a more appropriate name for a settlement?)

Phillip Island (Australia)
Phillip Island, at the entrance to Western Port on the south coast of **Victoria**, was discovered in 1798 by George Bass (see **Bass Strait**) and was originally known as Grant Island, after Lieutenant James Grant, who landed here in 1801. It was soon renamed, however, for Captain Arthur Phillip (1739–1814), the founder of **New South Wales** (in 1788). He also gave his name to **Port Phillip** Bay, where **Melbourne** arose.

Pickersgill Islands (South Atlantic)
The four Pickersgill Islands, southwest of **South Georgia**, in the South Atlantic, take their name from Lieutenant Richard Pickersgill (1749–1779), an officer on Captain Cook's ship, the *Resolution*, with Cook said to have given the name to the islands (or possibly to some other island or islands near here) during his expedition in the 1770s to discover the great southern continent that was believed to exist here.

Picton (New Zealand, Canada)
The town and port of Picton, in South Island, was originally called Newton when it arose here in 1848 on a site occupied by the Maoris. In 1858 it was renamed in honour of Sir Thomas Picton (1758–1815), a commander under Wellington (see **Wellington**) in the Peninsular War, in which he was killed at the Battle of

Waterloo. In Canada, the town that is the seat of **Prince Edward Island** was founded in 1786 and similarly named after the military hero.

Pinetown (South Africa)

The town in Natal, northwest of **Durban**, was laid out in 1848 and named after Sir Benjamin Pine (1809–1901), Lieutenant-Governor of Natal from 1849 to 1856 and then Governor from 1873 to 1875.

Pioneer River (Australia)

Pioneer River, which flows into the sea at Mackay, on the east **Queensland** coast, was named after the ship HMS *Pioneer*, which called here in 1862.

Pirie (South Africa)

Pirie is a forest region in Transkei, northwest of **King William's Town**. It was named after a mission station here, itself established in 1830 and named after Alexander Pirie, one of the founders of the Glasgow Missionary Society that was active here.

Pitcairn Island (South Pacific)

Pitcairn Island was discovered in 1767 by Philip Carteret, and is named after the sailor who first sighted it from the fore-topgallant-cross-trees of HMS *Swallow* in July that year. This was Midshipman Robert Pitcairn (1747–1770), son of a Scottish marine officer who would be killed at the Battle of Bunkers Hill (1775) in the American Revolution. The ship's log recorded the event of the naming: '[the island] having been sighted by a young gentleman, son to Major Pitcairn of the Marines, we called it Pitcairn's Island'. The name is remarkably suitable for a rocky, rugged island that is full of 'pits' and 'cairns'.

Pitt Island (South Pacific, Canada)

Pitt Island is one of the **Chatham** Islands, in the South Pacific. It was not named after William Pitt, who gave his name to **Pittsburgh** (see the next entry below), but after the ship *Pitt* that discovered it in 1791, the same year that the *Chatham* was here. Pitt Island off the west coast of **British Columbia**, however, *was* named after William Pitt ('the Younger') (1759–1806). The name was given by George Vancouver (see **Vancouver**) in 1793.

Pittsburgh (USA)

Pittsburgh, **Pennsylvania**, arose on the site of the French fort, Fort-Duquesne, captured by the British in 1758 after several years of fighting between the French and the English. The leader of the English troops was General John Forbes, and he renamed the site in honour of William Pitt ('the Elder') (1708–1778), the famous statesman who was effectively Prime Minister. When a new British fort was built here it was thus named Fort Pitt, and the present city was laid out round the fort in 1764 with the name of Pittsburgh. 'The Great Commoner', as he was called, also gave his name to other United States cities, notably Pittsburg, California, and Pittsburg, Kansas, although indirectly so, as these were named after the Pennsylvania settlement. On the other hand, some sources associate the names of these two industrial cities with the coalmining carried on there (formerly, if not now). Doubtless there is really a blend of both. Pittsylvania County, **Virginia** has a name that can be interpreted as 'Pitt's woods': compare **Pennsylvania** and see also **New Brunswick** and the next two entries below.

Pittsfield (USA)

The city of Pittsfield, Massachusetts, was settled in the 1740s as Pontoosuc Plantation, after an Indian name. When incorporated as a town in 1791 it was renamed after the well-known statesman William Pitt, who also gave his name to **Pittsburgh** (see entries above and below).

Pittston (USA)

The **Pennsylvania** city was settled in about 1762 and, like **Pittsburgh** and **Pittsfield** (see above), was named after the British statesman William Pitt, who was a good friend of the American colonies before the American Revolution (War of American Independence).

Plains of Abraham (Canada)
The plateau west of the old city of Quebec, the site of the battle of 1759 in which the British (under Wolfe) defeated the French (under Montcalm), takes its quasi-biblical name from an early settler here, one Abraham Martin (1589–1664), who may have been of Scottish origin. See also **Wolfe**.

Plymouth (USA)
This is the famous town where the 'Pilgrim Fathers', sailing in the *Mayflower* from Plymouth, England, arrived in 1620 to found a new colony and begin a new life free from religious intolerance. They were thus the first permanent British colony in **New England**. Naturally, they gave their new settlement the name of the town and port from which they had sailed. There are many other Plymouths in the United States, all directly deriving from this one in Massachusetts. For other exploitation of the Devonshire town's name, see **New Plymouth**.

Point Edward (Canada)
The Ontario village was originally called Huron, for the lake on which it lies. In 1860, however, it was renamed to mark the visit here by the then Prince of Wales, the future Edward VII (1841–1910).

Pomeroy (South Africa)
The town in Natal is named after Sir George Pomeroy Colley (1835–1881), the British general and Governor of Natal who was killed in the Battle of Amajuba in the First Boer War.

Pomfret (USA)
The residential town and resort in Connecticut is named after the English town of Pontefract, Yorkshire, doubtless through emigrant connections there. 'Pomfret' is a 'smoothed' version of the town's name, representing its former pronunciation. (Even now, the flat, round type of liquorice sweets called 'Pontefract cakes' are still alternatively known as 'Pomfret cakes'.)

Ponds Inlet (Canada)
The settlement on the inlet of the same name in northeast **Baffin** Island, Northwest Territories, was originally called Ponds Bay when first designated in 1828 after the Astronomer Royal, John Pond (1767–1836). The present name was officially adopted in 1951.

Porcher Island (Canada)
The **British Columbia** island north of **Pitt Island** was named after the British naval officer, Commander E. A. Porcher, who was in charge of this section of the Pacific station for the four years from 1865.

Port [. . .]
Some names formerly or still now alternatively beginning 'Port' will be found under the second word, e.g. Port Stanley (**Falkland Islands**) is under **Stanley**.

Port Alfred (South Africa)
The Cape Province town, at the mouth of the Kowie River, was originally known as Port Frances when founded in 1825, after the daughter-in-law of Lord Charles Somerset, Governor of the Cape Colony. It was renamed in 1860 after the visit here (and elsewhere in South Africa) of Prince Alfred (1844–1900), the second son of Queen Victoria. (See the next entry for his brother's similar visit.)

Port Arthur (China, Canada)
Port Arthur, the seaport town in northeast China, on a peninsula east of Beijing (Peking), is now usually known by its Chinese name of Lüda (or else either Lüshun or Dalian, whose first elements give this name). It has passed between many hands since it was first visited by the British in 1860, notably the Chinese, Japanese and Russians. Its English name derives from a Lieutenant Arthur, who was a member of a British naval survey party that came here in the year mentioned. Unfortunately, little seems to be known about him apart from his name and nationality. In Canada, Port Arthur is, with Fort William, one of the two twin cities that now form the city of Thunder

Bay, in southwest Ontario. Both cities arose in the nineteenth century, with Port Arthur developing in the 1850s as a silver-mining settlement. It takes its name from Prince Arthur, later the Duke of Connaught (1850–1942), the third son of Queen Victoria, who paid a visit here in 1866 (as a mere 16-year-old, like his brother Prince Alfred on his visit to South Africa: see entry above). The two cities amalgamated in 1970 to form a major transportation centre, taking their present name from Lake Superior's Thunder Bay.

Port Augusta (Australia)
The South Australia city and port, at the head of **Spencer** Gulf, was founded in 1852 and named after the wife, née Augusta Sophia Marryatt, of Sir Henry Edward Fox Young (1808–1870), Governor of South Australia from 1848 (the year he married) to 1855.

Port Beaufort (South Africa)
The seaside resort of Port Beaufort, Cape Province, was founded in about 1816 and was named by the Governor of the Cape Colony, Lord Charles Somerset, after his father, the Duke of Beaufort (who also gave his name to **Beaufort** West). See also **Port Alfred** and **Somerset**.

Port Blair (Bay of Bengal)
Port Blair is the capital of the Andaman and Nicobar Islands, Indian territory in the Bay of Bengal. The seaport town is named after the officer who first surveyed the islands in 1789, Lieutenant Blair of the Indian Navy.

Port Chalmers (New Zealand)
The borough in South Island, northeast of **Dunedin**, was named after Dr Thomas Chalmers (1780–1847), the Scottish theologian who led the breakaway Free Church of Scotland, formed by him in 1844 with a group of evangelical ministers from the Church of Scotland.

Port Chester (USA)
The residential suburb on Long Island, New York, was originally known as Saw Pits when founded in the 1660s, for its early timber industry. As it developed as a harbour, it changed its name in 1837 to Port Chester, after the English county of Cheshire (rather than the city of Chester), in which there were many noted ports, in particular Liverpool (now in Merseyside).

Port Colborne (Canada)
The Ontario port, on Lake Erie, was originally called Gravelly Bay when first settled in 1832. It was subsequently renamed in honour of Sir John Colborne, 1st Baron Seaton (1778–1863), the British general who became Lieutenant-Governor of Upper Canada (equivalent to modern south Ontario) in 1828 and Governor General ten years later. See also **Sarnia**.

Port Dalrymple (Australia)
The Tasmanian port, at the mouth of the **Tamar** River, is one of the earliest settlements on the island, founded in 1804. It was named after Alexander Dalrymple, who gave his name to Mount **Dalrymple** (which see for his particulars).

Port Davey (Australia)
This inlet of the Indian Ocean in southwest Tasmania was passed, but not named, by Matthew Flinders (see **Flinders**) in 1798. In 1815 it was entered by the British naval officer James Kelly, who named it after Colonel Thomas Davey, who was Lieutenant-Governor of Tasmania from 1813 to 1817, and before that, a marine officer who had fought under Nelson (see **Nelson**) at Trafalgar. (He was an eccentric man, described by Scott [see Bibliography, p. 219] as a 'rollicking Toby Belch' who was obliged to resign his post under pressure from Governor Macquarie [see **Macquarie**] because of his irresponsible manner and his blunt methods of maintaining authority.)

Port Douglas (Australia)
The **Queensland** port, up the east coast from **Cairns**, was named after John Douglas (1828–1904), Prime Minister of Queensland.

Port Durnford (South Africa)
Port Durnford, the anchorage in Natal, derives its name either from a Midshipman E.P. Durnford, who surveyed the coast here in about 1822, or from Captain A.W. Durnford of the Royal Engineers, who came to South Africa in 1871 and who was killed in 1879 in the Zulu War. The latter's activities seem rather on the late side for the place-name, however.

Port Edward (South Africa)
Port Edward, the coastal village south of **Margate** in Natal, was founded in 1924 and was named after the then Prince of Wales, who became Edward VIII (1894–1972).

Port Elgin (Canada)
The community of Port Elgin, Ontario, was originally known as Normanton. Its name was later changed in order to honour Lord Elgin, who was Governor General of Ontario from 1847 to 1854. For more about him, see **Elgin**.

Port Elizabeth (South Africa)
The Cape Province port arose round Fort Frederick, the oldest British building in Southern Africa, erected here in 1799 and itself named after Frederick Augustus, Duke of York and Albany (1763–1827), the second son of George III (see **Albany**, **Frederick**, **York**). The city was laid out in 1820 by Sir Rufane Donkin, Acting Governor of the Cape, and he named it after his late wife, née Elizabeth Markham, who had died of fever in India two years previously, at the age of 28.

Porterville (South Africa)
The town in Cape Province was laid out in 1863 and was named after William Porter (1805–1880), the Irish-born Attorney-General of the Cape Colony from 1839 to 1866.

Port Essington (Australia)
Port Essington is an inlet of the **Coburg Peninsula**, Northern Territory. It was discovered in 1818 by Philip Parker King (see **King**) who named it after Admiral Sir William Essington. The British government attempted to settle a colony here, in the belief that the harbour would be a good one, but although troops were stationed here from 1838 (when the settlement was named **Victoria**) to 1849, nothing came of it, largely because of the unhealthy climate.

Port Harcourt (Nigeria)
Port Harcourt, a seaport on the Bonny River in southern Nigeria, was founded in 1912 on the site of an abandoned African village and was named after Lewis Harcourt, 1st Viscount Harcourt (1863–1922), Colonial Secretary from 1910 to 1915.

Port Hawkesbury (Canada)
The **Nova Scotia** town at the south end of Cape Breton Island, was originally known as Ship Harbour. In 1860 it was renamed after Charles Jenkinson, 1st Baron Hawkesbury (1727–1808), for further details of whom see **Hawkesbury**.

Port Hood (Canada)
As the seat of **Inverness** County, **Nova Scotia**, Port Hood was named as a tribute to Samuel Hood, 1st Viscount Hood (1724–1816), the British admiral who was Commander-in-Chief on the North American station from 1767 to 1770. For more about him, see **Hood**.

Port Hope (Canada)
The town on the north shore of Lake Ontario, at the mouth of the Ganaraska River, was first known as Smith's Creek, after the post's proprietor, when it was established as a trading point in 1778. It was then renamed Toronto before becoming Port Hope in 1817, with this name given in (posthumous) honour to Colonel Henry Hope, the Scottish-born Lieutenant-Governor of Quebec from 1785 to his death four years later.

Port Jackson (Australia)
Port Jackson is an alternative name for **Sydney** Harbour, where it is the main port of **New South Wales**. The harbour, one of the finest natural harbours in the world, was discovered in 1770 by Cook,

and he named it after Sir George Jackson (1725–1822), a Secretary to the Admiralty. Cook probably did not realise what a fine harbour it was – he may not even have sailed into it – and if he had realised its ideal nature, he would doubtless have chosen a more propitious name for it, or at least a 'grander' one.

Port Keats (Australia)
The coastal community of Port Keats, southwest of **Darwin**, Northern Territory, was named after Admiral Sir Richard Goodwin Keats (1757–1834), rated by Nelson as 'one of the very best officers in his majesty's navy'.

Portland (USA, Canada, Australia, New Zealand)
In many instances, the name will be a purely descriptive one, denoting a port with a good land base. In others, however, the name may have been adopted from Portland, Dorset, whether specifically or not with reference to the Isle of Portland (the peninsula there), Portland Bill (the tip of this peninsula), Portland Harbour (artificially constructed), or even Portland Castle. There could equally be an implied reference to the stone quarries there, as there was for Portland, Connecticut, which had similar quarries. The city of Portland, Maine, which was settled by the English in 1632, had six different names before acquiring that of Portland in 1786. One of the names was Falmouth, after the port in Cornwall, because its harbour resembled that of the Cornish town. The same sort of physical resemblance seems to have motivated the new name of Portland, with the reference being to its own harbour. (There is indeed some similarity between Falmouth's natural harbour and Portland's artificial one.) But we must not forget the Dukes! And in Canada, the Portland Inlet, indenting western **British Columbia**, was so named in 1793 by George Vancouver (see **Vancouver**) after William Bentinck, 3rd Duke of Portland (1738–1809), twice Prime Minister of Britain. The Australian town of Portland, on the bay of the same name in **Victoria**, takes its name from the bay, which was itself discovered in 1800 by James Grant, a naval officer, and named after this same Duke, as also was Cape Portland, in Tasmania. But Portland Island, New Zealand, lying south of Mahia Peninsula, off the east coast of North Island, was so named by Cook in 1769 from the resemblance of the whole peninsula to the Isle of Portland in Dorset.

Port Lincoln (Australia)
Port Lincoln, west of **Adelaide** on the east coast of **Eyre** Peninsula, was so named by Matthew Flinders (see **Flinders**) in 1802 after his native Lincolnshire.

Port Lyttelton (New Zealand)
Port Lyttelton forms the harbour of **Lyttelton**, the shipping port of **Christchurch** in South Island, and is also named after Lord George Lyttelton.

Port Macquarie (Australia, New Zealand)
Port Macquarie, at the mouth of the **Hastings** River, **New South Wales**, was founded as a penal colony in 1818 and was named after Lachlan Macquarie, Governor of New South Wales (see **Macquarie**). In New Zealand, the port of Bluff in South Island was also formerly known as Port Macquarie when it was settled in 1813. The name lasted until a whaling station was built here in 1836, when the port became Campbelltown. It finally became Bluff in 1917.

Port Maitland (Canada)
Port Maitland, at the mouth of the Grand River on the north shore of Lake Erie, in Ontario, was named after Sir Peregrine Maitland, former Lieutenant-Governor of Upper Canada and **Nova Scotia**. See **Maitland** for further details.

Port Moody (Canada)
The city of Port Moody, east of **Vancouver**, **British Columbia**, was so named in 1859 after Colonel Richard Clement Moody (1813–1897), the former Commissioner of Lands and Works for British Columbia. It was Moody who selected the site of **New Westminster**.

Port Moresby (Papua New Guinea)
The capital of Papua New Guinea had its harbour explored in 1873 by Captain (later Admiral) John Moresby, and he named it after his father, Admiral Sir Fairfax Moresby (1786–1877). For more details about him, see **Moresby Island**.

Port Nelson (Canada)
Port Nelson is a trading post on the north bank of the mouth (itself known as Port Nelson) of the **Nelson** River, Manitoba, and so has the same origin for the name as that of the river (see for further information, and for confirmation of the fact that it was *not* named after the famous admiral!).

Port Nicholson (New Zealand)
Also known as **Wellington** Harbour, Port Nicholson is a fine natural harbour in the south of North Island, with Wellington itself located on it. It was explored by Captain Cook in 1773, and named by him after Captain John Nicholson, the harbourmaster at **Sydney**.

Port Nolloth (South Africa)
The coastal town of Port Nolloth, Cape Province, was originally known as Robbe Bay, after the bay on which it stands, the name meaning 'seal bay'. In 1855 it was renamed by Sir George Grey (see **Grey**, **Greytown**) after Commander M.S. Nolloth, captain of HMS *Frolic*, who had surveyed the coast here in this ship the previous year.

Port Orford (USA)
The Oregon city stands on a stretch of the Pacific coast which was sighted by George Vancouver (see **Vancouver**) in 1792. He named it as a tribute to Horace Walpole, 4th Earl of Orford (1717–1797), the politician and well-known man of letters (*The Castle of Otranto*), who had received his earldom the previous year, when he succeeded to the title held until then by his nephew.

Port Phillip (Australia)
Port Phillip Bay, **Victoria**, is the name of the inlet that is the harbour of **Melbourne**. It was discovered in 1802 by the naval officer Lieutenant John Murray, who originally named it Port King, after Philip Gidley King (see **King**), at that time Governor of **New South Wales** (then incorporating future Victoria). Subsequently, it was renamed for Captain Arthur Phillip (1738–1814), the actual founder of New South Wales (in 1788). Port Phillip District was the original name (from 1802 to 1851) of the present state of **Victoria** (which see for the history). See also **Melbourne**.

Port Pirie (Australia)
The city of Port Pirie is the next most important seaport of South Australia after **Adelaide**. It ws founded in 1848 and named after the ship *John Pirie*, which had brought settlers here three years earlier. The ship was herself named after Sir John Pirie (1781–1851), Lord Mayor of London.

Port Rex See **East London**.

Port Sandwich (South Pacific)
Port Sandwich is an island of Vanuatu (former **New Hebrides**), in the southwest Pacific, where its now more usual indigenous name is Malekula. It was given to the island in 1774 by James Cook 'in honour of his patron', in other words in honour of the man who had financially backed his memorable voyages of discovery. This was John Montagu, 4th Earl of Sandwich (1718–1792). See also **Montagu**, **Sandwich**, **South Sandwich Islands**.

Port Saunders (Canada)
Port Saunders, on the northwest coast of Newfoundland, was named as a compliment to Admiral Sir Charles Saunders (?1713–1775), who was Commander-in-Chief of the Newfoundland station in 1752.

Port Shepstone (South Africa)
Port Shepstone, at the mouth of the Umzimkulu River, Natal, was laid out in 1867 and named after Sir Theophilus Shepstone (1817–1893), Secretary for Native Affairs from 1856.

Portsmouth (USA)
The city of Portsmouth, appropriately in **New Hampshire**, is this state's oldest settlement, founded in 1624. It was initially known by the Indian name of Piscataqua before being called Strawbery Banke for a while. In 1653 it was incorporated as a town and renamed for the English city and port in Hampshire, while at the same time being understood, as the English name can be, as denoting a town at the 'mouth of the port', i.e. at the harbour. In the case of the American seaport, the town (with its harbour) lies also at the mouth of the Piscataqua River. Other United States ports so named, and also on rivers, are in Ohio, Rhode Island and **Virginia**. However, one or more of these may have been directly named after the New Hampshire city rather than the English port.

Port Stanley (Canada)
The Ontario village on Lake Erie, where it serves as a port of **London**, was so named in 1818 by Colonel John Bostwick for Edward George Geoffrey Smith Stanley, 14th Earl Stanley (1799–1869), father of the 16th Earl, who was Governor General of Canada from 1888 to 1893. The occasion of the naming is said to have been a visit paid by Stanley to Colonel Thomas Talbot, who at that time was enthusiastically if increasingly eccentrically colonising the northern shore of Lake Erie (where he founded Port Talbot, and a number of other settlements jointly known as Talbot Street). (For Port Stanley in the **Falkland Islands**, see **Stanley**.)

Port Stephens (Australia)
Port Stephens, a lagoon and inlet of the Tasman Sea in **New South Wales**, was discovered by Cook in 1770 and named by him after Sir Philip Stephens (1725–1809), Secretary of the Admiralty.

Port Swettenham (Malaysia)
Port Swettenham, the port for Kuala Lumpur, was developed by the Malayan Railway to join it to the Malaysian capital, and was named after Sir Frank Swettenham (1850–1946), the Scottish-born British resident here. The naming took place some time after 1882. The port was opened in 1901 but was closed because of malaria less than two months later, only being fully developed after the First World War.

Port Townsend (USA)
Port Townsend, the Washington city and port at the west side of the entrance to Puget Sound, was settled in 1851 and named by George Vancouver (see **Vancouver**) after George Ferrars Townshend, 3rd Marquis Townshend (1778–1855), with the name subsequently simplified in spelling (and pronunciation).

Potter County (USA)
Potter County, **Pennsylvania**, was originally given the Indian name of Sinnemahoning when first formed in 1804. It was subsequently renamed in honour of General James Potter (1729–1789), an Irishman who came to Pennsylvania in 1741 with his father, John Potter (who later became the first sheriff of **Cumberland** County). General Potter fought in the American Revolution (War of American Independence), after which he retired to his estate.

Poultney (USA)
Both the town of Poultney, Vermont, and the river of the same name on which it stands take their names from William Pulteney, Earl of Bath (1684–1764), the Whig politican and famous orator.

Prescott (Canada)
The town of Prescott, Ontario, and the county in which it is located (although not its seat), were named after Robert Prescott (1725–1815), the British general who was Lieutenant-Governor of Canada in 1796 and Governor General from 1797 to 1807. The town was founded in 1810, and was originally known as Johnstown.

Preston (Canada)
The town in Ontario was originally settled in 1805 and was at first called Cambridge Mills, after a gristmill here. In 1830 it was renamed for the Lancashire town, prob-

ably more for its manufacturing associations than for any specific emigrant ties. The Canadian town is now part of the **Guelph-Kitchener-Galt** industrial complex.

Prince Albert (Canada, South Africa, Antarctica)
In British royal history, there is only one Prince Albert of consequence, and that is the Prince Albert who married Queen Victoria, and who was thus the Prince Consort of England. He gave his name to several places, including the Saskatchewan city, founded in 1866 (five years after Albert's death), the Prince Albert Peninsula on (suitably) **Victoria** Island, Northwest Territories, where it was discovered in 1850 by Robert McClure (see **M'Clure Strait**), and the South African town of Prince Albert, Cape Province, which was established in 1843. In the Antarctic, the Prince Albert Mountains, **Victoria** Land (again, an apt pairing) were discovered by James Ross (see **Ross Sea**) during his expedition here of 1839–43, and he was their namer. See also **Albert** for further details.

Prince Charles Mountains (Antarctica)
The Prince Charles Mountains, to the west of **Princess Elizabeth Land**, and not far from the **Amery Ice Shelf**, were so named in 1956 by an Australian expedition carried out, as many others were by other countries at this time, in connection with the forthcoming International Geophysical Year, during which several nations undertook to cooperate in a geophysical research programme. The honour on this occasion was to Prince Charles (born 1948), the son of Queen Elizabeth II (the former Princess Elizabeth, hence the proximity of 'his' mountains to 'her' land).

Prince County (Canada)
Prince County, **Prince Edward Island**, was named both specifically in honour of Prince Edward (who gave his name to the island) and generally as a 'loyal tribute' to the Royal Family.

Prince Edward Island (Canada, Indian Ocean)
The Canadian province was settled in 1719 and became a British colony in 1758. It had been discovered by the French in 1534, however, and they were the original settlers, who named it Île-St-Jean. This name (translated by the English as Isle St John) was in use until 1799, when because of the interest he had shown in the fortifications of **Charlottetown**, the province was renamed for Prince Edward Augustus, Duke of Kent (1767–1820), the fourth son of George III and father of Queen Victoria. That year, too, was the one in which the Prince became Commander-in-Chief of the forces in British North America, and in which he was raised to the peerage (as the Duke of Kent and Strathearn). Ill health obliged him to return from Canada to England the following year. Prince Edward Island, in the Indian Ocean, is one of two islands (the other is Marion Island) in the Prince Edward Islands group, southeast of South Africa, and belonging to that country. The islands were discovered by the French in 1772 and originally named respectively as Île de L'Espérance ('Hope Island') and Île de la Caverne ('Cave Island'). Four years later, Captain Cook came upon the islands, and unaware that they had already been discovered, named the group of two in honour of Prince Edward (as for the Canadian province). (On subsequently learning of the earlier discovery, however, he restricted this name to the smaller island, and named the larger after the Frenchman who had made the initial discovery, Marion du Fresne.)

Prince Frederick (USA)
Prince Frederick, the town that is the seat of **Calvert** County, **Maryland**, was named after the eldest son of George II. Prince Frederick died in 1751, nine years before his father.

Prince George (USA, Canada)
Prince George County, **Virginia**, and its seat of the same name were so designated in honour of George, Prince of Denmark (1653–1708), the husband of Queen Anne

of England. In Canada, however, the city of Prince George in **British Columbia**, was named after George III (1738–1820). The town was founded in 1807 as a fur-trading post named Fort George. The founder was Simon Fraser, who gave his name to the **Fraser** River on which it stands. See also **George** and the next entry.

Prince Georges County (USA)

The **Maryland** county was named after George, Prince of Denmark. Compare the entry above.

Prince of Wales (USA, Canada, Australia, Malaysia)

The name is almost always given to a natural feature, such as an island or headland. In each case, however, one needs to determine precisely *which* Prince of Wales is being complimented, as the title is traditionally that of the eldest son of the reigning monarch, whoever he is, and thus that of the heir apparent. There are three places of the name in Alaska alone. The Prince of Wales Archipelago was named in 1793 by George Vancouver (see **Vancouver**), so was for the future George III. The same prince was honoured by the name of Cape Prince of Wales here, although the name was given earlier, by James Cook in 1778. Prince of Wales Island, however, was first recorded in 1825, so appears to have named after George IV, although he had come to the throne five years before this. In Canada, Prince of Wales Strait, between **Banks** Island and **Victoria** Island, Northwest Territories, was discovered in 1850 by Robert McClure (see **M'Clure Strait**), so was named after the future Edward VII, then a mere 9-year-old. Prince of Wales Island, also in the Canadian Arctic, between Victoria Island and **Somerset** Island, was discovered a year later by sledge parties searching for the missing explorer John Franklin (see **Franklin**), and was thus similarly named for the boy prince. In Australia, Prince of Wales Island in the Torres Strait, **Queensland**, was discovered by Cook in 1770, when the future George IV was still a small 8-year-old Prince of Wales. And in Malaysia, the Prince of Wales Island that is now known as Penang (or Pinang), was settled as a British colony in 1786, and this was named also for the future George IV. The name was in use for the island until about 1867. (See **Georgetown**, as the former name of its capital.) See also **George**.

Prince Patrick Island (Canada)

The island is the westernmost of the **Parry** Islands, in **Franklin** District, Northwest Territories. It was discovered in 1853 by Francis McClintock (see **M'Clintock Channel**) and was named after Prince Arthur Wiliam Patrick Albert, third son of Queen Victoria, the future Duke of Connaught, then a mere 3-year-old.

Prince Regent (Canada, Australia)

In Arctic Canada, Prince Regent Inlet lies between **Somerset** Island and **Baffin** Island, Northwest Territories, where it was discovered by William Parry (see **Parry**) in 1819. He named it after the most familiar Prince Regent of British royal history, otherwise George IV, who acted as regent (ruler) during the insanity of his father, George III, from 1811 to 1820. Prince Regent River in Australia will thus have the same dedication. It was named by Philip Parker King (see **King**) in 1820, after the same Prince. (King actually named the river in October 1820, ten months after the Regency had ceased, on 29 January that year. But he did not know of this, for news did not travel then with the instancy with which it is transmitted today!) The river is in northern Western Australia, where it flows into **Brunswick Bay**, also named by King.

Prince Rupert (Canada)

The city at the head of **Dixon Entrance**, **British Columbia**, arose as a tent town as recently as 1904, becoming a terminus of the Grand Trunk Pacific Railway (now Canadian National Railways) five years later. Despite this late start, the settlement was named after the first Governor of the Hudson's Bay Company, who was Prince Rupert (1619–1682), the nephew of Charles I and First Lord of the Admiralty from 1673 to 1679. He also gave his name to Prince Rupert's Land (or Rupert Land), the historic region of north and west Canada that comprised the basin of **Hudson** Bay and that was granted to the Hudson's Bay Company in 1670 by Charles II.

Princess Anne (USA)

The seat of **Somerset** County, **Maryland**, was named after Princess Anne (1665–1714), the daughter of James II who in 1702 became Queen Anne of England.

Princess Charlotte Bay (Australia)

The inlet of the Coral Sea in northeast **Queensland** was discovered in 1815 by the naval lieutenant, Charles Jeffreys, who named it after Princess Charlotte (1796–1817), the only daughter of George, Prince of Wales (the future George IV). The Princess died two years later in childbirth.

Princess Elizabeth Land (Antarctica)

The name was given to this stretch of land to the east of **Enderby** Land by the members of the **Banzare** expedition of 1929–31, as a royal compliment to Princess Elizabeth (born 1926), the future Queen Elizabeth II (from 1952). Compare **Prince Charles Mountains**.

Princess Royal Island (Canada)

The island, in **British Columbia**, lies in **Hecate Strait**, which separates the mainland here from **Queen Charlotte** Islands. It was named in 1788 by Captain Charles Duncan after his ship, the *Princess Royal*. The ship herself would have been named after Princess Charlotte, daughter of George III, who was Princess Royal until her death in 1828.

Princeton (USA, Canada)

Places with this name will either have honoured a particular prince or else have been intended as a general compliment to the royal family at the time. Princeton, **New Jersey**, was originally known as Stony Brook when first settled in 1681, this being the name of the Long Island home of one of the settlers. It was then renamed in 1724 in honour of Prince William, the future William III ('William of Orange'). Many other United States Princetons will have been directly named after the New Jersey town, but not later than the American Revolution (War of American Independence) (1775–83), unless 'retrospectively' for a hero of the Revolution, for example (as was the case with Princeton, West **Virginia**, which was settled in 1826 and named for the New Jersey town where the Revolutionary War general Hugh Mercer had been killed). In Canada, Princeton, **British Columbia**, was so named in 1863 by James Douglas, Governor of British Columbia, to mark the visit to Canada three years earlier by the then Prince of Wales, the future Edward VII.

Prince William (USA)

Prince William County, **Virginia**, was named for Prince William Augustus, Duke of Cumberland (see **Cumberland**), while Prince William Sound, Alaska, which was discovered by Cook in 1778, was named after the then Prince of Wales, the future William IV.

Q

Queen Alexandra Range
(Antarctica)
The Queen Alexandra Range, along the western edge of the Ross Ice Shelf (see **Ross Sea**), was discovered by Shackleton (see **Shackleton Glacier**) in 1908 and named after Alexandra (1844–1925), the Queen Consort of Edward VII.

Queen Annes County (USA)
Queen Annes County, **Maryland**, was named after Queen Anne, who came to the throne in 1702. Compare **Princess Anne**.

Queen Charlotte (Canada, New Zealand)
Canada has the Queen Charlotte Islands, in the western **British Columbia**, and the Queen Charlotte Sound, between these islands and **Vancouver** Island, as well as the Queen Charlotte Strait that links this sound with the Johnstone Strait. New Zealand also has a Queen Charlotte Sound, leading into **Cook** Strait, the channel between North and South Islands. The Canadian islands were sighted by the Spanish in 1774 and by Cook four years later. They were not named, however, until 1787, when Captain George Dixon (see **Dixon Entrance**) surveyed them and named them after his ship, the *Queen Charlotte*. The strait and the sound were then named after the islands. The New Zealand sound was also discovered by Cook, and when he landed here in 1770 (see **Cook**), he took possession of New Zealand, as it came to be called, in the name of George III, naming the sound after his wife, Queen Charlotte Sophia (1744–1818), whom he married in 1761. So she also gave the name of Dixon's ship. For more about her, see **Charlotte**, **Charlottesville** and **Charlottetown**.

Queen Elizabeth Islands (Canada)
The islands form a largish group in Arctic Canada, and include the **Parry** Islands, Sverdrup Islands, **Devon** Island and **Ellesmere** Island. They were explored in part by William Baffin (see **Baffin**) and Robert Bylot in 1615 and the following year, although they had probably been visited by the Vikings long before that. But despite the date, they were not named (posthumously) for Queen Elizabeth I but for Elizabeth II, for the name was not applied until 1953, and was given to mark her coronation that year.

Queen Mary Land (Antarctica)
Queen Mary Land, formerly Queen Mary Coast, to the west of Wilkes Land, was so named by Douglas Mawson (see **Mawson**) during his expedition of 1911–14 to eastern Antarctica, the royal honour being paid to Queen Mary (1867–1953), consort of George V, whom she had married in 1893.

Queen Maud Land (Antarctica)
Strictly speaking, Queen Maud Land should not be in this book. But the extensive Antarctic territory, to the west of **Enderby** Land, although claimed by Norway in 1939 and named after their Queen (1869–1938), wife of King Haakon VII, was at the same time named after a queen of English birth, for Maud (in full, Maud Charlotte Mary Victoria) was the youngest child of Edward VII. So she actually does have the accreditation to appear in this entry.

Queensburgh (South Africa)
The borough in Natal, northwest of **Durban**, was proclaimed a township in 1952 (comprising five formerly separate townships), and was named after Queen Elizabeth II (born 1926), who succeeded to the throne that year.

Queenscliff (Australia)
Formerly known as Whale Head and Shortland Bluff, the town to the west of the entrance to **Port Phillip** Bay, **Victoria**, was established as a fishing settlement in 1846 and named after Queen Victoria (see **Victoria** for much more).

Queens County (USA, Canada)
There is one Queens County in the United States, with three more in Canada. The first, in **New York**, where it is coterminous with the borough of the same name, was named after Catherine of Braganza (1638–1705), wife of Charles II. The Canadian counties, respectively in **New Brunswick**, **Nova Scotia** and **Prince Edward Island**, were all named after Queen Charlotte, wife of George III (see **Charlotte**, **Queen Charlotte**).

Queensland (Australia)
Which queen lies behind the name of the Australian state? The coast here had been first visited by Cook in 1770. Later, the first penal settlement was opened (on **Moreton Bay**) in 1824. Free settlers were admitted in 1842, when **Brisbane** was opened up. The colony was part of **New South Wales** until 1859, and that was when it received its separate identity, and was named. So the royal compliment is due to Queen Victoria (just as it is for the state in the southeast of the country). At first, a proposal had been made to name the new state as Cooksland, after the famous explorer who discovered it. But the queen won the day. (And Cook does have a good range of 'possessions' of his own: see **Cook**.)

Queenstown (Australia, New Zealand, South Africa)
The Tasmanian town was founded in 1897, so was named for Queen Victoria. The New Zealand community, however, in South Island, arose somewhat earlier, as a result of the goldrush of the 1860s. And although this is a good date to fit a tribute to Queen Victoria also, some sources claim that the name was given more because the place was 'fit for a queen'. Its setting is certainly magnificent, by Lake Wakatipu, amid forest and mountain scenery. But there must surely have been a nod in Victoria's direction. There certainly was in South Africa, where the Cape Province town was founded in 1853 and named for the Queen of England who that year had been on the throne for sixteen years.

Queen Victoria Sea (Arctic Ocean)
There is no doubt who is the royal subject of this naming! The name was given to the expanse of water discovered immediately to the north of Franz Josef Land, now in the Arctic territory of the USSR, by Frederick Jackson during his expedition to this region in the three years from 1894. In his account of his time there, *A Thousand Days in the Arctic*, published in 1899, he describes the discovery and the naming (in 1895): 'We were fortunate in thus being the discoverers of this new country and of the sea to the north and north-west, which I named after our Queen – Queen Victoria Sea.' (See also Appendix II, pp. 208–15.) The name is no longer regularly found on the map, however, and this area is now simply part of the Arctic Ocean.

R

Radnor (USA)

The **Pennsylvania** township was settled in 1683 by Quakers from the Welsh county of Radnorshire (now absorbed into Powys), and they gave it the name of their native county.

Raglan (New Zealand)

The town and seaside resort in North Island was founded as a mission settlement in 1835 and was established as a community by European immigrants in 1854. Its name is a tribute to the British field marshal Lord Raglan (1788–1855), son of the 5th Duke of Beaufort (see **Beaufort**, **Somerset**), who commanded the British troops in the Crimean War (and who took his title from the Welsh town of the name).

Rainier, Mount (USA)

For the ultimate source of the name of this mountain in Washington, see **Mount Rainier**, the **Maryland** city named after it.

Raleigh (USA)

It would have been surprising if Sir Walter Raleigh (1554–1618) had not had his name preserved on the map of the English-speaking world. The famous naval commander, courtier and colonist gave his name to several places in the United States, among them Raleigh, the capital of North **Carolina**, whose site was selected in 1778, and Raleigh County, West **Virginia**, as well as the Mississippi town of the same name. Raleigh Bay, North Carolina, is also named for the great pioneer, and it was through his efforts that the colony of Virginia was established, with Raleigh himself as the first proprietor (from 1584 to 1603).

Ramsgate (South Africa)

The seaside resort in Natal arose some time in 1922 or shortly after, and the local surveyor apparently named the place for its proximity to **Margate**. This duplicated that of the English resorts in Kent, which are almost exactly the same distance from each other (around four miles) as their South African counterparts.

Rankin Inlet (Canada)

The settlement of Rankin Inlet, on the inlet of the same name on the northwest shore of **Hudson** Bay, Northwest Territories, was named after John Rankin, who discovered the inlet in 1741, as a lieutenant on board the *Furnace*, commanded by the Arctic explorer, Christopher Middleton. The settlement is comparatively recent, and arose round a nickel mine here in the mid-1950s.

Rawsonville (South Africa)

The Cape Province town was named in 1858 after Sir Rawson W. Rawson, Colonial Secretary at the Cape from 1854 to 1864.

Raynham (USA)

The Massachusetts town was settled in 1731 and apparently named either for one of the villages of Raynham (East, South or West) in Norfolk, or for the town of Rainham, Essex (now in Greater London), or even the Kent village of Rainham that is now a district of Gillingham. Presumably there must have been an emigrant link with one of these.

Reading (USA)

The name is found for more than one community in the United States. Most obviously, it occurs for the **Pennsylvania** city, which was laid out in 1748 by Thomas and Richard Penn (the sons of William Penn, who founded Pennsylvania) and named for the Berkshire town that was the hometown of the Penn family. In Ohio, the city of Reading was so named by an early citizen, one Harvey Redinbo, who was a son-in-law of William Penn and who similarly wished to honour the founder's hometown. The Pennsylvania Reading is appropriately the seat of **Berks** County.

Redvers (Canada)
The community of Redvers, Saskatchewan, was named for General Sir Redvers Buller (1839–1908), who commanded the British forces in South Africa in the second Boer War (1899–1902).

Regina (Canada)
The city of Regina, the capital of Saskatchewan, was originally known as either Waskana, after the river here, or as Pile o' Bones, for some local incident. In 1882 it was named Regina, the Latin word for 'queen', by the Governor General, the Marquess of Lorne (see **Lorneville**), in honour of his wife's mother, who was Queen Victoria. The Marquess's wife was Princess Louise (see **Louise**). The name was partly prompted by the fact that **Victoria** itself already existed in Canada for the capital of **British Columbia**, but also because 'Victoria Regina' was a commonly found Latin designation for the Queen on coins and official documents.

Renfrew (Canada)
The Ontario town, the seat of Renfrew County, arose some time in the 1830s and was named after the Scottish town of Renfrew, or the county of Renfrewshire (now Strathclyde), from which early settlers had come.

Rennell Island (South Pacific)
The island is in the Solomon Islands, where it was named after the geographer and hydrographer, James Rennell (1742–1830), who was Surveyor-General of Bengal and who accompanied Alexander Dalrymple (see Mount **Dalrymple**) to the Philippines.

Rennick Glacier (Antarctic)
The glacier, one of the largest in the Antarctic, is on the **Oates Coast** and is named after Lieutenant Henry Rennick, an officer on board the *Terra Nova* who accompanied Scott on his Antarctic expedition of 1910–12. A bay here is also named after him. See also **Pennell Coast**.

Resolution Island (Canada, New Zealand)
This is a ship name. The Canadian island, at the entrance to **Hudson** Strait, Northwest Territories, was named after the *Resolution* that was one of the ships in Thomas Button's voyage here in 1612 (see **Button Bay**). The New Zealand island, off the southwest coast of South Island, was named after James Cook's principal ship, in which he discovered it during his second expedition of 1771–4.

Reston (Canada)
The Manitoba community is named after the Scottish village of Reston, near Eyemouth, Berwickshire (now in the Borders), from which several early settlers had emigrated.

Revelstoke (Canada)
The city in **British Columbia**, on the Columbia River, was originally known as Farwell, for the first settler, Arthur Farwell. When he made too extravagant a demand for a station site here, the Canadian Pacific Railway chose a slightly different location (at first known as Second Crossing), and named it after one of the financial backers of the venture, the British banker Edward Charles Baring, Lord Revelstoke (1828–1897).

Rexton (Canada)
The **New Brunswick** community was originally known as Kingston, apparently after the Yorkshire village of Kingstone that is now a district of Barnsley. Because the name was common, however, and caused confusion in the mails, it was re-

rendered as Rexton, by adopting the Latin word for 'king'.

Rhodes (South Africa)
The Cape Province village was originally known as Rossville, after David Ross, the minister of the Dutch Reformed Church at nearby **Lady Grey** for much of the second half of the nineteenth century. The name was then changed to honour Cecil Rhodes, the statesman and politician, for further details of whom see the next entry.

Rhodesia (Africa)
The African country, formerly familiar as Northern Rhodesia (modern Zambia) and Southern Rhodesia (now Zimbabwe), originated as a territory first administered in 1889 by the British Africa Company managed by the British statesman and financier Cecil John Rhodes (1853–1902), Prime Minister of the Cape Colony, South Africa, from 1890 to 1896. Southern Rhodesia became simply Rhodesia in 1964 when Northern Rhodesia gained independence as Zambia. It then itself gained independence as Zimbabwe in 1980. Cecil Rhodes's name still survives in South Africa, as shown in the previous entry above. The slightly Greek-looking surname has nothing to do with Rhodes: it is a genuine Old English name meaning 'dweller at the clearings' (Old English *rod*, 'clearing', as in such names as Ackroyd ('oak clearing') or Murgatroyd ('Margaret's clearing')).

Riccarton (New Zealand)
Riccarton is a suburb of **Christchurch**, South Island. The name was given by two of the original settlers here, the Scottish brothers John and William Dean, and they named it after their native village of Riccarton, Ayrshire (now a residential suburb of Kilmarnock, Strathclyde).

Richards Bay (South Africa)
The town in Natal takes its name from the bay on which it stands. This in turn was named after Sir Frederick Richards (1833–1912), the British admiral who commanded the Cape station of the Royal Navy and who aided the land forces against the Zulus in 1879.

Richardson (Canada)
Canada has four Richardson locations in its Arctic territory: Richardson River, Richardson Bay, Richardson Islands (south of **Victoria** Island) and Richardson Mountains (in the Yukon). All four honour one man: Dr (later Sir) John Richardson (1787–1866), the surgeon and naturalist on John Franklin's expeditions (see **Franklin**) to the Arctic in 1819–20 and 1825–6.

Richmond (USA, Canada, Australia, New Zealand, South Africa)
The name has always been popular, largely because of its favourable associations: of richness, of height (like Richmond in Yorkshire), of a river setting (like Richmond upon Thames, Surrey), of the dukes so titled, and simply for its satisfying sound. Many United States Richmonds took their names from the famous Richmond that is the capital of **Virginia**. This was originally a trading post set up in 1637, but the town was not laid out and named until exactly a hundred years later. In this case, one of the leading associations seems to have been the river, for the Virginian town was located on the **James** River just as the Surrey town was on the Thames. However, in some instances actual Dukes of Richmond were complimented by the name, such as Charles Lennox, 1st Duke of Richmond (1672–1723) for the three Richmond Counties respectively in **Georgia**, **New York** and North **Carolina**, and Charles Lennox, 4th Duke of Richmond (1764–1819), who was Governor-in-Chief of Canada from 1818 to 1819, for the two Canadian counties of the name in **Nova Scotia** and Quebec, and the towns in Quebec (as the seat of the county) and Ontario. (See also **Lennox and Addington County** and **Lenox**.) In Australia, Richmond, **New South Wales**, is not only situated on a hill (as it were, a 'rich mound'), but was actually named (in 1789) after the 4th Duke already mentioned. The New Zealand Richmond, however, in northern South Island, was

named allusively for the town near London (actually now within Greater London). Finally, but by no means exhaustively for this far-flung and desirable name, the South African town in Cape Province, *and* the one in Natal, were both named Richmond for the same Lennox family who were Dukes of Richmond, as Sir Peregrine Maitland, Governor of the Cape Colony from 1844 to 1847 (see **Maitland**), was related to this family by marriage. See also the next entry below.

Richmond Hill (Canada)

The Ontario town, now a northern suburb of Toronto, was originally called Miles Hill, then Mount Pleasant, before being renamed in 1819 for the 4th Duke of Richmond (see entry above).

Ripon (USA)

The city of Ripon, Wisconsin, is named after the Yorkshire town, doubtless through emigrant home ties there. Ripon, California, was named after the Wisconsin town.

Robbins Island (Australia)

Robbins Island, off northwest Tasmania, was discovered in 1804 by Lieutenant Charles Robbin, an officer on HMS *Buffalo*, and is thus named after him.

Robertson (South Africa)

The Cape Province town was established in 1853 and named after Dr William Robertson (1805–1879), the minister of the Dutch Reformed Church at **Clanwilliam**.

Robinson Crusoe Island (South Pacific)

There really is such an island, although it is now more usually known by its Spanish name of Más a Tierra. It lies in the Juan Fernández group, situated some distance west of Chile in the South Pacific, and belonging to that country. It is the island on which Alexander Selkirk, the original of Defoe's literary hero Robinson Crusoe, lived from October 1704 to February 1709. Another island in the small group, now usually known as Más Afuera, has the alternative name of Alejandro Selkirk. The Spanish names respectively mean 'more to the land' and 'further out', indicating their geographical positions with regard to the South American mainland.

Rochester (USA)

All the New York Rochesters, and also the city in Minnesota, are named after an American army colonel, so cannot properly be represented here. However, Rochester, **New Hampshire**, incorporated as a town in 1722, was named for Laurence Hyde, 1st Earl of Rochester (1641–1711), who was a friend of Samuel Shute, governor of New Hampshire, and he it was who named the town after his English associate.

Rockhampton (Australia)

The Queensland city, at the head of the **Fitzroy** River, was originally named Gracemere Station when founded in 1855. Two years later it was renamed as now, with the name combining a reference to the rocks in the river here with a compliment to the London Hampton of Hampton Court fame. The tribute seems to have been purely a 'prestige' one, although both places are located attractively on a river. Compare **Hampton**.

Rockingham (USA, Canada, Australia)

Many places of the name, such as the three Rockingham Counties, respectively in **New Hampshire**, North **Carolina** and **Virginia**, and also the city of Rockingham, North Carolina (not in the county of the same name), all pay a compliment to Charles Watson-Wentworth, 2nd Marquis of Rockingham (1730–1782), the statesman (and, briefly, Prime Minister) who opposed a severe policy in the American colonies and who was influential in repealing the Stamp Act of 1765 (which obliged all publications and legal documents in the colonies to bear a tax stamp). In Canada, Rockingham, **Nova Scotia**, also honours this statesman, and the name was given by a relation of his, Sir John Wentworth, who was governor of Nova Scotia from 1792 to 1808. In Australia,

Rockingham Bay, northeast **Queensland**, was discovered by Cook in 1770 and named after the same marquis who gave his title to the American locations.

Rodney (USA, Canada, New Zealand)
Cape Rodney, in the Bering Strait, Alaska, the community of Rodney, Ontario, and Cape Rodney, northeast North Island, New Zealand, are all named after the famous English admiral, George Brydges Rodney, 1st Baron Rodney (1712–1792), who was Governor of Newfoundland from 1748 to 1752 and who won several historic victories in maritime engagements subsequently.

Roes Welcome (Canada)
The strait so named between **Southampton** Island and the mainland, Northwest Territories, pays a tribute to the traveller and diplomat, Sir Thomas Roe (?1581–1644), who in 1641 backed the expedition of Luke Foxe (see **Foxe**) to search for a Northwest Passage here. The name was given to the strait either by Thomas Button (see **Button Bay**) or by Foxe himself, originally to a small island here, and originally as 'Sir Thomas Roe's Welcome'.

Roma (Australia)
The **Queensland** town is not named for Rome but for Roma, otherwise Diamantina, Countess Roma, daughter of Candiano, Count Roma, who as Lady Diamantina Roma Bowen was the wife of Queensland's first Governor, Sir George Ferguson Bowen (see **Bowen**). They married in 1856 (and he remarried after her death in 1893). The town was surveyed in 1862 and declared a municipality five years later.

Romney (USA)
The West **Virginia** city was so named in 1762 by Thomas Fairfax, 6th Baron Fairfax (see **Fairfax**), after the Kent seaport of Romney, or for the region known as Romney Marsh there, which was in the same county as the estates (which included Leeds Castle) inherited by his mother from her father, Lord Thomas Culpeper. The West Virginian city was itself in the similar American estate, the so-called 'Fairfax Proprietory'.

Rooke Island (Papua New Guinea)
The island, at the western end of **New Britain** in the Bismarck Archipelago, was so named by Wiliam Dampier (see **Dampier**) in 1700 after the English admiral Sir George Rooke (1650–1709), a victor in several sea battles against the French (but not quite so many against the Spanish). The island is now usually known by its indigenous name of Umboi.

Roscommon (USA)
The Michigan county and its seat of the same name were so designated by Irish settlers, after their native Co. Roscommon. The town was so named in 1843.

Rosebery (Australia)
The Tasmanian town was founded in 1900 after the discovery of gold nearby and was named after the British Prime Minister at the time of the discovery, Archibald Philip Primrose, 5th Earl of Rosebery (1847–1929). The Earl's title comes from his family estate of Rosebery, Scotland, west of Edinburgh.

Rosmead (South Africa)
The village in Cape Province was originally known as Middelburg Road when founded in 1880. Three years later, however, it was renamed after Sir Hercules George Robert Robinson, Baron Rosmead (1824–1897), Governor of the Cape Colony from 1880 to 1889.

Ross Sea (Antarctica, Canada)
All the places of the name in Antarctica honour the Scottish polar explorer Sir James Ross (1800–1862), who after making four expeditions to the Arctic, led an Antarctic expedition of geographical discovery in 1839–43 and in 1841 first penetrated to the Ross Sea, as it is now known, in his ships HMS *Erebus* (see **Erebus**) and HMS *Terror* (see **Terror**). Also named after him here are Ross Island, the Ross Ice Shelf (formerly the Ross Barrier), and Ross Dependency, the latter containing

wholly or partly all the former features, and so named as it is under the jurisdiction of New Zealand. Not all the names were given at the time of discovery, or even by Ross himself. Ross Island, for example, was so named by Captain Scott during his first Antarctic expedition of 1901–4. In Canada, Ross River, in the Yukon, is named after another Ross, however. This was Donald Ross, the chief factor of the Hudson's Bay Company (see **Hudson**). The name was given in 1843. See also **James Ross Island**.

Rothesay (Canada)
The community of Rothesay, northeast of Saint John, **New Brunswick**, was so named for one of the titles (Duke of Cornwall and Rothesay) of Edward, Prince of Wales, the future Edward VII, who embarked from here for **Fredericton** during his royal visit of 1860. Rothesay itself is the chief town on the Scottish island of Bute, now in Strathclyde.

Roxboro (USA)
The city in North **Carolina** is named after the former Scottish county of Roxburgh (or the village of Roxburgh there), both now being in the district of Borders. Doubtless there were emigrant connections there. Compare the next entry below.

Roxburgh (New Zealand)
The community in southeast South Island is named for its Scottish emigrant links with the county of the same name. Compare the entry above.

Royal Oak (USA)
The Michigan city, now a residential suburb of Detroit, was first settled in 1819 and was named for the supposed 'Royal Oak' in Shropshire whose foliage is popularly said to have hidden Charles II after his defeat at the Battle of Worcester in 1651. The name is thus a sort of royal compliment. The name is equally popular in Britain as a public house name, with the same allusion.

Rugby (USA)
The city in North Dakota was founded in 1885 and was so named by English stockholders who had come from this city in England and who were investing in the new railroad here.

Runnemede (USA)
The residential borough near **Camden**, **New Jersey**, was named as a royal and historic tribute to Runnymede, the meadows near Egham, Surrey, where King John signed the Magna Carta in 1215.

Rupert River (Canada)
The river in Quebec was discovered by Henry Hudson (see **Hudson**) who wintered at its mouth in 1610–11 and who named it after Prince Rupert (see **Prince Rupert**), one of the founders of the Hudson's Bay Company. See also the next entry below.

Rupert's Land (Canada)
This is an alternative name for Prince Rupert's Land, for details of which see **Prince Rupert**.

Russell (Canada, New Zealand)
Most United States Russells are named after Americans. But Russell County, Ontario, was named after the Irish-born statesman, the Hon. Peter Russell (1733–1803), who was administrator of the government of Upper Canada from 1796 to 1799. In New Zealand, the town of Russell in northern North Isand was originally known by its Maori name of Okiato when it was chosen in 1840 by William Hobson, the Lieutenant-Governor of New Zealand, to be the country's first capital. He duly renamed it after the then Colonial Secretary, Lord John Russell, 1st Earl Russell (1792–1878). However, the settlement had barely been established when Hobson realised its unfavourable geographical location, and he therefore moved the capital south and renamed it **Auckland** (which see for the origin of the name). But although Russell was destroyed by fire in 1841, it had been rebuilt on its original site five years later and now remains as a seaside resort with a road link to Auckland, some 165 miles south of it.

Rutherglen (Australia)
The town in **Victoria**, near the border with **New South Wales**, was named after the Scottish royal burgh of Rutherglen, Lanarkshire (now in Strathclyde), no doubt having emigrant ties with that location.

Rutland (USA)
The city of Rutland, Vermont, the seat (from 1784) of the identically named county, arose in 1761 from an outpost on the military road built here to connect up forts by the British general Sir Jeffrey Amherst (see **Amherst**). The site's grantee came from Rutland, Massachusetts, however, so that is the direct source of the name. The Massachusetts town was founded in 1714 and named either for the former English county, or else as a tribute to one of the Dukes of Rutland (or even both, unless there were specific home ties for early settlers in Massachusetts).

Rye (USA)
The **New York** city was originally settled in 1660 by men from Greenwich, Connecticut, and they named it five years later after the town in Sussex, with which one or more of them must have had emigrant connections.

S

Sabine (Canada, Antarctica)
Cape Sabine, on **Ellesmere** Island, in Canada's Northwest Territories, and Mount Sabine, in the Admiralty Mountains, **Victoria** Land, Antarctica, are both named for the same man. This was Sir Edward Sabine (1788–1883), the multi-talented British general who was also explorer, astronomer and scientist, and President of the Royal Society from 1861 to 1871. Earlier, in 1818, he had served as astronomer to John Ross, uncle of James Ross (see **Ross Sea**), in his expedition to the Arctic to search for the Northwest Passage, and the following year he acted in the same capacity in another Arctic expedition under William Parry (see **Parry**).

Sabrina Coast (Antarctica)
Sabrina Coast (formerly Sabrina Land) is a section of Wilkes Land south of Australia. The name is that of the ship *Sabrina* which, together with the *Eliza Scott*, sailed to this part of Antarctica from Tasmania in 1839 under the command of the British naval officer John Balleny (see **Balleny Islands**). The expedition ended in tragedy, when the two ships became separated in a storm and the *Sabrina* was lost with all her crew, leaving the *Eliza Scott* to return alone. The name was thus given as a memorial to the ship and her men.

Sackville (Canada)
The **New Brunswick** town arose on the site of three destroyed French villages in 1761, when New England immigrants named it after George Sackville Germain, 1st Viscount Sackville (1716–1785), who was Colonial Secretary from 1775 to 1782 and who virtually directed the war against the American colonists.

St Albans (USA)
The Vermont town of St Albans took its name from the English city, perhaps for emigrant links there. The town was chartered in 1763 and organised in 1788, late enough for such an ostensibly 'Catholic' name to be adopted. Earlier, the Puritan emigrants of the seventeenth century would not have considered such a name. The date of naming seems too late for a tribute to the Duke of St Albans, who died in 1726, to be considered, as some sources suggest. In the case of St Albans West **Virginia**, it is possible that the name derived from the home town of one of the engineers who helped build the railroad here in 1871. Earlier names of the city, which was laid out in 1816, were Philippi, Coalsmouth, and Kanawha City.

St Catherines (Canada)
The city in Ontario was named after Catherine Askin Hamilton (died 1798), the first wife of Robert Hamilton, member of the first legislative council of Upper Canada, and mother of George Hamilton, who founded **Hamilton**. The 'Saint' is therefore purely for prestige purposes.

St Clair (USA)
The Scottish-born American soldier, General Arthur St Clair (1736–1818), has given his name to several places in the United States, from the St Clair River, that forms the international boundary between Michigan and Ontario, to the four St Clair Counties in the country. Lake St Clair, in Michigan, had originally been named for St Clare, the saint, but the

name was adapted to honour the general. The name is specially associated with **Pennsylvania**, where General St Clair settled, hence the name of the borough of St Clair in that state.

Saint-Éphrem-de-Tring (Canada)
The province of Quebec is unique in having a number of communities with compound place-names, usually with a fairly fixed formula such as the word 'Saint' plus the name of a (French) settler and an (English) location, the two usually not connected. Thus, in the name cited, 'Éphrem' represents the settler Éphrem Poulx, who donated money for the church here, and 'Tring' represents the Hertfordshire town from which English emigrants will have come. There is no space to give more than a very few such names, but examples of others are Saint-Léon-de-Standon (for the settler Léon Rousseau and the village of Standon, Hertfordshire) and Saint-Germain-de-Grantham (where the settler is not French but English, as Edward Granville Eliot, 3rd Earl of St Germain, with Grantham as the town in Lincolnshire). Such bilingual names reflect the essential dual Franco-English nature of Quebec.

St George (USA)
Inasmuch as St George is the patron saint of England, it can be said that many places of the name in the United States will have been chosen to express an English loyalty by the emigrants from there who came to settle in the American colonies. It is worth pointing out that Point St George, on the Pacific coast in California, was named by George Vancouver (see **Vancouver**), who thus blended his personal name with that of 'his' saint. See also the next two entries below, as well as the popular name **George**, with its additional royal links.

St George's Bay (Canada)
The **Nova Scotia** bay was originally known as both George Bay and Georges Bay. But the intention has always been to honour the patron saint of England, as expressed by the original namer, the English military engineer Joseph Frederick Walsh (or Wallet) Des Barres (1722–1824), Lieutenant-Governor of Cape Breton from 1784 to 1805, and of **Prince Edward Island** from 1805 to 1813.

St George's Channel (Papua New Guinea)
St George's Channel is the name of the strait between **New Britain** and **New Ireland**, in the Bismarck Archipelago, where it mirrors the British St George's Channel that lies between mainland Britain (more precisely, Wales) and Ireland. It was Carteret who confirmed that the channel was a strait, not a bay, as originally supposed. See **New Ireland**.

St Helens (USA)
Mount St Helens, Washington, was so named by George Vancouver (see **Vancouver**) after Alleyne Fitzherbert, Baron St Helens (1753–1839), British ambassador to Spain from 1790 to 1794. The city of St Helens, Oregon, was named after the mountain.

Saint Vincent (Australia)
Both the Gulf of Saint Vincent, South Australia, east of the **Yorke Peninsula**, and Point Saint Vincent, Tasmania, were named by Matthew Flinders (see **Flinders**) after Admiral John Jervis, 1st Earl of St Vincent (1735–1823), First Lord of the Admiralty from 1801 to 1804. The Earl took his title from the Portuguese Cape St Vincent, off which in 1797 he and Nelson had won an important victory over the Spanish (who were numerically superior). Flinders named the cape first, in 1798, just one year after this victory, and then the gulf, in 1802.

Sale (Australia)
The coastal city in **Victoria** was founded in 1845 and named for Sir Robert Sale, nicknamed 'Fighting Bob' (1782–1845), the British general who fought in India and became famous for his defence of Jalalabad in 1841–42. He died in India when his leg was shattered by grapeshot in the Battle of Mudki, the victory of the English over the Sikhs in 1845, and it was thus as

a memorial to him that the Australian town was so named.

Salisbury (USA, Australia, Zimbabwe, South Africa, USSR)
Another of the 'dual' names that could derive from a place or a person. If the former, it will almost certainly be the cathedral city in Wiltshire. If the latter, it is more than likely to be Lord Salisbury, otherwise Robert Arthur Talbot Gascoyne-Cecil, 3rd Marquis of Salisbury (1830–1903), three times Prime Minister (1885–6, 1886–92, 1895–1902). In the United States, the name refers to the city, with the best-known examples being the following towns (with settlement year): Salisbury, Massachusetts (1640), Salisbury, **Maryland** (1732), Salisbury, Connecticut (1738), Salisbury, North **Carolina** (1753), this last directly deriving from the Maryland town. It is right to suppose an emigrant connection for the earliest names. In Australia, the city that is now a suburb of **Adelaide** was founded in 1856 and was named after the Wiltshire birthplace of an early settler's wife. Salisbury, the capital of Zimbabwe, was renamed Harare in 1982. The town originated as Fort Salisbury in 1890, in what was then the embryo country of **Rhodesia**. The name was chosen as a partriotic tribute to the then Prime Minister, Lord Salisbury. (The name was shortened to simply Salisbury in 1897.) But although this name has now been superseded by Harare (after a local chief), Salisbury still exists in South Africa, where it is found in Salisbury Island, in the Bay of Natal at **Durban**. The island was named neither for the city nor for the statesman, but for a ship, the *Salisbury*, in which British explorers visited it in 1823, and which thus brought them to found a mission station at Port Natal (as Durban was then) the following year. The ship herself (a brig) would have been named after the city. Finally, Salisbury Island, in Franz Josef Land, in Soviet Arctic territory (where its official Russian name is Ostrov Solsberi), appears to have been named after the Prime Minister. The namer seems to have been Frederick Jackson, who explored the territory here in his expedition of 1894–7, and who named many newly discovered islands. But although he makes no mention of naming Salisbury Island in his account of his discoveries, *A Thousand Days in the Arctic* (see Appendix II, p. 210), it does not appear on his map of the area as it stood before his expedition, but does appear on the map at the end of his time there, which includes all newly discovered and named features. So one must assume that he omitted to record the naming. Certainly the dating is exactly right, for Lord Salisbury was then in his third and most influential period as Premier, and Jackson named other features after similar statesmen of standing (e.g. Peel, Rhodes, Chamberlain).

Saltcoats (Canada)
The community in Saskatchewan was originally named Stirling, after the Scottish town (see **Stirling**). This name was then changed to Saltcoats, for an alternative Scottish town (and port), then in Ayrshire (now in Strathclyde). Doubtless the change was made to avoid confusion with exisiting places of the name, such as Stirling, **Alberta**, or Stirling, Ontario. The change itself was proposed by Sir Hugh Allan (1810–1882), the Scottish financier and shipowner who was closely associated with Canada and who was one of the projectors of the Canadian Pacific Railway.

Sandringham (Canada)
The Newfoundland community is named for the royal residence of Sandringham House, in Norfolk, and was perhaps named soon after this house became one of the country homes of the British royal family (in 1861, when Queen Victoria bought the estate there for her eldest son, the future Edward VII). Compare **Balmoral**.

Sandwich (USA, Canada, Pacific Ocean, Australia)
Rather like **Salisbury** (see above), this name is one that could derive from a town or a title. In this case, the town is that of the port in Kent, and the title is invariably

that of John Montagu, 4th Earl of Sandwich (1718–1792), three times First Lord of the Admiralty between 1748 and 1782, and a man much admired by contemporary navigators and explorers, such as Cook. Lord Montagu took his title from the town, and it was this port that gave the names of the two United States Sandwiches, the town in Massachusetts (settled in about 1637) and the city in Illinois (derived from this). In Canada, Sandwich Bay, Labrador, was named for the Earl, however, as was Cape Sandwich in **Queensland**, Australia. The latter was named by Cook who also named **Hinchinbrook** Island, on which the cape is located. (Hinchinbrook was not only the name of the family seat of his patron, George Montagu Dunk, but the title of his father, Edwin Richard Montagu, Viscount Hinchinbrook, for the two Montagu families were related.) It was Cook, too, who named the Sandwich Islands in the northern Pacific Ocean, where they are now known as the Hawaiian Islands, and form a state of the USA. Lord Sandwich was Cook's patron for many of his voyages of discovery, including this one which was to end fatally. Cook discovered and named the islands in 1778 and was killed here the following year in a squabble with the local (Polynesian) inhabitants about a boat. Earlier, he had given the same name, 'in honour of his noble patron', to Sandwich Island, in the **New Hebrides**, where it is now usually known by its indigenous name of Efate or Vaté. And as if that was not enough, he similarly named the **South Sandwich Islands**. It was this particular Lord Sandwich who gave his name to the homely sandwich. For the background to this, see **Montague**. See also, for related namings, **Dunk** and **Halifax**.

Sarnia (Canada)

The Ontario city was first settled in 1807, and the present town was established in 1833. Two years later it was named Sarnia, after the Roman name for Guernsey, in the Channel Islands. The namer was Sir John Colborne (1778–1863), the British general who was Lieutenant-Governor of Upper Canada from 1828 to 1838 and who earlier had been Lieutenant-Governor of Guernsey (see **Port Colborne**).

Saunders (New Zealand, South Atlantic)

Cape Saunders, near **Dunedin**, South Island, New Zealand, was so named by James Cook after his friend Sir Charles Saunders (?1717–1775), the British admiral, and he also gave his name (in 1775) to Saunders Island, in the **South Sandwich Islands**, as well as another Cape Saunders there in the **Falklands Islands** Dependencies, on the northern coast of **South Georgia**. Cook had served under Admiral Saunders when surveying the St Lawrence Channel, Canada, in 1759.

Saybrook (USA)

The residential town in Connecticut, where it is officially known as Old Saybrook, was founded in 1635 by colonists sent here by William Fiennes, 1st Viscount Saye and Sele (1582–1662) and Robert Greville, 2nd Baron Brooke (1608–1643), and the name is a blend of both their titles. As far as is known, this is the earliest example of such a blend of names, described by Taylor (see Bibliography, p. 217) as a 'vicious practice'.

Scarborough (Canada, USA)

The Ontario borough, which with four other boroughs and the City of Toronto constitute the Municipality of Metropolitan Toronto, was originally known as Glasgow. In 1793, however, it was renamed at the suggestion of the wife of the Lieutenant-Governor of Ontario, John Simcoe (see **Simcoe**), because its cliffs (Scarborough Bluffs) here on the shores of Lake Ontario seemed to her to resemble those at Scarborough, Yorkshire, on the North Sea coast. In the United States, Scarborough, Maine (also spelt Scarboro) was similarly named, with its location on the Atlantic coast also rocky. Compare the next entry below.

Scarbro (USA)

The community of Scarbro, West **Virginia**, is believed to have been named after the many families here of the name (in this spelling or in a more usual variant), with their names in turn suggesting, and even deriving from, that of the Yorkshire town.

Scarsdale (USA)
The **New York** town was settled in 1701, following its purchase by one Caleb Heathcote, and he named it after the Manor of Scarsdale that he owned in his native Derbyshire.

Schooleys Mountain (USA)
The **New Jersey** mountain takes its name (with a modification in spelling) from Thomas Scholey, who came to this area from England in 1677 to join a Quaker colony.

Scilly Isles (South Pacific)
The name is that of a group in the **Society Islands**, in French Polynesia, which were so called in 1767 by the circumnavigator Samuel Wallis (see **Wallis Islands**) because they appeared to him to resemble the rocky and (to shipping) potentially dangerous Isles of Scilly off the coast of Cornwall.

Scone (Australia)
The **New South Wales** town was originally known by the Scottish name of Invermein when first gazetted in 1837. It was subsequently renamed after another Scottish location, the village of Scone (either Old Scone or New Scone, or even the famous Palace of Scone there) in Perthshire (now in Tayside). The link would have been a Scottish emigrant one.

Scoresby Sound (Greenland)
There are not many English names in Greenland, but this is one that remains. The deep inlet of Scoresby Sound (or, in Danish, Scoresby Sund) on the eastern coast is named after the man who charted it in 1822, the Yorkshire-born explorer and clergyman, William Scoresby (1789–1857). There is a hunting and fishing settlement here named Scoresbysund, founded in 1924. Coincidentally, the name would not seem too outlandish for Danes, who are used to the place-name suffix '-by' in their own country to mean 'settlement' (as at Lyngby or Lundby). Indeed Scoresby's own surname derives from an English place-name that is itself Scandinavian in origin, and that was included in the Danelaw (that part of northern and eastern England where the Danes had settled, bringing their language and place-names with them).

Scotch Plains (USA)
The residential township in **New Jersey** was settled in 1684 by Scottish emigrants, and was named as much for them as for their leader, one George Scot (who died on the way). The 'Plains' are those south of the Watchung Mountains here.

Scotia Sea (South Atlantic)
The Scotia Sea lies between the **Falkland Islands** Dependencies and the southern tip of South America. It was named after the ship *Scotia*, the vessel of the Scottish National Antarctic Expedition led here by William Bruce from 1902 to 1904 as the first oceanographic survey of the **Weddell Sea**. The ship's name is itself one of the Latin names for Scotland. Compare **Nova Scotia**.

Scotland (USA)
There are two Scotland Counties in the United States, respectively in Missouri and North **Carolina**. Both were named for (and by) settlers from Scotland, as was the community of this name in **Pennsylvania**, where the Scottish namer was one Alexander Thompson. Compare the next two entries below.

Scotsburn (Canada)
The community in **Nova Scotia** was originally named Roger's Hill. It was renamed in 1867 by a Scot, High Ross, after his native village of Scotsburn in Ross-shire (now in Grampian).

Scotstown (Canada)
The Quebec community was so named for the Scottish settlers brought here in the 1830s by the British American Land Company, a colonist organisation.

Scottburgh (South Africa)
The seaside resort of Scottburgh, Natal, was surveyed in 1860 and named after Sir John Scott (1814–1898), Lieutenant-Governor of Natal from 1856 to 1864.

Scott Coast (Antarctica)
The Scott Coast is a region of **Victoria** Land, where it stands as a memorial to Robert Falcon Scott, who discovered it here in 1911 on board the *Terra Nova*, before continuing his journey by sledge with four companions to the South Pole, from which none were to return alive. The four have their names similarly commemorated in Antarctica as the **Bowers Mountains**, **Evans Glacier**, **Oates Coast**, and **Wilson** Hills.

Seaford (USA)
The city of Seaford, **Delaware**, has a name that was adopted from the English coastal resort of Seaford in Sussex. (The Delaware Seaford is also in **Sussex** County.) The reason for the adoption of this particular name may be partly through its suitability as an equally descriptive name, for the city lies at the head of navigation on the Nanticoke River, and is thus a sort of 'sea ford' over this river. The town was laid out in 1799.

Sedgefield (South Africa)
The Cape Province resort was founded early in the twentieth century and was named after the home village of its founder, one Henry Barrington, which was Sedgefield near Stockton-on-Tees, Co. Durham (now Cleveland).

Selkirk (Canada)
The town of Selkirk, Manitoba, on the Red River, was settled in 1812 and named for Thomas Douglas, 5th Earl of Selkirk (1771–1820), who founded the Red River Settlement locally in the period from 1811 to 1820. (See also **Douglas**.) The Selkirk Mountains, in the Rockies, **British Columbia**, are also named for the Earl.

Selma (USA)
This is a Scottish literary name. The city of Selma, Alabama, was originally known as Moore's Bluff or Moore's Landing when first settled in 1815. On its incorporation five years later it was renamed after the poem 'The Song of Selma' in the Ossianic poems by James Macpherson, where Selma is the name of a 'high seat or throne'. For the Alabama town, this is appropriate for its location on the high northern bank of the Alabama River.

Severna Park (USA)
The **Maryland** community is located on, and named after, the Severn River, which was itself named for the river in England and Wales, perhaps because an early settler was familiar with it. Compare the next entry below.

Severn River (Canada)
The Severn River, Ontario, was so named after the English (and Welsh) river by its discoverer in 1631, Captain Thomas James, who gave his name to the **James** River. He originally called it the New Severn. Not much is known about James, but he was familiar with the English port of Bristol, which stands on the mouth of the Severn, and he was certainly personally acquainted with the river. Compare the entry above.

Seymour (Australia, South Africa)
The town of Seymour, **Victoria**, was founded in 1837 and proclaimed a town four years later, when it was named in honour of Edward Adolphus Seymour, 12th Duke of Somerset (1804–1885), who was First Lord of the Admiralty from 1859 to 1866. The South African town of the name, in Cape Province, pays a compliment to Colonel Charles Seymour, Military Secretary to the Governor of the Cape, Sir George Cathcart (see **Cathcart**). The town was founded in 1853.

Shackleton Glacier (Antarctica)
The Irish-born Antarctic explorer, Sir Ernest Shackleton (1874–1922), has given his name to more than one natural feature in the continent, including the Shackleton Glacier, descending to the Ross Ice Shelf (see **Ross Sea**), the extensive Shackleton Ice Shelf itself, in eastern Antarctica, and

the Shackleton Range, **Coats Land**. This last was first sighted from the air by members of the British–New Zealand expedition of 1955–8. Shackleton made three expeditions to the Antarctic, and died during the last of these when on the island of **South Georgia**. For the continuing polar exploration undertaken by his son, see **Oxford**.

Shakespeare Island (Canada)

It is perhaps surprising that such a famous, quintessentially English name is not found much more frequently on the world map. Yet *The Times Atlas of the World* (see Bibliography, p. 217), which contains over 200,000 place-names, lists only one occurrence, and that is the island in Lake Nipigon, north of Lake Superior, Ontario. True, the name has been proposed on more than one occasion when an important new settlement was to be named (one such proposal was for the Australian capital, Canberra), but for some reason it has never ultimately been adopted. Perhaps the association was felt to be too 'literary'. Some places have honoured the playwright by calling themselves **Stratford**.

Shaunavon (Canada)

The town in Saskatchewan is believed to have been named in 1913 by Thomas George Shaughnessy, 1st Baron Shaughnessy (1853–1923), who was himself born in Milwaukee, Wisconsin, for his ancient family home in Ireland, or a region near it. (This was presumably somewhere near Ashford, Co. Limerick, where his father, later a detective in the Milwaukee police, had been born.) Lord Shaughnessy was latterly a President of the Canadian Pacific Railway, and it is possible that this particular place-name is actually a combination of his own and that of Sir William Cornelius Van Horne. He was the man who had promoted Shaughnessy (in 1879) to the post of general storekeeper with the Milwaukee and St Paul Railway, for which he had been working since 1869.

Sheffield (USA, Canada)

Most United States places of the name give recognition to the Yorkshire city, in some instances as a specific 'industrial' reference. This was so for Sheffield, Alabama, where in 1816 the future US President Andrew Jackson made land purchases for such an 'industrial city', as he defined it. Today the city has a diversified industry, although it is nothing like the size of its English counterpart. In Canada, on the other hand, the community of Sheffield, **New Brunswick**, was named as a tribute to John Baker Holroyd, Lord Sheffield (1735–1821), Member of Parliament for Coventry. The Earl's title, however, does not come from the Yorkshire city but from his estate (which he had purchased in 1769) of Sheffield Park in Sussex.

Shefford County (Canada)

The Ontario county takes its name from the small town of Shefford, Bedfordshire, where there must have been home links for some of the early settlers here.

Shelburne (USA, Canada)

The reference for virtually all places in North America will be to Sir William Petty, 2nd Earl of Shelburne (1737–1805), the English statesman who was President of the Board of Trade and who opposed the government on its American colonial policies. The name is found, among other places, in the town of Shelburne, Vermont (settled in 1761) and in the identically named town in **Nova Scotia**, Canada, where it was settled in 1783 by Loyalists who had fled from the States after the Revolutionary War (War of American Independence). The Earl was Prime Minister at this stage (for the two years from 1782).

Sherborn (USA)

The Massachusetts town was originally named Sherburne when settled in 1674, and the reference is to the home town of one of the settlers, Sherborne in Dorset.

Sherbrooke (Canada)

Sherbrooke County, Quebec, with its seat of the same name, honours Sir John Coape Sherbrooke (1764–1830), Governor General of Canada from 1816 to 1818. It took the name in the latter year, having earlier been a fur-trading post.

Sheridan (USA)
The name will usually pay a compliment to the famous American general. In Sheridan, **New York**, however, the tribute was deliberately made (in 1824) to the dramatist, Richard Brinsley Sheridan (1751–1816), known for his support for the French Revolution.

Shrewsbury (USA)
Many early settlers in colonial America were natives of the English town of Shrewsbury, Shropshire, and this will therefore be the motivation for the name in several instances. At the same time, a compliment may have been additionally intended to Charles Talbot, Duke of Shrewsbury (1660–1718), who was Lord Lieutenant of Ireland and one of those who invited William of Orange to seize power from the Catholic king James II and thus to succeed him (which he did, as William III, in 1689). Compare **Orange**, **Williamsburg**. Shrewsbury, **Pennsylvania**, was settled by emigrants from the English town in 1739.

Sidney (USA)
For most places of the name there will have been an implied tribute to Sir Philip Sidney (1554–1586), the English poet and statesman who was killed fighting the Spanish. In the case of the Ohio city, however, there may have been an additional prompting for this particular name as the namer, who donated land for the town site, was Charles Sidney Starrett. The Sidney in **New York**, too, may have been derived from the name of the English vice-admiral, William Sidney (1764–1840).

Simcoe (Canada)
Wherever it is found in Canada, the place-name will be sure to honour John Graves Simcoe (1752–1806), the British soldier and statesman who became the first Lieutenant-Governor of Upper Canada (modern Ontario). However, in the case of Lake Simcoe, Ontario, which was named by Simcoe himself, the tribute was paid to his father, Captain John Simcoe, a naval officer. Before he renamed the lake, it was known by its French name of Lac aux Claies.

Simpson (Canada)
Two typical instances of the name can be seen in Simpson Strait, between **King William** Island and **Adelaide** Peninsula,Northwest Territories, and Simpson Peninsula, also in Arctic Canada, in the Gulf of **Boothia**. The name is a compliment to Sir George Simpson (1792–1860), who administered the territory of the Hudson's Bay Company (see **Hudson**) from 1821 to 1856.

Simsbury (USA)
The Connecticut town is probably named for the Dorset village of Symondsbury, near Bridport, from which an early settler must have come. On the other hand, the name of one Simon Wolcott has been recorded as that of one of the original pioneers. Either is possible. However, the Dorset name is pronounced with a short 'i', as in 'Simmonds', not a long one, as in 'Simon', and so is a more likely derivation than the personal name.

Sir Edward Pellew Group (Australia)
This is the modern version of the name of the **Pellew Islands**, with the name deliberately altered to prevent confusion with another, similarly named group.

Smith (Canada, Pacific Ocean, Australia)
Smith Sound, at the northern end of **Baffin** Bay, Northwest Territories, Canada, where it forms an Arctic passage between **Ellesmere** Island and Greenland, was discovered by Baffin (of the bay) in 1616 and named by him after Sir Thomas Smith (?1558–1625), the English merchant and benefactor who was the main founder of the East India Company. In the Pacific, the former Smith Islands are now the Johnston Islands. These are now named after Captain Johnston (see

Johnston Island), but he had originally named them after his First Lieutenant on board the *Cornwallis*, whose name was Smith. Then Smith River, Western Australia, was named after Frederick Smith, who accompanied George (later Sir George) Grey here on his expedition of the 1830s (see **Grey**, **Greytown**). That by no means exhausts the Smiths, but gives something of a sample of their ubiquitousness in place-names!

Smithers (Canada)

The village of Smithers, **British Columbia**, was named in 1913 for Sir Alfred Waldron Smithers (1850–1824), a director of the Grand Trunk Pacific Railway.

Smithfield (South Africa)

The town of Smithfield, Orange Free State, was laid out in 1849 and was named after Sir Harry Smith (1787–1860), Governor of the Cape Colony from 1847 to 1852. The name thus belongs to the fairly large 'family' of names that compliment him and his wife, the other members including **Harrismith**, **Ladismith** and **Ladysmith**.

Society Islands (South Pacific)

The islands were visited by James Cook in 1769 with a scientific expedition commissioned (to observe the transit of Venus) by the Royal Society. Hence the name and Cook's compliment to his sponsors.

Somerset (USA, Canada)

Such names have the implied selection between county or courtier, otherwise place or person. Many United States counties and communities are named after the English county, from which early settlers will have come. Equally, some will have originated with a name that compliments a Duke of Somerset. And in certain instances, the reference could be to both, as it apparently is for the Kentucky city, with an implied additional acknowledgment to an existing place of the name, here, Somerset, **Pennsylvania** (which is the seat of the county of the same name). Somerset County was the last of the Pennsylvania counties to take its name from an English county (in 1795), with earlier ones being **Bedford**, **Berks**, **Bucks**, **Chester** and **York**, among others. Somerset County, **Maryland**, has a precise reference to Edward Somerset, Marquis of Worcester (?1601–1667), but in Canada, Somerset Island, east of **Prince of Wales** Island, Northwest Territories, was named by William Parry (see **Parry**) after his native English county. See also the next two entries below.

Somerset East (South Africa)

The town of Somerset East, Cape Province, was founded in 1825 and named after Lord Charles Henry Somerset (1767–1831), Governor of the Cape Colony from 1814 to 1826 and owner of the farm here (Somerset Farm) on which the town was originally laid out. 'East' was added to distinguish the settlement from **Somerset West**.

Somerset West (South Africa)

The Cape Province town was founded in 1822 (originally as Somerset) and named after Lord Somerset, Governor of the Cape at the time. 'West' was added later to distinguish this town from **Somerset East**.

Sorell (Australia)

The Tasmanian town, northeast of **Hobart**, was originally known as Pittwater when founded in 1819, with this name referring to the lagoon here and intended to compliment William Pitt ('the Younger') (see **Pitt Island**). Three years later, however, the settlement was renamed by Lachlan Macquarie (see **Macquarie**) as Sorell, after William Sorell, the Lieutenant-Governor of **New South Wales**.

Southampton (USA, Canada)

Some places of the name undoubtedly borrowed it from the English city and port in Hampshire, and in Massachusetts, the town of Southampton is actually in **Hampshire** County. At the same time, its name could well refer to the fact that originally the community was the southern section of the town of Northampton.

Southampton County, **Virginia**, however, was named for Henry Wriothesley, 3rd Earl of Southampton (1573–1624), the English statesman who helped to send an expedition to Virginia (in 1603) and who was an active member of the Virginia and East India companies. (He is more popularly known, though, for being a patron of Shakespeare.) In Canada, similarly, Southampton Island, in Keewatin District, Northwest Territories, was so named in 1613 by Thomas Button (see **Button Bay**) for the same Earl.

Southgate (USA)

Whereas the city of Southgate, Michigan, is so named because it is south of Detroit, there is some evidence that suggests that Southgate, Kentucky, was named after the London district of Southgate, possibly for emigrant connections. At the time of naming, the English Southgate would have been little more than a village in Middlesex.

South Georgia (South Atlantic)

South Georgia is the most prominent of all the islands in the **Falkland Islands** Dependencies. It was visited by James Cook in 1775 and claimed by him for Britain. He named it 'Isle of Georgia', therefore, as a tribute to the reigning monarch, George III (1738–1820). The present version of the name is not recorded until the nineteenth century. (Compare **George**, **Georgia**.) The island was first crossed in 1916 by Shackleton (see **Shackleton Glacier**), who died there, and the interior was not further explored until the 1960s.

South Orkney Islands (Antarctica)

The islands lie south of the **Scotia Sea** to the northeast of the Antarctic Peninsula. They were discovered by British and American sealers in 1821, in particular by George Powell (British) and Nathaniel Palmer (American, who gave his name to Palmer Land on the peninsula). They were so named for their proximity to the **South Shetland Islands**, which had been discovered two years previously, with the grouping ultimately referring to that of the Orkney and Shetland Islands north of the Scottish mainland.

South Sandwich Islands (South Atlantic)

The islands are in the **Falkland Islands** Dependencies, where they lie southeast of **South Georgia**. They were discovered by James Cook in 1775 and at first named by him (rather uncharacteristically) as Snowland. Later, however, he altered this to 'Sandwich Land', after John Montagu, 4th Earl of Sandwich (1718–1792), who had sponsored his many voyages of discovery. (Subsequently, he named the **Sandwich** Islands after him.) Cook also named the individual island of Montagu (see **Montague**) here after his patron, and that of **Saunders** Island after the famous admiral.

South Shetland Islands (Antarctica)

The islands lie to the north of the Antarctic Peninsula, where they were discovered and named in 1819 by the British sealer William Smith, who likened their appearance and proximity to the Antarctic mainland to that of the Shetland Islands, off the Scottish mainland. (Although he would have done better to call them the Orkneys, as these correspond more exactly in their geographical relationship with the main landmass.)

Southwark (USA)

The district of Philadelphia, **Pennsylvania**, was incorporated in 1794 and named after the London borough. The district lies by the **Delaware** River, just as London's Southwark lies by the Thames. However, the London borough is (as its name suggests) *south* of the river, whereas the Philadelphia district is not!

Southwick (USA)

The Massachusetts town was so named in 1771, probably for an English Southwick, although it is not certain which. Again, it may have been the surname of an early settler.

Spencer (Australia)
Australia has two noted features of the name: Spencer Gulf, the inlet in South Australia, and Cape Spencer at its entrance, as the southern tip of the **Yorke Peninsula**. Both gulf and cape were discovered in 1802 by Matthew Flinders (see **Flinders**), and he named them in honour of the 'respectable nobleman' (as he called him), George John Spencer, 2nd Earl Spencer (1758–1834), who was First Lord of the Admiralty at the time when Flinders's ship was commissioned. The Earl's courtesy title of Viscount Althorp gave the name of the **Althorpe Islands**.

Spotswood (USA)
The **New Jersey** borough was named after the Scottish estate of Spottiswoode, near Lauder in Berwickshire (now in Borders), from which had come the first white settler here, James Johnstone. The Scottish name is frequently pronounced as 'Spotswood'. Compare the next entry below.

Spotsylvania (USA)
The county and its seat of this name in **Virginia** pay a compliment to Alexander Spotswood (1676–1740), the English Lieutenant-Governor of the colony of Virginia from 1710 to 1722 (who moreover actually took on the duties of the nominal governor, who was the Earl of Orkney). The second half of the place-name is intended to suggest 'woodlands', just as it does for **Pennsylvania** and **Pittsylvania**. In this instance however, there is an added significance, or pleasant pun, for the second half of the Lieutenant Governor's name was 'wood' in any case! (The surname itself derives from a place-name that probably means 'small piece of woodland'.)

Springfield (USA)
Although many places of the name acquired it purely descriptively, for a 'spring by a field' (or something similar), there are certain instances where the name is known to have derived from an English place. This is certainly so for the city of Springfield, Massachusetts, which was founded on the Connecticut River in 1635 by William Pynchon, one of the original patentees of the Massachusetts Bay Company. He named it for his birthplace in Essex, where the original village of Springfield is now a northeast suburb of Chelmsford. Both Springfield, Minnesota and Springfield, Vermont, adopted their names from the Massachusetts settlement. The original (Indian) name of the Massachusetts city was Agawam.

Stafford (USA)
Most places of the name seem to have derived it from the English town of Stafford or the county of Staffordshire, almost certainly for emigrant ties with one or the other, although some sources claim that Stafford, **Virginia**, named in 1661, honours William Howard, Viscount Stafford (1614–1680) (who was beheaded for treason).

Stamford (USA)
The Connecticut city, now a residential suburb of **New York**, was founded in 1641 and named for the town in Lincolnshire from which early settlers had emigrated. The Texas city of Stamford took its name from the Connecticut town.

Standish (USA)
The town of Standish in Maine was named in honour of Miles Standish (?1584–1656), the English soldier who was a pioneer of the **Plymouth** colony and whose family seat gave the name of **Duxbury**, Massachusetts, where he died.

Stanley (Zaire, Australia, Falkland Islands)
There are two men of note named Stanley who have given their names to different places in the world. First, there was Sir Henry Morton Stanley (1841–1904), the famous explorer of Central Africa, who rescued Livingstone there (see **Livingstone**). Then, there was Edward George Geoffrey Smith Stanley, 14th Earl of Derby (1799–1869), styled 'Lord Stanley' (until 1851), who was both Colonial Secretary (twice, between 1833 and 1844) and Prime Minister (three times, between

1852 and 1868). As is to be expected, all the African Stanleys will have been named after the explorer. Some have subsequently been renamed indigenously, but they include: Mount Stanley, on the Zaire/Uganda border, which Stanley discovered in 1889 (and which is now known as Mount Ruwenzori, or Mount Ngaliema in Zaire); the Stanley Falls on the Congo (Zaire) River, Zaire; Stanley Pool, on this same river, between Congo and Zaire (and known in the latter country as Malebo Pool). (See also the next entry below for another place formerly named after him.) In Australia, the Tasmanian town of Stanley, on the other hand, is named after Lord Stanley. It arose as a penal colony and was the first settlement (in 1826) of the Van Dieman's Land Company (after the former name of Tasmania) in the island. (It was originally called Circular Head, for the promontory where it is located, this extending into **Bass Strait**.) It received its present name in 1833. Then there is Stanley, still also known as Port Stanley, the chief town and capital (since 1842) of the **Falkland Islands**. It was so named by Major-General Richard Moody, Lieutenant-Governor and Vice-Admiral of the Falkland Islands (from 1841 to 1847), who took up his official residence in the settlement in 1844 and named it after the Colonial Secretary. It was Lord Stanley himself, in fact, who ordered the transfer of the chief settlement on the island from Port Louis to Stanley. (Stanley Harbour was originally called Jackson Harbour, probably after the American President, Andrew Jackson. American whalers frequently visited the Falklands in the first half of the nineteenth century.)

Stanleyville (Zaire)

Stanleyville is the former name of the Zaire city now called Kisangani (since 1966). It was established in 1883 by Europeans and was at first called Falls Station, for its location just below **Stanley** Falls on the Congo (Zaire) River. It was then subsequently renamed for Sir Henry Morton Stanley, who explored and navigated the Congo River in the 1870s (and who named Stanley Pool and the **Livingstone** Falls).

Stanstead County (Canada)

The Quebec county is named after one of the English places called Stanstead (or Stansted). Perhaps the most likely is the Essex village of Stansted, now famous for its airport.

Starbuck Island (Pacific Ocean)

The island, now one of the Line Islands, belonging to Kiribati, was discovered in 1823 by Valentine Starbuck, the British captain of a whaling ship, and is thus named after him. As a remote island (it is an uninhabited coral atoll), it has also been known by several others names, including Volunteer Island, Starve Island, Low Island, Hero Island, Barren Island and Coral Queen Island. These are mostly descriptive, although one or two undoubtedly 'tell a tale'.

Staunton (USA)

The city in **Virginia** was founded by one John Lewis in 1736 and was named after Lady Rebecca Staunton, wife of Sir William Gooch (1681–1751), the British Lieutenant-Governor of Virginia. The town was the capital of Virginia for a brief period in 1781.

Stawell (Australia)

The town in **Victoria** arose in the gold rush of 1853 and was at first known as Pleasant Creek. It was subsequently renamed in honour of Sir William Foster Stawell (1815–1889), the Irish-born Chief Justice of Victoria from 1857 to 1873 and later Governor of the colony.

Stewart Island (New Zealand)

Stewart Island, south of South Island, was sighted by James Cook in 1770, when he believed it to be a peninsula, not noticing Foveaux Strait that separates it from South Island. He therefore named it Cape South. The error was corrected in 1809 when one Captain William Stewart, about whom little is known, surveyed the island and discovered the strait to the north of it. He may have been here earlier as a sealer and whaler. Whoever he was, he gave his name to the island, while his ship, the *Pegasus*, has had her name preserved in Pegasus Bay, on the island.

Stirling (Australia, New Zealand, Canada)
The Stirling Range of mountains, in Western Australia, was discovered in 1802 by Matthew Flinders (see **Flinders**) and named after Sir James Stirling (1791–1865), the first Governor of Western Australia (from 1828 to 1839), who was active in the establishment of **Fremantle** and **Perth**. The New Zealand community of Stirling, southeast of **Balclutha**, South Island, was however named by Scottish settlers after their native town (or county of Stirlingshire, now in Central). In Canada, Stirling, Ontario, was also named by Scottish emigrants, who are recorded as having noted a resemblance between the landscape here and that of their native country.

Stockport (USA)
Stockport, **New York**, is a community that was so named by an English mill owner, one James Wild, after his home town of Stockport in Cheshire (now in Greater Manchester).

Stokes, Mount (New Zealand)
Mount Stokes, north of **Wellington** at the northern end of South Island, was so named after the British admiral and explorer John Lort Stokes (1812–1885), who himself named Mount **Cook** (in 1851) and Mount **Peel** (also about this time).

Stormont County (Canada)
The county of this name in Ontario honours David Murray, 1st Viscount Stormont (died 1631), Comptroller of Scotland. The name was given by patriotic Scots settlers.

Stoughton (USA)
The Massachusetts town, in the **Boston** metropolitan area, was settled in 1713 as part of **Dorchester** and when incorporated in 1726 was named for William Stoughton (1631–1701), the first Lieutenant-Governor of the Massachusetts Bay Colony (from 1692 to 1701). His father, Israel Stoughton, was the founder of Dorchester.

Strafford (USA)
The title of Earl of Strafford was held by the Wentworth family, with the first of the name being Sir Thomas Wentworth, 1st Earl of Strafford (1593–1641), the Lord Deputy of Ireland who was impeached for treason and executed on Tower Hill. Two of his descendants were Benning Wentworth and John Wentworth, governors of **New Hampshire**. It is thus in this state that one finds the county and town of Strafford (the latter not the seat of the former, however). But it is likely that these place-names honour not so much the 1st Earl as the 4th, William Wentworth, who was a cousin of John Wentworth. See also **Wentworth**.

Strahan (Australia)
The Tasmanian town arose in the 1870s as the result of a goldrush near here. The name is a compliment to Major Sir George C. Strahan, who was Governor of Tasmania from 1881 to 1886.

Stratford (USA, Canada, New Zealand)
One cannot always assume a Shakespearean compliment for the name, but in many cases this is what one nevertheless finds, and the name of the great playwright's birthplace, Stratford-on-Avon, is a highly suitable one for adoption for a new overseas settlement, especially if there is a river that can be conveniently substituted for the 'Avon'. In some instances, indeed, the English name has had a genuine literary influence, and both Stratford, Connecticut, and Stratford, Ontario, now have thriving Shakespeare Festival Theatres to more than justify the name. The Connecticut town was settled in 1639, originally under the Indian name of Cupheag, and was given its present name four years later. (Some sources see the origin, moreover, in Stratford-le-Bow, London, rather than the Warwickshire town, which if so makes the place's present

Shakespearean reputation all the more remarkable.) The city in Ontario was founded in 1832 and was at first named Little Thames, after the river here (which was itself renamed the Avon by the Canada Company, a development organisation). The present name was given three years later. In New Zealand, the town of Stratford, North Island, has a different sort of modern Shakespearean reputation. Although named for his birthplace, it was at first called Stratford-on-Patea, after the river on which it stands. This was then shortened as at present. But the Bard lives on visibly here in the streets, many of which are named after characters from his plays. The town was actually founded in 1877. See also **Avon**.

Strathmore (Canada)
The community in **Alberta** has a specific noble if not royal compliment to pay. It was named for Claud Bowes-Lyon, Earl of Strathmore (1824–1904), whose granddaughter, Elizabeth Bowes-Lyon (born 1900), married the future George VI, and became Elizabeth, the Queen Mother.

Strathroy (Canada)
The town in Ontario was founded in the early nineteenth century, originally as Strath Valley or Red Valley, and when the land here was bought by John Stewart Buchanan in 1832 he renamed it after his native town, the small seaport of Strathroy, in Co. Antrim, Northern Ireland.

Stuart Island (USA)
Stuart Island, in **Norton** Sound, Alaska, was named by James Cook in 1778, although it is not clear whom he was complimenting. Perhaps he intended a general tribute to the royal house of Stuart? On the other hand, this had ended in 1714 with the death of Queen Anne, the last of the Stuarts. But the surname is common enough, and Cook may have meant a personal tribute to someone of the name.

Sturbridge (USA)
The town in Massachusetts was settled in about 1729 and incorporated nine years later, when it was named for the English town of Stourbridge, Worcestershire (now in West Midlands). There must have been an emigrant link here, unless the aim was to found a similar industrial settlement.

Sturt Desert (Australia)
The Sturt Desert, that extends across the border between South Australia and **Queensland**, is named after the explorer, Charles Sturt (1795–1869), whose expedition down the Murrumbidgee and **Murray** Rivers is generally regarded as one of the major explorations in the history of Australia. It seems unfair that the Murray, the country's greatest river, should not bear the name of the man who had toiled to chart its course, but instead that of the Colonial Secretary of the day, who had never even been to Australia.

Sudbury (USA, Canada)
Both Sudbury, Massachusetts, and Sudbury, Ontario, are named after the town in Suffolk, from which English colonists must have originally come. The United States town was settled in 1638, and the Canadian city in 1883, when rich copper and nickel ores were discovered during the construction of the Canadian Pacific Railway.

Suffolk (USA)
Although a potential 'title' name, for once there does not appear to be a Duke or Earl of Suffolk in sight, and the places of the name, such as the two Suffolk Counties (respectively in Massachusetts and **New York**), and the city in **Virginia**, were named after the English county, probably with colonist home ties there.

Sumner (New Zealand)
The seaside district of **Christchurch**, South Island, is named after John Bird Sumner (1780–1862), the Archbishop of Canterbury who was the President of the Canterbury Association (see **Canterbury**) formed in 1848 to establish a Church of England colony in New Zealand.

Sunbury (USA)
The **Pennsylvania** city was laid out on

the site of an Indian village known as Shamokin in 1772 and was named Sunbury, after the town in Surrey. The man who laid out the settlement was John Lukens, the Surveyor-General for Pennsylvania, but the actual giver of the name was the Governor, Richard Penn, son of the founder of Pennsylvania, William Penn. The association seems to have been a purely geographical one, with the new settlement located on the Susquehanna River just as the Surrey town is on the Thames. The suggestion of 'sun' may have helped, of course.

Sunderland (Canada)
The Ontario community was originally known as Brock. In 1868 the name was changed to Sunderland, after the coastal town in Co. Durham (now in Tyne and Wear). The Canadian Sunderland is not on the coast, although it lies about thirty miles from Lake Ontario and about half this distance from Lake **Simcoe**.

Sundridge (Canada)
The community in Ontario was apparently named after the village of Sundridge near Sevenoaks, Kent. But perhaps this particular name was chosen simply because it happened to suggest a 'sunny ridge', and there could be no actual link with the English place.

Surrey (Canada)
The municipality in **British Columbia**, where it forms a southwest suburb of **Vancouver**, was named after the English county of Surrey because it lies to the south of **New Westminster** in the same way that the English Surrey is to the south of Westminster, London. The Canadian community was incorporated in 1879. Compare the next entry below.

Surry (USA)
Surry County, **Virginia**, with its seat of the same name, is named after the English county of Surrey, as is Surry County, North **Carolina**. The name was probably selected to accord with the general pattern of English county names for their Virginian equivalents (compare **Bedford**, **Buckingham**, **Cumberland**, **Middlesex**, **Sussex**, etc.), with the spelling modified slightly, however. The Virginia county was formed in 1652 with this spelling, and the North Carolina county followed with it when it was formed in 1770.

Sussex (USA, Canada)
The name of the English county was adopted for three counties in the United States, respectively in **Delaware**, **New Jersey** and **Virginia**, in which last the seat has the same name. There may have been no actual connection with the English county, and in the case of Virginia the name was doubtless chosen to blend in with the many other counties that are named after their English counterparts (see **Surry**).

Sutherland (Australia, New Zealand)
We could have a duke to consider here, as well as a Scottish county. But in fact, at least in these two instances, we have neither! Sutherland that is now a southern district of **Sydney**, Australia, is so named because it is located by Sutherland Point, on Botany Bay, with the point being named after Forby Sutherland, one of James Cook's seamen who was buried here in 1770. In New Zealand, the Sutherland Falls, on the Arthur River, South Island, are named after the first European to see them, who was Donald Sutherland, a prospector who came here in 1880.

Sutton (USA, Canada)
Although in some instances the name derives from an early (or even a later) settler, in many others it seems to have been given after an English Sutton, even if it is now not certain exactly which. The Massachusetts town of Sutton was laid out in 1715, and *may* have additionally been so named because it lies immediately to the south of **Worcester**, which dates from 1684. This is to exploit the literal sense of the name as 'southern town'. In Canada, Sutton, Quebec, is probably more generally named. If a particular reference is needed, it may be to the town of Sutton in Surrey (now in Greater London). But

there are over at least thirty other Suttons in Britain as possibilities!

Swansea (USA, Australia)

One would expect Welsh connections for this name, and one finds them. The village of Swansea, Illinois, was so named by Welsh miners who settled here in the early years of the nineteenth century, while the larger town of Swansea, Massachusetts, had a Welshman as its first minister when it was founded in about 1667, and he came from the Glamorganshire seaport (now in West Glamorgan). In Australia, the Tasmanian town of Swansea was originally called Waterloo Point when it arose as a military garrison in the early nineteenth century. It was renamed in 1842 after the Welsh town from which the settlement's original land grantee had come.

Swift's Creek (USA)

The Kentucky community is named after one Jonathan Swift, an English sea captain who had visited the area. (This was *not* the famous author of *Gulliver's Travels*, however appropriate this would seem to be!) The name coincidentally suggests a fast-flowing stream.

Sydney (Australia, Canada)

Australia does not have a monopoly of the name, but it does have the best-known instance of it, so a very brief history is in order. The English explorer Captain Arthur Phillip (see **Phillip Island**, **Port Phillip**) had been sent to Botany Bay (discovered by Cook in 1770) by the British government to found a settlement. That was in 1788. On arriving, however, he found the bay to be too exposed for him to anchor safely, while the surrounding terrain did not appear congenial for settlement. He therefore looked further to the north and came to the entrance to **Port Jackson** (what is now Sydney Harbour), which had been named by Cook but not explored by him. Philip felt that the site would make a good anchorage ('in which a thousand sail of the line may ride in the most perfect security', he wrote in a despatch to Lord Thomas Sydney, the Home Secretary), and that a cove here would be suitable for a settlement. He thus named the cove Sydney Cove after the Home Secretary, and that was the first step in the founding of the city that today is the capital of **New South Wales**. Sydney Cove is now the chief overseas shipping terminal of the city, lying immediately to the west of the famous (or infamous) Sydney Opera House. (This potted history does not relate that the purpose of the settlement was to serve as a penal colony. But this was 1788, after all). Other places in other countries founded at about this time are thus also likely to have been named after Thomas Townsend (or Townshend), 1st Viscount Sydney (1733–1800), and they may be found in Canada, for example, notably in the city of Sydney, **Nova Scotia**, which was founded in 1783 as a place of refuge for Loyalists, and which was the capital of Nova Scotia until 1820. Sydney Harbor here, too, serves as a double of its Australian namesake. But the object here was not to found a penal settlement, and the founder, Joseph Desbarres (see **Northumberland**), had not left England with 11 ships, 200 marines, and 776 convicts, as Arthur Phillip had done when he set sail for Australia in 1787. See also **Townsend**, **Townshend**.

T

Talbot (USA, Australia)
Talbot County, **Maryland**, was named after Grace Talbot, daughter of George Calvert (see **Calvert**), 1st Baron Baltimore (see **Baltimore**), and sister of Cecilius Calvert, the first proprietor of the colony of Maryland. Cape Talbot, on the north coast of Western Australia, was so named in 1819 by Philip Parker King (see **King**) after Charles Chetwynd Talbot, Earl of Talbot (1777–1849), Lord Lieutenant of Ireland.

Tamar River (Australia)
The river in northern Tasmania was named after the river Tamar in southwest England, where it forms the boundary between Devon and Cornwall. It is in effect a tidal estuary, at the mouth of which stands **Port Dalrymple**, the first Tasmanian settlement (in 1804). The Tamar is navigable as far as **Launceston**, whose Cornish namesake lies similarly near the English river of the name.

Tamworth (Australia)
The **New South Wales** city was founded in 1838 by a British land development company and was named after the Staffordshire town of Tamworth, which at the time of naming was the parliamentary constituency of the Prime Minister, Sir Robert Peel (see **Peel**).

Taunton (USA)
The city of this name in Massachusetts was organised as a town in 1639 on land purchased from the Indians the previous year by a Somerset lady, Elizabeth Poole (1589–1654), who so designated it after her family seat in that English county.

Temora (Australia)
The **New South Wales** town was founded in the goldrush of 1879 and was given this Celtic literary name. *Temora* is one of the Ossianic epic poems written by Macpherson, where it features as the name of the palace of the kings of Ulster. In the original Gaelic, it means 'great house' (*Taigh-mòr*), which if interpreted as 'elevated place with a fine view' is an appropriate description of the Australian town on the western slopes of the Great Dividing Range, where it overlooks (to the west) the flat, fertile plains of the Riverina district.

Temple, Mount (Canada)
The mountain in **Alberta**, in the **Banff** National Park, was so named by the Canadian geologist and explorer, Dr George Mercer Dawson, for the English administrator (in India) and historian, Sir Richard Temple (1826–1902), who in 1884 led an expedition to the Rocky Mountains on behalf of the British Association, as President of its Section of Economic Science and Statistics.

Templeton (Canada)
The village in Quebec is believed to have been named after the village of Templeton near Tiverton, Devon. Presumably there were emigrant links there.

Tenterfield (Australia)
The town in northeast **New South Wales** was founded in 1848 and named after the Scottish home of one of the early settlers. This was Tentfield, near the Antonine Wall in Stirlingshire (now in Central).

Terra Nova Bay (Antarctica)
This is the name of a large inlet in the **Ross Sea**, off **Victoria** Land, which was discovered by Captain Scott in his first expedition of 1901–4 and named after the *Terra Nova*, one of the two support ships (the other was the *Morning*) that accompanied the *Discovery*. What more appropriate name (Latin for 'new land') for a ship used to explore and chart new territory? See also **Pennell Coast**.

Terror (Antarctica, Canada)
Mount Terror is an extinct volcano on Ross Island in the **Ross Sea**, off **Victoria** Land. It was so named after the *Terror*, one of the two ships in which James Ross explored this area of Antarctica in 1841. (The other ship, the *Erebus*, gave its name to Mount **Erebus**, the active volcano on this same island.) The ship's name is more classical than contemporary, and derives from the mythological personification of fear or fright. Ironically, in view of their doomladen names, the *Erebus* and the *Terror* were the two ships that were abandoned in the ice during John Franklin's final, fatal expedition to the Arctic in 1845, and two bays on **King William** Island there have been named respectively Erebus Bay and Terror Bay as a memorial to them. See **Franklin**.

Tewksbury (USA)
The town of Tewksbury, Massachusetts, was settled in 1734 and named after the English town of Tewkesbury in Gloucestershire, from which early settlers must have emigrated.

Thames (USA, Canada, New Zealand)
It is not so surprising that the name of Britain's best-known river should have been duplicated in the New World. In the United States, the Thames River is found in Connecticut, and was so named after the settlement of the town of **New London** at its mouth. The two names thus match there, as they do in Canada, where in Ontario the city of **London** (in **Middlesex** County) lies on the Thames River. Here, though, the town was named after the river, not the other way round. The Thames was so named in 1792, with the former name of the river being La Tranche. In New Zealand, the Waihou River in North Island was renamed by Cook in 1769 because it seemed to him to be as wide as the London Thames at Greenwich. The Maori name is still in use for the river as an alternative (sometimes preferred). And the small industrial town of Thames, at its mouth, is named after the river. It has no London, however!

Thetford Mines (Canada)
The Quebec city has asbestos mines that produce about half the world's supply of the mineral. The first deposits were discovered here in 1876, and the town was originally known as Kingsville, after the proprietor of the mines, a Mr King. Later, the name was changed to Thetford, after the town in Norfolk, presumably for emigrant connections there, perhaps through Mr King himself.

Thistle Island (Australia)
The island, at the entrance to **Spencer** Gulf, South Australia, was so named by Matthew Flinders (see **Flinders**) after John Thistle, one of the officers on board Flinders's ship *Investigator*. John Thistle had been the officer in charge of a ship's boat that went missing with all its crew in an attempt to land here.

Thompson (USA, Canada)
The town of Thompson in Connecticut was named after an Englishman, Robert Thompson, who owned much property in the town but who did not live there. In Canada, the Thompson River, in **British Columbia**, was discovered in 1808 by Simon Fraser (see **Fraser**) and was named after a fellow Scot, David Thompson, who is now wrongly credited with having reached its upper course, as it was initially claimed he had.

Thorold (Canada)
The industrial town of Thorold, Ontario, was named after Sir John Thorold, a Member of Parliament from Lincolnshire, who opposed the war against the American colonies and who was similarly

against the Constitutional Act of 1791. (This was passed by the British Parliament to give the same constitution in Canada to the colonies of Upper Canada, now Ontario, and Lower Canada, now Quebec.)

Thurso (Canada)
The Quebec town is named after the Scottish town of Thurso, Caithness (now in Highland), for what must have been emigrant links there.

Tilbury (Canada)
The town in Ontario lies at the mouth of the **Thames** River not far from **Chatham**, and is not only named after the English port of Tilbury, Essex, also on the Thames, but has a name that accords with all the others here that form the 'London neighbourhood' (see **London**). The town was originally known as Tilbury Centre, but the latter word was dropped from the name in 1895.

Tipton (USA)
Many Tiptons are named for local citizens and officials, but Tipton, Kansas, was apparently named for Tipton, Staffordshire, now a district of West Bromwich (West Midlands). There must have been emigrant connections with the place.

Tisbury (USA)
The town of Tisbury, Massachusetts, which was settled in about 1671, was named after an English Tisbury, probably the village near Wilton, Wiltshire. As always in such cases, without further evidence one must assume an emigrant link here.

Tiverton (USA)
Tiverton, Rhode Island, was settled in 1694 and named after the town of Tiverton, Devon, from which an early settler probably came.

Todd River (Australia)
The Todd River, in Northern Territory, was named in 1870 by surveyors for the Overland Telegraph Line after Sir Charles Todd (1826–1910), the English astronomer who organised the meteorological service and who was Postmaster General for South Australia from 1870 to 1905.

Toms River (USA)
The Toms River, **New Jersey**, was named for an early settler, one Thomas Luker, who came to America from England on the ship *Falcon* in 1685 to marry an Indian chieftain's daughter, Princess Ann, and who settled to live in a wigwam near the bridge over the river at what is now the resort of Toms River near its mouth.

Topsham (USA)
The town in Maine was settled in 1764 and named after the village of Topsham in Devon, which is now a suburb of Exeter. Many of the original settlers had come from there.

Torrens (Australia)
Lake Torrens, in South Australia, was discovered in 1839 by Edward Eyre (see **Eyre**) while seeking new pastures, and was named after Colonel (later Sir) Robert Torrens (1814–1884), who was Premier of South Australia for a brief time in 1857. He was the Irish-born son of the identically named Sir Robert Torrens who was one of the founders of South Australia in 1836. The Torrens River is similarly named after him. (The name should not be confused with that of the Torres Strait, between northern **Queensland** and Papua New Guinea. This was named after its Spanish discoverer.)

Torrington (USA)
The industrial city in Connecticut was originally settled in about 1735 under the name of New Orleans Village or Mast Swamp. In 1732 it was renamed after the Devon town of Torrington (also known as Great Torrington), from which some of the original settlers had come. (For much of the nineteenth century it was further renamed as Wolcottville, after a family named Wolcott who built a woollen mill here. The name reverted to Torrington, however, in 1883.) Torrington, Wyoming, was laid out in 1908 and named after the Connecticut town.

Townsend (USA)
The Massachusetts town was named for Charles Townsend (or Townshend), 2nd Viscount Townsend (1674–1738), a statesman and diplomat who went over from the Tories to the Whigs and who was twice Secretary of State for the Northern Department. His son, Thomas Townsend, was the cabinet minister who gave his name to **Sydney**, Australia. Compare the next entry.

Townshend (Australia)
Townshend Island and its headland of Cape Townshend, off the eastern coast of **Queensland**, are both named after Thomas Townshend (also spelt Townsend), 1st Viscount Sydney, who gave the name of **Sydney**. The cape was named first, by Cook in 1770. Later, in 1802, Matthew Flinders (see **Flinders**) extended the name to the whole island, which Cook did not seem to have sighted. Compare the entry above.

Townsville (Australia)
Taken at its face value, the name seems a toponymical tautology! However, the **Queensland** city and port, founded in 1864, was actually named after Robert Towns (1791–1873), an English sailor who settled in **Sydney** in 1842 and who commissioned one John Black to find a suitable port and harbour here for northern livestock owners.

Tredyffrin (USA)
The **Pennsylvania** community, in **Chester** County, has an artificially devised Welsh name which means 'township in the valley' and which is descriptive of its location. Some colonial documents record the place under the equivalent English name of Valleytown.

Trent (USA)
North **Carolina** has two rivers of the name, which seems to derive more or less arbitrarily from the English river Trent that flows into the Humber.

Trotwood (USA)
A Dickensian compliment! The village in Ohio was so named by the postmaster, a lover of Dickens, after Betsey Trotwood, David Copperfield's aunt in the novel that bears his name.

Truro (USA, Canada)
The name, wherever it occurs, derives from the Cornish cathedral town. Truro, Illinois and Truro, Massachusetts are two examples in the United States. In Canada, the **Nova Scotia** town originally had the Indian name of Cobequid ('end of flowing water', for its location at the head of Cobequid Bay). In 1759, at the suggestion of New Englanders and Scottish-Irish settlers from Northern Ireland, the name was changed to Truro, presumably for its Celtic connotation.

Tryon (Canada)
The **Prince Edward Island** community was so named in honour of William Tryon (1725–1788), the British general who was Governor of North **Carolina** in 1765 and of **New York** in 1771.

Tunbridge (USA)
The **New Hampshire** community was named after the same Viscount Tunbridge and Baron Enfield and Colchester who gave the names of **Colchester** and **Enfield**.

Tweed River (Australia)
The **New South Wales** river was discovered in 1823 by the English explorer John Oxley, who named it in a fairly random manner after the Tweed in Scotland. It was Oxley who also named the **Peel** and **Hastings** Rivers and **Port Macquarie**.

Tyndall (USA, New Zealand)
Tyndall County, South Dakota, is named after John Tyndall (1820–1893), an English physicist who came to lecture in the United States. (His special interest was glaciers.) Mount Tyndall, in the Southern Alps, South Island, New Zealand, was also named after him (in 1861).

Tyrone (USA)
The **Pennsylvania** borough was named for the Irish county of Tyrone. Emigrants from Northern Ireland had settled in this particular region early.

Tyrrell, Lake (Australia)
The lake was visited in 1838 by Edward Eyre (see **Eyre**) when he was in search of new grazing grounds, and he named it after an early settler in the **Port Phillip** area.

U

Ugie (South Africa)
The Cape Province town owes its origin to the Scottish missionary William Murray, who when working among the Griquas in the area was reminded of his native land and named his station, set up in 1863, after the river Ugie, Aberdeenshire (now in Grampian). The mission station was thus the nucleus that gave the town of Ugie, established in 1874.

Ulverstone (Australia)
The Tasmanian town was surveyed some time before 1855 and named after the town of Ulverston, Lancashire (now in Cumbria). Perhaps the adoption of the name was more for a geographical affinity than an emigrant link: the Tasmanian town is near the mouth of the Leven River on **Bass Strait**, while its English counterpart is also near the mouth of the river Leven which flows into Morecambe Bay near here.

Union Jack (Canada)
The community in Saskatchewan was originally known as Verendrye. In 1928 this name was changed to Union Jack 'for patriotic reasons' (Hamilton: see Bibliography, p. 219). The British national flag does not feature as any part of the Canadian flag, although it still appears as a quarter of the Australian and New Zealand flags, and as a small but distinct element within the national flag of South Africa.

Upington (South Africa)
The Cape Province town was originally known as Olijvenhoutsdrift, after the mission station founded in 1871 from which it developed. In 1884 it was renamed after Sir Thomas Upington (1844–1898), the Prime Minister of the Cape Colony (from 1884 to 1886) who visited it that year.

Upton (USA, Canada)
Although the name could be purely descriptive, for a 'hill town', both Upton, Maine, and Upton, Massachusetts, appear to be named specifically after the village of Upton near Elmsall, Yorkshire. This particular Upton seems the most likely, but it is fair to point out, however, that there are many other Uptons in England from where any original settlers could have come! (Nor should one overlook the fact that Upton is also a surname, and could similarly have originated from a settler's family.) In Canada, the community of Upton in Quebec was established in 1800 and is probably named, with emigrant links, after Upton in Cheshire, where it is now a northern suburb of Chester.

Uxbridge (USA, Canada)
The Massachusetts town may perhaps be named after Uxbridge, Middlesex, now in Greater London. But the naming took place relatively late, in 1727, and is more likely to be a tribute to Henry Paget, 1st Earl of Uxbridge (died 1743), who was a member of the Privy Council. In Canada, however, the town of Uxbridge was specifically named after its English counterpart by its founder, Joseph Gould, who had family ties there. (A local legend, however, claims that the town was originally nicknamed Oxbridge, and that this was subsequently changed to Uxbridge. But there is no basis for the tale.)

V

Valleyfield (Canada)

The city in Quebec, on the St Lawrence River, arose on a group of islands here after a paper mill was built in 1870. The mill was operated by the Scottish company of Valleyfield Paper Mills, of Edinburgh, so this therefore is the ultimate source of the name. (The Scottish mill was the one in Penicuik, ten miles from Edinburgh, where it was built in 1709, trading as Alexander Cowan & Sons.)

Vancouver (Canada, USA)

British Columbia is famous for its city of Vancouver and for its Vancouver Island, the largest island off the west coast of Canada. Both are named for the British navigator and explorer George Vancouver (1758–1798), who first went to sea at the age of 13 under James Cook (see **Cook**), and who subsequently, between 1790 and 1795, explored both the western coast of North America and the Australian area, circumnavigating the world in the process. He and members of his crew named many features in the regions they explored and surveyed, although he did not name the city of Vancouver. The name was actually proposed by Sir William Cornelius Van Horne, who was General Manager of the Canadian Pacific Railway at the time (in 1887) when the railroad reached the western coast here. He therefore wanted a suitably 'western' name, and made the wise choice of George Vancouver's surname for the railroad terminus built at this site that year. (Earlier, the sawmill settlement here, with its fine natural harbour, had been known as Granville.) Vancouver Island, opposite which the city lies, was surveyed by Cook in 1792, but had been earlier visited by him in 1776, with Vancouver present on board (the first time as a midshipman) on both occasions. He was thus credited with discovering the strait (now known as **Queen Charlotte** Sound in its northern extent, and the Strait of Georgia in its southern part) that separates the island from the mainland. Vancouver therefore named the island after himself, so that the name was an obvious choice for Van Horne a hundred years later. In the United States, all the places of the name are usually a direct tribute to George Vancouver rather than a derivative from the city, and indeed they will have arisen long before its late development. The city of Vancouver in Washington, for example, was founded as a trading post of the Hudson's Bay Company (see **Hudson**) in 1824 under the name of Fort Vancouver, while the many places of the name in Alaska (such as Mount Vancouver, Vancouver Island and Cape Vancouver) are also a direct tribute to him. George Vancouver, despite the fact that he was a true Englishman (born in Norfolk, died in Surrey), has a family name that hardly appears typically English! But it is, despite its ultimate Dutch origin, and is thus similar to names such as Vansittart and Vanderfelt (or Vanderbilt) that have been assimilated as English over the past three centuries. (Look in *Who's Who*, for example, and you will find many such names beginning with 'Van-'.) Compare also the next entry below.

Vansittart (Australia, Canada)

Both Vansittart Bay, in Western Australia, and Vansittart Island, south of **Melville** Peninsula, Northwest Territories, Canada, are named after Nicholas

Vansittart, Baron Bexley (1766–1851), Chancellor of the Exchequer from 1812 to 1822. He gave his title to Cape **Bexley**.

Victor Harbour (Australia)

The town and seaside resort in South Australia was founded in 1839 and named after HMS *Victor*, a British ship that had called here two years earlier.

Victoria (worldwide)

Although Queen Victoria (1819–1901) has now been dead for the best part of a century, her prodigious reign (from 1837 to 1901, and the second longest in British history), coupled with her prestigious name (implying 'victory' and the conquests of the British Empire), have assured her commemoration in many place-names round the world, from states to cities and rivers to mountains. *The Times Atlas of the World* (see Bibliography, p. 217) has over seventy Victorias or Victoria-related names playing compliment to the Queen, and it is clearly impossible to detail here more than a fraction of these. Suffice it to say that they will all have originated in (or in a few cases after) her reign and will all have been given in her honour but at the same time will have had the associations of 'greatness' and 'victory' already mentioned. Here, then, are some of the major places of the name, together with the year of naming (if known) and any other relevant details. The Australian state of Victoria, originally part of **New South Wales**, was set off from that colony in 1851. Victoria, the capital of **British Columbia**, Canada, was founded in 1834 as a fur-trading post of the Hudson's Bay Company (see **Hudson**) under the name of Fort Camosun, but was renamed (originally as Fort Victoria) in 1843. Victoria, the capital of Hong Kong, was founded in 1842. Victoria (originally Port Victoria), the capital of the Seychelles, was founded in 1841. Lake Victoria, the largest lake in Africa, mainly in Tanzania and Uganda, was discovered by the British explorer John Speke in 1858 and named by him that year. The Victoria Falls on the Zambezi, on the Zambia/Zimbabwe border, were sighted by Livingstone (see **Livingstone**) in 1855 and named by him that year. (The town of Victoria Falls here, in Zimbabwe, was founded during the building of the Victoria Falls Bridge in 1905). Victoria Island in the Canadian Arctic was discovered by Thomas Simpson in 1838. Victoria Land, in the Antarctic, was discovered in 1841. Victoria River in Northern Territory, Australia, was discovered in 1839 by Captain J.C. Wickham of the *Beagle*. In Canada, there are three Victoria Counties, respectively in **New Brunswick**, **Nova Scotia** and Ontario. In South Africa, the Ciskei district of Victoria East was named in 1847, while the town of Victoria West, in Cape Province, was laid out in 1844 (originally as Victoria, adding 'West' in 1855 to distinguish it from the district). Some places of the name have now taken an indigenous name, such as Victoria, the town and port in Cameroon, West Africa, which is now Limbe, and the former town of Fort Victoria in **Rhodesia** that is now Masvingo, Zimbabwe. But by no means all places named Victoria will have honoured the British Queen, and Victoria County, Texas, for example, pays tribute to a Mexican president, while others will have simply commemorated a victory. (In this respect it is significant that the Queen's name was also that of the Roman goddess of victory in classical mythology, the equivalent of the Greek goddess Nike. As such, the goddess Victoria was worshipped by the army.) How fortunate she was, therefore, to have been given a name that in more senses than one would 'send her victorious' round the world. See also **Regina** and the next entry below.

Victoriaville (Canada)

The Quebec town was originally known as Demersville after a French bishop. This was altered to the present name (retaining the French '-ville') in 1861 in honour of Queen Victoria (see previous entry).

Virden (Canada)

The Manitoba town was originally known as Gopher Creek before it was renamed Manchester by officials of the Canadian Pacific Railway in 1882. Later, it was further renamed as now, after the Scottish estate of George Stephen, 1st Baron Mount Stephen (1829–1921), whose family already lived here in Canada at the time of the settlement of the town. Stephen himself had gone to Canada in 1850, where he became President of the Bank of Montreal and an influential figure in the construction of the Canadian Pacific Railway.

Virginia (USA)

A *British* name, the reader may wonder? Yes, or rather, a British nickname. The state of Virginia was named for Queen Elizabeth I (1533–1603), the 'Virgin Queen' who came to the throne in 1558. The name, as often in such 'territorial' cases (compare **New South Wales**), originally applied to a much larger area than that of the present state, and indeed was used of all lands claimed by the British in North America. The first (unsuccessful) attempt at colonisation was made in 1584 at Roanoke Island (now in North **Carolina**), and there is documentary evidence that the name was given that year to the territory by the Queen herself, with a reference to 'now called Virginia Anno 1584'. Elizabeth would certainly have been aware of the nickname, or the poetic designation, that described her unmarried state. The name was singularly appropriate, too, for what was then a 'virgin land', and doubtless the Queen, if she did give the name, was aware of this also. The first permanent English settlement was not made until after her death, however, at **Jamestown** in 1607. Various parts of the original colony were subsequently ceded as other states were formed, including **West Virginia** (which see below) in 1863.

Viscount Melville Sound
(Canada)

Formerly Melville Sound, the arm of the Arctic Ocean in **Franklin** District, Northwest Territories, was so named by William Parry (see **Parry**) during his exploratory voyage here of 1819–20 in honour of Viscount Melville, for details of whom see **Melville**.

Wager Bay (Canada)
The inlet in **Roes Welcome**, Northwest Territories, was named in 1742 after Sir Charles Wager (1666–1743), the English admiral.

Wakefield (New Zealand)
The New Zealand community, in the north of South Island, is not named for the famous New Zealand coloniser, Edward Gibbon Wakefield (1796–1862), who organised the New Zealand Association and who was prominent in the Canterbury Association that settled **Canterbury**, but for his younger brother Arthur Wakefield (1799–1843), who was instrumental in founding **Nelson** but who was killed by Maoris near here in what has gone down in New Zealand history as the Wairu Massacre.

Wake Island (Pacific Ocean)
The island is one of three, comprising an atoll in the central Pacific, where it is United States territory. It is named after the British sailor William Wake, who visited it in 1796. The atoll was not properly charted, however, until 1841 (by an American expedition).

Wales (USA, Canada)
The city of Wales on Cape **Prince of Wales**, Alaska, is named after the Prince's title (for the particular prince involved, see the entry). In Canada, however, Wales Point, Manitoba, was named after William Wales (?1734–1798), the British astronomer who was sent to **Churchill** near here in 1769 to observe the transit of Venus that year. The name was adopted only as recently as 1948.

Walkerton (Canada)
The Ontario town is named after an Irish miller, Joseph Walker, who settled here in 1850 and built the first sawmill.

Wallaceburg (Canada)
The town in Ontario was originally known as The Forks, for its location at the confluence of the two branches of the Sydenham River. It was subsequently renamed by the first postmaster, a Scot, after Sir William Wallace (?1272–1305), the famous Scottish patriot and guardian of Scotland (familiar from Robert Burns's line, 'Scots, wha hae wi' Wallace bled').

Wallingford (USA)
The Connecticut town was founded on land purchased from Indians in 1638, and was opened to white settlers in 1667. Its original name was East River (also New Haven Village), and in 1670, when it was incorporated, it was renamed for the Berkshire (now Oxfordshire) town of Wallingford. It is not clear what the connections were, if any, with the English counterpart, unless there were colonist ties there.

Wallis Islands (Pacific Ocean)
The Wallis Islands, to the west of Western Samoa in the southwest Pacific, are a part of the French territory of Wallis and Futuna Islands. They were visited in 1767 by the British navigator Samuel Wallis (1728–1795), and are named after him. The islands came under French control, with no change of name, in 1842.

Walmer (South Africa)
Walmer is a western residential district of **Port Elizabeth**, Cape Province, where it was named after Walmer Castle, Kent,

the seat of the Duke of Wellington (see **Wellington**).

Walpole (USA, Pacific Ocean)

Both towns of the name in Massachusetts and **New Hampshire** were named after Sir Robert Walpole (1676–1745), regarded as the first modern British Prime Minister, holding this post, and that of Chancellor of the Exchequer, twice between 1715 and 1742, in which time he did much to encourage both colonial and international trade. Walpole, Massachusetts was first settled in 1659, but was given its present name on being separately incorporated from Dedham in 1724. Walpole, **New Hampshire** was not named until 1752, so is a posthumous commemoration. Walpole Island, **New Caledonia**, in the southwest Pacific, was discovered by the captain of the ship *Walpole* in 1794, and was named after her. The ship was herself named after the famous statesman.

Walsingham, Cape (Canada)

The cape, on the eastern coast of **Baffin** Island, Northwest Territories, was discovered and named by John Davis (of the **Davis** Strait here) in 1585, with the name given as a tribute to one of his patrons, Sir Francis Walsingham (?1530–1590), Secretary of State from 1573 to his death.

Waltham (USA)

The city of Waltham, Massachusetts, was settled in the 1630s and named after the town of Waltham Abbey, Essex, from which several of the early emigrants had come.

Wareham (USA)

The Massachusetts town was settled in 1739 and named after the town of Wareham, Dorset, from which a number of the original residents had come.

Warkworth (New Zealand)

The town of Warkworth, north of **Auckland**, North Island, was so named by two early settlers from Northumberland, after their native village of Warkworth. The geographical locations of the two places near the sea may have served as an additional motive for the naming.

Warren (USA)

Most places of the name in the United States are commemorative of the great American Revolutionary leader, Joseph Warren. In Rhode Island, however, the town of Warren is named after Admiral Sir Peter Warren (1703–1752), who played an important part in the French and Indian Wars and who commanded the British fleet in the victory at Fort Louisburg in 1745 (see **Nova Scotia**).

Warrenton (South Africa)

The Cape Province town was laid out in 1884 and was named after Sir Charles Warren (1840–1927), the British colonel who commanded the expedition to Bechuanaland that year.

Warwick (USA, Canada, Australia)

The city of Warwick, Rhode Island, was first settled in 1643, and subsequently was named for Robert Rich, 2nd Earl of Warwick (1587–1658), who played an influential part in the founding of Rhode Island and who was a defender of religious freedom. Both Warwick, **New York**, and Warwick, **Pennsylvania**, appear to be named for the English city, however, or for the county of Warwickshire, from which doubtless early settlers had come. In Canada, the town in Quebec is known to have been named after the county in 1804, while in Australia, the **Queensland** city of Warwick appears to have been named after its English counterpart, also probably for an early settler's links with the town. The American places of the name are usually pronounced as if two words ('war wick').

Waterford (USA)

The **Pennsylvania** community was established in 1795 and named after the town (or county) in Ireland, from which some of the first Irish settlers here had come.

Waterloo (USA, Canada)

There are many places of the name in both the United States and Canada, as well as in other countries, and they all without exception commemorate the Duke of Wellington's victory, together with allied forces, over the forces of Napoleon in 1815 at (or near) the village of Waterloo in Belgium. Among some of the best known are the city of Waterloo, Iowa, and the town of Waterloo, Ontario. The name is coincidentally easily assimilated into English, and is suitable for a settlement by the water or on a river. See also **Wellington**.

Waterton (Canada)
The Waterton Lakes National Park, **Alberta**, established in 1895, takes its name from the lakes that are a major feature here, and that were themselves named after Charles Waterton (1782–1865), the English naturalist and traveller. The namer was Thomas Blakiston, who was a member of John Palliser's expedition to western British America in the 1840s and 1850s. The name happens to be entirely suitable for its 'watery' location.

Watling Island (Bahamas)
The island is now usually known by the name that Columbus gave it when he landed here in 1592, San Salvador. The English name commemorates one John Watling (died 1681), a 'hardened old pirate' who settled here in the West Indies in the seventeenth century.

Waverley (Canada, New Zealand)
The community in **Nova Scotia** derives its name from a cottage here, which was itself named by its owner, Charles P. Allen, after the *Waverley* novels of Walter Scott. In New Zealand, the town of Waverley in southwest North Island was originally known by the common placename of Wairoa ('high waterfall'). This was changed fairly arbitrarily to Waverley in order to avoid confusion with other places of the name. Compare the next entry below.

Waverly (USA)
Although spelt without the second 'e' of the original, places named Waverly pay a compliment (more romantic than literary, one suspects) to Walter Scott's *Waverley* novels, the first of which was published in 1814. The best-known places of the name are the city in Iowa, the town in Tennessee, and the two villages respectively in **New York** and Ohio. There is a tale that the Iowa city was mistakenly named by a Scott devotee during a speech in which he should have named the settlement after its founder, one William P. Harmon. Compare the entry above.

Weddell Sea (Antarctica)
Weddell Sea, east of the Antarctic Peninsula, is named after the British sealer and explorer, James Weddell (1787–1834), who in 1823, on board the *Jane*, succeeded in finding an open route to the southeast here, where others before him had failed, and managed to reach farther south (to 74° 15′S, 34° 17′W) than any previous explorer had yet penetrated. Weddell himself loyally named the sea George IV Sea, after his reigning monarch, and this name was in use until 1900 when it was proposed that the sea should be more properly named after the man who had discovered it.

Welland (Canada)
The Ontario city of Welland, the seat of Welland County, is on the Welland River and the Welland Ship Canal. It was originally named The Aqueduct when it arose round the first Welland Canal, completed here in 1829, then it was renamed Merrittsville, after William Merritt, one of the canal's builders. Finally, it was renamed in 1856 for the canal, which had itself been named at the time of its projection after the river Welland, in Lincolnshire, by John Simcoe (see **Simcoe**), the first Lieutenant-Governor of Upper Canada (now Ontario). Simcoe himself was born in north Northamptonshire, only a few miles from the Welland as it flows through south Lincolnshire.

Wellesley (USA, Australia)
Wellesley Island, **New York**, where it is one of the major Thousand Islands in the upper St Lawrence River, was named after

Sir Arthur Wellesley, otherwise the famous Duke of Wellington (for details of whom see the next entry below). However, the Wellesley Islands in the Gulf of Carpentaria, Australia, were so named in 1802 by Matthew Flinders (see **Flinders**) after Richard Colley Wellesley, Marquess of Wellesley (1760–1842), the noted Governor General of India. His second title, as Earl of Mornington, gave the name of **Mornington** Island here, the largest in the group. The Marquess's younger brother Arthur was the renowned 'Hero of Waterloo' of the next entry.

Wellington (New Zealand, Australia, USA, Canada, South Africa)
Wherever one finds the name, it will honour the 'Iron Duke', Arthur Wellesley, 1st Duke of Wellington (1769–1853), famous for his victory with the allied forces over Napoleon at the Battle of Waterloo in 1815 (see **Waterloo**). New Zealand's capital city of Wellington, in the extreme south of North Island, was so named in 1840, honouring not so much the battle as the generous aid given by the Duke to the New Zealand Company, whose colonist members had arrived the previous year with the task of finding a suitable site for their first settlement. (The Company was a development from the earlier New Zealand Association: see **Wakefield**.) Wellington was not immediately the capital, however, for that was **Auckland** until 1865. Australia's town of the name, in **New South Wales**, arose from the exploration base set up here in 1817 by the English explorer John Oxley. The settlement was first a penal colony before it was proclaimed a town in 1846. In the United States, both Wellington, Kansas, and Wellington, Texas, were named to honour theDuke, the former being given the name by its original settlers in 1871, and the latter by British cattlemen and promoters. (However, Wellington, Ohio, was probably not named for the Duke but for an early settler, one William Welling.) In Canada, the Duke's title can be found in Wellington Channel, between **Cornwallis Island** and **Devon** Island, Northwest Territories. And in South Africa, the town of Wellington in the Cape was established in 1840 and likewise compliments the same Duke, whose own title derives from the market town of Wellington, Somerset.

Wells (USA)
Several places of the name honour local American citizens and leaders, but the town of Wells, Maine, settled in 1635, took the name of the cathedral city in Somerset, doubtless through emigrant connections there.

Wenham (USA)
The Massachusetts community, which was settled in 1643, took its name from either Great or Little Wenham, villages in Suffolk near Hadleigh. Early colonists must have come from this area.

Wentworth (USA, Canada, Australia)
The village of Wentworth, North **Carolina**, was named for Charles Wentworth, Marquis of Rockingham (see **Rockingham** for details about him), while Lake Wentworth, **New Hampshire**, was named after a former governor of the state, Benning Wentworth (who although a colonial governor with English family ties was actually born in America). In Canada, Wentworth County, **Nova Scotia**, was named for another member of this same family, Sir John Wentworth (1737–1820), Lieutenant-Governor of Nova Scotia from 1792 to 1808. (He was Benning Wentworth's nephew.) In Australia, the **New South Wales** town of Wentworth was named after quite a different Wentworth. This was William Charles Wentworth (1793–1872), born to an Irish surgeon on what was at the time the penal colony of Norfolk Island, Australia. He became known as 'The Australian Patriot', and was the founder of colonial self-government in Australia, as well as of **Sydney** University. The town of his name arose in 1859 around a store that had been set up at a point where the explorer Charles Sturt (see **Sturt Desert**) had ended his journey down the **Darling** River in 1829.

Wesley (South Africa)
The village of Wesley, Ciskei, was founded in 1823 by a member of the Wesleyan Missionary Society here and was almost certainly named after John Wesley (1703–1791), the founder of Methodism. Compare the next entry below.

Wesleyville (USA, Canada)
The borough of Wesleyville, **Pennsylvania** was laid out in 1828 by one John Shadduck, who built a Methodist church here and named the settlement after John Wesley, the founder of Methodism (see entry above). Similarly named for him is the community of Wesleyville, Newfoundland, which was known as Coal Harbour until 1884 but was then renamed as now.

Westbury (USA)
The **New York** residential village of Westbury was named after one of the places of this name in England, although which is not certain. The best known is the town of Westbury, Wilshire, but there are also several villages of the name.

West Chester (USA)
Whether West Chester (two words) or Westchester (one word), places of the name usually derive from either the city of Chester or its county of Cheshire, from which many early colonists had emigrated. 'West' implies a transatlantic settlement. Two of the best known are the **Pennsylvania** borough of West Chester (in **Chester** County), and the village of Westchester, Illinois, where it is now a suburb of Chicago.

Westcliffe (USA)
The Colorado town was so named by an early settler who had come from the village (now town) of Westcliff-on-Sea, Essex (now a district of Southend-on-Sea).

Westminster (USA, South Africa)
In most cases, the name will relate to London's Westminster, or to something connected with it, such as Westminster Abbey or the so-called Westminster Catechism. The latter was the religious formulation drawn up during the English Civil War that was subsequently adopted by Presbyterians. The association will thus usually be religious, not political, as one might suppose from the name, and the city of Westminster, California, for example, was specifically so named by Presbyterian settlers, while the South **Carolina** town was named for its church (so that the association was with Westminster Abbey). In South Africa, however, the village of Westminster, Orange Free State, was named after the Duke of Westminster when it was founded by him to settle British ex-soldiers after the second Boer War (1899–1902). Compare **New Westminster**.

Westmoreland (USA, Canada)
There are two counties of the name in the United States, and one in Canada. Westmoreland County, **Pennsylvania** was named after the (now former) English county, but at the same time had a descriptive name for its location in the west of the state. Westmoreland County, **New Brunswick**, was given a similar name of dual significance, coming from the English county but also alluding to the Canadian county's location next to **Cumberland** County, as its English counterpart used to be. The Kansas city of Westmoreland was named after the Pennsylvania County. The remaining county of the name is in **Virginia**. The English county, abolished in 1974, was spelt without the second 'e' (i.e. as Westmorland), and was pronounced with the 'West-' accented unlike the American pronunciation, which stresses the second syllable (as if it was 'west moorland'). This is actually appropriate geographically for the Canadian county, which has moors and marshes.

Westport (New Zealand)
The borough and port in northwest South Island arose after gold and coal were discovered locally in the late 1850s, and it is said to take its name from the Irish port of Westport, Co. Mayo. Both places are geographically descriptive of their location and operation as ports on the western coast.

West Virginia (USA)
The state of West Virginia was part of **Virginia** until the Civil War (of 1861–5 between the North and the South), when it was admitted to the Union (in 1863) and so named for its location to the west of what remained of Virginia. There is thus (as there often is, by implication) no 'East Virginia'. Compare North **Carolina**, South Carolina; North Dakota, South Dakota.

Wethersfield (USA)
The town in Connecticut was settled in 1634 as the oldest permanent English settlement in the future state, and was originally known as Watertown, for its location on the Connecticut River. Three years later it was renamed after the English village of Wethersfield, Essex, from which one or more of the original residents must have come.

Wexford County (USA)
Wexford County, Michigan, was named after the Irish town or county, from which some of the original settlers had emigrated.

Weymouth (USA)
The Massachusetts town was settled in 1635 and named for the port of Weymouth, Dorset, from which many of the early colonists had set sail for America.

Whitby (Canada)
The Ontario town was first settled in about 1794, and became known as Perry's Corner after one Peter Perry arrived here in 1836. In 1855 the name was changed to Whitby, after the English town and port in Yorkshire, presumably as there had been emigrant ties here, although the Ontario town is also a port (on Lake Ontario).

Whitehall (USA)
There are several places of the name in the United States, in each case having a direct or indirect reference to the London street, whose name is synonymous for the British government and its main offices.

Whittlesea (South Africa)
The Ciskei village, south of **Queenstown**, was founded in 1849 and named after the village (now town) of Whittlesey (as it is usually spelt) in Cambridgeshire, which was the birthplace of Sir Harry Smith (see **Harrismith**), the Cape Governor. The English town has a pub, the 'Hero of Aliwal', named after him (see **Aliwal North**).

Wiarton (Canada)
The town in Ontario is named after Wiarton Place, near Maidstone, Kent, which was the birthplace of Sir Edmund Walker Head (1805–1868), Governor General of Canada from 1854 to 1861.

Wilberforce, Cape (Australia)
Cape Wilberforce, northwest of Cape Arnhem, Northern Territory, was named after the famous philanthropist and anti-slavery campaigner, William Wilberforce (1759–1833).

Wilbraham (USA)
The Massachusetts town, so named in 1763, probably honours the village of Great (or even Little) Wilbraham, near Cambridge, unless the tribute is to a Viscount Wilbraham.

Wilkes-Barre (USA)
The **Pennsylvania** city was settled in 1786 and was given the names of two British politicians who supported the cause of the American colonies in their speeches in Parliament. These were the outspoken journalist and polemicist (both popular and notorious), John Wilkes (1725–1797), who was repeatedly expelled from Parliament for his forthright stance as a 'champion of liberty' in the colonies, and the Irish-born soldier and Member of Parliament (the son of French parents), Isaac Barré (1726–1802), who equally opposed the taxation of the colonies under Lord North. The latter's name also gave that of the town of Barre, Massachusetts, and the city of the same name (after the Massachusetts town) in Vermont. The pronunciation of 'Barre' varies from 'Barrer' to 'Barry' to 'Barr'.

Williamsburg (USA)

The **Virginia** city of Williamsburg, with its famous College of William and Mary, one of the oldest in the United States, was first settled in 1633 as Middle Plantation. In 1699, after **Jamestown** had been burned down, the town became the capital of Virginia and was renamed to honour William III, who reigned with Mary from 1689 to 1702. Williamsburg is the oldest incorporated city in the United States. (Williamsburg, Kentucky is named for an American colonel.) In 1780, the Virginian capital was moved to **Richmond**, and Williamsburg declined in importance. Compare the next entry below.

Williamstown (Australia)

The town in **Victoria** was settled in 1835 and two years later was given its name in honour of William IV, the 'Sailor King' (or 'Silly Billy'), who reigned from 1830 to his death seven years later. His wife was Queen Adelaide, who gave her name to **Adelaide**. Today, Williamstown is a district of **Melbourne**. Compare the previous entry above.

Willingboro (USA)

The **New Jersey** township was first settled in about 1677 by English Quakers. In 1682 one Thomas Olive arrived here and named it for his native English town of Wellingborough, since when the name has been refashioned in its present spelling. (From 1959 to 1963 it was renamed Levittown, after a building firm that had played a part in community development. The name was temporary, however.) For a similar spelling adjustment, compare the next entry below.

Willington (USA)

The Connecticut town, incorporated in 1727, is named after the town of Wellington, Shropshire, from which early settlers had come. (Note that this is not the same town that gave the title of the Duke of Wellington, and thus the name of the many places called **Wellington**.) Compare also the next entry.

Wilmington (USA)

The **Delaware** city of Wilmington was founded by Swedish settlers in 1638 and initially called Fort Christina. The Dutch then captured it, and renamed it as Altena. Finally the English won it from the Dutch in 1664. It retained the Dutch name, however, until the 1730s, when the Quakers moved here. They secured a borough charter from Thomas Penn, the son of William Penn, the founder of **Pennsylvania**, and he renamed the town for his friend Spencer Compton, Earl of Wilmington (?1673–1743), Speaker of the House of Commons (until 1727) and then Lord Privy Seal (in 1730). (At first the name was officially Willington, but became as now in 1739.) In North **Carolina**, the city of Wilmington was formed from two existing communities in the 1730s, and was at first called New Town (or Newton). In 1740, on incorporation, it also was renamed after the Earl.

Wilson (Australia, Antarctica)

Wilson's Promontory, the southernmost point of the Australian mainland, in **Victoria**, was discovered in 1798 by the English explorer George Bass (see **Bass Strait**) and was initially called Furneaux Land after Tobias Furneaux (see **Furneaux Islands**), a member of Cook's second expedition (of 1772). It was renamed as a compliment to Thomas Wilson, a London merchant. In the Antarctic, the Wilson Hills, extending along the **Oates Coast**, were discovered by Pennell (see **Pennell Coast**) in 1911 from the *Terra Nova*, and he named them after Dr Edward Adrian Wilson (1872–1912), one of the four companions of Captain Scott who would all be fated to perish, with Scott himself, on their fearful return journey from the South Pole the following year. Wilson had joined Scott on board the *Terra Nova* as chief of the scientific staff. He also gave his name to a glacier on the **Ross Sea**. For the names of the other members of Scott's polar party, see **Bowers Mountains**, **Evans Glacier**, **Scott Coast**, and the **Oates Coast** already mentioned. See also **Terra Nova Bay**.

Wilton (USA)
The residential town in Connecticut was settled in 1726 and named after the town of Wilton, Wiltshire, with which early residents must have had home links. Compare the next entry below.

Wilton Manors (USA)
The Florida city was named after the same Wiltshire town as **Wilton** (see above), with 'Manors' added as a 'prestige' word, for promotional purposes. Oddly enough, the name of the English county of Wiltshire seems to have made no impact at all in North America, and any occurrences of the name (also in the spelling Wilshire) will have derived from a surname.

Winchendon (USA)
The Massachusetts town takes its name from the Buckinghamshire village of Winchendon (either Upper Winchendon, near Aylesbury, or Lower Winchendon, near Thame), with which there were known colonist links. The town was named in 1764.

Winchester (USA)
Many Americans can trace their ancestry back to the city of Winchester, Hampshire, and the name is found fairly widely in the United States. However, only the earliest namings will have derived direct from that of the city, and later namings will have occurred by transfer from existing places. The earliest naming of all is that of Winchester, Connecticut, where the town was laid out in 1732. The city of Winchester, **Virginia**, was founded in 1744 as Fredericktown (see **Frederick** for the tribute), and was renamed for the Hampshire city in 1752. And although one would expect the town of Winchester, **New Hampshire**, to be named after its English counterpart, especially in view of the correspondence between state name and county name, it was in fact a compliment, made in 1753, to Charles Paulet, 8th Marquis of Winchester and 3rd Duke of Bolton (1685–1754), Lord Lieutenant of Hampshire (the English county). Much later occurrences of the name will have been for the Winchester rifle, or rather for its manufacturer, who lived in the nineteenth century. Winchester, Indiana, and Winchester, Nevada, are both in this category.

Windham (USA)
Several places of the name, such as the town of Windham, Maine, or Windham County, Connecticut (with Windham in this county, although not its seat), will have been named after the town of Wymondham, Norfolk, through emigrant connections there. The name of this town is still regularly pronounced 'Windham' even today, except by those unfamiliar with it. The town of Windham, **New Hampshire**, however, was probably named as a compliment to Charles Wyndham (1710–1763), the Member of Parliament and Secretary of State who was a friend of the state governor, Benning Wentworth (see **Wentworth**) and who advocated a peaceful solution for any differences with the American colonies. This last town was named in 1741.

Windsor (USA, Canada, Australia)
Not surprisingly, this English name, with its royal associations, was seized on by several colonial namers in the New World. Although the name is found quite widely in the United States, for example Windsor, Connecticut, settled in 1635 and named two years later, Windsor, **Pennsylvania**, named in 1758, and Windsor, North **Carolina**, also named about this time, it is more fulsomely represented in Canada. In that country, the important city of Windsor, Ontario, was originally known as The Ferry (i.e. over the Detroit River here) before being renamed first as Richmond (see **Richmond** for the associations) and then finally as Windsor in 1836, after the Berkshire town with its royal castle. Windsor, **Nova Scotia**, was first settled by the French in 1703 with the Indian name of Piziquid. In 1750 it became known as Ford Edward, after the defence built here to protect property, and was then renamed with its present name in 1764. In Quebec, the town of Windsor, which was settled in about 1800, was also named for the English town. In Australia,

the **New South Wales** town of Windsor was founded in 1810 (near an earlier, low-lying settlement) by Lachlan Macquarie (see **Macquarie**) and was named directly after its royal counterpart. Most places of the name will of course have been established long before the British royal house of Windsor was proclaimed in 1917, although the Canadian town of Windsor, Newfoundland, may possibly have been named for this reason and with this particular compliment. It was first known as Grand Falls Station (after the falls here on the Exploits river) when it arose as a settlement in 1909 around the papermill at this location.

Wingate (Israel)
The village of this name arose on Mount Carmel in 1953, with the tribute made to the British soldier Orde Charles Wingate (1903–1944), who from 1936 to 1939 served as an intelligence officer in Palestine, where he organised patrols to repel Arab raids on Jewish communities. He was killed in an air crash in Burma.

Wingham (Canada)
The Ontario town is named after the villge of Wingham near Canterbury, Kent, probably for colonist connections there.

Winthrop (USA)
The Massachusetts town was settled in 1635, with its name honouring John Winthrop (1588–1649), the Suffolk-born first governor of the Massachusetts Bay Colony. His son of the same name (and also Suffolk-born) was a governor of Connecticut, where he was sponsored by Viscount Saye and Sele and Lord Brooke (see **Saybrook**).

Winton (Australia)
The town in **Queensland** was settled in 1873 and was at first known as Pelican Waterholes. It was subsequently proclaimed a village (in 1875) and then a town (1879) and was renamed Winton, after the birthplace of its postmaster, the village of Winton, Hampshire (now a district of Bournemouth, Dorset). This village was itself a nineteenth-century creation.

Woburn (USA)
The Massachusetts city was set off from **Charlestown** in 1642 and incorporated as a town that year, when it was named after the village of Woburn near Leighton Buzzard, Bedfordshire, where there were doubtless emigrant ties. The famous country mansion of Woburn Abbey had not yet been built at this date, although there was a house of the name in which, for example, Charles I was entertained three times in the 1640s.

Wolfe (Canada)
General James Wolfe (1727–1759), the English soldier who fought the French at Fort Louisbourg (see **Nova Scotia**) and who won a famous victory over Montcalm at the **Plains of Abraham** gave his name to a few places in Canada, such as Wolfe County, Quebec. Wolfe died of wounds sustained in his final engagement with the French general, who survived him by only a few hours. This capture of Quebec assured British supremacy in Canada. Doubtless the association of the name with the animal serves to give it added 'power' and belligerence.

Wollaston (Canada)
The name is found at various sites in Canada, such as Lake Wollaston, Saskatchewan and the Wollaston Peninsula, with Cape Wollaston, on **Victoria** Island, Northwest Territories. Each occurrence honours Dr William Hyde Wollaston (1766–1828), President of the Royal Society. The lake was discovered in about 1800 by the English fur trader and surveyor Peter Fidler. It was not named until John Franklin (see **Franklin**) explored it more thoroughly in 1821.

Wolseley (Canada, South Africa)
The community of Wolseley in Saskatchewan has a name that compliments Sir Garnet Joseph, 1st Viscount Wolseley (1833–1913), the British soldier who commanded the Red River Expedition in 1870. The South African town of Wolseley, in

the Cape Province, was laid out in 1875 and was named after the same man, who was a commander in the Zulu War of 1879.

Wolstenholme, Cape (Canada)
The cape of this name, in northwest Quebec, at the western end of the **Hudson** Strait, was discovered by Hudson in 1610 and named by him after Sir John Wolstenholme (1562–1639), a merchant adventurer who was also a generous promoter of Arctic exploration, especially attempts to discover a Northwest Passage. He had backed not only Hudson himself, but had also equipped the expedition of Button (see **Button Bay**), Baffin (see **Baffin**) and Luke Foxe (see **Foxe**). See also **London Coast**.

Woodbridge (USA)
The city of Woodbridge, **New Jersey**, was settled in 1665 by Puritans from Massachusetts Bay and **New Hampshire** and was named after the town of Woodbridge in Suffolk, from which some of them had originally come.

Woodbury (USA)
Many places of the name are so called descriptively, with reference to a wood, but Woodbury, **New Jersey** was settled in about 1683 by a group of Quakers led by one John Wood, who had come from Bury, Lancashire (now in Greater Manchester). The name is thus a tribute to him and his native town. How fortunate that his surname and the English place-name combined so readily and authentically!

Woodstock (USA, Canada)
In some instances, the name will have derived directly from the town of Woodstock in Oxfordshire as well as referring in romantic vein to Walter Scott's novel *Woodstock*, published in 1826. Before this year, however, the reference will naturally be to the town only. The name is first recorded in Maine, where it appeared in about 1690. In Canada, the city of Woodstock, Ontario was founded in 1834 by Rear-Admiral Henry Vansittart (1777–1843), who specifically had the Oxfordshire town in mind, perhaps implying a reference to Blenheim Palace nearby, and so using the name as an indirect military compliment to the Duke of Marlborough. The name Woodstock can also suggest a woodland, too, in a complimentary manner. Compare **Blenheim**, **Marlborough**.

Worcester (USA, South Africa)
If the name does not derive directly from the English city of Worcester, or its county of Worcestershire, from which early settlers may have emigrated, it could serve as a tribute to an Earl of Worcester. The latter is almost certainly the case for Worcester County, **Maryland**, where the reference is to Edward Somerset, 6th Earl and 2nd Marquis of Worcester (1601–1667), who was the son-in-law of Lord Baltimore. (see **Baltimore**, **Somerset**.) The Massachusetts city of Worcester dates from 1684, and may have a name that was given with an additional reference to the Battle of Worcester (1651), in which Charles II and his Scottish army were defeated by Cromwell and his Parliamentarians. This would have met with strong Puritan approval! In South Africa, the town of Worcester, Cape Province, was named by Lord Charles Somerset, who chose its site in 1817 and made the compliment to his brother, the Marquess of Worcester.

Wottonville (Canada)
The community in Quebec was founded in 1849 and named after the village of Wotton near Dorking, Surrey, from which one of the original settlers had presumably come.

Wrentham (USA)
The Massachusetts town was settled in 1669 and named after the village of Wrentham near Southwold, Suffolk, from where early colonists must have come.

Wyndham (Australia)
The northern port of Wyndham, Western Australia, was founded in 1885 and was named after the son, Wyndham, of the Governor of Western Australia at this

time, Sir Frederick Napier Broome (see **Broome**).

Wynnewood (USA)

The **Pennsylvania** community of Wynnewood preserves the name of Thomas Wynne, the Welsh president of the first colonial Assembly of Pennsylvania.

Wynyard (Australia, Canada)

The Tasmanian town of Wynyard was founded in 1841 and originally named Table Cape, after a promontory near here on **Bass Strait**. In 1861, when gazetted as a town, it was renamed in honour of Major-General Edward B. Wynyard, who in 1850 had been Commander-in-Chief of the British forces in Van Dieman's Land (as Tasmania was then known). In Canada, the Saskatchewan community of Wynyard, however, was named after the English family estate of Mrs F.W. Peters, whose husband was supervisor of the Land Department of the Canadian Pacific Railway. The precise location of the estate is uncertain.

Y

Yarmouth (USA, Canada)

As always with this sort of name, one can find a derivation from a place or a person. If the former, as is mostly the case, the reference will be to the town and port of Yarmouth (Great Yarmouth), Norfolk, as it certainly is for the Massachusetts town, named in 1638. But the Canadian town of Yarmouth, **Nova Scotia**, founded in 1761 by **New England** settlers, probably has a name that compliments Sir William Paston, 2nd Earl of Yarmouth (1652–1732), who was Treasurer of the Royal Household and the last of his family (that is, his title became extinct on his death).

York (USA, Canada, Australia, Greenland)

The name is common in North America, and it is a matter of establishing whether a reference to the city of York is meant or a compliment to a Duke of York, and in the latter case, to which particular Duke! The three York Counties respectively in Nabraska, **Pennsylvania**, and South **Carolina**, each having a seat named York, will almost certainly take the name from the English city, or from the county of Yorkshire, from which many emigrants are known to have come. York, Maine, was the first English city on the American continent when Sir Ferdinando Gorges (?1566–1647), English despite his name, endowed it with a city charter in 1641 under the name of Gorgeana. The Massachusetts Bay Company revoked the charter in 1652, however, and renamed the city after its English counterpart. The Pennsylvania city of the name was laid out much later, in 1741, but was still named after the English city, although by then the name was well established and could easily have been transferred from one York to another. However, some sources prefer to derive the Maine city from the title of the Duke of York, the future James II, who gave his title also much more memorably to **New York**, but it is likely that any York names in **Virginia**, such as York County (whose seat is **Yorktown**) and York River, will honour a later Duke, that is, Charles, Duke of York (1600–1649), the future Charles I (who was executed as a tyrant and an enemy of the nation). In Canada, York was the original name of Toronto, given the capital when it was founded in 1793 by Colonel John Simcoe (see **Simcoe**), Lieutenant-Governor of Upper Canada. In bestowing the name, he aimed to compliment the Duke of York of his time, who was Frederick Augustus, the second son of George III (see **Frederick**). The name remained York until 1834, when it reverted to the Indian name of Toronto that had originally applied to the site. (The name has survived, however, for York County, Ontario, and for the York that is now one of the five boroughs that with the City of Toronto constitute the municipality of Metropolitan Toronto.) In Australia, the town of York in southwest Western Australia was surveyed in 1831 and was named after the English county, from which settlers had emigrated. But Cape York, the northernmost point of Australia, at the tip of York Peninsula, **Queensland**, was so named by James Cook in 1770, when he sought to compliment the same Frederick Augustus who would give his title name to the Canadian capital, as mentioned above. (The Duke of York was still a small boy at this time, and indeed had celebrated his seventh birthday only five days before

Cook came on the cape and named it!) This York Peninsula, incidentally, should not be confused by non-Australians with its near namesake and virtual 'opposite number', the **Yorke Peninsula** in South Australia. There are many other Yorks of one kind and another in English-speaking countries, but one in a non-English-speaking land is the Cape York (or Kap York) that is on **Baffin** Bay in northwest Greenland. It was discovered and named by James Ross in 1818, and was yet again named after the same Duke of York. If the annals are accurate, Ross arrived here by coincidence on yet another birthday of the Duke, who that year reached the age of 55 (on 16 August, to be precise). For related names, see **Duke of York**, **New York**, and also **York Factory**, **Yorkton** and **Yorktown**.

Yorke Peninsula (Australia)

The Yorke Peninsula, on the south coast of South Australia, was sighted in 1802 by Matthew Flinders (see **Flinders**) and was named (somewhat confusingly, in view of the entry above) after Charles Philip Yorke, later 4th Earl of Hardwicke (1799–1873), subsequently a captain in the Royal Navy (and, as a retired rank, an admiral).

York Factory (Canada)

York Factory was a settlement in Manitoba at the mouth of **Hayes River**, on **Hudson** Bay, where it was the site of a trading post (Fort Nelson) of the Hudson's Bay Company, built in 1682. This post was destroyed by the French but a new one was built by the British, who named it Fort York for the Duke of York, the future James II (1633–1701), who came to the throne in 1685. Later, as York Factory, it became the chief port and depot for the fur trade of northern Canada. With the coming of the railroad, however, and especially the line to **Churchill**, on the Hudson Bay, its importance declined, so that in 1957 it eventually closed down. The location is now preserved as a historic site, however.

Yorkton (Canada)

The Saskatchewan city was originally settled in 1882 by families from **York** County, Ontario, and at first was known as York City. The name thus indirectly honours the Duke of York who was the second son of George III, even though it arose after his time. Compare **Yorktown**.

Yorktown (USA)

The town in **Virginia** was so named because it was the seat of **York** County. The name thus indirectly honours the Duke of York who was to become Charles I. The town is famous in American history for the siege of 1781 in which the British (under Cornwallis) surrendered to the French and Americans (under Washington and Rochambeau), thus effectively ending the American Revolution (War of American Independence). Places named Yorktown later than 1781 will almost certainly have been commemoratively named, therefore, for this victory, which assured the independence of America. Compare **Yorkton**.

Young (Australia)

The town of Young, **New South Wales**, arose in 1830 as a sheep station called Lambing Flat. Thirty years later the settlement was proclaimed a town and renamed for Sir John Young, 1st Lord Lisgar (1807–1876), Governor General of New South Wales from 1861 to 1867. Mount Young, west of the **Spencer** Gulf, South Australia, was named after Admiral Sir George Young (1732–1810), who in 1784 actively pursued a plan to establish a colony in New South Wales, and who backed the scheme that led to the expedition undertaken by Arthur Phillip (see **Port Phillip**), the founder of New South Wales in 1788. A small island off the **York** Peninsula, **Queensland**, is on record as having been named Young Island by Philip Parker King (see **King**) in 1819 because it appeared to him to be 'in an infant state' and thus unlikely to grow any larger. Taylor (see Bibliography, p. 217) comments scathingly: 'This is perhaps the silliest name on record.' But for a genuine 'Young' (i.e. youthful) name, see the next (and last) entry below.

Young Nick's Head (New Zealand) Young Nick's Head is a small promontory on the east coast of North Island, to the south of Poverty Bay, itself south of **Gisborne**. This headland was the first point of New Zealand made out by James Cook when he arrived off the coast here on 6 October 1769, and it is named after the member of his crew who actually spotted it. This was Cook's cabin boy, who was at the masthead at the time, Nicholas Young, nicknamed Young Nick, so the headland was quite rightly named after him. What a thrill for him, and what an honour! (Compare **Pitcairn Island**, similarly descried by a youthful member of the ship's company.)

APPENDIX I
CATEGORIES OF PLACE-NAMES

The object of this Appendix is to present the different categories of origin of the place-names in the Dictionary. When an explorer discovers a new geographical feature, or a colonist founds a new settlement, what is it to be named? The subject of study here is naturally restricted to names of British origin, but even so, it can be seen that existing place-names in the 'old country' form by far the largest source for new names, whether the latter are bestowed as direct, unaltered borrowings or transfers from the origin, whether they are taken over in slightly adopted form, or whether they are prefixed by 'New' or have some other addition.

Thus existing Boston has its name given to new **Boston**, and age-old Kent is transferred to the brand-new **Kent**. And although a county name is often used for a newly created county, equally, it can be given to any kind of settlement, so that Essex, for example, is an American town, not a county. On the other hand, British river names tend to be transferred to rivers, so the identity there is likely to be greater.

The four next largest categories of name (although only half the size of those in List 1) are those found respectively in Lists 2, 3, 10 and 14. List 2, names derived from aristocratic titles, contains many names that are themselves place-names, so provides a neat opportunity to honour both a person and a place. The fact that the name has the same 'aristocratic' aura as its original gives it added status, too. Much the same can be said of the 'royal' names of List 3, although these are less likely to resemble a true place-name in origin, unless they happen to coincide with a royal dukedom such as **Cornwall**, **Gloucester**, **Kent** or **York**. As with the aristocratic names, a new name that combines a royal name or title with a common place-name word or element will achieve something of a 'royal' status. Examples are **Cape Elizabeth**, **Louiseville**, **Prince Patrick Island** and **Williamsburg**.

List 10 comprises names derived from explorers and discoverers, and will be found to contain a higher proportion of natural features (mountains, rivers, islands, capes) than the categories already mentioned. Here the suggestion is frequently one of possession or acquisition: an explorer discovers a bay and it instantly becomes 'his' bay, or a lookout sights a headland and it immediately becomes 'his' property. Examples here are **Button Bay** and **Young Nick's Head**. List 14, on the other hand, consists of names derived from colonial officials, the people who first administrated, presided, officiated and governed. If the aristocratic titles from List 2 had been included here, the list would have been noticeably longer, and in 'weightiness' it must be considered as one of the most substantial categories. Although a name of royal origin (as in List 3) undoubtedly has a higher status value, at the same time it is more remote, for many royal personages never came near the new lands and settlements named after them. The governors and administrators certainly did, however, so that their names have a much more immediate and important impact when transferred for place-name use. Here, possession is a reality, and a man who administers a populated area, whether settlement or new colony, is much more obviously its 'owner'. He is, after all, resident there, and is seen to be so.

These last two categories, those of Lists 10 and 14, are therefore largely based on surnames (family names), as they are in some of the smaller categories not yet mentioned. Where a surname happens to coincide with a place-name anyway, it is an added advantage, and of course many surnames do in reality derive from place-names, so the likelihood of such occurrences is fairly great. Examples of such conveniences (new place-names derived from a surname that itself derives from an old place-name) can be seen in **Creighton**, **Hamilton**, **Hastings** and **Wentworth**, all of which exist in their own right as place-names in Britain. It should be noticed that many names that are clearly not of place-name origin usually have a generic place-name element added to give them a more suitable status for the place they designate. Examples are the many surnames to which an element such as '-ville', '-boro' or '-town' has been added.

Sometimes a person's name is fully exploited, with both forename and surname put to use. This happens, for instance, with Lachlan Macquarie, the British general who became the Governor of New South Wales. He is commemorated in both the **Lachlan River** and the two **Macquarie** Rivers, to say nothing of several other locations that adopted his surname (such as **Port Macquarie**). Perhaps one of the record-breakers in this respect was the Governor of the Cape Colony, Sir Harry Smith, who gave his surname to **Smithfield**, his forename and surname combined to **Harrismith**, his wife's name to **Ladismith** and **Ladysmith**, his Indian battle victory to **Aliwal North**, and his birthplace to **Whittlesea**!

The remaining categories in the Appendix are self-explanatory, and range from house names to ship names, and literary names to the names of financial backers and sponsors.

One difficulty in compiling a breakdown of some seventeen categories like this is that frequently it is hard to delegate a name to a single category. There are thus admirals (as in List 7) who are also explorers and discoverers (List 10), and there are founders and settlers (List 13) who go on to become colonial officials and administrators (List 14). In such instances, I have placed the person who gave the name in what I hope, even subjectively, to have been the more dominant role, or the more important position. It is thus likely that a person who was the first governor of a place will have his name remembered for that reason rather than for the fact that he happened to settle or colonise it, and for the discoverer or explorer of a new territory to have his name commemorated rather than that of the captain of the ship that took him there. Lieutenant Harry Pennell took Captain Scott to the Antarctic on board the *Terra Nova*, but it is Scott's name that is now widely known and that can be found in Antarctic place-names, rather than Pennell's (although he had a coast named after him).

Where a name appears in more than one category in this Appendix, it will usually not be because it was that of one person featuring in different roles, therefore, but because different people were involved. Thus the **Nelson** in List 7 is the famous admiral, the 'Victor of Trafalgar', but the **Nelson** in List 14 is the Lieutenant-Governor of British Columbia. Similarly, the **Wellington** in List 2 is the renowned 'Iron Duke', who fought and won at Waterloo, but the **Wellington** in List 13 is the settler of the place, a Mr Welling.

Finally, for ease of alphabetical reference, a generic term such as 'Cape' or 'Mount' is printed in roman (not italic) type where in the main entries of the Dictionary it follows the place-name (e.g. **Hermes**, Cape, but **Cape Elizabeth**).

Each category is preceded by a brief introductory paragraph designed to clarify or explain some of the more detailed aspects of the names in that category.

1 Place-names

This large and important category of name transfer embraces mainly towns and villages, but also includes larger features such as counties and island groups. Rivers, too, are fairly well represented. Distortions are sometimes found, with letters frequently omitted or added ('Beverly' for 'Beverley', 'Hemmingford' for 'Hemingford', for example), and historic or classical names used in some instances ('Clutha' for 'Clyde', 'Sarnia' for 'Guernsey'). The range of names included here extends from the national, at the largest (*British Empire Range, English Bazar, Nova Scotia*) to the very local, at the smallest (*Cynwyd, Orbost, Spotswood*). The smallest reference may thus be to an estate or even a street. Names transferred from houses or mansions, however, are presented separately at List 16.

Aberdeen, Abingdon, Abington, Acton, Acton Vale, Ailsa Craig, Airdrie, Albion, Albury, Aldershot, Allerton, Alliston, Alvinston, Amesbury, Andover, Anerley, Annandale, Antrim, Armagh, Armidale, Arnprior, Arundel, Ashburnham, Athelstan, Atholville, Attleboro, Avoca, Avon, Avondale, Ayr, Balclutha, Banff, Bangor, Barnstaple, Barrhead, Beaudesert, Bedford, Belfast, Ben Lomond, Berks, Berkshire, Berwick, Berwyn, Beverly, Bexley, Biddeford, Bideford, Billerica, Birmingham, Blantyre, Bolingbrook, Boston, Bothwell, Bowbells, Boxford, Braintree, Brampton, Branford, Brentwood, Bridgewater, Brighton, Bristol, British Channel, British Columbia, British Empire Range, Bromptonville, Bryn Mawr, Buckingham, Bucks, Burlington, Burnhamthorpe, Bury, Buxton, Caledonia, Calgary, Callander, Cambria, Cambridge, Camrose, Canterbury, Cardiff-by-the-Sea, Carleton Place, Carlisle, Carrick, Cathkin Peak, Chalfont, Charleville, Chelmsford, Chelsea, Cheshire, Chester, Cheviot, Clare, Clarendon Hills, Cloncurry, Clutha River, Clyde, Coalbrook, Colchester, Compton, Cornwall, Coventry, Cranbrook, Croydon, Cumberland, Cynwyd, Dalby, Dalton, Danbury, Darby, Darlington, Dartmouth, Dedham, Derry, Derwent, Devon, Didsbury, Donnybrook, Dorchester, Dover, Drayton, Dublin, Dundalk, Dundee, Dunedin, Dungarvan River, Dunmaglass, Dunvegan, Durham, Eardley, East Liverpool, East London, Easton, Edenburg, Edina, Edinboro, Edinburg, Edmonton, Eildon, Elgin, Emo, Enfield, English Bazar, Essex, Eston, Exeter, Fairfield, Falmouth, Fannettsburg, Farnham, Footscray, Framlingham, Gillitts-Emberton, Glasgow, Glastonbury, Glencoe, Gloucester, Goodwood, Grampian, Granby, Greenwich, Gretna, Grimsby, Groton, Guernsey County, Guilford, Hadley, Hampshire,

Hampstead, Hampton, Ham South, Hantsport, Harrow, Hartford, Harwich, Haverford, Haverhill, Hawarden, Hellam, Hemmingford, Hempstead, Henley-on-Klip, Hensall, Hereford, Hertford, Highland, Hilton, Hingham, Horsham, Hull, Humber River, Huntingdon, Huntington, Huntly, Hurley, Innisfail, Inverness, Ipswich, Isle of Wight, Islip, Jersey City, Jerseyside, Kearsney, Kelso, Kempsey, Kensington, Kent, Kildonan, Killaloe, Kilsyth, Kingsey Falls, Kinloch, Kinross, (Lake) *Kyle, Lac-Brôme,* (Cape) *Lambert, Lanark, Lancaster, Launceston, Leamington, Leeds, Leicester, Leominster, Leslie, Lewes, Lexington, Lincoln, Lismore, Litchfield, Liverpool, Llandudno, Lochaber, Lochgelly, Loddon River, Londina, London, Londonderry, Londres, Lorne, Lucan, Ludlow, Lynn, Maidstone, Maldon, Malton, Malvern,* (Isle of) *Man, Manchester, Margate, Marton, Maryborough, Melrose, Melsetter, Mersey River, Middlesboro, Middlesex, Milford, Monmouth, Mornington, Mount Ayr, Mount Pleasant, Mount Sterling, Mowbray, Needham, New Albion, New Annan, Newark, New Bedford, New Brighton, New Britain, Newburgh, New Caledonia, New Carlisle, Newcastle, New Castle, New England,* (Cape) *Newenham, New Glasgow, New Hampshire, New Haven, New Hebrides, Newington, New Ireland, New Jersey, New Kensington, New Liskeard, New London, Newmarket, New Plymouth, Newport, Newry, New Scotland, New South Wales, New Waterford, New Westminster, Nith River, Norfolk, Northam, Northampton, North Hatley, Northumberland, Norwich, Nottingham Road, Nova Scotia, Oban, Orbost, Orcadia, Orkney, Oxford, Penge, Penrith, Perth, Plymouth, Pomfret, Port Chester, Portland, Port Lincoln, Portsmouth, Preston, Radnor, Ramsgate, Raynham, Reading, Renfrew, Reston, Rexton, Riccarton, Richmond, Ripon, Rockhampton, Romney, Roscommon, Roxboro, Roxburgh, Rugby, Rutherglen, Rutland, Rye, St Albans, Saint-Éphrem-de-Tring, St Georges Channel, Salisbury, Saltcoats, Sarnia, Scarborough, Scilly Isles, Scone, Scotland, Scotsburn, Seaford, Sedgefield, Severna Park, Severn River, Sheffield, Shefford County, Sherborn, Shrewsbury, Simsbury, Somerset, Southampton, Southgate, South Orkney Islands, Southwark, Southwick, Spotswood, Springfield, Stafford, Stamford, Stanstead County, Stirling, Stockport, Stratford, Strathroy, Sturbridge, Sudbury, Suffolk, Sunbury, Sundridge, Surrey, Surry, Sussex, Sutton, Swansea, Tamar River, Tamworth, Taunton, Templeton, Tenterfield, Tewksbury, Thames, Thetford Mines, Thurso, Tilbury, Tipton, Tisbury, Tiverton, Topsham, Torrington, Trent, Truro, Tweed River, Tyrone, Ugie, Ulverstone, Upton, Uxbridge, Valleyfield, Virden, Wallingford, Waltham, Wareham, Warkworth, Warwick, Waterford, Welland, Wells, Wenham, Westbury, West Chester, Westcliffe, Westminster, Westmoreland, Westport, Wethersfield, Wexford County, Weymouth, Whitby, Whitehall, Whittlesea, Wilbraham, Willingboro, Willington, Wilton, Wilton Manors, Winchendon, Winchester, Windham, Windsor, Wingham, Winton, Woodbridge, Woodstock, Worcester, Wottonville, Wrentham, Wynyard, Yarmouth, York.*

2 Aristocratic titles

Many of the titles that follow will have derived direct from a place-name, and as such can be wrongly taken *as* a place-name unless the origin of the name is known. For such names, the reader will therefore need to see the appropriate main entry to discover the actual circumstances of the naming, and to find out why the particular person was so chosen for the name. A few aristocratic titles are the same as the person's family name, such as James Gambier, the naval commander, who had the title of Baron Gambier. But such titles are in a minority. All types of aristocratic title are included in the list except the 'royal' ones, which appear in List 3. This means that, proceeding down the scale from the top end, all dukes will be here except the 'royal' ones (such as *Cornwall, Gloucester, Kent, York*), followed by the marquesses (or marquises), earls, viscounts and barons, all of whom can be called 'Lord'.

Albany, Albermarle, (Mount) *Alverstone, Anne Arundel, Arlington, Ashburton River, Athol, Auckland, Aylesford, Baltimore, Barrington, Barrington Passage, Bedford, Bexley, Bristol, Buckingham, Caledon, Cambridge, Camden, Cardigan, Carnarvon, Chatham, Chester, Chesterfield, Clanwilliam, Claremont, Clarendon, Colchester,* (Cape) *Colville, Craven, Cumberland, Dalhousie, Dartmouth, De Grey River, Delaware, Derby, Dorchester, Dorset, Dufferin, Dunmore, Effingham, Egmont, Elgin, Ellesmere, Enfield, Exmouth Gulf, Fairfax, Falkland Islands, Fort Albany, Fort Beaufort, Fort Loudon, Gambier Islands, Glenelg, Goderich, Gosford, Grafton, Granby, Granville, Great Barrington, Grenville County, Grey, Greymouth, Greytown, Guilford, Halifax, Hampton, Hartington, Hastings, Hawkesbury, Hertford, Hillsboro, Hillsborough, Huntingdon, Kimberley, Kingston, Kinnaird, Lanesborough, Leeds, Ligonier, Liverpool, Lord Hill, Lord Howe Islands, Lorneville, Loudon, Lyndhurst, Malmesbury, Malvérnia, Mandeville, Mansfield, Marlboro, Marlborough, Melbourne, Melville, Milton, Minto, Moreton Bay, Mornington, Mount Gambier, Mulgrave, Newcastle, New Richmond, Norfolk, Normanby Island, Northampton, Northumberland, Palmerston, Pembroke, Perth Amboy, Peterborough, Port Beaufort, Port Elgin, Port Harcourt, Port Hawkesbury, Portland, Port Orford, Port Sandwich, Port Stanley, Port Townsend, Raglan, Richmond, Richmond Hill, Rochester, Rockingham, Rodney, Rosebery, Rosmead, Rutland, Sackville, St Helens, Saint Vincent, Salisbury, Sandwich, Saybrook, Selkirk, Shaunavon, Shelburne, Shrewsbury, Southampton, South Sandwich Islands, Spencer, Stafford, Stanley, Stormont County, Strafford, Strathmore, Sydney, Talbot, Tunbridge, Uxbridge, Viscount Melville Sound, Warwick, Wellesley, Wellington, Wilmington, Winchester, Wolseley, Worcester, Yarmouth.*

3 Royal names and titles

The list below contains the the personal names of both kings and queens and members of their immediate family (such as consorts, princes and princesses), and also includes the titles of royal dukes (such as *Cornwall, Gloucester, Kent, York*) as well as their personal names, where they have been used for a place-name. Similarly here are the names of royal houses (such as *Brunswick, Windsor*) and those words that denote royalty, such as 'King', 'Queen', 'Prince', 'Princess', 'Duke', 'Duchess'. A few names of royal residences will likewise appear, as their associations place them here rather than in List 16.

Adelaide, Albert, Alberton, Alexandra, (Lake) *Alexandrina, Alfred, Alice Springs, Amelia,* (Cape) *Ann, Annapolis, Augusta, Balmoral, Brunswick, Brunswick Bay, Cape Elizabeth, Carolina, Charles, Charleston, Charlestown, Charlotte, Charlottesville, Charlottetown, Clarence River, Cobourg, Coburg Peninsula, Cornwall, Coronation, Duke of York, Dutchess*

County, Edgartown, (Lake) *Edward, Edward VII Peninsula, Elizabeth, Fort George, Fort Prince of Wales, Fort Victoria, Frederick, Fredericksburg, Fredericton, George, Georgetown, Georgia, Georgian Bay, Glocester, Gloucester, Great Victoria Desert, Guelph, Hanover, Henrico County,* (Cape) *Henry, James, Jamesburg, Jamestown, Kent, Kentville, King and Queen,* (Mount) *King Edward, King George, King George IV Lake, King George's Islands, Kings, Kingston, Kingstown, King William, King William's Town, Kinston, Lake Arthur, Lake George, Lake Louise, Louisa, Louise, Louiseville, Lunenburg, Maryland, Mecklenburg, Nassau, New Brunswick, New Hanover, New York, North Kent Island, Orange, Orangeburg, Point Edward, Port Arthur, Port Edward, Prince Albert, Prince Charles Mountains, Prince County, Prince Edward Island, Prince Frederick, Prince George, Prince Georges County, Prince of Wales, Prince Patrick Island, Prince Regent, Prince Rupert, Princess Anne, Princess Charlotte Bay, Princess Elizabeth Land, Princeton, Prince William, Queen Alexandra Range, Queen Annes County, Queen Charlotte, Queen Elizabeth Islands, Queen Mary Land, Queen Maud Land, Queensburgh, Queenscliff, Queens County, Queensland, Queenstown, Queen Victoria Sea, Regina, Rothesay, Royal Oak, Runnemede, Rupert River, Rupert's Land, Sandringham, South Georgia, Victoria, Victoriaville, Virginia, Wales, West Virginia, Williamsburg, Williamstown, Windsor, York, York Factory, Yorkton, Yorktown.*

4 Statesmen and government officers

This list includes the names of noted ministers, especially those of prime ministers and colonial ministers, who will have been commemorated in a place-name. At times, the interest of such ministers in overseas development and 'empire-building' was active and genuine. On other occasions, one rather feels that it was more a matter of simply being in office at the time. Whatever the case, a good mix will be found below of the famous (such as *Churchill, Disraeli, Gladstone* and *Pitt*) with the less familiar official. Many ministers had aristocratic titles, and will have been commemorated in that form. Their titles will therefore have been included in List 2 above, and not here.

Addison, Althorpe Islands, Amery Ice Shelf, Ashley River, Baillie-Hamilton Island, Balfour, (Mount) *Bartle Frere, Bright,* (Mount) *Bryce, Burke, Buxton, Byam Martin Island, Canning, Carleton, Charlton, Churchill, Cobden, Conway, Croker, Cromwell, Disraeli, Dundas, Dunk, Edgecombe County, Foxborough, Gisborne, Gladstone, Goulburn, Graham, Hamden, Hamilton, Hampden, Hawke, Herbert, Hobart, Hollis, Horton River, Hotham Inlet, Howick, Lennox and Addington County, Lenox, Lytton, Meredith, Methuen, Middleton Island, Milne Bay, Monson, Montague, Murray River, Norton, Palliser, Peel, Pelham, Pitt Island, Pittsburgh, Pittsfield, Pittston, Port Jackson, Poultney, Seymour, Thorold, Townsend, Townshend, Vansittart, Walpole, Wilkes-Barre, Windham.*

5 Financial backer or sponsor

A few explorers and pioneer colonists were indebted enough, financially or morally, to the backers of their exploration or adventurous enterprise to name the place they discovered or founded after their sponsors. For the more obviously 'multiple' backers, such as firms and other bodies, see List 6.

Barrow, Beardmore Glacier, Bellingham, Birchenough Bridge, Boothia, Caird Coast, Carnegie, Coats Land, Dawson-Lambton Glacier, Durham, Enderbury Atoll, Enderby, (Cape) *Felix, Grenfell, Healdtown, Holliston, Hutt, Jones Sound, Lancaster, Revelstoke, Roes Welcome, Smith,* (Cape) *Walsingham,* (Cape) *Wolstenholme.*

6 Sponsoring firms and other bodies

The following short list includes firms or other bodies who commissioned or initiated an expedition, voyage of exploration, or pioneer settlement.

Admiralty Island, Banzare Coast, Bridgeport, English Company's Islands, Lewisporte, London Coast, Millertown, Society Islands.

7 Military leaders

This list includes the names of those military leaders, such as admirals and generals, who distinguished themselves in a particular battle or in war service generally, or who held important posts of authority, so that they have thus been commemorated in place-name form for their eminence in this way. The list will not include 'home' officers, such as Lords of the Admiralty, who more properly belong to List 4 above, or those seagoing officers who were either primarily explorers or discoverers (in which case they will be in List 10) or the captains of ships on various voyages (in which case they will be in List 11).

Amherst, Amherstberg, Anson, Back River, Baffin, Beaufort, Bigelow Mountain, Boscawen, Braddock, Charlestown, Clive, Cockburn, Collingwood, Cornwallis Island, Curtis, Douglastown, Duncan Island, Fitz-James, Gagetown, Goodenough Island, Havelock, Hervey, Hood, Hope Point, Howe, Jacobabad, Jervis Bay, Keppel, Kitchener, Lawford Islands, Lawrence, Mercer, Montgomery, Moresby Island, Mount Rainier, Mount Vernon, Napier, Nelson, Nelson-Miramichi, Otway, Peddie, Pellew Islands, Percy Islands, Picton, Porcher Island, Port Essington, Port Hood, Port Keats, Port Moresby, Port Saunders, Port Stephens, Redvers, Richards Bay, Rooke Island, St Clair, Sale, Saunders, Sidney, Somerset, Wager Bay, Warren, Warrenton, Wellesley, Wingate, Wolfe, Wynyard.

8 Tribute names

The list below contains names that have been given in a fairly general way as a tribute to a particular person, whether known or not to the namer. Usually, the person so favoured will have had nothing to do with the discovery or settling of the actual place that bears his or her name. Among such people are a range of more or less relevant occupations, including writers, artists, cartographers (more relevant than many), scientists, churchmen (also relevant for a place settled by a religious community), and simply friends or acquaintances who perhaps happened to be local 'worthies' in their own right, such as a Member of Parliament. There is even a prize boxer here, proving that it takes all sorts to make a new world for humans to inhabit.

Arrowsmith, Babbage River, Bell Lakes, Bendigo, Berkeley, Bessemer, Bingham, Buntingville, Burns, Burnshill, Butterworth, Byron, Calderwood, Carlyle, Clarkson, Colenso, Cudworth, Douglas, Dover, (Cape) *Dyer, Emmet County, Emmetsburg, Estcourt, Florenceville, Forbes, Glynn, Halley, Hankey, Herschel, Hobhouse, Howard, Inman River, Katherine, Kelvington, Kipling,* (Cape) *Lambert,* (Mount) *Leacock, Lyttelton, Macadam Range, Maclear, McPherson Range, Malone, Markham, Milton, Ministers Island, Minna Bluff, Mount Fletcher, Newton, Pennfield Ridge, Pirie, Ponds Inlet, Port Chalmers, Port Lyttelton, Port Nicholson, Shakespeare Island, Sheridan, Sidney, Stuart Island, Sumner, Tyndall, Wales, Wallaceberg, Waterton, Wesley, Wesleyville, Wollaston, Yorke Peninsula.*

9 Battle names

Tying in fairly closely with List 7, here is a list of places named after famous battles, whose victories (for the British) were regarded as worth commemorating in a place-name. For the two battles in England, it was a case of 'us' winning against 'them'.

Aliwal North, Blenheim, Camperdown, Monmouth, Naseby, Waterloo.

10 Explorers and discoverers

Here now are the men who made it happen. The explorers, discoverers, surveyors, prospectors, expedition leaders and members, and all others who found a new place to be settled (or not, in some cases). Sometimes the discovery was a fortuitous one. Sometimes the seekers found what they sought. And sometimes, the name given to the nearly discovered place was not that of the actual person who discovered it or surveyed it, but a member of his family, such as his wife or daughter. It will be noticed that many of the named objects here are ones that need a special effort to be 'captured': an island to be located and surveyed, a mountain to be sighted and possibly climbed, a river to be traced and charted, a desert to be crossed and measured.

Alexander Bay, (Cape) *Ann, Arthurs Pass, Balleny Islands, Banks, Bass Strait, Beechey Island, Belcher Islands,* (Mount) *Belinda, Biscoe Islands, Bowers Mountains, Bransfield Strait, Broughton Island,* (Mount and Point) *Brown, Buccaneer Archipelago, Bunbury, Burketown, Burnaby, Button Bay, Byron, Campbell River, Clipperton Island, Cook, Cook's Harbour, Cooktown,* (Mount) *Dalrymple, Dampier, Darwin, Davis, Dixon Entrance, Drake, Evans Glacier,* (Mount) *Everest, Eyre, Flinders, Fort Raleigh, Foxe, Franklin, Fraser, Frobisher Bay, Furneaux Islands, George, Gilbert Islands,* (Mount) *Godwin Austen,* (Mount) *Goodsir,* (Lake) *Gregory, Heaphy Track,* (Cape) *Hearne, Hepburn Island, Hicks, Hilton Head Island, Hood, Hooker, Hoppner River, Hudson,* (Cape) *Hurd, Jackson Island, James, James Ross Island, Johnston Island, Keeling Islands, Kemp, King, Livingston, Livingstone, Livingstonia, Logan, M'Clintock Channel, M'Clure Strait, Mackenzie, Marshall Islands, Mason and Dixon Line, Matthew Island, Mawson, Mitchell River,* (Mount) *Mudge, Muir, Murchison, Nelson, Oates Coast, Owen Sound, Owen Stanley Range, Parry, Peard Bay, Pickersgill Islands, Pitcairn Island, Port Arthur, Port Blair, Port Dalrymple, Port Durnford, Port Nelson, Rankin Inlet, Rennell Island, Rennick Glacier, Richardson, Robbins Island, Ross Sea, Sabine, Scoresby Sound, Scott Coast, Shackleton Glacier, Smith, Stanley, Stanleyville,* (Mount) *Stokes, Sturt Desert, Sutherland, Swift's Creek,* (Mount) *Temple, Thistle Island, Thompson, Vancouver, Wake Island, Wallis Islands, Weddell Sea, Wilson, Young Nick's Head.*

11 Ship's captains

As distinct from the naval commanders in List 7, or the explorers and hydrographers in List 10, the following list aims to single out those ship's captains who wittingly or unwittingly steered their ship to a newly discovered land or region. In one instance, the name is that of the captain's daughter.

Batemans Bay, Bligh Island, (Cape) *Colbeck, Courtenay, Crozier Channel, Fitzroy, Gilford Island, Manning Strait, Martha's Vineyard, Pennell Coast, Port Nolloth, Starbuck Island.*

12 Ship names

No overseas discoveries, at least in the pre-air era, could have been made without a ship, and it is only fitting that some of these should have had their names preserved in the places to which they took their crews and their navigators. Some are more specifically 'war' ships than others, however.

Ajax, Alert, Arniston, Beagle Bay, Beagle Channel, Bounty Islands, Challenger Deep, Chatham, Coromandel, Discovery, Dolphin and Union Strait, Duff Islands, Endeavour, Erebus, Fury and Hecla Strait, Hecate Strait, Hecla and Griper Bay, (Cape) *Henrietta*

Maria, Herald Island, (Cape) *Hermes, Investigator Group, Lark Harbour, Magnet Bay, Miranda,* (Mount) *Morning, Nassau, Nimrod Glacier, Northumberland, Penrhyn, Pioneer River, Pitt Island, Port Pirie, Princess Royal Island, Queen Charlotte, Resolution Island, Sabrina Coast, Salisbury, Scotia Sea, Terra Nova Bay, Terror, Victor Harbour.*

13 Founders and settlers

If the explorers and discoverers of List 10 found the places where human beings could settle or pursue their investigations, then the list below is of those who were men and women who were 'on the spot', the pioneers and colonists who actually lived and worked and strove (in most instances) to establish the new community. Sometimes they had a specialised role, such as a church minister or a postmaster, the one to set down the desired code of religious endeavour and fellowship, the other to set up an efficient means of communication with other settlements. Sometimes, again, the person who gave his name to the place may have simply chosen to live in the spot for mere convenience, without any particular thought of expansion or enterprise. But in many cases the names are those of the real all-round 'doers', who put the place (in their name) quite literally on the map. Some names are those of a person's close relation.

Alden, Alexandria, Alice Springs, Archbald, Baker Lake, Barkerville, Blackstone, Boalsburg, Brentwood, Bytown, Charters Towers, Clark Point, Dare, Digby, Douglas, Ebensburg, Edwardsville, Elizabethtown, Fergus, Fleetwood, Fort Garry, Fremantle, Galt, Georgetown, Gillitts-Emberton, Gilroy, Glasville, Godley Head, Graham, Haddonfield, Hamilton, Hannastown, Harrisburg, Helensville, Hollidaysburg, Invercargill, Jenkintown, Jermyn, Kingston, Livermore, Lloydminster, Loggieville, Lovelock, McAllen, McGregor, McKeesport, Mackenzie, Mac-Mac, Maryborough, Maugerville, Mirabel, Mount Pearl, Newport News, Norristown, Oglethorpe, Paterson, Paxton, Pennsylvania, Peterborough, Philippolis, Philipsburg, Phillip Island, Plains of Abraham, Port Phillip, Potter County, Raleigh, Rhodes, Rhodesia, Robertson, Scarbro, Schooleys Mountain, Scotch Plains, Scotstown, Standish, Stewart Island, Thompson, Toms River, Townsville, (Lake) *Tyrrell, Wakefield, Walkerton, Watling Island, Wellington, Woodbury, Wynnewood.*

14 Colonial officials

Once a place was established, it needed someone to supervise and administer it. This is where the colonial officials came in, the civilian or military overseers, from the Governor General downwards, depending on the size and importance of the place. Many of the most senior such men will have had titles, so will be found in List 2. In other instances, the names are those of members of the official's family, such as a wife or daughter. Here, therefore, are some of the most numerous and significant names of all, many of them the manmade forts and ports from which great cities grew, and a few the names of large territories that are famed internationally, such as *Alberta* and *Gippsland*.

Abbottabad, (Lake) *Ainslie, Alberta, Bagotville, Baillie Islands, Barkly Tableland, Barkly West, Berkeley, Berkeley Heights, Berkeley Springs, Bernardsville, Blackall, Blaketown, Bourke, Bowen, Brisbane, Brockville, Broome, Bulwer, Cairns, Calvert, Campbellton, Campbelltown, Carleton, Caroline, Carteret, Cathcart, Cecil, Charlestown, Churchill, Colesberg,* (Cape) *Colville, Condamine, Cooper River, Cradock, Creighton, Daly River, Darling, Denton, Dinwiddie, Douglastown, Drummond, Drummondville, Durban, Durbanville, Elizabeth, Elliot, Elliotdale, Fauquier County, Featherston, Fitzroy, Forbes, Fort Frances, Fort James, Fort Johnston, Fort Sandeman, Fort Smith, Fox Glacier, Foxton, Frankford,* (Mount) *Frere, Garry, Gawler, Georgina, Geraldine, Gippsland, Gladwin, Goochland, Gore, Guysborough, Haldimand, Hamilton, Hammond Plains, Harford County, Harrismith, Hastings, Havelock, Hayes River, Healesville, Herbert, Herberton, Hindmarsh, Hotham Heights, Hunter, Hunters Islands, Hutchinson, Hyde County, Hyde Park, Jesselton, Johnstown, Keene, Lachlan River, Lac-Kempt, Ladismith, Lady Frere, Lady Grey, Ladysmith, Lambton County, Latrobe, Lawley, Lawrencetown, Lennox and Addington County, Lennoxville, Leonardtown, Lyallpur, MacCarthy Island, Macdonnell Ranges, Macleantown, Macquarie, Maitland, Maria, Mary River, Maryborough, Melmoth, Milnerton, Molteno, Moncton, Montagu, Musgrave Ranges, Musgravetown, Nelson, Palk Strait, Palmerville, Parkes, Parrsboro, Pelly, Philipstown, Pinetown, Pomeroy, Port Augusta, Port Colborne, Port Davey, Port Douglas, Port Elizabeth, Porterville, Port Hope, Port Macquarie, Port Maitland, Port Moody, Port Shepstone, Port Swettenham, Prescott, Rawsonville, Roma, Russell, St Catherines, Scottburgh, Seymour, Sherbrooke, Simcoe, Simpson, Smithers, Smithfield, Somerset East, Somerset West, Sorell, Spotsylvania, Staunton, Stawell, Stirling, Stoughton, Strahan, Talbot, Todd River, Torrens, Tryon, Upington, Wentworth, Winthrop, Wyndham, Young.*

15 Literary names

This list comprises fictional names, of people (characters) or places,with the Scots particularly attracted to Walter Scott and his novels, as can be seen. (List 8 will be found to contain the names of one or two poets and novelists, additionally.)

Auburn, Avalon, Cessnock, Deloraine, Elsinore, Enid, Erewhon, Hermiston, Ivanhoe, Kenilworth, Lothair, Midlothian, Montrose, Nigel, Robinson Crusoe Island, Selma, Temora, Trotwood, Waverley, Waverly, Woodstock.

16 Names of buildings

Although more 'real' than the names of List 15 (above), the buildings listed here form a special category of place-name that in a sense combines the aristocratic titles of List 2 with the fictional castles and mansions of List 15, so that *Walmer*, for example, is a kind of equivalent of *Elsinore*. List 15, too, has a 'real' name behind its *Kenilworth*, while here, in this list, the name of *Mosgiel* is really a literary tribute to its resident, Robert Burns. Besides actual residences, the list also includes a few names of schools, colleges and other 'public' buildings.

Ashcroft, Carberry, Chatsworth, Christchurch, Claremont, Doonside, Drayton, Duxbury, Germiston, Guildhall, Haileybury, Hinchinbrook, Hughenden, Killingly, Kittery, Longacre, Melfort, Meriden, Mosgiel, Scarsdale, Walmer, Wiarton.

17 Other names

The final list contains just a few names that will not fit precisely into any of the categories above. Sometimes, they are an invented place-name, such as the Scottish *Brackenfell* or the Welsh *Tredyffrin*. Other names are patriotic tributes, such as *Imperial* and *Union Jack*. *St George* could have been included under List 3, as a 'royal' name, but this is a secondary association, and the primary sense is patriotic. For the other allusions, see the entries themselves.

Bairnsdale, Brackenfell, Darien, Delmarva Peninsula, Giant's Castle, Helen Furnace, Imperial, Inverell, Invermere, Mirror, St George, St Georges Bay, Tredyffrin, Union Jack.

APPENDIX II
THE NAMING PROCESS

How did the explorers and settlers of historic times actually set about naming the objects they discovered and colonised? The entries in the Dictionary give a general idea of the names that were chosen, depending on the namer and the period of naming. But it is interesting to study the naming system followed by a particular individual, especially when the naming procedure has been reasonably well documented.

By way of an example, then, this Appendix considers the names given by the Arctic explorer Frederick Jackson during his three-year survey of Franz Josef Land, from 1894 to 1897. This particular period is sufficiently close to our own times to make it more immediate than, say, a study of seventeenth-century American colonial naming. At the same time, the naming took place in a region of the world that had been only partially charted hitherto, and that therefore was virtually 'virgin land' for the namer and his companions. An added aspect of the area is that it is now part of the Soviet Union, so that its names usually appear in modern atlases in Russian form. However, it remains uninhabited, so has not been colonised on a permanent basis by Russians or anyone else.

First, a word about the territory involved. Franz Josef Land (in Russian: Zemlya Frantsa-Iosifa) is an archipelago of over a hundred islands, some fairly sizeable, north of the Arctic Circle in the Barents Sea. As such, it lies at a latitude roughly equivalent to that of Canada's Ellesmere Island. The largest island, over a thousand square miles in area, is George Land (Zemlya Georga). Any human activity here in modern times is restricted to meteorological observers, students of Arctic flora and fauna, and (Russian) fur trappers. The many lakes and glaciers abound in seals, polar bears and sea birds of various kinds.

The islands were discovered in 1873 by an Austro-Hungarian expedition led by Julius von Payer and Karl Weyprecht, and they named their find after Franz Josef, Emperor of Austria and King of Hungary. The archipelago was subsequently visited by various explorers, including the Briton, Leigh Smith, who partially charted it in the 1880s, but it fell to Frederick Jackson to make the most complete exploration and survey of the group when he arrived there on board the *Windward* with five companions in 1894.

Frederick George Jackson (1860–1938) was a typical late Victorian at this time, a manly but not insensitive bachelor adventurer (in the best sense), born into a family of good social standing, who having first sailed to Arctic waters in 1887 was inspired by the exploits of Fridtjof Nansen, the Norwegian polar explorer, to make his own attempt on the North Pole as soon as he realistically could. For this was the era when many of the main continents had already been explored and colonised, and man now turned his attention in earnest to the polar regions, with the focus on the very poles themselves. (The famous Northwest Passage that so many had sought for so long, some never to return, would soon be made by Amundsen in the earliest years of the twentieth century, and the Swede Nordenskjöld had already made the Northeast Passage by now, in the late 1870s.)

Jackson thus proposed to use Franz Josef Land as a base for his push to the North Pole. Having gained some Arctic experience in northern Russia, he was then fortunate enough to find a patron for his polar project in the publisher Alfred Harmsworth, later Lord Northcliffe, the newspaper magnate. His venture was thus officially entitled the Jackson-Harmsworth Polar Expedition.

On arriving in the archipelago, however, the party found their imagined overland route to the North Pole barred by an extensive expanse of water (which Jackson named Queen Victoria Sea). They therefore abandoned any attempt to travel further north, and confined their activities to exploring, mapping and *naming* the many features that they discovered, while at the same time making a number of valuable scientific observations, such as meteorological records, botanical studies and so on.

The story of the three-year stay was recorded in some detail by Jackson in his two-volume work, *A Thousand Days in the Arctic*, published in 1899, and it is in this 'diary' that we have the account of more than fifty naming acts, as quoted below in this Appendix. It will be seen that most of Jackson's names were given by way of a tribute to friends and acquaintances, even to members of his family, while outside his immediate circle he reserved the most important names (usually for the major features) for the rulers and statesmen of the day.

It will pay us to make a brief survey of some of the better-known names here, to see who exactly they were, and to note Jackson's own comments on the various personages he honoured in this way. (For ease of reference in the quotations below, individual names will be followed by the appropriate chronological number in square brackets, for example 'Henry Cooke [20]' refers to the entry No. 20 dated 18 July 1895.)

Quite clearly, pride of place had to be accorded to the reigning monarch, Queen Victoria [15], and Jackson's main record of naming for her is reproduced not here but under the entry **Queen Victoria Sea** in the main body of the Dictionary. It is obvious that Jackson's loyalty and allegiance to his queen was no mere formality, and he refers to the naming more than once in his book, and to the monarch similarly. His entry dated 25 December 1894, therefore, referring to his party's Christmas Dinner, reads: 'At dinner I proposed as the first toast "The health of Her Majesty the Queen of Great Britain, Ireland and Franz Josef Land, and may she live long enough to be proud of her possessions on or about the latitude of 90° north".' ('On or about 80° north' would have been more accurate, but at that stage he did not know that the Queen's eponymous sea would bar his way to more northerly latitudes.)

Later, in his entry for 12 May 1895, after he had named the sea, he took stock of his expedition to date as follows:

'The results of our journey are:

That we have entirely altered the map of Franz Josef Land, discovering islands and seas where terra firma had been laid down; have been able to discover the most northern sea in the eastern Polar area, and to name it after our Queen – Queen Victoria Sea.'

A third tribute to Her Majesty, apart from the actual name-giving, appears in the entry for 24 May 1897, quite close to the end of his expedition, when commenting 'We feel *especially* loyal today' (it was Victoria's 78th birthday), he notes: 'We are all very gratified that we have been able to give her name – Queen Victoria Sea – to the frozen ocean to the north of these islands.' (Alas, the name no longer appears on modern maps, and Victoria's sea has been swallowed up in the vast Arctic Ocean.)

The only other members of the royal family that Jackson so honoured were the future George V [35], a choice that in later years he must have felt appropriately prescient, and Prince Henry Maurice of Battenberg [45]. The latter's brother married Queen Victoria's granddaughter, which brought him into the English court from the German. (Their fourth child was Prince Louis of Battenberg, who after 1917 became better known as Lord Louis Mountbatten of Burma, the naval and military leader.) For more about George, see the main entry for **George** in the Dictionary.

When it comes to other public figures, and especially statesmen and politicians, we find Jackson honouring Joseph Chamberlain [41], the Liberal-Unionist leader, and Sir Robert Peel [6]. The latter would appear not to be the famous Prime Minister and founder of the Metropolitan Police Force, who had died 45 years earlier, but his identically named son (1822–1895), who was a Member of Parliament for Tamworth and Chief Secretary to the Lord Lieutenant of Ireland. Nor did Jackson overlook Cecil Rhodes [32] (see **Rhodesia**). But it would seem, to judge by his cartographical evidence, that he *did* overlook noting the fact that he named one of the larger islands here Salisbury Island, after Lord Salisbury, the Conservative Prime Minister of the day. He can hardly have deliberately omitted such an important statesman in his naming scheme. (see **Salisbury**.)

As is to be expected, there is a fair representation of admirals, generals and other military contemporaries, some of whom Jackson will have known personally, and many of whom were explorers in their own right. They include Sir Albert Hastings Markham [5] (1841–1918), the British admiral and writer on exploration, Sir Francis Leopold McClintock [12] (1819–1907), the admiral and explorer (see **M'Clintock Channel**), Admiral Sir Erasmus Ommanney [13] (1814–1904), who discovered the first traces of the missing explorer John Franklin in 1850 (see **Franklin**), Sir Allen William Young [18] (1827–1915), the seaman and polar explorer, Admiral Sir Richard Vesey Hamilton [27] (1829–1912), who also looked for Franklin in the Arctic, and Sir John Murray [38] (1841–1914), the Scottish explorer, oceanographer and naturalist who was active in Canada.

Jackson does not confine his tributes to his fellow countrymen, but equally is happy to honour Baron Ferdinand von Richthofen [8] (1833–1905), the German geographer and traveller, the Swedish Arctic explorer Baron Nordenskjöld [23] (1832–1901), already mentioned above, the two men who originally discovered Franz Josef Land, Von Payer [23] (1842–1915) and Weyprecht [23] (1838–1881), similarly mentioned, the great Nansen [23] (1861–1930), and the American explorer Robert Peary [23] (1856–1920), as well as the latter's wife Josephine [48] (1863–1955), who accompanied her husband on two of his Arctic expeditions, and whose daughter Marie was actually born in the Arctic, farther north than any other white child previously.

The name of Nansen [34] is especially important here, for he and Jackson met in 1896. The Norwegian explorer and one other man were returning from their northernmost point of 86° 14′ N, and had been wintering at Cape Norway [16] on what was later named Jackson Island [34] before continuing their journey, as they hoped, to Spitsbergen. It is likely that the chance encounter saved the lives of Nansen and his companion, Fredrik Hjalmar Johansen. At any rate, Jackson took the two men back to Norway in his ship and was later awarded the Norwegian order of St Olav. For other Nansen names, see [22], [29].

Quite rightly, Jackson also pays tribute to his patron, naming a bay after his wife Mary Harmsworth [23] and part of an island after his brother, Cecil Harmsworth [49]. He had already named his ship's boat after Mrs Harmsworth and similarly named a cape after her [21].

Other persons of note that can be duly identified here are Sir John Scott Keltie [4] (1840–1927), who was Secretary of the Royal Geographical Society at the time of Jackson's expedition, William Johnson Neale [13] (1812–1893), the author of books on the sea and maritime themes, and George Harley [13] (1829–1896), the English physician who lived in Harley Street (but did not give his name to it). His daughter, Ethel Harley, married Alec Tweedie [24], and made a name for herself as 'Mrs Alec Tweedie' the authoress (who died in 1940). She wrote an account of George Harley's life (published in 1899, the same year as Jackson's book), and otherwise led a busy and active life, travelling a good deal. (From *A Girl's Ride in Iceland*, published in 1890, she progressed to *Thirteen Years of a Busy Woman's Life*, which came out in 1912, and *Tight Corners of My Adventurous Life*, appearing in 1933.)

The names of Jackson's immediate companions on his expedition also feature, as will be seen, from the carpenter [2] to Harry Fisher [9], his botanist and zoologist, and his second-in-command and personal friend, Albert Borlase Armitage [43]. He also commemorates his mother [11] and his brother [39]. As mentioned, he had not married at this stage (although he would in 1898), so had no wife to whom he could accord a like honour.

Jackson compliments his old school [40], too, as well as three of his London clubs [42, 47, 51]. (He chose the name of the school's patron saint, St Chad, showing its link with Lichfield: it is a Church of England, so-called 'Woodard' school, and the Bishop of Lichfield is its visitor. St Chad was the first bishop of Lichfield.) Nor does he forget to acknowledge his predecessor, who prepared the way for him in Franz Josef Land, so that Leigh Smith [44] is duly acknowledged. Most of the British names on the partially completed map of the islands before Jackson's arrival will thus have been planted there by Leigh Smith, such as Alexandra Land (see **Alexandra**) and probably Nightingale Sound. Of the latter, Jackson writes that it is named 'after Miss Nightingale of Crimean fame', adding: 'Its appearance rather belies its name, no singing bird ever warbled sweet notes here, I fancy.' On the other hand, the obviously German names will have been given by Van Payer and Weyprecht, and include Austria Sound, for example.

It is clear that several names were given by Jackson some time after the discovery of the feature in question, or else that he forgot to note the name-giving at the time. This leads to a few inconsistencies, so that he records certain names twice, apparently forgetting on their second mention that he had already given the name. The naming of Smithson Channel is thus noted at [19], in the entry for 5 May 1895, and at [31], in the entry dated 3 April 1896, and he similarly twice records the naming of Guy's Head [7, 30]. If a name is recorded twice, it can equally be omitted once, and this serves to increase the suspicion that he forgot to note the naming of Salisbury Island, as already mentioned.

For the rest, the names are either self-explanatory or relate to persons known more intimately to Jackson than to the world at large. And if we cannot immediately identify them, we at least have enough documentary evidence to examine Jackson's general naming pattern, not forgetting the rather unoriginal Camp Point [3], or the slightly more imaginative Cape Norway [16], in honour of Nansen.

The nearest thing that Jackson and his party had to a settlement was their base hut, which they set up on Northbrook Island for their winter quarters. This was therefore the 'home settlement' for nearly three years for six men and a sizeable number of dogs and ponies. Jackson naturally named it, and his record of the event, dated 2 November 1894, runs: 'I decided, out of compliment to Mr. Harmsworth, to name our little settlement "Elmwood".' What he does not tell us is that Elmwood was the name of Alfred Harmsworth's house in St Peter's, near (and now a part of) Broadstairs, Kent. (As Lord Northcliffe, he took his title from a cliff of this name just to the north of the town.) Before him, Leigh Smith had named his own hut Eira House, after his ship.

Upon completion of his exploration, Jackson returned to England to lead a fairly conventional army and civilian life. He served in the Boer War, was invalided home during the First World War, supervised a number of Russian prisoner-of-war camps in Germany after the war, and then took up big-game hunting in Africa, where he further exploited his exploratory inclinations by visiting the sources of the Zambezi, the Nile and the Congo. He was thus an officer and a gentleman (he listed his recreations in *Who's Who* as 'big-game shooting, fishing, hunting, polo, and shooting'), and possibly a fairly unoriginal one. But he had at least had an important and creative spell in the Arctic as a discoverer, investigator and namer, and the results of the latter exercise are reproduced below for the perusal of the reader.

The dates are those of the appropriate entry, and not necessarily those of the naming. Jackson frequently appended the origin of the naming by way of a footnote on the relevant page. In such cases, his 'diary' reference to the name will be followed by an asterisk (*), and the footnote preceded by one. This convention has been reproduced in the instances where it occurs. Wording in square brackets has been added to or substituted for Jackson's original, although wording in quotes in square brackets (as for entry No. 1) is his own. Only entry No. 34 relates to a naming not made by Jackson.

The namings

1 (7 Sep 1894) : This ['an island about a mile long by half a mile broad'] I named Windward Island, after our ship.
2 (7 Oct 1894) : I named the rock, where the carpenter had his little adventure [with a polar bear], Sharpe's Rock, after him.
3 (10 Mar 1895) : Camped at 6.15 P.M. at Camp Point (north-west point of Northbrook Island), to which I gave this name.
4 (20 Apr 1895) : the long island* *Since named by me Scott Keltie Island.
5 (21 Apr 1895) : We camped at midnight near the bold rock* to the north of the island. *Named by me Cape Albert Markham, after Admiral Albert Hastings Markham.
6 (22 Apr 1895) : The new sound (named by me Robert Peel Sound, after the late Sir Robert Peel, Bart.)
7 (22 Apr 1895) : one cliff of weathered columnar basalt,* *Named by me Guy's Head in compliment to our doctor, who was at Guy's Hospital.
8 (26 Apr 1895) : We travelled due north toward a high bold cape,* *Named by me Cape Richthofen.
9 (27 Apr 1895) : a bold headland about ten or fifteen miles away – named by me Cape Fisher.
10 (29 Apr 1895) : [see **British Channel**]
11 (30 Apr 1895) : We are making for an island* *Mary Elizabeth Island, named by me after my mother.
12 (30 Apr 1895) : This cape I named Cape McClintock, after Sir F. Leopold McClintock.
13 (1 May 1895) : three islands* *Since named by me William Neale, George Harley, and Erasmus Ommanney Islands, after Dr. William Neale, Dr. George Harley, F.R.S. (since dead), and Admiral Sir Erasmus Ommanney.
14 (1 May 1895) : a bold headland* *Named by me Cape Mill.
15 (2 May 1895) : [see **Queen Victoria Sea**]
16 (2 May 1895) : The cape* where Nansen erected his hut *Named by me Cape Norway.
17 (4 May 1895) : I tried to strike straight across Brown Fjord* *So named by me after Captain Brown, the captain of the *Windward* in 1896 and 1897.
18 (5 May 1895) : Allen Young Sound* *Named by me after Captain Sir Allen Young.
19 (5 May 1895) : A long strait runs nearly South out of Allen Young Sound [. . .] this I have named Smithson Channel, after the energetic secretary of the Tyneside Geographical Society.
20 (18 Jul 1895) : moraine [. . .] on the Cape Grant side of the rocks* *Named by me the Cooke Rocks, after Mr. Henry Cooke, H.B.M. Vice-Consul at Archangel.
21 (22 Jul 1895) : We also discovered a cape to the west of Cape Lofley, which I named Cape Mary Harmsworth [. . .] after Mrs. Harmsworth and our boat.
22 (24 Jul 1895) : the bold headland to the northward, named by me Cape Fridtjof Nansen.
23 (30 Jul 1895) : The cape to the west of Cape Lofley I have named after Mrs. Alfred Harmsworth, "Cape Mary Harmsworth."

The bay between Cape Mary Harmsworth and Cape Lofley after Baron Nordenskjold, "Nordenskjold Bay."

The bay between Capes Lofley and Ludley after Carl Weyprecht, "Weyprecht Bay."

The glacier reaching from the west side of Cambridge Bay to Cape Mary Harmsworth after Julius von Payer, "Payer Glacier," who together with Weyprecht were the brave discoverers of Franz Josef Land.

The bold, prominent rock headland at the head of Cambridge Bay after Dr. Fridtjof Nansen, "Cape Fridtjof Nansen."

The glacier north of Capes Stephen, Grant, Crowther and Neale after Lieutenant Robert E. Peary, U.S.N., the well-known American explorer, "Peary Glacier."

24 (26 Mar 1896) : Alex Tweedie Bay* *So named by me after Mr. Alec Tweedie.

25 (27 Mar 1896) : to Markham Sound, the northern point of which I have named Cape Paterson.

26 (28 Mar 1896) : an island named by me David Wilton Island.

27 (1 May 1896) : the centre of Vesey Hamilton Channel, named by me after the Arctic explorer, Admiral Sir Vesey Hamilton.

28 (2 Apr 1896) : a bold, high, basaltic rocky headland, which I named Cape Taylor after General Sir Richard Taylor.

29 (3 Apr 1896) : Fridtjof Nansen* Island *Afterwards named by me after Dr. Nansen.

30 (3 Apr 1896) : Guy's Head [. . .] which I named after Guy's Hospital, out of compliment to our doctor who studied there.

31 (3 Apr 1896) : Smithson Channel* *Named by me after Mr. G.E.T. Smithson, Secretary of the Tyneside Geographical Society.

32 (11 Jun 1896) : an island in Cecil Rhodes Fjord (named by me).

33 (11 Jun 1896) : Gore-Booth Fjord* *Named by me after Sir Henry Gore-Booth.

34 (6 Jul 1896) : He [Nansen] asked me about naming a cape after Armitage and a rock after Blomkvist in the large bay in the neighbourhood of his hut[. . .]* Should he do this? I told him I thought it very kind of him. *On reading Dr. Nansen's book "Farthest North", I find he has only availed himself of my offer so far by naming one of these spots – Frederick Jackson Island – after me, which I should never have consented to had I known of his intention to reject the rest. Reading his book was the first intimation I had of this.

35 (19 Mar 1897) : the rolling glacier-slopes of Prince George's Land* *So named by me after H.R.H. Prince George of Wales [see **George** Land].

36 (23 Mar 1897) : Brown Fjord* *So named by me after Captain Brown, skipper of the *Windward* in 1896 and 1897.

37 (23 Mar 1897) : Cape Farman* *Called by me after Mr. Edgar Farman.

38 (25 Mar 1897) : a plateau, strewn with jagged basaltic boulders to a height of 300 ft [. . .] which I have named Cape John Murray, after Dr., now Sir John Murray.

39 (27 Mar 1897) : Arthur Island to the north,* *Named by me after my brother, Arthur Jackson.

40 (27 Mar 1897) : a rocky headland [. . .] of weathered columnar basalt [. . .] which I named St Chad's Head, after my old school, Denstone College.

41 (27 Mar 1897) : This fjord I named after The Right Honourable Joseph Chamberlain, M.P., Chamberlain Fjord.

42 (27 Mar 1897) : The cape at the northern entrance of Chamberlain Fjord I have named Cape Grosvenor, after the London club that has shown me so much kindness.

43 (28 Mar 1897) : Albert Armitage Island* *Named by me after my comrade, Mr. Albert B. Armitage.

44 (28 Mar 1897) : Leigh Smith Sound – named so by me after the gentleman whose bold and successful voyages and excellent geographical work paved the way for my own expedition.

45 (28 Mar 1897) : This headland I named Cape Battenberg, after Prince Henry of Battenberg, who sacrificed his life in serving Great Britain, his adopted country.

46 (30 Mar 1897) : the [. . .] bay named by me Crichton Somerville Bay* *After Mr. D.M.M. Crichton Somerville.

47 (8 Apr 1897) : I named this spot Cape Nimrod after the London club under the hospitable roof of which I have spent many pleasant hours and where I have met with very much kindness.

48 (4 May 1897) : the bay to the west of Cape Stephen, which I named Josephine Peary Bay, after Mrs Peary, the wife of the Arctic explorer.

49 (20 May 1897) : the south-east corner of Hooker Island, which I named Cape Cecil Harmsworth.
50 (21 May 1897) : Cape Lewis-Poole* *Named by me after Mr. D. Lewis-Poole.
51 (21 May 1897) : Royal Societies* [Island] *Named by me after the club in London which has done so much to aid the cause of science.
52 (18 Jul 1897) : Capt. Robertson tells me he has seen two very small rocky islands just to the north of Cape Barents, and has asked me to include them in my map. This I have done, naming them the Robertson Islands.
53 (6 Aug 1897) : Peary Glacier* *Named by me after the Arctic Explorer, Mr. Peary, U.S.N.

Bibliography

The subject of this Dictionary is such a vast one – in effect, place-names round the world, albeit those of British origin – that any bibliography could be equally extensive, if it claimed to be anything like comprehensive.

Clearly, this is undesirable in a book whose very entries have had to be presented on a selective basis. The Bibliography that follows is therefore intended to include only those sources that will offer the reader three basic lines of pursuit, designated by the three letters of the alphabet,(a), (b) and (c), into which the main English-speaking countries of the world (Parts 2 to 7) are divided, with the world itself treated under Part 1 and Antarctica under Part 9.

Works listed under (a) are of a *general* nature, and give a wide range of information about the background of the country or countries concerned.

Books listed under (b) are basically about *place-names* and their origins, so will have the most immediate relevance to the overall subject of the Dictionary. Even here, however, the selection of titles is restricted to those works that bear most obviously on names of British origin. This means that in the United States (Part 3), books on place-name origins will on the whole be restricted to those states that have a significant number of British-derived names, which will mean basically the New England states. A selection of similar books is given for the United Kingdom itself (Part 2) as it is possible that some of the first settlers and namers may have taken the original meaning of a name into account when bestowing it. For example, the name Bristol, which means basically 'bridge place', may have been chosen for its aptness in designating a new settlement by a bridge over a river, and names of Celtic origin (Scottish, Welsh, Irish) may have had a similar appropriateness when translated.

Those titles listed under letter (c) are essentially *biographical* in nature. This subsection is most significant for the United Kingdom (Part 2), as it was from there that the names of many 'worthies' were transferred. Most of the other headings in the Bibliography, therefore, will not need this third category.

If a reader wishes a concise summary of a particular English-speaking country's history or geography, he or she could really do no better than consult the appropriate entry in any of the encylopaedias listed in subsection (a), or for an even briefer summary, extending to merely a few lines of print, the relevant entry in *Webster's New Geographical Dictionary* (see Part 1, subsection (b)). This particular work also give salient historical facts for many individual places, such as the years of foundation, change of status, or renaming.

Part 10 gives particulars of the title that is the subject of Appendix II, pp. 208–15.

Non-English titles are translated in square brackets for ease of reference.

1 The World

(a) *Encyclopaedia Britannica*, 30 vols, Encylopaedia Britannica, Chicago etc., 15th edn, 1976.
McCrum, Robert, Cran, William, and MacNeil, Robert, *The Story of English*, Faber & Faber/BBC Publications, London, 1986.

(b) Matthews, C.M., *Place-Names of the English-Speaking World*, Weidenfeld & Nicholson, London, 1972.
Meynen, Emil, *Gazetteers and Glossaries of Geographical Names*, Franz Steiner Verlag, Wiesbaden, 1984.
Muir's Historical Atlas: Medieval and Modern, ed. by the late R.F. Treharne and Harold Fullard, George Philip & Son, London, 11th edn, 1969.
Paxton, John (ed.), *The Statesman's Year-Book World Gazetteer*, Macmillan, London and Basingstoke, 3rd edn, 1986.
Room, Adrian, *Place-Name Changes Since 1900: A World Gazetteer*, Routledge & Kegan Paul, London, 1979.
Room, Adrian, *Place-Names of the World*, Angus & Robertson, North Ryde, Australia, and London, 1987.
Stewart, George, R., *Names on the Globe*, Oxford University Press, New York, 1975.
Taylor, Isaac, *Names and their Histories*, Rivington, Percival & Co., London, 1898.
The Times Atlas of the World,Times Books/John Bartholomew & Son, London, 7th edn, 1985.
Webster's New Geographical Dictionary, Merriam-Webster, Springfield, Mass., 1980.
Where's Where: A Descriptive Gazetteer, Eyre Methuen, London, 1974.
Wilcocks, Julie, *Countries and Islands of the World*, Clive Bingley, London, 2nd edn, 1985.

(c) Carrington, Charles Edmund, *The British Overseas: Exploits of a Nation of Shopkeepers. Part 1: The Making of the Empire*, Cambridge University Press, Cambridge, 1968.
Hyamson, Albert M., *A Dictionary of Universal Biography of All Ages and All Peoples*, Routledge & Kegan Paul, London, 2nd edn, 1951.
Webster's Biographical Dictionary, Merriam-Webster, Springfield, Mass., 1976.

2 United Kingdom

(a) Isaacs, Alan and Monk, Jennifer, *The Cambridge Illustrated Dictionary of British Heritage*, Cambridge University Press, Cambridge, 1986.
Room, Adrian, *Dictionary of Britain*, Oxford University Press, Oxford, 2nd edn, 1987.

(b) *Cassell's Gazetteer of Great Britain and Ireland*, 6 vols, Cassell, London, 1893–8.
Davies, Elwyn (ed.), *A Gazetteer of Welsh Place-Names*, University of Wales Press, Cardiff, 1975.
Davies, E.M., *Welsh Place Names*, Celtic Educational, Swansea, 1978.
Ekwall, Eilert, *The Concise Oxford Dictionary of English Place-Names*, Oxford University Press, Oxford, 4th edn, 1960.
Field, John, *Place-Names of Great Britain and Ireland*, David & Charles, Newton Abbot, 1980.
Forster, Klaus, *A Pronouncing Dictionary of English Place-Names*, Routledge & Kegan Paul, London, 1981.
Johnston, James, B., *Place-Names of Scotland*, S.R. Publishers, East Ardsley, 1970 [1934].

Johnston's Gazetteer of Scotland, rev. by R.W. Munro, Johnston & Bacon, Edinburgh, 3rd edn, 1973.

Mason, Oliver (comp.), *Bartholomew Gazetteer of Places in Britain*, John Bartholomew & Son, Edinburgh, rev. edn, 1986.

Nicolaisen, W.F.H., *Scottish Place-Names*, Batsford, London, 1976.

Room, Adrian, *A Dictionary of Irish Place-Names*, Appletree Press, Belfast, 1986.

(c) *Dictionary of National Biography*, from the earliest times to 1900, 22 vols, Oxford University Press, 1908; Supplements: 1901–11 (1920), 1912–21 (1927), 1922–30 (1937), 1931–40 (1949), 1941–50 (1959), 1951–60 (1971), 1961–70 (1981), 1971–80 (1986).

Who Was Who, A. & C. Black, London, vol. 1, 1897–1915 (1967), vol. 2, 1916–28 (1967), vol. 3, 1929–40 (1967), vol. 4, 1941–50 (1981), vol. 5, 1951–60 (1967), vol. 6, 1961–70 (1979), vol. 7, 1971–80 (1981).

3 United States of America

(a) *Encyclopedia Americana*, 30 vols, Grolier, Danbury, Conn., 1985.

(b) Alotta, Robert I., *Old Names and New Places*, Westminster Press, Philadelphia, Pa., 1979.

Baker, Ronald L. and Carmony, Marvin, *Indiana Place Names*, Indiana University Press, Bloomington, Ind., 1974.

Bloodworth, Bertha E. and Morris, Alton C., *Places in the Sun: The History and Romance of Florida Place-Names*, University Presses of Florida, Gainesville, Fla., 1978.

Espenshade, Abraham H., *Pennsylvania Place Names*, Gale Research, Detroit, 1969 [1925].

Forbes, A., *Towns of New England and Old England*, 2 vols, State Street Trust, Boston, Mass., 1921.

Gannett, Henry, *The Origin of Certain Place Names in the United States*, Genealogical Publishing, Baltimore, Md., 1977 [1905].

Gudde, Erwin G., *California Place-Names*, Irvington Publishers, New York, 1986 [1949].

Harder, Kelsie B. (ed.), *Illustrated Dictionary of Place Names: United States and Canada*, Van Nostrand Reinhold, New York, 1976.

Holt, Alfred H., *American Place-Names*, Gale Research, Detroit, 1969 [1938].

Hunt, Elmer M., *New Hampshire Town Names and Whence They Came*, Noone House, Peterborough, N.H., 1971.

Janssen, Quinith and Fernbach, William, *West Virginia Place Names*, J. and F. Enterprises, Shepherdstown, W.Va., 1984.

Kaminkow, Marion J., *Maryland A to Z: A Topographical Dictionary*, Magna Carta Book Co., Baltimore, Md., 1985.

Kenny, Hamill, *West Virginia Place Names: Their Origin and Meaning*, Place Names Press, Piedmont, W.Va., 1945.

Orth, Donald J., *Dictionary of Alaska Place-Names*, Government Printing Office, Washington, D.C., 1967.

Phillips, James W., *Washington State Place Names*, University of Washington Press, Seattle, rev. edn, 1971.

Romig, Walter, *Michigan Place Names*, Wayne State University Press, Detroit, 1986.

Rutherford, Philip R., *The Dictionary of Maine Place-Names*, Bond Wheelwright Co., Freeport, Me., 1971.

Schorr, Alan Edward (ed.), *Alaska Place Names*, Library Occasional Papers No. 1, University of Alaska, Juneau, 2nd edn, 1980.

Sealock, Richard B., *et al.*, *Bibliography of Place-Name Literature: United States and Canada*, American Library Association, Chicago, 3rd edn, 1982.
Shirk, George H., *Oklahoma Place Names*, University of Oklahoma Press, Norman, Okla., 1965.
Stewart, George R., *American Place-Names*, Oxford University Press, New York, 1970.
Stewart, George R., *Names on the Land*, Lexikos, San Francisco, 4th edn, 1982.
Wolk, Allan, *The Naming of America*, Thomas Nelson, Nashville, Tenn., 1977.

4 Canada

(a) *Encyclopaedia Canadiana*, 10 vols, Grolier, Danbury, Conn., 1977.

(b) Akrigg, G.P.V. and Helen B., *1001 British Columbia Place Names*, Discovery Press, Vancouver, 3rd edn, 1973.
Armstrong, G.H., *The Origin and Meaning of Place Names in Canada*, Macmillan of Canada, Toronto, 1930.
Brown, Thomas, J., *Nova Scotia Place Names*, Royal Print, Halifax, 1922.
Dawson, R. MacG., 'Place Names in Nova Scotia', in *Onomastica* (Ukrainian Free Academy of Sciences) No. 19, Winnipeg, 1960, pp. 5–16.
Douglas, Robert, *Place Names of Prince Edward Island*, King's Printer, Ottawa, 1925.
Fergusson, Bruce, *Place Names of Nova Scotia*, Public Archives of Nova Scotia, Halifax, 1967.
Fraser, Ian A., 'Placenames of Scottish Origin in Nova Scotia', in *Names* (*Journal of the American Name Society*), vol. 34, no. 4, December 1986, pp. 364–72.
Hamilton, William B., *The Macmillan Book of Canadian Place Names*, Macmillan of Canada, Toronto, 1978.
Holmgren, E.J. and P.M., *2000 Place Names of Alberta*, Modern Press, Saskatoon, 1972.
Kerfoot, Helen, 'Naming the Islands of Canada's Arctic' in *Canoma*, vol. 6, no. 2, Surveys and Mapping Branch, Energy Mines and Resources, Ontario, December 1980, pp. 35–6.
Mardon, Ernest G.,'The History of Place Names in Southern Alberta', in *Onomastica* (Canadian Institute of Onomastic Sciences) no. 43, Winnipeg, 1972, pp. 5–20.
Rayburn, Alan, *Geographical Names of Prince Edward Island*, Survey and Mapping Branch, Department of Energy, Mines and Resources, Ottawa, 1973.
Rayburn, Alan, *Geographical Names of New Brunswick*, Survey and Mapping Branch, Department of Energy, Mines and Resources, Ottawa, 1975.
Rudnyc'kij, J.B., *Manitoba: Mosaic of Place-Names*, Canadian Institute of Onomastic Sciences, Winnipeg, 1970.
Walbran, John T., *British Columbia Coast Names*, J.J. Douglas, West Vancouver, 1971.

5 Australia

(a) *The Australian Encyclopaedia*, 10 vols, Grolier, Sydney, 1965.
The Modern Encyclopaedia of Australia and New Zealand, Horwitz-Grahame, Cammeray, 1964.
Scott, Ernest, *A Short History of Australia*, Oxford University Press, Melbourne, 1920.

(b) Martin, A.E., *One Thousand and More Place Names in New South Wales*, Bookstall, Sydney, 1943.
Martin, A.E., *Twelve Hundred and More Place Names in South Australia, Western Australia and the Northern Territory*, Bookstall, Sydney, 1943.
Martin, A.E., *Place Names in Victoria and Tasmania*, Bookstall, Sydney, 1944.
Praite, Ronald and Tolley, J.C., *Place Names of South Australia*, Rigby, Adelaide, 1970.
Reed, A.W., *Place-Names of New South Wales: Their Origins and Meanings*, Reed, Sydney, 1969.

6 *New Zealand*

(a) *An Encyclopedia of New Zealand*, 3 vols, R.E. Owen, Wellington, 1966.
Melvin, Kenneth, *New Zealand*, Collins, Auckland, 1962.
The Modern Encyclopaedia of Australia and New Zealand, Horwitz-Grahame, Cammeray, 1964.
Sinclair, Keith, *History of New Zealand*, Allen Lane, London, rev. edn, 1980.

(b) Dollimore, E.S., *The New Zealand Guide*, A. Wise and Co., Dunedin, 3rd edn, 1962.
McLintock, A.H, (ed.), *A Descriptive Atlas of New Zealand*, R.E. Owen, Wellington,1959.
Shadbolt, Maurice (ed.), *The Shell Guide to New Zealand*, Michael Joseph, London, 1969.

7 *South Africa*

(a) Rosenthal, Eric, *Encyclopaedia of Southern Africa*, Juta and Co., Cape Town, 7th edn, 1978.

(b) Holt, B.F., *Place Names in the Transkeian Territories*, Africana Museum, Johannesburg, 1959.
Nienaber, P.J., *Suid-Afrikaanse Pleknaamwoordeboek* [South African Place-Name Dictionary], Suid-Afrikaanse Boekensentrum, Kaapstadt, 1963.
Pettman, Charles, *South African Place Names Past and Present*, Lowry Publishers, Johannesburg, 1931.
Raper, P.E., *Dictionary of Southern African Place Names*, Lowry Publishers, Johannesburg, 1987.
Reader's Digest Illustrated Guide to Southern Africa, Reader's Digest, Cape Town, 3rd edn, 1982.

8 *South America*

(b) McEwen, Alec, 'The English Place-Names of the Galápagos', in *The Geographical Journal*, vol. 154, part 2, July 1988, pp. 234–42.

9 Antarctica

(a) United States Naval Photographic Interpretation Center, *Antarctic Bibliography*, Greenwood Press, London, 1951.

(b) Boumphrey, R.S., Hamilton, J.E., and Busbie, Major, 'Preliminary Derivations of Some Falkland Islands Place-Names', unpublished typescript, 1950.

Dubrovin, L.I. and Preobrazhenskaya, M.A., *O chem govorit karta Antarktiki* [What the Map of the Antarctic Has to Tell], Gidrometeoizdat, Leningrad, 1987.

Hattersley-Smith, G., *The History of Place-Names in the Falkland Islands Dependencies (South Georgia and the South Sandwich Islands)*, British Antarctic Survey Scientific Reports No. 101, Cambridge, 1980.

Hattersley-Smith, G., *The History of Place-Names in the British Antarctic Territory*, British Antarctic Survey Scientific Reports No. 113, Cambridge, 1989.

Law, Phillip, *Antarctic Odyssey*, Heinemann, Richmond, Victoria, 1983.

Spence, S.A. (ed.), *Antarctic Miscellany: Books, Periodicals and Maps Relating to the Discovery and Exploration of Antarctica*, J. Simper, Mitcham, 1980.

10 The Arctic

The following title is the sole subject of Appendix II, pp. 208–15:

Jackson, Frederick, G., *A Thousand Days in the Arctic*, Harper & Brothers, London, 1899.